Lecture Notes in Computer Science 6590

Commenced Publication in 1973
Founding and Former Series Editors:
Gerhard Goos, Juris Hartmanis, and Jan van Leeuwen

Per Stenström (Ed.)

Transactions on High-Performance Embedded Architectures and Compilers III

 Springer

Volume Editor

Per Stenström
Chalmers University of Technology
Department of Computer Science and Engineering
412 96 Gothenburg, Sweden
E-mail: per.stenstrom@chalmers.se

ISSN 0302-9743 (LNCS)   e-ISSN 1611-3349 (LNCS)
ISSN 1864-306X (THIPEAC)   e-ISSN 1864-3078 (THIPEAC)
ISBN 978-3-642-19447-4   e-ISBN 978-3-642-19448-1
DOI 10.1007/978-3-642-19448-1

Springer Heidelberg Dordrecht London New York

Library of Congress Control Number: 2007923068

CR Subject Classification (1998): B.2, C.1, D.3.4, B.5, C.2, D.4

Typesetting: Camera-ready by author, data conversion by Scientific Publishing Services, Chennai, India

Printed on acid-free paper

Springer is part of Springer Science+Business Media (www.springer.com)

Editor-in-Chief's Message

It is my pleasure to introduce you to the third volume of *Transactions on High-Performance Embedded Architectures and Compilers*. This journal was created as an archive for scientific articles in the converging fields of high-performance and embedded computer architectures and compiler systems. Design considerations in both general-purpose and embedded systems are increasingly being based on similar scientific insights. For example, a state-of-the-art game console today consists of a powerful parallel computer whose building blocks are the same as those found in computational clusters for high-performance computing. Moreover, keeping power/energy consumption at a low level for high-performance general-purpose systems as well as in, for example, mobile embedded systems is equally important in order to either keep heat dissipation at a manageable level or to maintain a long operating time despite the limited battery capacity. It is clear that similar scientific issues have to be solved to build competitive systems in both segments. Additionally, for high-performance systems to be realized – be it embedded or general-purpose – a holistic design approach has to be taken by factoring in the impact of applications as well as the underlying technology when making design trade-offs. The main topics of this journal reflect this development and include (among others):

- Processor architecture, e.g., network and security architectures, application specific processors and accelerators, and reconfigurable architectures
- Memory system design
- Power, temperature, performance, and reliability constrained designs
- Evaluation methodologies, program characterization, and analysis techniques
- Compiler techniques for embedded systems, e.g, feedback-directed optimization, dynamic compilation, adaptive execution, continuous profiling/optimization, back-end code generation, and binary translation/optimization
- Code size/memory footprint optimizations

This volume contains 14 papers divided into four sections. The first section is a special section containing the top four papers from the Third International Conference on High-Performance and Embedded Architectures and Compilers - HiPEAC. I would like to thank Manolis Katevenis (University of Crete and FORTH) and Rajiv Gupta (University of California at Riverside) for acting as guest editors of that section. Papers in this section deal with cache performance issues and improved branch prediction

The second section is a set of four papers providing a snapshot from the Eighth MEDEA Workshop. I am indebted to Sandro Bartolini and Pierfrancesco Foglia for putting together this special section.

The third section contains two regular papers and the fourth section provides a snapshot from the First Workshop on Programmability Issues for Multicore Computers (MULTIPROG). The organizers – Eduard Ayguade, Roberto

Gioiosa, and Osman Unsal – have put together this section. I thank them for their effort.

The editorial board has worked diligently to handle the papers for the journal. I would like to thank all the contributing authors, editors, and reviewers for their excellent work.

Per Stenström, Chalmers University of Technology
Editor-in-chief
Transactions on HiPEAC

Editorial Board

Per Stenström is a professor of computer engineering at Chalmers University of Technology. His research interests are devoted to design principles for high-performance computer systems and he has made multiple contributions to especially high-performance memory systems. He has authored or co-authored three textbooks and more than 100 publications in international journals and conferences. He regularly serves Program Committees of major conferences in the computer architecture field. He is also an associate editor of *IEEE Transactions on Parallel and Distributed Processing Systems*, a subject-area editor of the *Journal of Parallel and Distributed Computing*, an associate editor of the *IEEE TCCA Computer Architecture Letters*, and the founding Editor-in-Chief of *Transactions on High-Performance Embedded Architectures and Compilers*. He co-founded the HiPEAC Network of Excellence funded by the European Commission. He has acted as General and Program Chair for a large number of conferences including the ACM/IEEE Int. Symposium on Computer Architecture, the IEEE High-Performance Computer Architecture Symposium, and the IEEE Int. Parallel and Distributed Processing Symposium. He is a Fellow of the ACM and the IEEE and a member of Academia Europaea and the Royal Swedish Academy of Engineering Sciences.

Koen De Bosschere obtained his PhD from Ghent University in 1992. He is a professor in the ELIS Department at the Universiteit Gent where he teaches courses on computer architecture and operating systems. His current research interests include: computer architecture, system software, code optimization. He has co-authored 150 contributions in the domain of optimization, performance modeling, microarchitecture, and debugging. He is the coordinator of the ACACES research network and of the European HiPEAC2 network. Contact him at Koen.DeBosschere@elis.UGent.be.

Jose Duato is a professor in the Department of Computer Engineering (DISCA) at UPV, Spain. His research interests include interconnection networks and multiprocessor architectures. He has published over 340 papers. His research results have been used in the design of the Alpha 21364 microprocessor, the Cray T3E, IBM BlueGene/L, and Cray Black Widow supercomputers. Dr. Duato is the first author of the book *Interconnection Networks: An Engineering Approach.* He has served as associate editor of IEEE TPDS and IEEE TC. He was General Co-chair of ICPP 2001, Program Chair of HPCA-10, and Program Co-chair of ICPP 2005. Also, he has served as Co-chair, Steering Committee member, Vice-Chair, or Program Committee member in more than 55 conferences, including HPCA, ISCA, IPPS/SPDP, IPDPS, ICPP, ICDCS, Europar, and HiPC.

Manolis Katevenis received his PhD degree from U.C. Berkeley in 1983 and the ACM Doctoral Dissertation Award in 1984 for his thesis on "Reduced Instruction Set Computer Architectures for VLSI." After a brief term on the faculty of Computer Science at Stanford University, he has been in Greece, with the University of Crete and with FORTH since 1986. After RISC, his research has been on interconnection networks and interprocessor communication. In packet switch architectures, his contributions since 1987 have been mostly in per-flow queueing, credit-based flow control, congestion management, weighted round-robin scheduling, buffered crossbars, and non-blocking switching fabrics. In multiprocessing and clustering, his contributions since 1993 have been on remote-write-based, protected, user-level communication.

His home URL is http://archvlsi.ics.forth.gr/~kateveni

Michael O'Boyle is a professor in the School of Informatics at the University of Edinburgh and an EPSRC Advanced Research Fellow. He received his PhD in Computer Science from the University of Manchester in 1992. He was formerly a SERC Postdoctoral Research Fellow, a Visiting Research Scientist at IRISA/INRIA Rennes, a Visiting Research Fellow at the University of Vienna and a Visiting Scholar at Stanford University. More recently he was a Visiting Professor at UPC, Barcelona.

Dr. O'Boyle's main research interests are in adaptive compilation, formal program transformation representations, the compiler impact on embedded systems, compiler directed low-power optimization and automatic compilation for parallel single-address space architectures. He has published over 50 papers in international journals and conferences in this area and manages the Compiler and Architecture Design group consisting of 18 members.

Cosimo Antonio Prete is a full professor of computer systems at the University of Pisa, Italy, faculty member of the PhD School in Computer Science and Engineering (IMT), Italy. He is Coordinator of the Graduate Degree Program in Computer Engineering and Rector's Adviser for Innovative Training Technologies at the University of Pisa. His research interests are focused on multiprocessor architectures, cache memory, performance evaluation and embedded systems. He is an author of more than 100 papers published in international journals and conference proceedings. He has been project manager for several research projects, including: the SPP project, OMI, Esprit IV; the CCO project, supported by VLSI Technology, Sophia Antipolis; the ChArm project, supported by VLSI Technology, San Jose, and the Esprit III Tracs project.

André Seznec is "directeur de recherches" at IRISA/INRIA. Since 1994, he has been the head of the CAPS (Compiler Architecture for Superscalar and Special-purpose Processors) research team. He has been conducting research on computer architecture for more than 20 years. His research topics have included memory hierarchy, pipeline organization, simultaneous multithreading and branch prediction. In 1999–2000, he spent a sabbatical year with the Alpha Group at Compaq.

Olivier Temam obtained a PhD in computer science from the University of Rennes in 1993. He was assistant professor at the University of Versailles from 1994 to 1999, and then professor at the University of Paris Sud until 2004. Since then, he is a senior researcher at INRIA Futurs in Paris, where he heads the Alchemy group. His research interests include program optimization, processor architecture, and emerging technologies, with a general emphasis on long-term research.

Theo Ungerer is Chair of Systems and Networking at the University of Augsburg, Germany, and Scientific Director of the Computing Center of the University of Augsburg. He received a Diploma in Mathematics at the Technical University of Berlin in 1981, a Doctoral Degree at the University of Augsburg in 1986, and a second Doctoral Degree (Habilitation) at the University of Augsburg in 1992. Before his current position he was scientific assistant at the University of Augsburg (1982–1989 and 1990–1992), visiting assistant professor at the University of California, Irvine (1989–1990), professor of computer architecture at the University of Jena (1992–1993) and the Technical University of Karlsruhe (1993–2001). He is Steering Committee member of HiPEAC and of the German Science Foundation's priority programme on "Organic Computing." His current research interests are in the areas of embedded processor architectures, embedded real-time systems, organic, bionic and ubiquitous systems.

Mateo Valero obtained his PhD at UPC in 1980. He is a professor in the Computer Architecture Department at UPC. His research interests focus on high-performance architectures. He has published approximately 400 papers on these topics. He is the director of the Barcelona Supercomputing Center, the National Center of Supercomputing in Spain. Dr. Valero has been honored with several awards, including the King Jaime I award by the Generalitat Valenciana, and the Spanish national award "Julio Rey Pastor" for his research on IT technologies. In 2001, he was appointed Fellow of the IEEE, in 2002 Intel Distinguished Research Fellow and since 2003 a Fellow of the ACM. Since 1994, he has been a foundational member of the Royal Spanish Academy of Engineering. In 2005 he was elected Correspondant Academic of the Spanish Royal Academy of Sciences, and his native town of Alfamén named their public college after him.

Georgi Gaydadjiev is a professor in the computer engineering laboratory of the Technical University of Delft, The Netherlands. His research interests focus on many aspects of embedded systems design with an emphasis on reconfigurable computing. He has published about 50 papers on these topics in international refereed journals and conferences. He has acted as Program Committee member of many conferences and is subject area editor for the *Journal of Systems Architecture*.

Table of Contents

Third International Conference on High-Performance and Embedded Architectures and Compilers (HiPEAC)

Eighth MEDEA Workshop (Selected Papers)

Regular Papers

First Workshop on Programmability Issues for Multi-core Computers (MULTIPROG)

Third International Conference on High-Performance and Embedded Architectures and Compilers (HiPEAC)

Dynamic Cache Partitioning Based on the MLP of Cache Misses

Miquel Moreto[1], Francisco J. Cazorla[2], Alex Ramirez[1,2], and Mateo Valero[1,2]

[1] Universitat Politècnica de Catalunya, DAC, Barcelona, Spain
HiPEAC European Network of Excellence
[2] Barcelona Supercomputing Center – Centro Nacional de Supercomputación, Spain
{mmoreto,aramirez,mateo}@ac.upc.edu, francisco.cazorla@bsc.es

Abstract. Dynamic partitioning of shared caches has been proposed to improve performance of traditional eviction policies in modern multi-threaded architectures. All existing Dynamic Cache Partitioning (DCP) algorithms work on the number of misses caused by each thread and treat all misses equally. However, it has been shown that cache misses cause different impact in performance depending on their distribution. Clustered misses share their miss penalty as they can be served in parallel, while isolated misses have a greater impact on performance as the memory latency is not shared with other misses.

We take this fact into account and propose a new DCP algorithm that considers misses differently depending on their influence in performance. Our proposal obtains improvements over traditional eviction policies up to 63.9% (10.6% on average) and it also outperforms previous DCP proposals by up to 15.4% (4.1% on average) in a four-core architecture. Our proposal reaches the same performance as a 50% larger shared cache. Finally, we present a practical implementation of our proposal that requires less than 8KB of storage.

1 Introduction

The limitation imposed by instruction-level parallelism (ILP) has motivated the use of thread-level parallelism (TLP) as a common strategy for improving processor performance. TLP paradigms such as simultaneous multithreading (SMT) [1,2], chip multiprocessor (CMP) [3] and combinations of both offer the opportunity to obtain higher throughputs. However, they also have to face the challenge of sharing resources of the architecture. Simply avoiding any resource control can lead to undesired situations where one thread is monopolizing all the resources and harming the other threads. Some studies deal with the resource sharing problem in SMTs at core level resources like issue queues, registers, etc. [4]. In CMPs, resource sharing is focused on the cache hierarchy.

Some applications present low reuse of their data and pollute caches with data streams, such as multimedia, communications or streaming applications, or have many compulsory misses that cannot be solved by assigning more cache space to the application. Traditional eviction policies such as Least Recently

P. Stenström (Ed.): Transactions on HiPEAC III, LNCS 6590, pp. 3–23, 2011.

Used (LRU), pseudo LRU or random are demand-driven, that is, they tend to give more space to the application that has more accesses and misses to the cache hierarchy [5, 6]. As a consequence, some threads can suffer a severe degradation in performance. Previous work has tried to solve this problem by using static and dynamic partitioning algorithms that monitor the L2 cache accesses and decide a partition for a fixed amount of cycles in order to maximize throughput [7,8,9] or fairness [10]. Basically, these proposals predict the number of misses per application for each possible cache partition. Then, they use the cache partition that leads to the minimum number of misses for the next interval.

A common characteristic of these proposals is that they treat all L2 misses equally. However, in out-of-order architectures L2 misses affect performance differently depending on how clustered they are. An isolated L2 miss has approximately the same miss penalty than a cluster of L2 misses, as they can be served in parallel if they all fit in the reorder buffer (ROB) [11]. In Figure 1 we can see this behavior. We have represented an *ideal* IPC curve that is constant until an L2 miss occurs. After some cycles, commit stops. When the cache line comes from main memory, commit ramps up to its steady state value. As a consequence, an isolated L2 miss has a higher impact on performance than a miss in a burst of misses as the memory latency is shared by all clustered misses.

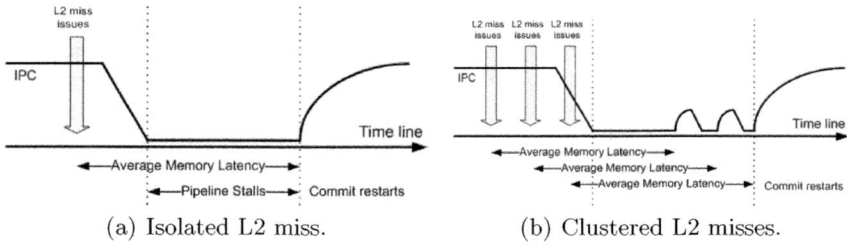

(a) Isolated L2 miss.   (b) Clustered L2 misses.

Fig. 1. Isolated and clustered L2 misses

Based on this fact, we propose a new DCP algorithm that gives a cost to each L2 access according to its impact in final performance. We detect isolated and clustered misses and assign a higher cost to isolated misses. Then, our algorithm determines the partition that minimizes the total cost for all threads, which is used in the next interval. Our results show that differentiating between clustered and isolated L2 misses leads to cache partitions with higher performance than previous proposals. The main contributions of this work are the following.

1) A runtime mechanism to dynamically partition shared L2 caches in a CMP scenario that takes into account the MLP of each L2 access. We obtain improvements over LRU up to 63.9% (10.6% on average) and over previous proposals up to 15.4% (4.1% on average) in a four-core architecture. Our proposal reaches the same performance as a 50% larger shared cache.

2) We extend previous workloads classifications for CMP architectures with more than two cores. Results can be better analyzed in every workload group.

3) We present a sampling technique that reduces the hardware cost in terms of storage to less than 1% of the total L2 cache size with an average throughput degradation of 0.76% (compared to the throughput obtained without sampling). We also show that scalable algorithms to decide cache partitions give near optimal partitions, 0.59% close to the optimal decision.

The rest of this paper is structured as follows. Section 2 introduces the methods that have been previously proposed to decide L2 cache partitions and related work. Next, Section 3 explains our MLP-aware DCP algorithm. Section 4 describes the experimental environment and in Section 5 we discuss simulation results. Finally, Section 6 summarizes our results.

2   Prior Work in Dynamic Cache Partitioning

Stack Distance Histogram (SDH). Mattson et al. introduce the concept of stack distance to study the behavior of storage hierarchies [12]. Common eviction policies such as LRU have the *stack property*. Thus, each set in a cache can be seen as an LRU stack, where lines are sorted by their last access cycle. In that way, the first line of the LRU stack is the Most Recently Used (MRU) line while the last line is the LRU line. The position that a line has in the LRU stack when it is accessed again is defined as the *stack distance* of the access. As an example, we can see in Table 1(a) a stream of accesses to the same set with their corresponding stack distances.

Table 1. Stack Distance Histogram

(a) Stream of accesses to a given cache set.

# Reference	1	2	3	4	5	6	7	8
Cache Line	A	B	C	C	A	D	B	D
Stack Distance	-	-	-	1	3	-	4	2

(b) SDH example.

Stack Distance	1	2	3	4	>4
# Accesses	60	20	10	5	5

For a K-way associative cache with LRU replacement algorithm, we need $K + 1$ counters to build SDHs, denoted $C_1, C_2, \ldots, C_K, C_{>K}$. On each cache access, one of the counters is incremented. If it is a cache access to a line in the ith position in the LRU stack of the set, C_i is incremented. If it is a cache miss, the line is not found in the LRU stack and, as a result, we increment the miss counter $C_{>K}$. SDH can be obtained during execution by running the thread alone in the system [7] or by adding some hardware counters that profile this information [8, 9]. A characteristic of these histograms is that the number of cache misses for a smaller cache with the same number of sets can be easily computed. For example, for a K'-way associative cache, where $K' < K$, the new number of misses can be computed as $misses = C_{>K} + \sum_{i=K'+1}^{K} C_i$.

As an example, in Table 1(b) we show an SDH for a set with 4 ways. Here, we have 5 cache misses. However, if we reduce the number of ways to 2 (keeping the number of sets constant), we will experience 20 misses (5 + 5 + 10).

Minimizing Total Misses. Using the SDHs of N applications, we can derive the L2 cache partition that minimizes the total number of misses: this last number corresponds to the sum of the number of misses of each thread for the given configuration. The optimal partition in the last period of time is a suitable candidate to become the future optimal partition. Partitions are decided periodically after a fixed amount of cycles. In this scenario, partitions are decided at a *way granularity*. This mechanism is used in order to minimize the total number of misses and try to maximize throughput. A first approach proposed a static partitioning of the L2 cache using profiling information [7]. Then, a dynamic approach estimated SDHs with information inside the cache [9]. Finally, Qureshi et al. presented a suitable and scalable circuit to measure SDHs using sampling and obtained performance gains with just 0.2% extra space in the L2 cache [8]. Throughout this paper, we will call this last policy *MinMisses*.

Fair Partitioning. In some situations, *MinMisses* can lead to unfair partitions that assign nearly all the resources to one thread while harming the others [10]. For that reason, the authors propose considering fairness when deciding new partitions. In that way, instead of minimizing the total number of misses, they try to equalize the statistic $X_i = \frac{misses_{shared_i}}{misses_{alone_i}}$ of each thread i. They desire to force all threads to have the same increase in percentage of misses. Partitions are decided periodically using an iterative method. The thread with largest X_i receives a way from the thread with smallest X_i until all threads have a similar value of X_i. Throughout this paper, we will call this policy *Fair*.

Table 2. Different Partitioning Proposals

Paper	Partitioning	Objective	Decision	Algorithm	Eviction Policy
[7]	Static	Minimize Misses	Programmer	–	Column Caching
[9]	Dynamic	Minimize Misses	Architecture	Marginal Gain	Augmented LRU
[8]	Dynamic	Maximize Utility	Architecture	Lookahead	Augmented LRU
[10]	Dynamic	Fairness	Architecture	Equalize X_1^i	Augmented LRU
[13]	Dynamic	Maximize reuse	Architecture	Reuse	Column Caching
[14]	Dyn./Static	Configurable	Operating System	Configurable	Augmented LRU

Other Related Work. Several papers propose different DCP algorithms in a multithreaded scenario. In Table 2 we summarize these proposals with their most significant characteristics. Settle et al. introduce a DCP similar to *MinMisses* that decides partitions depending on the average data reuse of each application [13]. Rafique et al. propose to manage shared caches with a hardware cache quota enforcement mechanism and an interface between the architecture and the OS to let the latter decide quotas [14]. We have to note that this mechanism is completely orthogonal to our proposal and, in fact, they are compatible as we can let the OS decide quotas according to our scheme. Hsu et al. evaluate different cache policies in a CMP scenario [15]. They show that none of them is optimal among all benchmarks and that the best cache policy varies depending on the performance metric being used. Thus, they propose to use a thread-aware cache resource allocation. In fact, their results reinforce the motivation of our paper: if we do not consider the impact of each L2 miss in performance, we can decide suboptimal L2 partitions in terms of throughput.

Cache partitions at a way granularity can be implemented with *column caching* [7], which uses a bit mask to mark reserved ways, or by augmenting the LRU policy with counters that keep track of the number of lines in a set belonging to a thread [9]. The evicted line will be the LRU line among its owned lines or other threads lines depending on whether it reaches its quota or not.

In [16] a new eviction policy for *private* caches was proposed in single-threaded architectures. This policy gives a weight to each L2 miss according to its MLP when the block is filled from memory. Eviction is decided using the LRU counters and this weight. This idea was proposed for a different scenario as it focus on single-threaded architectures.

3   MLP-Aware Dynamic Cache Partitioning

3.1   Algorithm Overview

Algorithm 3.1 shows the necessary steps to dynamically decide cache partitions according to the MLP of each L2 access. At the beginning of the execution, we decide an initial partition of the L2 cache. As we have no prior knowledge of the applications, we evenly distribute ways among cores. Hence, each core receives $\frac{Associativity}{Number\ of\ Cores}$ ways of the shared L2 cache.

Algorithm 3.1. MLP-AWARE DCP()

> *Step 1:* Establish an initial even partition for each core.
> *Step 2:* Run threads and collect data for the MLP-aware SDHs.
> *Step 3:* Decide new partition.
> *Step 4:* Update MLP-aware SDHs.
> *Step 5:* Go back to Step 2.

Afterwards, we begin a period where we measure the total MLP cost of each application. The histogram of each thread containing the total MLP cost for each possible partition is denoted *MLP-aware SDH*. For a K-way associative cache, exactly K registers are needed to store this histogram. For short periods, dynamic cache partitioning (DCP) algorithms react quicker to phase changes. Our results show that, for different periods from 10^5 to 10^8 cycles, small performance variations are obtained, with a peak for a period of 5 million cycles.

At the end of each interval, MLP-aware SDHs are analyzed and a new partition is decided for the next interval. We assume that running threads will have a similar pattern of L2 accesses in the next measuring period. Thus, the optimal partition for the last period is chosen for the following period. Evaluating all possible cache partitions gives the optimal partition. This evaluation is done concurrently with a dedicated hardware, which sets the partition for each process in the next period. Having old values of partitions decisions does not impact correctness of the running applications and does not affect performance as deciding new partitions typically takes few thousand cycles and is invoked once every 5 million cycles.

Since characteristics of applications dynamically change, MLP-aware SDHs should reflect these changes. However, we also wish to maintain some history of the past MLP-aware SDHs to make new decisions. Thus, after a new partition is decided, we multiply all the values of the MLP-aware SDHs times $\rho \in [0, 1]$. Large values of ρ have larger reaction times to phase changes, while small values of ρ quickly adapt to phase changes but tend to forget the behavior of the application. Small performance variations are obtained for different values of ρ ranging from 0 to 1, with a peak for $\rho = 0.5$. Furthermore, this value is very convenient as we can use a shifter to update histograms. Next, a new period of measuring MLP-aware SDHs begins. The key contribution of this paper is the method to obtain MLP-aware SDHs that we explain in the following Subsection.

3.2   MLP-Aware Stack Distance Histogram

As previously stated, *MinMisses* assumes that all L2 accesses are equally important in terms of performance. However, it has been shown that cache misses affect differently the performance of applications, even inside the same application [11, 16]. An isolated L2 data miss has a penalty cost that can be approximated by the average memory latency. In the case of a burst of L2 data misses that fit in the ROB, the penalty cost is shared among misses as L2 misses can be served in parallel. In case of L2 instruction misses, they are serialized as fetch stops. Thus, L2 instruction misses have a constant miss penalty and MLP.

We want to assign a cost to each L2 access according to its effect on performance. In [16] a similar idea was used to modify LRU eviction policy for single core and single threaded architectures. In our situation, we have a CMP scenario where the shared L2 cache has a number of reserved ways for each core. At the end of each period, we decide either to continue with the same partition or change it. If we decide to modify the partition, a core i that had w_i reserved ways will receive $w_i' \neq w_i$. If $w_i < w_i'$, the thread receives more ways and, as a consequence, some misses in the old configuration will become hits. Conversely, if $w_i > w_i'$, the thread receives less ways and some hits in the old configuration will become misses. Thus, we want to have an estimation of the performance effects when misses are converted into hits and vice versa. Throughout this paper, we will call this impact on performance MLP_cost.

MLP_cost of L2 misses. In order to compute the MLP_cost of an L2 miss with stack distance d_i, we consider the situation shown in Figure 2(a). If we force an L2 configuration that assigns exactly $w_i' = d_i$ ways to thread i with $w_i' > w_i$, some of the L2 misses of this thread will become hits, while other will remain being misses, depending on their stack distance. In order to track the stack distance

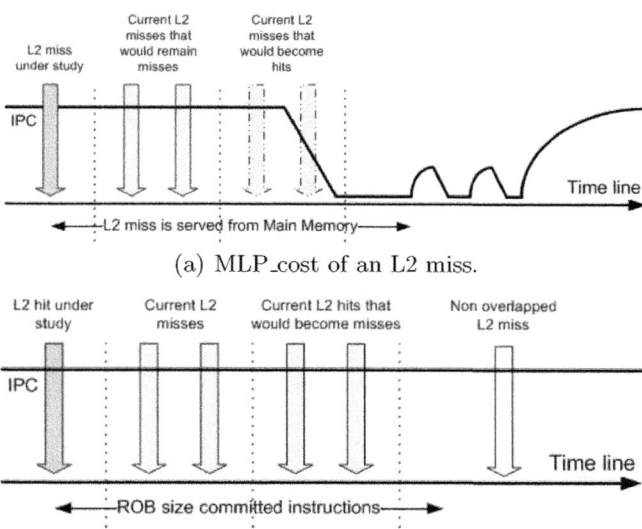

(a) MLP_cost of an L2 miss.

(b) Estimated MLP_cost when an L2 hit becomes a miss.

Fig. 2. MLP_cost of L2 accesses

and *MLP_cost* of each L2 miss, we have modified the L2 Miss Status Holding Registers (MSHR) [17]. This structure is similar to an L2 miss buffer and is used to hold information about any load that has missed in the L2 cache. The modified L2 MSHR has one extra field that contains the *MLP_cost* of the miss as can be seen in Figure 3(b). It is also necessary to store the stack distance of each access in the MSHR. In Figure 3(a) we show the MSHR in the cache hierarchy.

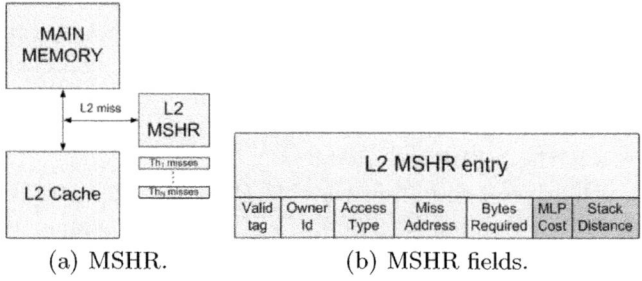

(a) MSHR.   (b) MSHR fields.

Fig. 3. Miss Status Holding Register

When the L2 cache is accessed and an L2 miss is determined, we assign an MSHR entry to the miss and wait until the data comes from Main Memory. We initialize the *MLP_cost* field to zero when the entry is assigned. We store the access stack distance together with the identifier of the owner core. Every cycle, we obtain N, the number of L2 accesses with stack distance greater or equal to d_i. We have a hardware counter that tracks this number for each possible number of d_i, which means a total of *Associativity* counters. If we have N L2 misses that are being served in parallel, the miss penalty is shared. Thus, we assign an equal share of $\frac{1}{N}$ to each miss. The value of the MLP_cost is updated until the data comes from Main Memory and fills the L2. At this moment we can free the MSHR entry.

The number of adders required to update the MLP_cost of all entries is equal to the number of MSHR entries. However, this number can be reduced by sharing several adders between valid MSHR entries in a round robin fashion. Then, if an MSHR entry updates its MLP_cost every 4 cycles, it has to add $\frac{4}{N}$. In this work, we assume that the MSHR contains only four adders for updating MLP_cost values, which has a negligible effect on the final MLP_cost [16].

MLP_cost of L2 hits. Next, we want to estimate the MLP_cost of an L2 hit with stack distance d_i when it becomes a miss. If we forced an L2 configuration that assigned exactly $w_i' = d_i$ ways to the thread i with $w_i' < w_i$, some of the L2 hits of this thread would become misses, while L2 misses would remain as misses (see Figure 2(b)). The hits that would become misses are the ones with stack distance greater or equal to d_i. Thus, we count the total number of accesses with stack distance greater or equal to d_i (including L2 hits and misses) to estimate the length of the cluster of L2 misses in this configuration.

Deciding the moment to free the entry used by an L2 hit is more complex than in the case of the MSHR. As it was said in [11], in a balanced architecture, L2 data misses can be served in parallel if they all fit in the ROB. Equivalently, we say that L2 data misses can be served in parallel if they are at ROB distance smaller than the ROB size. Thus, we should free the entry if the number of committed instructions since the access has reached the ROB size or if the number of cycles since the hit has reached the average latency to memory. The first condition is clear as L2 misses can overlap only if their ROB distance is less than the ROB size. When the entry is freed, we have to add the number of pending cycles divided by the number of misses with stack distance greater or equal to d_i. The second condition is also necessary as it can occur that no L2 access is done for a period of time. To obtain the average latency to memory, we add a specific hardware that counts and averages the number of cycles that a given entry is in the MSHR.

We use new hardware to obtain the MLP_cost of L2 hits. We denote this hardware Hit Status Holding Registers (HSHR) as it is similar to the MSHR. However, the HSHR is private for each core. In each entry, the HSHR needs an identifier of the ROB entry of the access, the address accessed by the L2 hit, the stack distance value and a field with the corresponding MLP_cost as can be seen in Figure 4(b). In Figure 4(a) we show the HSHR in the cache hierarchy.

When the L2 cache is accessed and an L2 hit is determined, we assign an HSHR entry to the L2 hit. We initialize the fields of the entry as in the case of the MSHR. We have a stack distance d_i and we want to update the MLP_cost field in every cycle. With this objective, we need to know the number of active entries with stack distance greater or equal to d_i in the HSHR, which can be tracked with one hardware counter per core. We also need a ROB entry identifier

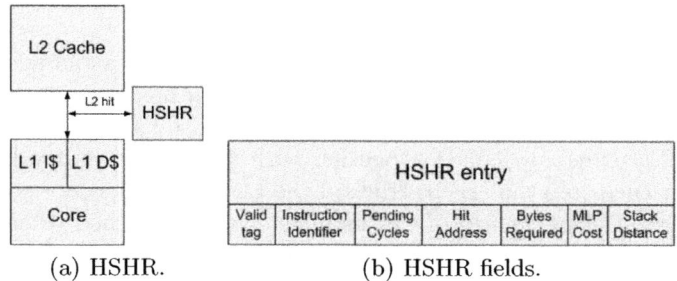

(a) HSHR.   (b) HSHR fields.

Fig. 4. Hit Status Holding Register

for each L2 access. Every cycle, we obtain N, the number of L2 accesses with stack distance greater or equal to d_i as in the L2 MSHR case. We have a hardware counter that tracks this number for each possible number of d_i, which means a total of *Associativity* counters.

In order to avoid array conflicts, we need as many entries in the HSHR as possible L2 accesses in flight. This number is equal to the L1 MSHR size. In our scenario, we have 32 L1 MSHR entries, which means a maximum of 32 in flight L2 accesses per core. However, we have checked that we have enough with 24 entries per core to ensure that we have an available slot 95% of the time in an architecture with a ROB of 256 entries. If there are no available slots, we simply assign the minimum weight to the L2 access as there are many L2 accesses in flight. The number of adders required to update the MLP_cost of all entries is equal to the number of HSHR entries. As we did with the MSHR, HSHR entries can share four adders with a negligible effect on the final MLP_cost.

Quantification of MLP_cost. Dealing with values of MLP_cost between 0 and the memory latency (or even greater) can represent a significant hardware cost. Instead, we decide to quantify this MLP_cost with an integer value between 0 and 7 as was done in [16]. For a memory latency of 300 cycles, we can see in Table 3 how to quantify the MLP_cost. We have split the interval $[0; 300]$ with 7 intervals of equal length.

Table 3. MLP_cost quantification

MLP_cost	Quantification	MLP_cost	Quantification
From 0 to 42 cycles	0	From 171 to 213 cycles	4
From 43 to 85 cycles	1	From 214 to 256 cycles	5
From 86 to 128 cycles	2	From 257 to 300 cycles	6
From 129 to 170 cycles	3	300 or more cycles	7

Finally, when we have to update the corresponding MLP-aware SDH, we add the quantified value of MLP_cost. Thus, isolated L2 misses will have a weight of 7, while two overlapped L2 misses will have a weight of 3 in the MLP-aware SDH. In contrast, *MinMisses* always adds one to its histograms.

3.3   Obtaining Stack Distance Histograms

Normally, L2 caches have two separate parts that store data and address tags to know if the access is a hit. Basically, our prediction mechanism needs to track every L2 access and store a separated copy of the L2 tags information in an *Auxiliary Tag Directory* (ATD), together with the LRU counters [8]. We need an ATD for each core that keeps track of the L2 accesses for any possible cache configuration. Independently of the number of ways assigned to each core, we store the tags and LRU counters of the last K accesses of the thread, where K is the L2 associativity. As we have explained in Section 2, an access with stack distance d_i corresponds to a cache miss in any configuration that assigns less than d_i ways to the thread. Thus, with this ATD we can determine whether an L2 access would be a miss or a hit in all possible cache configurations.

3.4   Putting All Together

In Figure 5 we can see a sketch of the hardware implementation of our proposal. When we have an L2 access, the ATD is used to determine its stack distance d_i. Depending on whether it is a miss or a hit, either the MSHR or the HSHR is used to compute the MLP_cost of the access. Using the quantification process we obtain the final MLP_cost. This number estimates how performance is affected when the applications has exactly $w_i' = d_i$ assigned ways. If $w_i' > w_i$, we are estimating the performance benefit of converting this L2 miss into a hit. In case $w_i' < w_i$, we are estimating the performance degradation of converting this L2 hit into a miss. Finally, using the stack distance, the MLP_cost and the core identifier, we can update the corresponding MLP-aware SDH.

We have used two different partitioning algorithms. The first one, that we denote *MLP-DCP* (standing for MLP-aware Dynamic Cache Partitioning), decides

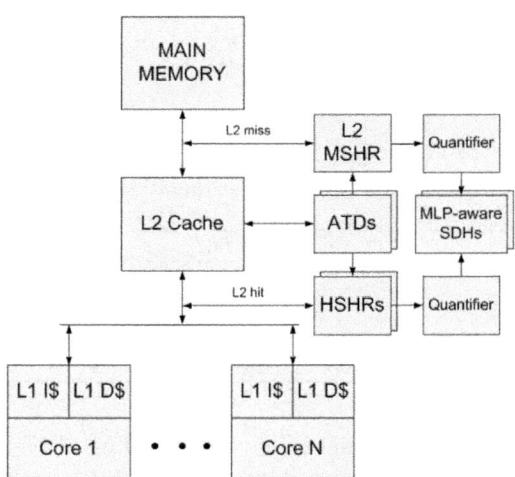

Fig. 5. Hardware implementation

the optimal partition according to the MLP_cost of each way. We define the total MLP_cost of a thread i that uses w_i ways as $TMLP(i, w_i) = MLP\_SDH_{i,>K} + \sum_{j=w_i}^{K} MLP\_SDH_{i,j}$. We denote the total MLP_cost of all accesses of thread i with stack distance j as $MLP\_SDH_{i,j}$. Thus, we have to minimize the sum of total MLP_costs for all cores:

$$\sum_{i=1}^{N} TMLP(i, w_i), \text{ where } \sum_{i=1}^{N} w_i = \text{Associativity}.$$

The second one consists in assigning a weight to each total MLP_cost using the IPC of the application in core i, IPC_i. In this situation, we are giving priority to threads with higher IPC. This point will give better results in throughput at the cost of being less fair. IPC_i is measured at runtime with a hardware counter per core. We denote this proposal $MLPIPC\text{-}DCP$, which consists in minimizing the following expression:

$$\sum_{i=1}^{N} IPC_i \cdot TMLP(i, w_i), \text{ where } \sum_{i=1}^{N} w_i = \text{Associativity}.$$

3.5   Case Study

We have seen that SDHs can give the optimal partition in terms of total L2 misses. However, total number of L2 misses is not the goal of DCP algorithms. Throughput is the objective of these policies. The underlying idea of *MinMisses* is that while minimizing total L2 misses, we are also increasing throughput. This idea is intuitive as performance is clearly related to L2 miss rate. However, this heuristic can lead to inadequate partitions in terms of throughput as can be seen in the next case study.

In Figure 6, we can see the IPC curves of benchmarks `galgel` and `gzip` as we increase L2 cache size in a way granularity (each way has a 64KB size). We also show throughput for all possible 15 partitions. In this curve, we assign x ways to `gzip` and $16-x$ to `galgel`. The optimal partition consists in assigning 6 to `gzip` and 10 ways to `galgel`, obtaining a total throughput of 3.091 instructions per cycle. However, if we use *MinMisses* algorithm to determine the new partition, we will choose 4 to `gzip` and 12 ways to `galgel` according to the SDHs values. In Figure 6 we can also see the total number of misses for each cache partition as well as the per thread number of misses.

In this situation, misses in `gzip` are more important in terms of performance than misses in `galgel`. Furthermore, `gzip` IPC is larger than `galgel` IPC. As a consequence *MinMisses* obtains a non optimal partition in terms of IPC and its throughput is 2.897, which is a 6.3% smaller than the optimal one. In fact, `galgel` clusters of L2 misses are, in average, longer than the ones from `gzip`. In that way, *MLP-DCP* assigns one extra way to `gzip` and increases performance by 3%. If we use *MLPIPC-DCP*, we are giving more importance to `gzip` as it has a higher IPC and, as a consequence, we end up assigning another extra way to `gzip`, reaching the optimal partition and increasing throughput an extra 3%.

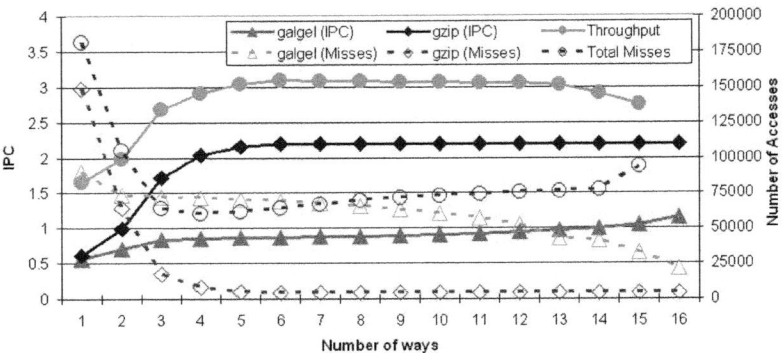

Fig. 6. Misses and IPC curves for `galgel` and `gzip`

4 Experimental Environment

4.1 Simulator Configuration

We target this study to the case of a CMP with two and four cores with their respective own data and instruction L1 caches and a unified L2 cache shared among threads as in previous studies [8, 9, 10]. Each core is single-threaded and fetches up to 8 instructions each cycle. It has 6 integer (I), 3 floating point (FP), and 4 load/store functional units and 32-entry I, load/store, and FP instruction queues. Each thread has a 256-entry ROB and 256 physical registers. We use a two-level cache hierarchy with 64B lines with separate 16KB, 4-way associative data and instruction caches, and a unified L2 cache that is shared among all cores. We have used two different L2 caches, one of size 1MB and 16-way associativity, and the second one of size 2MB and 32-way associativity. Latency from L1 to L2 is 15 cycles, and from L2 to memory 300 cycles. We use a 32B width bus to access L2 and a multibanked L2 of 16 banks with 3 cycles of access time.

We extended the SMTSim simulator [2] to make it CMP. We collected traces of the most representative 300 million instruction segment of each program, following the SimPoint methodology [18]. We use the FAME simulation methodology [19] with a Maximum Allowable IPC Variance of 5%. This evaluation methodology measures the performance of multithreaded processors by reexecuting all threads in a multithreaded workload until all of them are fairly represented in the final IPC taken from the workload.

4.2 Workload Classification

In [20] two metrics are used to model the performance of a partitioning algorithm like *MinMisses* for pairings of benchmarks in the SPEC CPU 2000 benchmark suite. Here, we extend this classification for architectures with more cores.

Metric 1. The $w_{P\%}(B)$ metric measures the number of ways needed by a benchmark B to obtain at least a given percentage $P\%$ of its maximum IPC (when it uses all L2 ways).

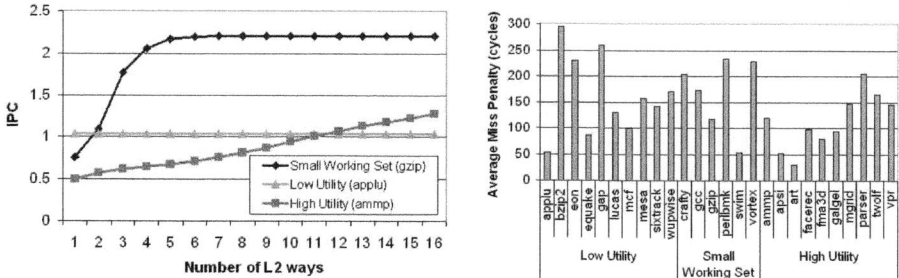

(a) IPC as we vary the number of assigned ways of a 1MB 16-way L2 cache.

(b) Average miss penalty of an L2 miss with a 1MB 16-way L2 cache.

Fig. 7. Benchmark classification

The intuition behind this metric is to classify benchmarks depending on their cache utilization. Using $P = 90\%$ we can classify benchmarks into three groups: *Low utility* (L), *Small working set* or *saturated utility* (S) and *High utility* (H). L benchmarks have $1 \leq w_{90\%} \leq \frac{K}{8}$ where K is the L2 associativity. L benchmarks are not affected by L2 cache space because nearly all L2 accesses are misses. S benchmarks have $\frac{K}{8} < w_{90\%} \leq \frac{K}{2}$ and just need some ways to have maximum throughput as they fit in the L2 cache. Finally, H benchmarks have $w_{90\%} > \frac{K}{2}$ and always improve IPC as the number of ways given to them is increased. Clear representatives of these three groups are `applu` (L), `gzip` (S) and `ammp` (H) in Figure 7(a). In Table 4 we give $w_{90\%}$ for all SPEC CPU 2000 benchmarks.

Table 4. The applications used in our evaluation. For each benchmark, we give the two metrics needed to classify workloads together with IPC for a 1MB 16-way L2 cache.

Bench	$w_{90\%}$	APTC	IPC	Bench	$w_{90\%}$	APTC	IPC	Bench	$w_{90\%}$	APTC	IPC
ammp	14	23.63	1.27	applu	1	16.83	1.03	apsi	10	21.14	2.17
art	10	46.04	0.52	bzip2	1	1.18	2.62	crafty	4	7.66	1.71
eon	3	7.09	2.31	equake	1	18.6	0.27	facerec	11	10.96	1.16
fma3d	9	15.1	0.11	galgel	15	18.9	1.14	gap	1	2.68	0.96
gcc	3	6.97	1.64	gzip	4	21.5	2.20	lucas	1	7.60	0.35
mcf	1	9.12	0.06	mesa	2	3.98	3.04	mgrid	11	9.52	0.71
parser	11	9.09	0.89	perl	5	3.82	2.68	sixtrack	1	1.34	2.02
swim	1	28.0	0.40	twolf	15	12.0	0.81	vortex	7	9.65	1.35
vpr	14	11.9	0.97	wupw	1	5.99	1.32				

The average miss penalty of an L2 miss for the whole SPEC CPU 2000 benchmark suite is shown in Figure 7(b). We note that this average miss penalty varies a lot, even inside each group of benchmarks, ranging from 30 to 294 cycles. This Figure reinforces the main motivation of the paper, as it proves that the clustering level of L2 misses changes for different applications.

Metric 2. The $w_{LRU}(th_i)$ metric measures the number of ways given by LRU to each thread th_i in a workload composed of N threads. This can be done simulating all benchmarks alone and using the frequency of L2 accesses for each thread [5]. We denote the number of L2 Accesses in a Period of one Thousand Cycles for thread i as $APTC_i$. In Table 4 we list these values for each benchmark.

$$w_{LRU}(th_i) = \frac{APTC_i}{\sum_{j=1}^{N} APTC_j} \cdot Associativity$$

Next, we use these two metrics to extend previous classifications [20] for workloads with more than two benchmarks.

Case 1. When $w_{90\%}(th_i) \leq w_{LRU}(th_i)$ for all threads. In this situation LRU attains 90% of each benchmark performance. Thus, it is intuitive that in this situation there is very little room for improvement.

Case 2. When there exists two threads A and B such that $w_{90\%}(th_A) > w_{LRU}(th_A)$ and $w_{90\%}(th_B) < w_{LRU}(th_B)$. In this situation, LRU is harming the performance of thread A, because it gives more ways than necessary to thread B. Thus, in this situation LRU is assigning some shared resources to a thread that does not need them, while the other thread could benefit from these resources.

Case 3. Finally, the third case is obtained when $w_{90\%}(th_i) > w_{LRU}(th_i)$ for all threads. In this situation, our L2 cache configuration is not big enough to assure that all benchmarks will have at least a 90% of their peak performance. In [20] it was observed that pairings belonging to this group showed worse results when the value of $|w_{90\%}(th_1) - w_{90\%}(th_2)|$ grows. In this case, we have a thread that requires much less L2 cache space than the other to attain 90% of its peak IPC. LRU treats threads equally and manages to satisfy the less demanding thread necessities. In case of *MinMisses*, it assumes that all misses are equally important for throughput and tends to give more space to the thread with higher L2 cache necessity, while harming the less demanding thread. This is a problem due to *MinMisses* algorithm. We will show in next Subsections that MLP-aware partitioning policies are available to overcome this situation.

Table 5. Workloads belonging to each case for a 1MB 16-way and a 2MB 32-way shared L2 caches

#cores	1MB 16-way			2MB 32-way		
	Case 1	Case 2	Case 3	Case 1	Case 2	Case 3
2	155 (48%)	135 (41%)	35 (11%)	159 (49%)	146 (45%)	20 (6.2%)
4	624 (4%)	12785 (86%)	1541 (10%)	286 (1.9%)	12914 (86%)	1750 (12%)
6	306 (0.1%)	219790 (95%)	10134 (5%)	57 (0.02%)	212384 (92%)	17789 (7.7%)
8	19 (0%)	1538538 (98%)	23718 (2%)	1 (0%)	1496215 (96%)	66059 (4.2%)

In Table 5 we show the total number of workloads that belong to each case for different configurations. We have generated all possible combinations without repeating benchmarks. The order of benchmarks is not important. In the case of a 1MB 16-way L2, we note that Case 2 becomes the dominant case as the number of cores increases. The same trend is observed for L2 caches with larger associativity. In Table 5 we can also see the total number of workloads that belong to each case as the number of cores increases for a 32-way 2MB L2 cache. Note that with different L2 cache configurations, the value of $w_{90\%}$ and $APTC_i$ will change for each benchmark. An important conclusion from Table 5 is that as we increase the number of cores, there are more combinations that belong to the second case, which is the one with more improvement possibilities.

To evaluate our proposals, we randomly generate 16 workloads belonging to each group for three different configurations. We denote these configurations $2C$ (2 cores and 1MB 16-way L2), $4C$-1 (4 cores and 1MB 16-way L2) and $4C$-2 (4 cores and 2MB 32-way L2). We have also used a 2MB 32-way L2 cache as future CMP architectures will continue scaling L2 size and associativity. For example, the IBM Power5 [21] has a 10-way 1.875MB L2 cache and the Niagara 2 has a 16-way 4MB L2.

4.3   Performance Metrics

As performance metrics we have used the IPC throughput, which corresponds to the sum of individual IPCs. We also use the harmonic mean of relative IPCs to measure fairness, which we denote *Hmean*. We use *Hmean* instead of weighted speed up because it has been shown to provide better fairness-throughput balance than weighted speed up [22].

Average improvements do consider the distribution of workloads among the three groups. We denote this mean *weighted mean*, as we assign a weight to the speed up of each case depending on the distribution of workloads from Table 5. For example, for the $2C$ configuration, we compute the weighted mean improvement as $0.48 \cdot x_1 + 0.41 \cdot x_2 + 0.11 \cdot x_3$, where x_i is the average improvement in Case i.

5   Evaluation Results

5.1   Performance Results

Throughput. The first experiment consists in comparing throughput for different DCP algorithms, using LRU policy as the baseline. We simulate *MinMisses* and our two proposals with the 48 workloads that were selected in the previous Subsection. We can see in Figure 8(a) the average speed up over LRU for these mechanisms. *MLPIPC-DCP* systematically obtains the best average results, nearly doubling the performance benefits of *MinMisses* over LRU in the four-core configurations. In configuration $4C$-1, *MLPIPC-DCP* outperforms *MinMisses* by 4.1%. *MLP-DCP* always improves *MinMisses* but obtains worse results than *MLPIPC-DCP*.

All algorithms have similar results in Case 1. This is intuitive as in this situation there is little room for improvement. In Case 2, *MinMisses* obtains a relevant improvement over LRU in configuration $2C$. *MLP-DCP* and *MLPIPC-DCP* achieve an extra 2.5% and 5% improvement, respectively. In the other

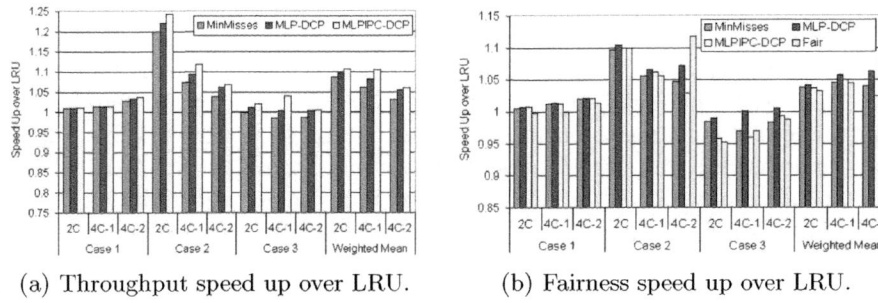

(a) Throughput speed up over LRU.   (b) Fairness speed up over LRU.

Fig. 8. Average performance speed ups over LRU

configurations, *MLP-DCP* and *MLPIPC-DCP* still outperform *MinMisses* by a 2.1% and 3.6%. In Case 3, *MinMisses* presents larger performance degradation as the asymmetry between the necessities of the two cores increases. As a consequence, it has worse average throughput than LRU. Assigning an appropriate weight to each L2 access gives the possibility to obtain better results than LRU using *MLP-DCP* and *MLPIPC-DCP*.

Fairness. We have used the harmonic mean of relative IPCs [22] to measure fairness. The relative IPC is computed as $\frac{IPC_{shared}}{IPC_{alone}}$. In Figure 8(b) we show the average speed up over LRU of the harmonic mean of relative IPCs. *Fair* stands for the policy explained in Section 2. We can see that in all situations, *MLP-DCP* always improves over both *MinMisses* and LRU (except in Case 3 for two cores). It even obtains better results than *Fair* in configurations *2C* and *4C-1*. *MLPIPC-DCP* is a variant of the *MLP-DCP* algorithm optimized for throughput. As a consequence, it obtains worse results in fairness than *MLP-DCP*.

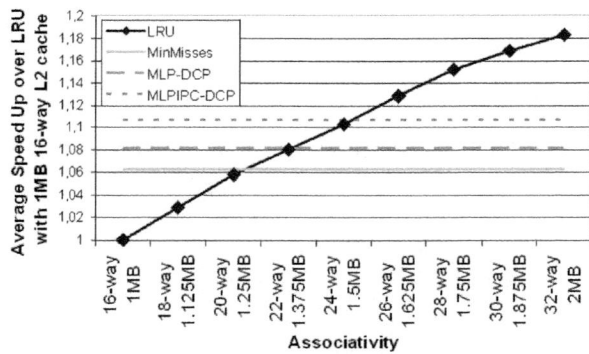

Fig. 9. Average throughput speed up over LRU with a 1MB 16-way L2 cache

Equivalent cache space. DCP algorithms reach the performance of a larger L2 cache with LRU eviction policy. Figure 9 shows the performance evolution when the L2 size is increased from 1MB to 2MB with LRU as eviction policy. In this experiment, the workloads correspond to the ones selected for the configuration *4C-1*. Figure 9 also shows the average speed up over LRU of *MinMisses*, *MLP-DCP* and *MLPIPC-DCP* with a 1MB 16-way L2 cache. *MinMisses* has the same average performance as a 1.25MB 20-way L2 cache with LRU, which means that *MinMisses* provides the performance obtained with a 25% larger shared cache. *MLP-DCP* reaches the performance of a 37.5% larger cache. Finally, *MLPIPC-DCP* doubles the increase in size of *MinMisses*, reaching the performance of a 50% larger L2 cache.

5.2   Design Parameters

Figure 10(a) shows the sensitivity of our proposal to the period of partition decisions. For shorter periods, the partitioning algorithm reacts quicker to phase changes. Once again, small performance variations are obtained for different periods. However, we observe that for longer periods throughput tends to decrease. As can be seen in Figure 10(a), the peak performance is obtained with a period of 5 million cycles.

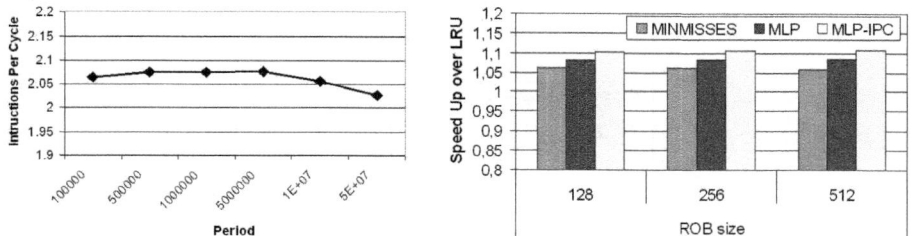

(a) Average throughput for different periods for the *MLP-DCP* algorithm with the *2C* configuration.

(b) Average speed up over LRU for different ROB sizes with the *4C-1* configuration.

Fig. 10. Sensitivity analysis to different design parameters

Finally, we have varied the size of the ROB from 128 to 512 entries to show the sensitivity of our proposals to this parameter of the architecture. Our mechanism is the only one which is aware of the ROB size: The higher the size of the ROB, the larger size of the cluster of L2 misses. Other policies only work with the number of L2 misses, which will not change if we vary the size of the ROB. When the ROB size increases, clusters of misses can contain more misses and, as a consequence, our mechanism can differentiate better between isolated and clustered misses. As we show in Figure 10(b), average improvements in the *4C-1* configuration are a little bit higher for a ROB with 512 entries, while *MinMisses* shows worse results. *MLPIPC-DCP* outperforms LRU and *MinMisses* by 10.4% and 4.3% respectively.

5.3   Hardware Cost

We have used the hardware implementation of Figure 5 to estimate the hardware cost of our proposal. In this Subsection, we focus our attention on the configuration *2C*. We suppose a 40-bit physical address space. Each entry in the ATD needs 29 bits (1 valid bit + 24-bit tag + 4-bit for LRU counter). Each set has 16 ways, so we have an overhead of 58 Bytes (B) for each set. As we have 1024 sets, we have a total cost of 58KB per core.

The hardware cost that corresponds to the extra fields of each entry in the L2 MSHR is 5 bits for the stack distance and 2B for the *MLP_cost*. As we have 32 entries, we have a total of 84B. Four adders are needed to update the *MLP_cost* of the active MSHR entries. HSHR entries need 1 valid bit, 8 bits to identify the ROB entry, 34 bits for the address, 5 bits for the stack distance and 2B for the *MLP_cost*. In total we need 64 bits per entry. As we have 24 entries in each HSHR, we have a total of 192B per core. Four adders per core are needed to update the *MLP_cost* of the active HSHR entries. Finally, we need 17 counters of 4B for each MLP-Aware SDH, which supposes a total of 68B per core. In addition to the storage bits, we also need an adder for incrementing MLP-aware SDHs and a shifter to halve the hit counters after each partitioning interval.

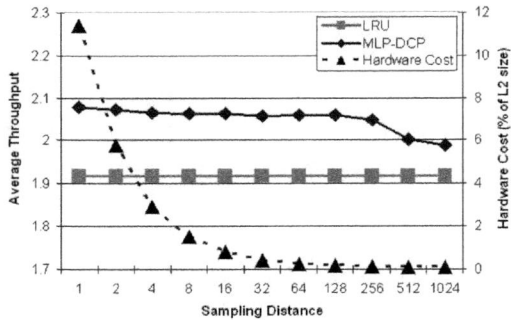

Fig. 11. Throughput and hardware cost depending on d_s in a two-core CMP

Sampled ATD. The main contribution to hardware cost corresponds to the ATD. Instead of monitoring every cache set, we can decide to track accesses from a reduced number of sets. This idea was also used in [8] with *MinMisses* in a CMP environment. Here, we use it in a different situation, say to estimate MLP-aware SDHs with a sampled number of sets. We define a *sampling distance* d_s that gives the distance between tracked sets. For example, if $d_s = 1$, we are tracking all the sets. If $d_s = 2$, we track half of the sets, and so on. Sampling reduces the size of the ATD at the expense of less accuracy in MLP-aware SDHs predictions as some accesses are not tracked, Figure 11 shows throughput degradation in a 2 cores scenario as the d_s increases. This curve is measured on the left y-axis. We also show the storage overhead in percentage of the total L2 cache size, measured on the right y-axis. Thanks to the sampling technique, storage overhead drastically decreases. Thus, with a sampling distance of 16 we obtain average throughput degradations of 0.76% and a storage overhead of 0.77% of the L2 cache size, which is less than 8KB of storage. We think that this is an interesting point of design.

5.4   Scalable Algorithm to Decide Cache Partitions

Evaluating all possible combinations allows determining the optimal partition for the next period. However, this algorithm does not scale adequately when associativity and the number of applications sharing the cache is raised. If we have a K-way associativity L2 cache shared by N cores, the number of possible partitions without considering the order is $\binom{N+K-1}{K}$. For example, for 8 cores and 16 ways, we have 245157 possible combinations. Consequently, the time to decide new cache partitions does not scale. Several heuristics have been proposed to reduce the number of cycles required to decide the new partition [8,9], which can be used in our situation. These proposals bound the length of the decision period by 10000 cycles. This overhead is very low compared to 5 million cycles (less than 0.2%).

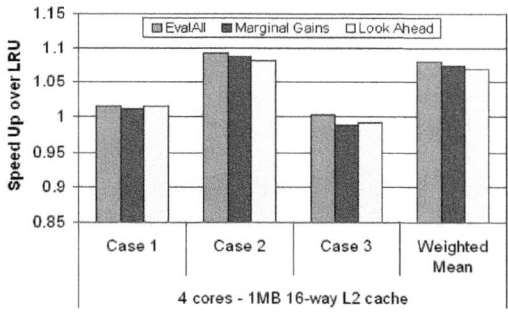

Fig. 12. Average throughput speed up over LRU for different decision algorithms in the *4C-1* configuration

Figure 12 shows the average speed up of *MLP-DCP* over LRU with the *4C-1* configuration with three different decision algorithms. Evaluating all possible partitions (denoted *EvalAll*) gives the highest speed up. The first greedy algorithm (denoted *Marginal Gains*) assigns one way to a thread in each iteration [9]. The selected way is the one that gives the largest increase in *MLP_cost*. This process is repeated until all ways have been assigned. The number of operations (comparisons) is of order $K \cdot N$, where K is the associativity of the L2 cache and N the number of cores. With this heuristic, an average throughput degradations of 0.59% is obtained. The second greedy algorithm (denoted *Look Ahead*) is similar to *Marginal Gains*. The basic difference between them is that *Look Ahead* considers the total *MLP_cost* for all possible number of blocks that the application can receive [8] and can assign more than one way in each iteration. The number of operations (add-divide-compare) is of order $N \cdot \frac{K^2}{2}$, where K is the associativity of the L2 cache and N the number of cores. With this heuristic, an average throughput degradations of 1.04% is obtained.

6   Conclusions

In this paper we propose a new DCP algorithm that assigns a cost to each L2 access according to its impact in final performance: isolated misses receive higher costs than clustered misses. Next, our algorithm decides the L2 cache partition that minimizes the total cost for all running threads. Furthermore, we have classified workloads for multiple cores into three groups and shown that the dominant situation is precisely the one that offers room for improvement.

We show that our proposal reaches high throughput for two- and four-core architectures. In all evaluated configurations, our proposal consistently outperforms both LRU and *MinMisses*, reaching a speed up of 63.9% (10.6% on average) and 15.4% (4.1% on average), respectively. With our proposals, we reach the performance of a 50% larger cache. Finally, we used a sampling technique to propose a practical implementation with a storage cost to less than 1% of the total L2 cache size and a scalable algorithm to determine cache partitions with nearly no performance degradation.

Acknowledgments

This work is supported by the Ministry of Education and Science of Spain under contracts TIN2004-07739, TIN2007-60625 and grant AP-2005-3318, and by SARC European Project. The authors would like to thank C. Acosta, A. Falcon, D. Ortega, J. Vermoulen and O. J. Santana for their work in the simulation tool. We also thank F. Cabarcas, I. Gelado, A. Rico and C. Villavieja for comments on earlier drafts of this paper and the reviewers for their helpful comments.

References

1. Serrano, M.J., Wood, R., Nemirovsky, M.: A study on multistreamed superscalar processors, Technical Report 93-05, University of California Santa Barbara (1993)
2. Tullsen, D.M., Eggers, S.J., Levy, H.M.: Simultaneous multithreading: maximizing on-chip parallelism. In: ISCA (1995)
3. Hammond, L., Nayfeh, B.A., Olukotun, K.: A single-chip multiprocessor. Computer 30(9), 79–85 (1997)
4. Cazorla, F.J., Ramirez, A., Valero, M., Fernandez, E.: Dynamically controlled resource allocation in SMT processors. In: MICRO (2004)
5. Chandra, D., Guo, F., Kim, S., Solihin, Y.: Predicting inter-thread cache contention on a chip multi-processor architecture. In: HPCA (2005)
6. Petoumenos, P., Keramidas, G., Zeffer, H., Kaxiras, S., Hagersten, E.: Modeling cache sharing on chip multiprocessor architectures. In: IISWC, pp. 160–171 (2006)
7. Chiou, D., Jain, P., Devadas, S., Rudolph, L.: Dynamic cache partitioning via columnization. In: Design Automation Conference (2000)
8. Qureshi, M.K., Patt, Y.N.: Utility-based cache partitioning: A low-overhead, high-performance, runtime mechanism to partition shared caches. In: MICRO (2006)
9. Suh, G.E., Devadas, S., Rudolph, L.: A new memory monitoring scheme for memory-aware scheduling and partitioning. In: HPCA (2002)

10. Kim, S., Chandra, D., Solihin, Y.: Fair cache sharing and partitioning in a chip multiprocessor architecture. In: PACT (2004)
11. Karkhanis, T.S., Smith, J.E.: A first-order superscalar processor model. In: ISCA (2004)
12. Mattson, R.L., Gecsei, J., Slutz, D.R., Traiger, I.L.: Evaluation techniques for storage hierarchies. IBM Systems Journal 9(2), 78–117 (1970)
13. Settle, A., Connors, D., Gibert, E., Gonzalez, A.: A dynamically reconfigurable cache for multithreaded processors. Journal of Embedded Computing 1(3-4) (2005)
14. Rafique, N., Lim, W.T., Thottethodi, M.: Architectural support for operating system-driven CMP cache management. In: PACT (2006)
15. Hsu, L.R., Reinhardt, S.K., Iyer, R., Makineni, S.: Communist, utilitarian, and capitalist cache policies on CMPs: caches as a shared resource. In: PACT (2006)
16. Qureshi, M.K., Lynch, D.N., Mutlu, O., Patt, Y.N.: A case for MLP-aware cache replacement. In: ISCA (2006)
17. Kroft, D.: Lockup-free instruction fetch/prefetch cache organization. In: ISCA (1981)
18. Sherwood, T., Perelman, E., Hamerly, G., Sair, S., Calder, B.: Discovering and exploiting program phases. IEEE Micro (2003)
19. Vera, J., Cazorla, F.J., Pajuelo, A., Santana, O.J., Fernandez, E., Valero, M.: FAME: Fairly measuring multithreaded architectures. In: PACT (2007)
20. Moreto, M., Cazorla, F.J., Ramirez, A., Valero, M.: Explaining dynamic cache partitioning speed ups. IEEE CAL (2007)
21. Sinharoy, B., Kalla, R.N., Tendler, J.M., Eickemeyer, R.J., Joyner, J.B.: Power5 system microarchitecture. IBM J. Res. Dev. 49(4/5), 505–521 (2005)
22. Luo, K., Gummaraju, J., Franklin, M.: Balancing throughput and fairness in SMT processors. In: ISPASS (2001)

Cache Sensitive Code Arrangement for Virtual Machine[*]

Chun-Chieh Lin and Chuen-Liang Chen

Department of Computer Science and Information Engineering,
National Taiwan University, Taipei,
10764, Taiwan
{d93020,clchen}@csie.ntu.edu.tw

Abstract. This paper proposes a systematic approach to optimize the code layout of a Java ME virtual machine for an embedded system with a cache-sensitive architecture. A practice example is to run JVM directly (execution-in-place) in NAND flash memory, for which cache miss penalty is too high to endure. The refined virtual machine generated cache misses 96% less than the original version. We developed a mathematical approach helping to predict the flow of the interpreter inside the virtual machine. This approach analyzed both the static control flow graph and the pattern of bytecode instruction streams, since we found the input sequence drives the program flow of the virtual machine interpreter. Then we proposed a rule to model the execution flows of Java instructions of real applications. Furthermore, we used a graph partition algorithm as a tool to deal with the mathematical model, and this finding helped the relocation process to move program blocks to proper memory pages. The refinement approach dramatically improved the locality of the virtual machine thus reduced cache miss rates. Our technique can help Java ME-enabled devices to run faster and extend longer battery life. The approach also brings potential for designers to integrate the XIP function into System-on-Chip thanks to lower demand for cache memory.

Keywords: cache sensitive, cache miss, NAND flash memory, code arrangement, Java virtual machine, interpreter, embedded system.

1 Introduction

Java platform extensively exists in all kinds of embedded and mobile devices. The Java™ Platform, Micro Edition (Java ME) [1] is no doubt a de facto standard platform of smart phone. The Java virtual machine (it is KVM in Java ME) is a key component that affects performance and power consumptions.

NAND flash memory comes with serial bus interface. It does not allow random access, and the CPU must read out the whole page at a time, which is a slow operation compared to RAM. This property leads a processor hardly to execute programs stored

---

[*] We acknowledge the support for this study through grants from National Science Council of Taiwan (NSC 95-2221-E-002 -137).

P. Stenström (Ed.): Transactions on HiPEAC III, LNCS 6590, pp. 24–42, 2011.

in NAND flash memory using the "execute-in-place" (XIP) technique. In the meanwhile, NAND flash memory offers fast write access time, and the most important of all, the technology has advantages in offering higher capacity than NOR flash technology does. As the applications of embedded devices become large and complicated, more mainstream devices adopt NAND flash memory to replace NOR-flash memory.

In this paper, we tried to offer an answer to the question: can we speed up an embedded device using NAND flash memory to store programs? "Page-based" storage media, like NAND flash memory, have higher access penalty than RAM does. Reducing the page miss becomes a critical issue. Thus, we set forth to find way to reduce the page miss rate generated by the KVM. Due to the unique structure of the KVM interpreter, we found a special way to exploit the dynamic locality of the KVM that is to trace the patterns of executed bytecode instructions instead of the internal flow of the KVM. It turned out to be a combinatorial optimization problem because the code layout must fulfill certain code size constraints. Our approach achieved the effect of static page preloading by properly arranging program blocks. In the experiment, we implemented a post-processing program to modify the intermediate files generated by the C compiler. The post-processing program refined machine code placement of the KVM based on the mathematical model. Finally, the obtained tuned KVMs dramatically reduced page accesses to NAND flash memories. The outcome of this study helps embedded systems to boost performance and extend battery life as well.

2 Related Works

Park *et al.*, in [2], proposed a hardware module to allow direct code execution from NAND flash memory. In this approach, program codes stored in NAND flash pages will be loaded into RAM cache on-demand instead of moving entire contents into RAM. Their work is a universal hardware-based solution without considering application-specific characteristics.

Samsung Electronics offers a commercial product called "OneNAND" [3] based on the same. It is a single chip with a standard NOR flash interface. Actually, it contains a NAND flash memory array for storage. The vendor intent was to provide a cost-effective alternative to NOR flash memory used in existing designs. The internal structure of OneNAND comprises a NAND flash memory, control logic, hardware ECC, and 5KB buffer RAM. The 5KB buffer RAM is comprised of three buffers: 1KB for boot RAM, and a pair of 2KB buffers used for bi-directional data buffers. Our approach is suitable for systems using this type of flash memories.

Park *et al.*, in [4], proposed yet another pure software approach to achieve execute-in-place by using a customized compiler that inserts NAND flash reading operations into program code at proper place. Their compiler determines insertion points by summing up sizes of basic blocks along the calling tree. Special hardware is no longer required, but in contrast to earlier work [2], there is still a need for tailor-made compiler.

Typical studies of refining code placement to minimize cache misses can apply to NAND flash cache system. Parameswaran *et al.*, in [5], used the bin-packing approach. It reorders the program codes by examining the execution frequency of basic blocks. Code segments with higher execution frequency are placed next to each other within the cache. Janapsatya *et al.*, in [6], proposed a pure software heuristic approach to reduce number of cache misses by relocating program sections in the main memory.

Their approach was to analyze program flow graph, identify and pack basic blocks within the same loop. They have also created relations between cache miss and energy consumption. Although their approach can identify loops within a program, breaking the interpreter of a virtual machine into individual circuits is hard because all the loops share the same starting point.

There are researches in improving program locality and optimizing code placement for either cache or virtual memory environment. Pettis [7] proposed a systematic approach using dynamic call graph to position procedures. They tried to place two procedures as close as possible if one of the procedure calls another frequently. The first step of Pettis' approach uses the profiling information to create weighted call graph. The second step iteratively merges vertices connected by heaviest weight edges. The process repeats until the whole graph composed of one or more individual vertex without edges.

However, the approach to collect profiling information and their accuracy is yet another issue. For example, Young and Smith in [8] developed techniques to extract effective branch profile information from a limited depth of branch history. Ball and Larus in [9] described an algorithm for inserting monitoring code to trace programs. Our approach is very different by nature. Previous studies all focused in the flow of program codes, but we tried to model the profile by input data.

This research project created a post-processor to optimize the code arrangements. It is analogous to "Diablo linker" [10]. They utilized symbolic information in the object files to generate optimized executable files. However, our approach will generate feedback intermediate files for the compiler, and invoke the compiler to generate optimized machine code.

3   Background

3.1   XIP with NAND Flash

NOR flash memory is popular as code memory because of the XIP feature. There are several approaches designed for using NAND flash memory as an alternative to NOR flash memory. Because NAND flash memory interface cannot connect to the CPU host bus, there has to be a memory interface controller to move data from NAND flash memory to RAM.

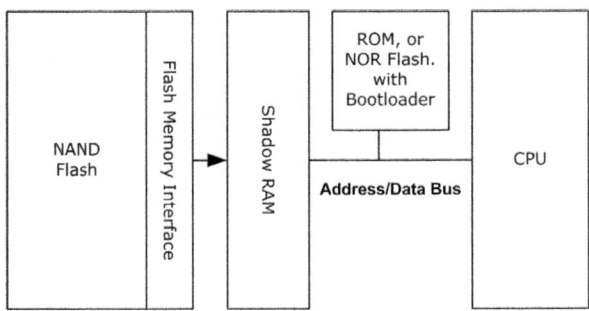

Fig. 1. Access NAND flash through shadow RAM

In system-level view, Figure 1 shows a straightforward design which uses RAM as the shadow copy of NAND flash. The system treats NAND flash memory as secondary storage device [11]. There should be a boot loader or RTOS resided in ROM or NOR flash memory. It copies program codes from NAND flash to RAM, then the processor executes program codes in RAM [12]. This approach offers best execution speed because the processor operates with RAM. The downside of this approach is it needs huge amount of RAM to mirror NAND flash. In embedded devices, RAM is a precious resource. For example, the Sony Ericsson T610 mobile phone [13] reserved 256KB RAM for Java heap. In contrast to using 256MB for mirroring NAND flash memory, all designers should agree that they would prefer to retain RAM for Java applets rather than for mirroring. The second pitfall is the implementation takes longer time to boot because the system must copy contents to RAM prior to execution.

Figure 2 shows a demand paging approach uses limited amount of RAM as the cache of NAND flash. The "romized" program codes stay in NAND flash memory, and a MMU loads only portions of program codes which is about to be executed from NAND into the cache. The major advantage of this approach is it consumes less RAM. Several kilobytes of RAM are enough to mirror NAND flash memory. Using less RAM means integrating CPU, MMU and cache into a single chip (the shadowed part in Figure 2) can be easier. The startup latency is shorter since the CPU is ready to run soon after the first NAND flash page is loaded into the cache. The component cost is lower than in the previous approach. The realization of the MMU might be either hardware or software approach, which is not covered in this paper.

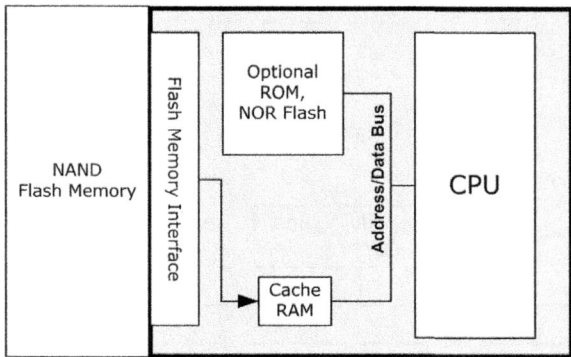

Fig. 2. Using cache unit to access NAND flash

However, performance is the major drawback of this approach. The penalty of each cache miss is high, because loading contents from a NAND flash page is nearly 200 times slower than doing the same operation with RAM. Therefore reducing cache misses becomes a critical issue for such configurations.

3.2 KVM Internals

Source Level. In respect of functionality, the KVM can be broken down into several parts: startup, class files loading, constant pool resolving, interpreter, garbage collection, and KVM cleanup. Lafond *et al.*, in [14], have measured the energy consumptions of each part in the KVM. Their study showed that the interpreter consumed more than 50% of total energy. In our experiments running Embedded Caffeine Benchmark [15], the interpreter contributed 96% of total memory accesses. These evidences lead to the conclusion that the interpreter is the performance bottleneck of the KVM, and they motivated us to focus on reducing the cache misses generated by the interpreter.

Figure 3 shows the program structure of the interpreter. It is a loop enclosing a large switch-case dispatcher. The loop fetches bytecode instructions from Java applications, and each "case" sub-clause deals with one bytecode instruction. The control flow graph of the interpreter, as illustrated in Figure 4, is a flat and shallow spanning tree. There are three major steps in the interpreter,

```
ReschedulePoint:
RESCHEDULE
opcode = FETCH_BYTECODE ( ProgramCounter );
switch ( opcode )
{
            case ALOAD: /* do something */
              goto ReschedulePoint;
            case IADD: /* do something */
              ...
            case IFEQ: /* do something */
              goto BranchPoint;
              ...
}
BranchPoint:
            take care of program counter;
            goto ReschedulePoint;
```

Fig. 3. Pseudo code of KVM interpreter

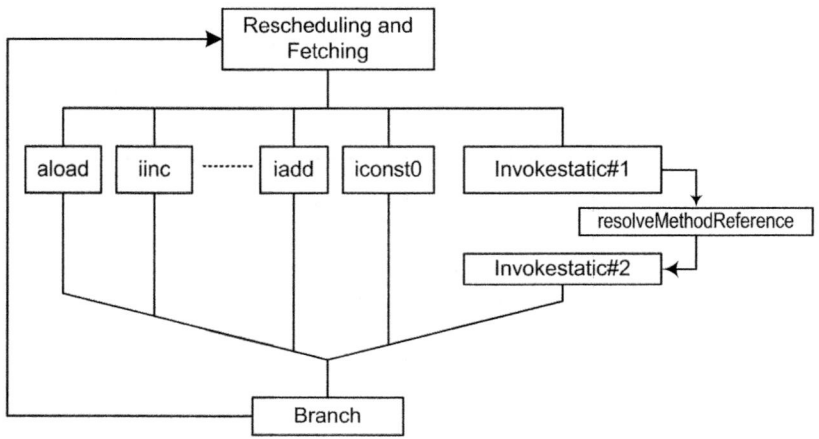

Fig. 4. Control flow graph of the interpreter

(1) Rescheduling and Fetching. In this step, KVM prepares the execution context and the stack frame. Then it fetches a bytecode instruction from Java programs.

(2) Dispatching and Execution. After reading a bytecode instruction from Java programs, the interpreter jumps to corresponding bytecode handlers through the big "switch...case..." statement. Each bytecode handler carries out the function of the corresponding bytecode instruction.

(3) Branching. The branch bytecode instructions may bring the Java program flow away from original track. In this step, the interpreter resolves the target address and modifies the program counter.

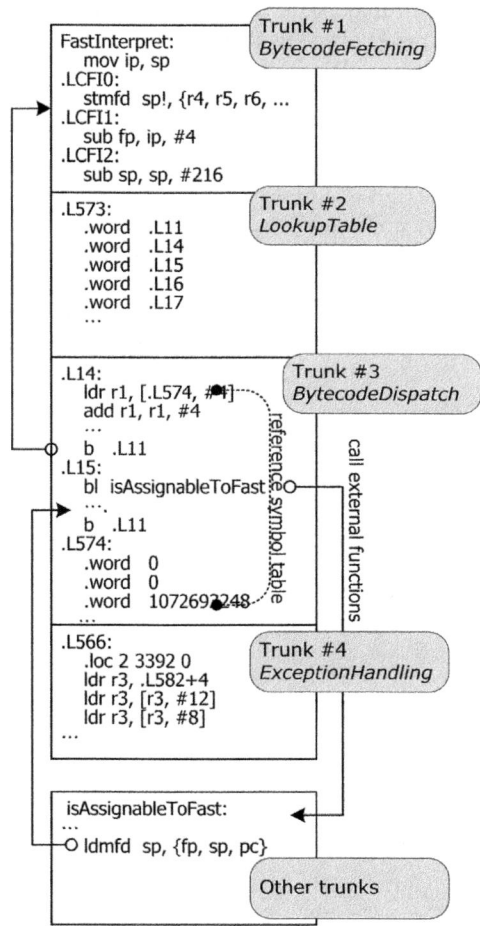

Fig. 5. The organization of the interpreter at assembly level

Assembly Level. Our analysis of the source files revealed the peculiar program structure of the VM interpreter. Analyzing the code layout in the compiled executables of the interpreter helped this study to create a code placement strategy. The assembly code analysis in this study is restricted to ARM and *gcc* for the sake of demonstration, but applying our theory to other platforms and tools is an easy job. Figure 5 illustrates the layout of the interpreter in assembly form (FastInterpret() in interp.c). The first trunk *BytecodeFetching* is the code block for rescheduling and fetching, it is exactly the first part in the original source code. The second trunk *LookupTable* is a large lookup table used in dispatching bytecode instructions. Each entry links to a bytecode handler. It is actually the translated result of the "switch...case...case" statement.

The third trunk *BytecodeDispatch* is the aggregation of more than a hundred bytecode handlers. Most bytecode handlers are self-contained which means a bytecode handler occupies a contiguous memory space in this trunk, and it does not jump to program codes stored in other trunks. There are only a few exceptions which call functions stored in other trunks, such as "invokevirtual." Besides, there are several constant symbol tables spread over this trunk. These tables are referenced by the program codes within the *BytecodeDispatch* trunk.

The last trunk *ExceptionHandling* contains code fragments for exception handling. Each trunk occupies a number of NAND flash pages. In fact, the total size of *BytecodeFetching* and *LookupTable* is about 1200 bytes (compiled with *arm-elf-gcc-3.4.3*), which is almost small enough to fit into two or three 512-bytes-page. Figure 6 shows the size distribution of bytecode handlers. The average size of a bytecode handler is 131 bytes, and there are 79 handlers smaller than 56 bytes. In other words, a 512-bytes-page could gather 4 to 8 bytecode handlers. The inter-handler execution flow dominates the number of cache misses generated by the interpreter. This is the reason that our approach tries to rearrange bytecode handlers within the *BytecodeDispatch* trunk.

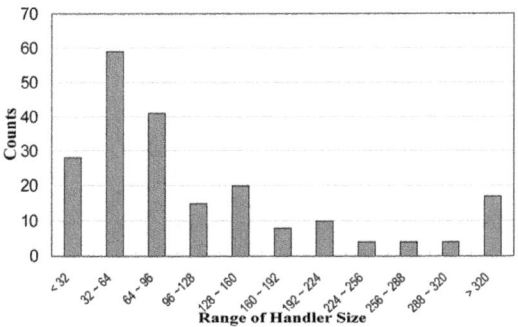

Fig. 6. Distribution of Bytecode Handler Size (compiled with *gcc-3.4.3*)

4 Analyzing Control Flow

4.1 Indirect Control Flow Graph

Static branch-prediction and typical code placement approaches derive the layout of a program from its control flow graph (CFG). However, the CFG of a VM interpreter is a special case, its CFG is a flat spanning tree enclosed by a loop. The CFG does not provide sufficient information to distinguish the temporal relations of each bytecode handler pair. If someone wants to improve the program locality by observing the dynamic execution order of program blocks, the CFG is apparently not a good tool to this end. Therefore, we propose a concept called "Indirect Control Flow Graph" (ICFG); it uses the real bytecode instruction sequences to construct the dual CFG of the interpreter. Consider a simplified virtual machine with 5 bytecode instructions: A, B, C, D, and E, and use the virtual machine to run a very simple user applet. Consider the following short alphabetic sequence as the instruction sequence of the user applet:

A-B-A-B-C-D-E-C

Each alphabet in the sequence represents a bytecode instruction. In Figure 7, the graph connected with the solid lines is the CFG of the simplified interpreter. By observing the flow in the CFG, the program flow becomes:

[Dispatch] – [Handler A] – [Dispatch] – [Handler B]…

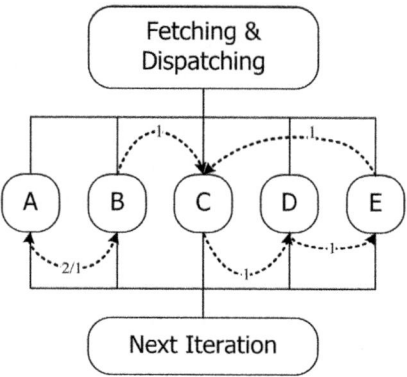

Fig. 7. The CFG of the simplified interpreter

It is hard to tell the relation between handler-A and handler-B because the loop header hides it. In other words, this CFG cannot easily present which handler would be invoked after handler-A is executed. The idea of the ICFG is to observe the patterns of the bytecode sequences executed by the virtual machine, not to analyze the structure of the virtual machine itself. Figure 8 expresses the ICFG in a readable way, it happens to be the sub-graph connected by the dashed directed lines in Figure 7.

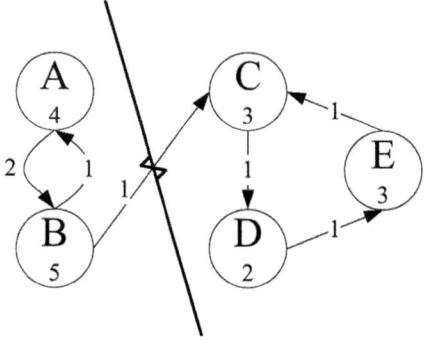

Fig. 8. An ICFG example. The number inside the circle represents the size of the handler

4.2   Tracing the Locality of the Interpreter

As stated, the Java applications that a KVM runs dominate the temporal locality of the interpreter. Precisely speaking, the incoming Java instruction sequence dominates the temporal locality of the KVM. Therefore, the first step to exploit the temporal locality is to consider the bytecode sequences executed by the virtual machine. Consider the previous example sequence, the order of accessed NAND flash pages is supposed to be:

[*BytecodeFetching*]–[*LookupTable*]–[A]–[*BytecodeFetching*]–[*LookupTable*]–
[B]–[*BytecodeFetching*]–[*LookupTable*]–[A]...

Obviously, memory pages containing *BytecodeFetching* and *LookupTable* are much often to appear in the sequence than those containing *BytecodeDispatch*. As a result, pages containing *BytecodeFetching* and *LookupTable* are favorable to last in the cache. Pages holding bytecode handlers have to compete with each other to stay in the cache. Thus, we induced that the order of executed bytecode instructions is the key factor impacts cache misses.

Consider an extreme case: In a system with three cache blocks, two cache blocks always hold memory pages containing *BytecodeFetching* and *LookupTable* due to the stated reason. Therefore, there is only one cache block available for swapping pages containing bytecode handlers. If all the bytecode handlers were located in distinct memory pages, processing a bytecode instruction would cause a cache miss. This is because the next-to-execute bytecode handler is always located in an uncached memory page. In other words, the sample sequence causes at least eight cache misses. Nevertheless, if both the handlers of A and B are grouped to the same page, cache misses will decline to 5 times, and the page access trace becomes:

fault-A-B-A-B-*fault*-C-*fault*-D-*fault*-E-*fault*-C

If we extend the group (A, B) to include the handler of C, the cache miss count would even drop to four times, and the page access trace looks like the following one:

fault-A-B-A-B-C-*fault*-D-*fault*-E-*fault*-C

Therefore, the core issue of this study is to find an efficient code layout method partitioning all bytecode instructions into disjoined sets based on their execution relevance. Each NAND flash page contains one set of bytecode handlers. We propose partitioning the ICFG reaches this goal.

Back to Figure 8, the directed edges represent the temporal order of the instruction sequence. The weight of an edge is the transition count for transitions from one bytecode instruction to the next. If we remove the edge (B, C), the ICFG is divided into two disjoined sets. That is, the bytecode handlers of A and B are placed in one page, and the bytecode handlers of C, D, and E are placed in the other. The page access trace becomes:

fault-A-B-A-B-*fault*-C-D-E-C

This placement causes only two cache misses, which is 75% lower than the worst case! The next step is to transform the ICFG diagram to an undirected graph by merging reversed edges connecting same vertices, and the weight of the undirected edge is the sum of weights of the two directed edges. The consequence is actually a variation of the classical MIN *k*-CUT problem. Formally speaking, we can model a given graph $G(V, E)$ as:

- V_i – represents the i-th bytecode instruction.
- $E_{i,j}$ – the edge connecting i-th and j-th bytecode instruction.
- $F_{i,j}$ – number of times that two bytecode instructions i and j executed after each other. It is the weight of edge $E_{i,j}$.
- K – number of expected partitions.
- $W_{x,y}$ – the inter-set weight. $\forall\ x \neq y$, $W_{x,y} = \Sigma F_{i,j}$ where $V_i \in P_x$ and $V_j \in P_y$.

The goal is to model the problem as the following definition:

Definition 1. The MIN k-CUT problem is to divide G into K disjoined partitions $\{P_1, P_2,\ldots,P_k\}$ such that $\Sigma W_{i,j}$ is minimized.

4.3 The Mathematical Model

Yet there is an additional constraint in our model. It is impractical to gather bytecode instructions to a partition regardless of the sum of the program size of consisted bytecode handlers. The size of each bytecode handler is distinct, and the code size of a partition cannot exceed the size of a memory page (e.g. NAND flash page). Our aim is to distribute bytecode handlers into several disjoined partitions $\{P_1, P_2,\ldots,P_k\}$. We define the following notations:

- S_i – the code size of bytecode handler V_i.
- N – the size of a memory page.
- $M(P_k)$ – the size of partition P_k. It is ΣS_m for all $V_m \in P_k$.
- $H(P_k)$ – the value of partition P_k. It is $\Sigma F_{i,j}$ for all V_i, $V_j \in P_k$.

Our goal is to construct partitions that satisfy the following constraints.

Definition 2. The problem is to divide G into K disjoined partitions $\{P_1, P_2,\ldots,P_k\}$. For each P_k that $M(P_k) \leq N$ such that $W_{i,j}$ is minimized, and maximize $\Sigma H(P_i)$ for all $P_i \in \{P_1, P_2,\ldots,P_k\}$.

This rectified model is exactly an application of the graph partition problem, i.e., the size of each partition must satisfy the constraint (size of a memory page), and the sum of inter-partition path weights is minimal. The graph partition problem is NP-complete [16]. However, the purpose of this paper was neither to create a new graph partition algorithm nor to discuss the difference between existing algorithms. The experimental implementation just adopted the following algorithm to demonstrate our approach works. Other implementations based on this approach may choose another graph partition algorithm that satisfies specific requirements.

Partition (G)

1. Find the edge with maximal weight $F_{i,j}$ among graph G, while the $S_i + S_j \leq N$. If there is no such an edge, go to step 4.
2. Call *Merge* (V_i, V_j) to combine vertices V_i and V_j.
3. Remove both V_i and V_j from G, go to step 1.
4. Find a pair of vertices V_i and V_j in G such that $S_i + S_j \leq N$. If there isn't any pair satisfied the criteria, go to step 7.
5. Call *Merge* (V_i, V_j) to combine vertices V_i and V_j.
6. Remove both V_i and V_j out of G, go to step 4.
7. End.

The procedure of merging both vertices V_i and V_j is:

Merge (V_i, V_j)

    1. Add a new vertex V_k to G.
    2. Pickup an edge E connects V_t with either V_i or V_j. If there is no such an edge, go to step 6.
    3. If there is already an edge F connects V_t to V_k.
    4.   Then, add the weight of E to F, and discard E.
    5.   Else, replace one end of E which is either V_i or V_j with V_k.
    6. End.

Finally, each vertex in G is a collection of several bytecode handlers. The refinement process is to collect bytecode handlers belonging to the same vertex and place them into one memory page.

5   The Process of Rewriting the Virtual Machine

Our approach emphasizes that the arrangements of bytecode handlers affects cache miss rate. In other words, it implies that programmers should be able to speed up their programs by properly changing the order of the "case" sub-clauses in the source files. Therefore, this study tries to optimize the virtual machine in two distinct ways. The first approach revises the order of the "case" sub-clauses in the sources of the virtual machine. If our theory were correct, this tentative approach should show that the modified virtual machine performs better in most test cases. The second version precisely reorganizes the layout of assembly code blocks of bytecode handlers, and this approach should be able to generate larger improvements than the first version.

5.1 Source-Level Rearrangement

The concept of the refining process is to arrange the order of these "case" statements in the source file (execute.c). The consequence is that after translating the rearranged source files, the compiler will place bytecode handlers in machine code form in meditated order. The following steps are the outline of the refining procedures.

A. Profiling. Run the Java benchmark program on the unmodified KVM. A custom profiler traces the bytecode instruction sequence, and it generates the statistics of inter-bytecode instruction counts. Although we can collect some patterns of instruction combinations by investigating the Java compiler, using a dynamic approach can capture further application-dependent patterns.

B. Measuring the size of each bytecode handler. The refining program compiles the KVM source files and measures the code size of each bytecode handler (i.e., the size of each 'case' sub-clause) by parsing intermediate files generated by the compiler.

C. Partitioning the ICFG. The previous steps collect all necessary information for constructing the ICFG. Then, the refining program partitions the ICFG by using a graph partition algorithm. From that result, the refining program knows the way to group bytecode handlers together. For example, a partition result groups (A, B) to a bundle and (C, D, E) to another as shown in Figure 8.

D. Rewriting the source file. According to the computed results, the refining program rewrites the source file by arranging the order of all "case" sub-clauses within the interpreter loop. Figure 9 shows the order of all "case" sub-clauses in the previous example.

```
switch ( opcode ) {
        case B:          ...;
        case A:          ...;
        case E:          ...;
        case D:          ...;
        case C:          ...;
}
```

Fig. 9. The output of rearranged case statements

5.2 Assembly-Level Rearrangement

The robust implementation of the refinement process consists of two steps. The refinement process acts as a post processor of the compiler. It parses intermediate files generated by the compiler, rearranges program blocks, and generates optimized assembly codes. Our implementation is inevitably compiler-dependent and CPU-dependent. Current implementation tightly is integrated with *gcc* for ARM, but the approach is easy to apply to other platforms. Figure 10 illustrates the outline of the processing flow, entities, and relations between each entity. The following paragraphs explain the functions of each step.

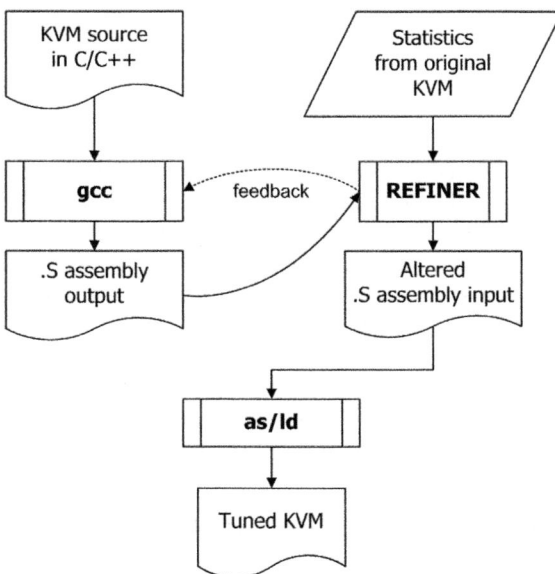

Fig. 10. Entities in the refinement process

A. Collecting dynamic bytecode instruction trace. The first step is to collect statistics from real Java applications or benchmarks, because the following steps will need these data for partitioning bytecode handlers. The modified KVM dumps the bytecode instruction trace while running Java applications. A special program called TRACER analyzes the trace dump to find the transition counts for all instruction pairs.

B. Rearranging the KVM interpreter. This is the core step and is realized by a program called REFINER. It acts as a post processor of *gcc*. Its duty is to parse bytecode handlers expressed in the assembly code and organize them into partitions. Each partition fits into one NAND flash page. The program consists of several sub tasks described as follows.

(i) Parsing layout information of the original KVM. The very first thing is to compile the original KVM. REFINER parses the intermediate files generated by *gcc*. According to structure of the interpreter expressed in assembly code introduced in §3.2, REFINER analyzes the jump table in the *LookupTable* trunk to find out the address and size of each bytecode handler.

(ii) Using the graph partition algorithm to group bytecode handlers into disjoined partitions. At this stage, REFINER constructs the ICFG with two key parameters: (1) the transition counts of bytecode instructions collected by TRACER; (2) the machine code layout information collected in the step A. It uses the approximate algorithm described in §4.3 to divide the undirected ICFG into disjoined partitions.

(iii) Rewriting the assembly code. REFINER parses and extracts assembly codes of all bytecode handlers. Then, it creates a new assembly file and dumps all bytecode handlers partition by partition according to the result of (ii).

(iv) Propagating symbol tables to each partition. As described in §3.2, there are several symbol tables distributed in the *BytecodeDispatch* trunk. For most RISC processors like ARM and MIPS, an instruction is unable to carry arbitrary constants as operands because of limited instruction word length. The solution is to gather used constants into a symbol table and place this table near the instructions that will access these constants. Hence, the compiler generates instructions with relative addressing operands to load constants from the nearby symbol tables. Take ARM for example, its application binary interface (ABI) defines two instructions called LDR and ADR for loading a constant from a symbol table to a register [17]. The ABI restricts the maximal distance between a LDR/ADR instruction and the referred symbol table to 4K bytes.

Besides, it would cause a cache miss if a machine instruction in page X loads a constant s_i from symbol table S_Y located in page Y. Our solution is to create a local symbol table S_X in page X and copy the value s_i to the new table. Therefore, the relative distance between s_i and the instruction never exceeds 4KB neither causes cache misses when the CPU tries to load s_i.

(v) Dumping contents in partitions to NAND flash pages. The aim is to map bytecode handlers to NAND flash pages. Its reassembled bytecode handlers belong to the same partition in one NAND flash page. After that, REFINER refreshes the address and size information of all bytecode handlers. The updated information helps REFINER to add padding to each partition and enforce the starting address of each partition to align to the boundary of a NAND flash page.

6 Evaluation

In this section, we start from a brief introduction of the environment and conditions used in the experiments. The first part of the experimental results is the outcome of source-level rearranged virtual machine. Those positive results prove our theory works. The next part is the experiment of assembly-level rearranged virtual machine. It further proves our refinement approach is able to produce better results than the original version.

6.1 Evaluation Environment

Figure 11 shows the block diagram of our experimental setup. In order to mimic real embedded applications, we have implanted Java ME KVM into uClinux for ARM7 in the experiment. One of the reasons to use this platform is that uClinux supports FLAT executable file format which is perfect for realizing XIP. We ran KVM/uClinux on a customized *gdb*. This customized *gdb* dumped memory access traces and performance statistics to files. The experimental setup assumed there was a specialized hardware unit acting as the NAND flash memory controller, which loads program codes from NAND flash pages to the cache. It also assumed all flash access operations worked transparently without the help from the operating system. In other words, modifying the OS kernel for the experiment is unnecessary. This experiment used "Embedded Caffeine Mark 3.0" [15] as the benchmark.

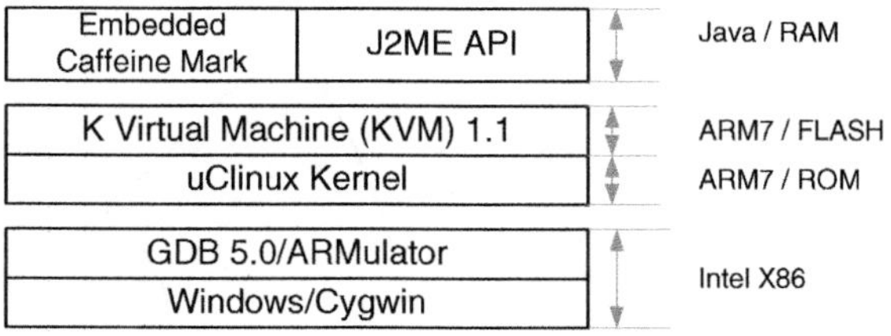

Embedded Caffeine Mark	J2ME API
K Virtual Machine (KVM) 1.1	
uClinux Kernel	
GDB 5.0/ARMulator	
Windows/Cygwin	

Java / RAM
ARM7 / FLASH
ARM7 / ROM
Intel X86

Title	Version
arm-elf-binutil	2.15
arm-elf-gcc	3.4.3
uClibc	0.9.18
J2ME (KVM)	CLDC 1.1
elf2flt	20040326

Fig. 11. Hierarchy of simulation environment

There are several kinds of NAND flash commodities in the market: 512-bytes, 2048-bytes, and 4096-bytes per page. In this experiment, we model the cache simulator after the following conditions:

1. There were four NAND flash page size options: 512, 1024, 2048 and 4096.
2. The page replacement policy was full associative, and it is a FIFO cache.
3. The number of cache memory blocks varied from 2, 4 ... to 32.

6.2 Results of Source-Level Rearrangement

First, we rearranged the "case" sub-clauses in the source codes using the introduced method. Table 1 lists the raw statistics of cache miss rates, and Figure 12 plots the charts of normalized cache miss rates from the optimized KVM. The experiment assumed the maximal cache size is 64K bytes. For each NAND flash page size, the number of cache blocks starts from 4 to (*64K / NAND flash page size*).

In Table 1, each column is the experimental result from a kind of the KVM. The "original" column refers to statistics from the original KVM, in which bytecode handlers is ordered by in machine codes. The second column "optimized" is the result from the KVM refined with our approach.

For example, in the best case (2048 bytes per page, 8 cache pages), the optimized KVM generates 105,157 misses, which is only 4.5% of the misses caused by the original KVM, and the improvement ratio is 95%.

Broadly speaking, the experiment shows that the optimized KVM outperforms the original KVM in most cases. Looking at the charts in Figure 12, the curves of normalized cache miss rates (i.e., *optimized_miss_rate / original_miss_rate*) tend to be concave. It means the improvement for the case of eight pages is greater than the one of four pages. It benefits from the smaller "locality" of the optimized KVM. Therefore, the cache could hold more localities, and this is helpful in reducing cache misses. After touching the bottom, the cache is large enough to hold most of the KVM program code. As the cache size grows, the numbers of cache misses of all configurations converge.

However, the miss rate at 1024 bytes * 32 blocks is an exceptional case. This is because our approach rearranges the order of bytecode handlers at source level, and it hardly predicts the precise starting address and code size of a bytecode handler. This is the drawback of the approach.

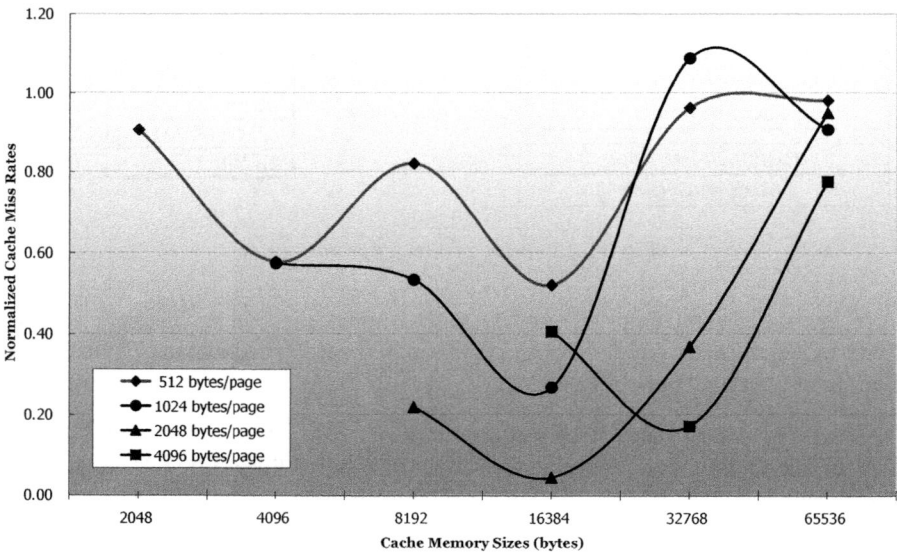

Fig. 12. The charts of normalized cache-miss rates from the source-level refined virtual machine. Each chart is an experiment performs on a specific page size. The *x*-axis is the size of the cache memory (*number_of_pages * page_size*).

Table 1. Normalized cache miss rates generated from source-level modified virtual machines

512 Bytes/Page		Miss Count	
# Pgs	Improve.	Original	Optimized
4	9.39%	25,242,319	22,871,780
8	42.25%	11,269,029	6,508,217
16	17.94%	2,472,373	2,028,834
32	47.84%	145,005	75,632
64	3.75%	11,933	11,485
128	1.91%	2,507	2,459
Total Access		567,393,732	567,393,732

1024 Bytes/Page		Miss Count	
# Pgs	Improve.	Original	Optimized
4	42.58%	15,988,106	9,180,472
8	46.58%	5,086,130	2,717,027
16	73.10%	486,765	130,921
32	-8.63%	23,395	25,413
64	9.35%	3,230	2,928
Total Access		567,393,732	567,393,732

2048 Bytes/Page		Miss Count	
# Pgs	Improve.	Original	Optimized
4	78.05%	10,813,688	2,373,841
8	95.51%	2,341,042	105,157
16	63.08%	68,756	25,388
32	4.98%	4,294	4,080
Total Access		567,393,732	567,393,732

4096 Bytes/Page		Miss Count	
# Pgs	Improve.	Original	Optimized
4	59.33%	4,899,778	1,992,734
8	82.82%	422,512	72,580
16	22.37%	8,995	6,983
Total Access		567,393,732	567,393,732

6.3   Results of Assembly-Level Rearrangement

The last experiment proved the theory should work except a few cases. The assembly-level rearrangement method is a remedy. We tuned four versions of KVM; each of them suited to one kind of page size. All the experimental measurements are compared

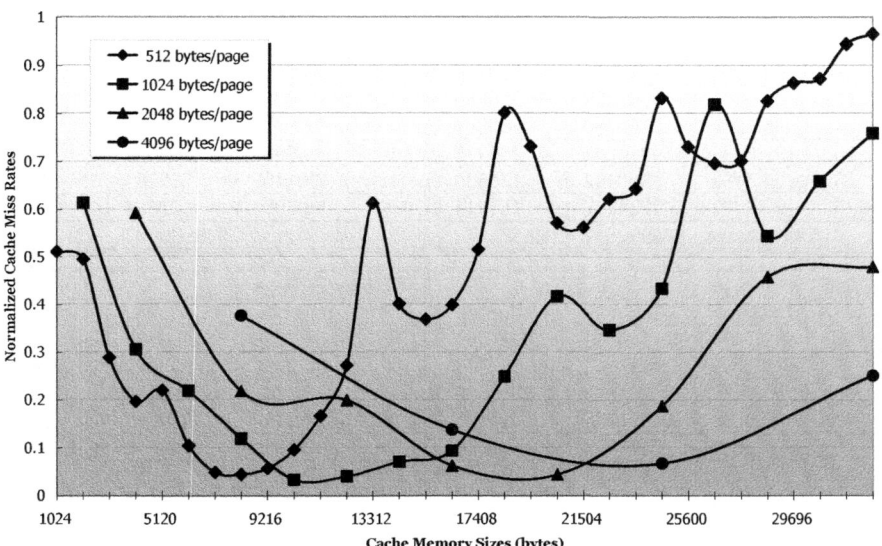

Fig. 13. The chart of normalized cache-miss rates from assembly-level rearranged virtual machines. Each chart is an experiment performs on a specific page size. The *x*-axis is the size of the cache memory (*number_of_pages * page_size*).

to those from the original KVM. Table 2 is the highlight of the experimental results and shows the extent of improvement of the optimized versions as well.

In the test case with 4KB/512-bytes per page, the cache miss rate of the tuned KVM is less than 1%, in contrast to the cache miss rate of the original KVM that is greater than 3%. In the best case, the cache miss rate of the tuned KVM is 96% lower than the value from the original one. Besides, in the case with only two cache blocks (1KB/512-bytes per page), the improvement is about 50%. It means the tuned KVMs outperform on devices with limited cache blocks.

Figure 13 is the chart of the normalized miss rates. The envelope lines of these charts are tending to be concave. In the conditions that the amounts of cache blocks is small, the cache miss rates of the tuned KVM decline faster than the rates of the original version, and the curve goes downward. Once there is enough cache blocks to hold the entire locality of the original KVM, the tuned version gradually loses its advantages, and the curve turns upward.

In both experiments, the normalized miss rate curves are tending to be concave. We conclude this is a characteristic of our approach.

Table 2. Experimental cache miss counts. Data of 21 to 32 pages are omitted due to being less relevant.

512 Bytes/Page		Miss Count		1024 Bytes/Page		Miss Count	
# Pgs	Improve.	Original	Optimized	# Pgs	Improve.	Original	Optimized
2	48.94%	52106472	25275914	2	38.64%	29760972	17350643
4	50.49%	34747976	16345163	4	69.46%	21197760	6150007
6	71.19%	26488191	7249424	6	78.15%	13547700	2812730
8	80.42%	17709770	3294736	8	88.11%	8969062	1013010
10	78.02%	12263183	2560674	10	96.72%	6354864	197996
12	89.61%	9993229	986256	12	96.02%	3924402	148376
14	95.19%	6151760	280894	14	92.97%	1735690	115991
16	95.63%	4934205	204975	16	90.64%	1169657	104048
18	94.37%	3300462	176634	18	75.11%	380285	89934
20	90.48%	1734177	156914	20	58.30%	122884	48679
	Total Access	548980637	521571173		Total Access	548980637	521571046

2048 Bytes/Page		Miss Count		4096 Bytes/Page		Miss Count	
# Pgs	Improve.	Original	Optimized	# Pgs	Improve.	Original	Optimized
2	40.74%	25616314	14421794	2	62.32%	14480682	5183539
4	78.17%	14733164	3055373	4	86.32%	7529472	978537
6	80.10%	8284595	1566059	6	93.27%	2893864	185037
8	93.80%	4771986	281109	8	74.91%	359828	85762
10	95.66%	2297323	94619	10	33.39%	88641	56096
12	81.33%	458815	81395	12	-89.68%	25067	45173
14	54.22%	96955	42166	14	0.08%	16547	15708
16	52.03%	62322	28403	16	-33.81%	7979	10144
18	24.00%	26778	19336	18	-17.08%	5484	6100
20	10.08%	18390	15710	20	-24.69%	3536	4189
	Total Access	548980637	521570848		Total Access	548980637	521570757

7 Conclusion

In this study, we present a refinement process to distribute bytecode handlers into logical partitions that can map to pages of NAND flash memory. The technique we used to profile the virtual machine analyzes not only the CFG of the interpreter but also the patterns of bytecode instruction streams, since we observe the input sequence drives the program flow. From this point of view, we conclude it is a kind of graph partition problem.

We use two different approaches in the experiments. By modifying either source codes or assembly codes, the refined KVMs effectively cause lower cache misses than the unmodified version. The success in source code modification even implies that our technique can help programmers to write efficient programs without the knowledge of modifying compiler-backend. Certainly, the assembly-level (or machine-code-level) rewriting tool is definitely the best solution and provides the ultimate performance.

The most important of all, the refined virtual machine has excellent performance on the devices with limited cache memory blocks. Consider the case of 8KB/512-bytes per page, the cache miss rate of the tuned KVM is 0.6%. Compare to the 3.2% of the original KVM, this is a significant improvement. Undoubtedly, if the cache size is large, the miss rate will not be an issue. However, our approach can ensure that the KVM generates lower cache misses at smaller cache sizes. This technique also enables SOC to integrate a small block of embedded cache RAM and still execute the KVM efficiently.

Comparing our improvement on the KVM interpreter with JIT (dynamic compilation) is an interesting issue. The outcome of JIT is usually good so that it seems the effort on improving interpreter is in vain. However, a JIT VM usually consumes huge amount of memory that a small-scaled embedded device cannot afford, it is still worthwhile to refine the interpreter VM. The experimental results in [18] by Anderson Faustino da Silva *et al.* suggest that an interpreter VM is between 3 to 11 times slower than a JIT VM. However, by taking timing parameters of real NAND flash memory and DRAM into our formula, the performance boost by our improvement helps an interpreter VM runs as faster as a JIT VM.

Actually, our approach is not exclusively for interpreters. Our investigation shows our approach is applicable to the part of translating bytecodes to native codes in a JIT VM. We left this issue for future development.

Furthermore, our systematic method can apply to any program with the following two properties. First, its program flow branches to a large number of sibling sub-blocks, i.e., a big "switch… case… case…" compound statement in the interpreter. Second, the input data patterns drive the execution flows of those sibling sub-blocks, so that we can plot an ICFG to capture the dynamic trace. In practice, our approach can apply to other virtual machines, like Microsoft .NET Common Language Runtime, or an XML-driven processing program besides KVM.

References

1. Sun Microsystem. J2ME Building Blocks for Mobile Devices. Sun Microsystems, Inc. (May 19, 2000)
2. Park, C., Seo, J., Bae, S., Kim, H., Kim, S., Kim, B.: A Low-Cost Memory Architecture with NAND XIP for Mobile Embedded Systems. In: ISSS+CODES 2003: First IEEE/ACM/IFIP International Conference on Hardware/Software Codesign and System Synthesis. ACM Press, New York (2003)

 3. Samsung Electronics. OneNAND Features & Performance. Samsung Electronics (November 4, 2005)
 4. Park, C., Lim, J., Kwon, K., Lee, J., Min, S.L.: Compiler Assisted Demand Paging for Embedded Systems with Flash Memory. In: Proceedings of the 4th ACM international Conference on Embedded Software (EMSOFT 2004), Pisa, Italy, September 27-29, pp. 114–124. ACM Press, New York (2004)
 5. Parameswaran, S., Henkel, J.: I-CoPES: Fast Instruction Code Placement for Embedded Systems to Improve Performance and Energy Efficiency. In: Proceedings of the 2001 IEEE/ACM International Conference on Computer-Aided Design, pp. 635–641. IEEE Press, Piscataway (2001)
 6. Janapsatya, A., Parameswaran, S., Henkel, J.: REMcode: relocating embedded code for improving system efficiency. In: IEE Proc.-Comput. Digit. Tech., vol. 151(6) (November 2004)
 7. Pettis, K., Hansen, R.: Profile-guided code positioning. In: The Proceedings of the ACM SIGPLAN 1990 Conference on Programming Language Design and Implementation PLDI 1990, vol. 25(6), pp. 16–27. ACM Press, New York (1990)
 8. Young, C., Smith, M.D.: Improving the Accuracy of Static Branch Prediction Using Branch Correlation. In: Proceedings of the 6th International Conference on Architectural Support for Programming Languages and Operating Systems (ASPLOS VI) (October 1994)
 9. Ball, T., Larus, J.R.: Optimally profiling and tracing programs. ACM Transactions on Programming Languages and Systems 16(4), 1319–1360 (1994)
10. Van Put, L., Chanet, D., De Bus, B., De Sutler, B., De Bosschere, K.: DIABLO: a reliable, retargetable and extensible link-time rewriting framework. In: The Proceedings of the Fifth IEEE International Symposium on Signal Processing and Information Technology, pp. 7–12. IEEE Press, Piscataway (2005)
11. Santarini, M.: NAND versus NOR-Which flash is best for bootin' your next system? In: EDN, Reed Business Information, a division of Reed Elsevier Inc., October 13, pp. 41–48 (2005)
12. Micron Technology, Inc. Boot-from-NAND Using Micron® MT29F1G08ABA NAND Flash with the Texas Instruments™ (TI) OMAP2420 Processor, Micron Technology, Inc. (2006)
13. Sony Ericsson. Java™ Support in Sony Ericsson Mobile Phones. Sony Ericsson Mobile Communications AB (2003)
14. Lafond, S., Lilius, J.: An Energy Consumption Model for Java Virtual Machine. Turku Centre for Computer Science TUCS Technical Report No 597, TUCS (March 2004)
15. CaffeineMark 3.0, Pendragon Software Corp., http://www.benchmarkhq.ru/cm30
16. Garey, M.R., Johnson, D.S.: Computer and Intractability - A Guide to the Theory of NP-Completeness. Bell Telephone Laboratories (1979)
17. Fuber, S.: ARM System-on-Chip Architecture, 2 edn. August 25, pp. 49–72. Addison-Wesley Professional, Reading (2000)
18. da Silva, A.F., Costa, V.S.: An Experimental Evaluation of JAVA JIT Technology. Journal of Universal Computer Science 11(7), 1291–1309 (2005)

Data Layout for Cache Performance on a Multithreaded Architecture

Subhradyuti Sarkar and Dean M. Tullsen

Department of Computer Science and Engineering,
University of California, San Diego

Abstract. High performance embedded architectures will in some cases combine simple caches and multithreading, two techniques that increase energy efficiency and performance at the same time. However, that combination can produce high and unpredictable cache miss rates, even when the compiler optimizes the data layout of each program for the cache.

This paper examines data-cache aware compilation for multithreaded architectures. Data-cache aware compilation finds a layout for data objects which minimizes inter-object conflict misses. This research extends and adapts prior cache-conscious data layout optimizations to the much more difficult environment of multithreaded architectures. Solutions are presented for two computing scenarios: (1) the more general case where any application can be scheduled along with other applications, and (2) the case where the co-scheduled working set is more precisely known.

It is shown that these techniques reduce data cache misses for a variety of cache architectures, multithreading environments, and cache latencies.

1 Introduction

High performance embedded architectures seek to accelerate performance in the most energy-efficient and complexity-effective manner. Cacheing and multithreading are two technologies that improve performance and energy efficiency at the same time. However, when used in combination, these techniques can be in conflict, as unpredictable interactions between threads can result in high conflict miss rates. It has been shown that in large and highly associative caches, these interactions are not large; however, embedded architectures are more likely to combine multithreading with smaller, simpler caches. This paper demonstrates techniques which allow the architecture to maintain these simpler caches, rather than necessitating more complex and power-hungry caches. It does so by solving the problem in software via the compiler and the runtime, rather than through more complex hardware.

Cache-conscious Data Placement (CCDP) [1] is a technique which finds an intelligent layout for the data objects of an application, so that at runtime objects which are accessed in an interleaved pattern are not mapped to the same cache blocks. On a processor core with a single execution context, this technique has been shown to significantly reduce the cache conflict miss rate and improve performance over a wide set of benchmarks.

P. Stenström (Ed.): Transactions on HiPEAC III, LNCS 6590, pp. 43–68, 2011.

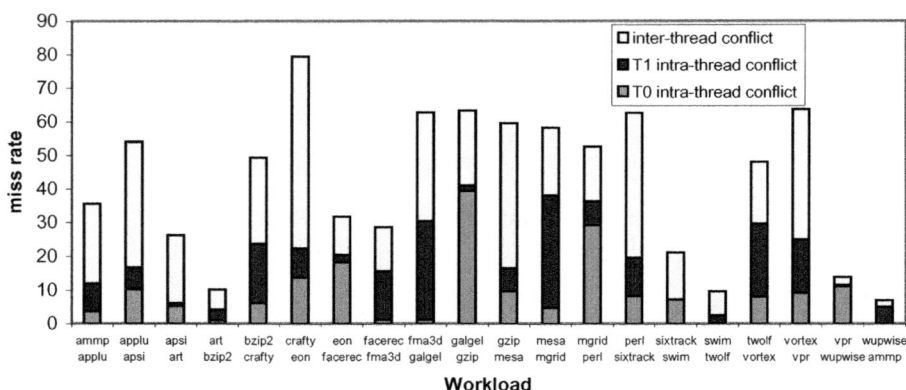

Fig. 1. Percentage of data cache misses that are due to conflict. The cache is 32 KB direct-mapped, shared by two contexts in an SMT processor. The program listed on top is T1.

However, in a multithreaded environment, such as simultaneous multithreading (SMT) [2,3], CCDP can lose much of its benefit, or even reduce performance. In an SMT processor multiple threads run concurrently in separate hardware contexts. This architecture has been shown to be a much more energy efficient approach to accelerate processor performance than other traditional performance optimizations [4,5]. In a simultaneous multithreading processor with shared caches, however, objects from different threads compete for the same cache lines – resulting in potentially expensive inter-thread conflict misses. These conflicts cannot be analyzed in the same manner that was applied successfully by prior work on intra-thread conflicts. This is because inter-thread conflicts are not deterministic.

Figure 1, shows the percentage of conflict misses for various pairs of co-scheduled threads. This figure shows two important trends. First, inter-thread conflict misses are just as prevalent as intra-thread conflicts (26% vs. 21% of all misses). Second, the infusion of these new conflict misses significantly increases the overall importance of conflict misses, relative to other types of misses.

Inter-thread cache conflicts are not strictly confined to multithreaded architectures. We also see this phenomenon in multi-core architectures. Multi-cores may share on-chip L2 caches, or possibly even L1 caches [6,7]. A data-layout strategy that reduces both intra-thread and inter-thread conflict misses will be helpful in those architectural scenarios as well. However, in this work we focus in particular on multithreaded architectures, because they interact and share caches at the lowest level.

In this paper, we develop new techniques that allow the ideas of CCDP to be extended to multithreaded architectures, and be effective. We consider the following compilation scenarios:

(1) In the most general case, we cannot assume we know which applications will be co-scheduled. This may occur, even in an embedded processor, if we have a set of applications that can run in various combinations. In this scenario, the

compiler does not know which applications are going to be co-scheduled by the operating system or runtime system, and in fact the combination of co-scheduled threads may even change over the lifetime of a particular thread.

(2) In more specialized environments, we will be able to more precisely exploit specific knowledge about the applications and how they will be run. We may have *a priori* knowledge about application sets to be co-scheduled in the multithreaded processor. In these situations, it should be feasible to co-compile, or at least cooperatively compile, these concurrently running applications.

This paper makes the following contributions: (1) It shows that traditional multithreading-oblivious cache-conscious data placement is not effective in a multithreading architecture. In some cases, it does more harm than good. (2) It proposes two extensions to CCDP that can identify and eliminate most of the inter-thread conflict misses for each of the above mentioned scenarios. We show as much as a 26% average reduction in misses after our placement optimization. (3) It shows that even for applications with many objects and interleavings, temporal relationship graphs of reasonable size can be maintained without sacrificing performance and quality of placement. (4) It presents several new mechanisms that improve the performance and realizability of cache conscious data placement (whether multithreaded or not). These include object and edge filtering for the temporal relationship graph. (5) We show that these algorithms work across different cache configurations. We show results for various caches and cache latencies, including set-associative caches. Previous CCDP algorithms have targeted direct-mapped caches – we show that they do not translate easily to set-associative caches. We present a new mechanism that eliminates set-associative conflict misses much more effectively. (6) Additionally, we extend these techniques to higher numbers of threads.

The rest of the paper is organized as follows. Section 2 discusses related work. Our simulation environment and benchmarks are described in Section 3. Section 4 and Section 5 provide algorithms and results for independent and co-ordinated data placement methods respectively. Section 6 shows that these techniques can work across a broad range of cache and processor configurations. We conclude in Section 7.

2 Related Work

Direct-mapped caches, although faster and simpler than set-associative caches, are prone to conflict misses. Consequently, much research has been directed toward reducing conflicts in a direct-mapped cache. Several papers [8,9,10] explore unconventional line-placement policies to reduce conflict misses. Lynch, *et al.* [11] demonstrate that careful virtual to physical translation (page-coloring) can reduce the number of cache misses in a physically-indexed cache. Rivera and Tseng [12] predict cache conflicts in a large linear data structure by computing expected conflict distances, then use intra- and inter-variable padding to eliminate those conflicts. A compiler-directed partitioning of the process address-space for a real-time system is described in [13], such that no pre-emptible process will share cache location with other processes.

The Split Cache [14] is a technique to virtually partition the cache through special hardware instructions, which the compiler can exploit to put potentially conflicting data structures in isolated virtual partitions.

Other works [15,16] dynamically detect and remove conflict misses, without requiring any support from the compiler. These methods logically partition the cache into *pages*, and can recolor conflicting pages to reduce conflict misses. This research attempts to reduce cache conflict misses without specialized hardware, or reducing the ability of any single thread to use the entire cache.

In a simultaneous multithreading architecture [2,3],various threads share execution and memory system resources on a fine-grained basis. Sharing of the L1 cache by multiple threads usually increases inter-thread conflict misses [2,17,18]. Until now, few studies have been conducted which try to improve cache performance in an SMT processor, particularly without significant hardware support. It has been shown [19] that partitioning the cache into per-thread local regions and a common global region can avoid some inter-thread conflict misses. Compiler directed cache partitioning for SMT processors has been explored by May, *et al.* [20]. However, static partitioning reduces the amount of cache memory available to a particular thread, which is undesirable. Traditional code transformation techniques (tiling, copying and block data layout) have been applied, along with a dynamic conflict detection mechanism to achieve significant performance improvement [21]; however, these transformations yield good results only for regular loop structures. Lopez, *et al.* [22] also look at the interaction between caches and simultaneous multithreading in embedded architectures. However, their solutions also require dynamically reconfigurable caches to adapt to the behavior of the co-scheduled threads.

This research builds on the profile-driven data placement proposed by Calder, *et al.* [1]. The goal of this technique is to model temporal relationships between data objects through profiling. The temporal relationships are captured in a *Temporal Relationship Graph* (TRG), where each node represents an object and edges represent the degree of temporal conflict between objects. Hence, if objects P and Q are connected by a heavily weighted edge in the TRG, then placing them in overlapping cache blocks is likely to cause many conflict misses. The TRG is constructed by keeping a queue of objects accessed in the recent past. The queue is examined at each memory reference to check if the newly accessed object has a previous occurrence. Accessing other objects between two successive accesses to the same object indicates a temporal conflict. A simple example of a TRG and a possible resulting cache mapping is shown in Figure 2.

We have extended this technique to SMT processors and set associative caches. Also, we have introduced the concept of object and edge trimming - which significantly reduces the time and space complexity of our placement algorithm. Kumar and Tullsen [23] describe techniques, some similar to this paper, to minimize instruction cache conflicts on an SMT processor. However, the dynamic nature of the sizes, access patterns, and lifetimes of memory objects makes the data cache problem significantly more complex.

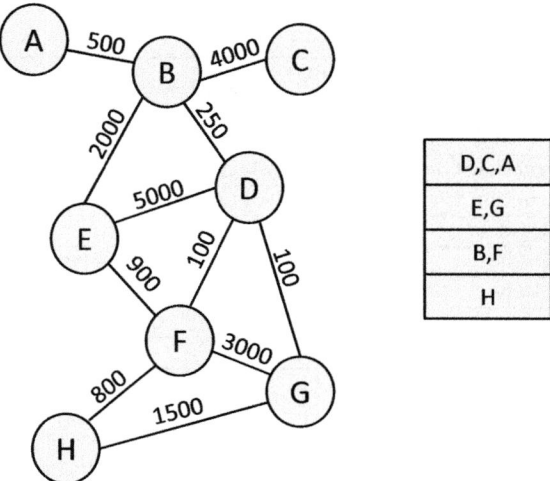

Fig. 2. A simplified Temporal Relationship Graph of the interleavings of 8 equal-sized objects (left), and a mapping of those objects (right) into a cache big enough to hold four objects, which minimizes conflicts between objects.

This paper contains several enhancements over a prior published version [24]. For example, this version contains more detailed descriptions of the compiler algorithms used, and several new results, particularly in Section 6.

3 Simulation Environment and Benchmarks

We run our simulations on SMTSIM [25], which simulates an SMT processor. The detailed configuration of the simulated processor is given in Table 1. For most portions of the paper, we assume the processor has a 32 KB, direct-mapped data cache with 64-byte blocks. We also model the effects on set associative caches in Section 6, but we focus on a direct-mapped cache both because the effects of inter-thread conflicts are more severe, and because direct-mapped caches can be an attractive design point for many embedded designs. We assume the address mappings resulting from the compiler and dynamic allocator are preserved in the cache. This would be the case if the system did not use virtual to physical translation, if the cache is virtually indexed, or if the operating system uses page coloring to ensure that our cache mappings are preserved.

The fetch unit in our simulator fetches from the available execution contexts based on the ICOUNT fetch policy [3] and the *flush* policy from [26], a performance optimization that reduces the overall cost of any individual miss. The ICOUNT fetch policy gives fetch priority to that thread which has the fewest instructions in the front end (fetch/decode/rename/queue) stages of the pipeline, thus always seeking to provide an even mix of instructions in the instruction window to maximize parallelism. The *flush* policy recognizes that in the presence of very long memory latencies, it is better for a stalled thread to release all held resources for use by non-stalled threads.

Table 1. SMT Processor Details

Parameter	Value
Fetch Bandwidth	2 Threads, 4 Instructions Total
Functional Units	4 Integer, 4 Load/Store, 3 FP
Instruction Queues	32 entry Integer, 32 entry FP
Instruction Cache	32 KB, 2-way set associative
Data Cache	32 KB, direct-mapped
L2 Cache	512 KB, 4-way set associative
L3 Cache	1024 KB, 4-way set associative
Miss Penalty	L1 15 cycles, L2 80 cycles, L3 500 cycles
Pipeline Depth	9 stages

It is important to note that a multithreaded processor tends to operate in one of two regions, in regards to its sensitivity to cache misses. If it is latency-limited (no part of the hierarchy becomes saturated, and the memory access time is dominated by device latencies), sensitivity to the cache miss rate is low, because of the latency tolerance of multithreaded architectures. However, if the processor is operating in bandwidth-limited mode (some part of the subsystem is saturated, and the memory access time is dominated by queuing delays), the multithreaded system then becomes very sensitive to changes in the miss rate. For the most part, we choose to model a system that has plenty of memory and cache bandwidth, and never enters the bandwidth-limited regions. This results in smaller observed performance gains for our placement optimizations, but we still see significant improvements. However, real processors will likely reach that saturation point with certain applications, and the expected gains from our techniques would be much greater in those cases.

Table 2 alphabetically lists the 20 SPEC2000 benchmarks that we have used. The SPEC benchmarks represent a more complex set of applications than represented in some of the embedded benchmark suites, with more dynamic memory usage; however, these characteristics do exist in real embedded applications. For our purposes, these benchmarks represent a more challenging environment to apply our techniques. In our experiments, we generate a k-threaded workload by picking each benchmark along with its $(k-1)$ successors (modulo the size of the table) as they appear in Table 2. Henceforth we shall refer to a workload by the ID of its first benchmark. For example, workload 10 (at two threads) would be the combination {*galgel gzip*}. Our experiments report results from a simulation window of two hundred million instructions; however, the benchmarks are fast-forwarded by ten billion dynamic instructions beforehand to ensure that we are executing in the main execution body of the application. Table 2 also lists the L1 hit rate of each application when run independently. All profiles (used to drive the compiler and layout optimizations) are generated running the SPEC *train* inputs, and simulation and measurement with the *ref* inputs. We also profile and optimize for a much larger portion of execution than we simulate.

Table 2. Simulated Benchmarks

ID	Benchmark	Type	Hit Rate(%)	ID	Benchmark	Type	Hit Rate(%)
1	ammp	FP	84.19	11	gzip	INT	95.41
2	applu	FP	83.07	12	mesa	FP	98.32
3	apsi	FP	96.54	13	mgrid	FP	88.56
4	art	FP	71.31	14	perl	INT	89.89
5	bzip2	INT	94.66	15	sixtrack	FP	92.38
6	crafty	INT	94.48	16	swim	FP	75.13
7	eon	INT	97.42	17	twolf	INT	88.63
8	facerec	FP	81.52	18	vortex	INT	95.74
9	fma3d	FP	94.54	19	vpr	INT	86.21
10	galgel	FP	83.01	20	wupwise	INT	51.29

This type of study represents a methodological challenge in accurately reporting performance results. In multithreaded experimentation, every run consists of a potentially different mix of instructions from each thread, making relative IPC a questionable metric. In this paper we use weighted speedup [26] to report our results.

Weighted speedup (WS) is given by

$$WS = \frac{1}{number\ of\ threads} \sum_{threads} \frac{IPC_{new}}{IPC_{baseline}}$$

Weighted speedup much more accurately reflects system-level performance improvements, and makes it more difficult to create artificial speedups by changing the bias of the processor toward certain threads.

4   Independent Data Placement

The next two sections handle two different execution scenarios. In this first section, we solve the more general and difficult scenario, where the compiler actually does not know which applications will be scheduled together dynamically, or the set of co-scheduled threads changes frequently; however, we assume all applications will have been generated by our compiler. In the following section, we handle the case where we have specific knowledge about which jobs will be co-scheduled.

In the current execution scenario, then, co-scheduling will be largely unpredictable and dynamic. However, we can still compile programs in such a way that conflict misses are minimized. Since all programs would essentially be compiled in the same way, some support from the operating system, runtime system, or the hardware is required to allow each co-scheduled program to be mapped onto the cache differently.

CCDP techniques tend to create balanced access across the cache. We have modified CCDP techniques to create an intentionally unbalanced utilization of the cache, mapping objects to a *hot* portion and a *cold* portion. This does not necessarily imply more intra-thread conflict misses. For example, the two most heavily accessed objects in the program can be mapped to the same cache index without a loss in performance, if they are not typically accessed in an interleaved pattern – this is the point of using the temporal relationship graph of interleavings to do the mapping, rather than just using reference counts. CCDP would typically create a more balanced distribution of accesses across the cache; however, it can be tuned to do just the opposite. This is a similar approach to that used in [23] for procedure placement, but applied here to the placement of data objects.

However, before we present the details of the object placement algorithm, we first describe the assumptions about hardware or OS support, how data objects are identified and analyzed, and some options that make the CCDP algorithms faster and more realizable.

4.1   Support from Operating System or Hardware

Our independent placement technique (henceforth referred to as IND) repositions the objects so that they have a *top-heavy* access pattern, i.e. most of the memory accesses are limited to the *top portion* of the cache. Let us consider an SMT processor with two hardware contexts, and a shared L1 cache (whose size is at least twice the virtual-memory page size). If the architecture uses a virtual cache, the processor can xor the high bits of the cache index with a hardware context ID (e.g., one bit for 2 threads, 2 bits for 4 threads), which will then map the hot portions of the address space to different regions of the cache.

In a physically indexed cache, we don't even need that hardware support. When the operating system loads two different applications in the processor, it ensures (by page coloring or otherwise) that heavily accessed virtual pages from the threads do not collide in the physically indexed cache.

For example, let us assume an architecture with a 32 KB data cache and 4 KB memory pages – so the cache can accommodate 8 memory pages. Physical pages whose page number is from the set $L = \{0, 1, 2, 3\}$ (modulo 8) map to the *top half* of the cache. Similarly, pages having page-numbers from the set $U = \{4, 5, 6, 7\}$ (modulo 8) map to the *bottom half*. The compiler creates an unbalanced partition by placing most of the heavily accessed objects in virtual pages having page-number from set L (modulo 8). During execution, before the OS allocates a physical page for the virtual page V of process p, it examines the virtual page number of V and the hardware context in which p is running. If the page-number of V is in the set L and p is running in context 0, the OS tries to allocate a physical page whose page number is from the set L. If p is running in context 1 instead, the OS tries to allocate a physical page having page-number from the set U. Thus, the mapping assumed by the compilers is preserved, but with each thread's *hot* area mapped to a different half of the cache. This is simply an application of page coloring, which is a common OS function.

4.2   Analysis of Data Objects

To facilitate data layout, we consider the address space of an application as partitioned into several *objects*. An *object* is loosely defined as a contiguous region in the (virtual) address space that can be relocated with little help from the compiler and/or the runtime system. The compiler typically creates several objects in the code and data segment, the starting location and size of which can be found by scanning the symbol table. A section of memory allocated by a malloc call can be considered to be a single *dynamic object*, since it can easily be relocated using an instrumented front-end to malloc. However, since the same invocation of malloc can return different addresses in different runs of an application – we need some extra information to identify the dynamic objects (that is, to associate a profiled object with the same object at runtime). Similar to [1], we use an additional tag (henceforth referred to as HeapTag) to identify the dynamic objects. HeapTag is generated by xor-folding the top four addresses of the return stack and the call-site of malloc.

Reordering the objects in the stack segment can be more difficult. First, no symbol table entry is created for the objects that are allocated in stack frames. Second, addresses on the stack are specified relative to the stack or frame pointer – so the same variable can be assigned different virtual addresses at different points of execution, based on the current call stack. Hence, in this analysis we treat the whole stack segment as a single object. To place stack objects more finely could require adding significant padding to the stack, which would reduce spatial locality, and increase stack overflow events. As a result, our techniques are not expected to be particularly effective for stack objects. However, stack objects tend to be short-lived and accessed with high temporal locality. Therefore, our techniques tend to still be effective overall for two reasons. First, stack objects tend to have low miss rates, and second, short-lived objects tend to be ignored (marked as unimportant) in our placement algorithm, anyway.

After the objects have been identified, their reference count and lifetime information over the simulation window can be retrieved by instrumenting the application binary with a tool such as ATOM [27]. Also found are the temporal relationships between the objects, which can be captured using a temporal relationship graph (henceforth referred to as TRGSelect graph). The TRGSelect graph contains nodes that represent objects (or portions of objects) and edges between nodes contain a weight which represents how many times the two objects were interleaved in the actual profiled execution.

Temporal relationships are collected at a finer granularity than full objects – mainly because some of the objects are much larger than others, and usually only a small portion of a *bigger* object has temporal association with the *smaller* one. It is more logical to partition the objects into fixed size chunks, and then record the temporal relationship between chunks. Though all the chunks belonging to an object are placed sequentially in their original order, having finer-grained temporal information helps us to make more informed decisions when two conflicting objects must be put in an overlapping cache region. The size of the chunk used for tracking conflicts is an important policy

decision – smaller chunks capture more information at the expense of a larger
TRGSelect graph. We have set the chunk size equal to the block size of the targeted cache. This provides the best performance, as we now track conflicts at
the exact same granularity that they occur in the cache.

4.3   Object and Edge Filtering

Profiling a typical SPEC2000 benchmark, even for a few millions of committed
instructions, involves tens of thousands of objects, and generates hundreds of millions of temporal relationship edges between objects. To make this analysis manageable, we must reduce both the number of nodes (the number of objects) as well
as the number of edges (temporal relationships between objects) in the TRGSelect
graph. This is possible because finding a suitable placement for all the identifiable
objects is not necessary. Most of these objects are rarely accessed and/or have a
very short life-time – hence their relative placement with respect to other objects
has little effect on L1 miss rates. We classify objects as *unimportant* if their reference count is zero, or the sum of the weights of incident edges in TRGSelect graph
lies below a certain threshold. In our experiment, that threshold was set to be either first percentile or fifth percentile – depending on the total number of objects
enumerated for a particular workload. Object filtering follows Algorithm 1.

If a HeapTag assigned to a heap object is non-unique, we mark all but the
most frequently accessed object having that HeapTag as unimportant. Multiple
objects usually have the same HeapTag when dynamic memory is being allocated
in a loop and they usually have similar temporal relationship with other objects.
Since heap objects with the same HeapTag would be indistinguishable from one
another to the customized memory allocator, making a placement decision based
on the most prominent member of the group seems to be a logical choice.

A similar problem exists for building the TRGSelect graph. Profiling creates
a TRGSelect graph with a very large number of edges. Since it is desirable to
store the entire TRGSelect graph in memory, keeping all these edges would not
be practical. Fortunately, we have noted that in a typical profile more than 90%
of all the edges are *light-weight*, having an edge weight less than one tenth of
the heavier edges. We use the following epoch-based heuristic to periodically
trim off the *potentially* light-weight edges, limiting the total number of edges to
a preset maximum value. In a given epoch, edges with weight below a particular
threshold are marked as *potentially light-weight*. In the next epoch, if the weight
of an edge marked as *potentially light-weight* does not increase significantly from
the previous epoch, it is deleted from the TRGSelect graph. The threshold is
liberal when the total number of edges is low, but made more aggressive when
the number of edges nears our preset limit on the number of edges. Algorithm 2
describes the edge trimming more precisely. In practice, we have noticed that a
TRGSelect graph with an upper threshold of 10 million edges can capture all
the important temporal relationships between the object-chunk pairs.

In this algorithm, then, we prune the edges dynamically during profiling,
and prune the objects after profiling, but before the placement phase. We find
pruning has little impact on the quality of our results.

1: mark all objects as important
2: **if** an object has a reference count of zero **then**
3:      mark the object is unimportant
4: **end if**
5: **for all** object o with nonzero reference count **do**
6:      TRGSum[o] $\leftarrow$ sum of TRG edge weights incident on this object
7: **end for**
8: **if** total number of objects is less than 4096 **then**
9:      find the objects below 1 percentile (based on TRGSum)
10:     mark these objects as unimportant
11: **else**
12:     find the objects below 5 percentile (based on TRGSum)
13:     mark these objects as unimportant
14: **end if**
15: **for all** non-unique HeapTag **do**
16:     add all objects having that HeapTag to a list L
17:     find the object p in L having maximum reference count
18:     delete p from L
19:     mark all objects in L as unimportant
20: **end for**

Algorithm 1. Object Filtering

The various parameters that we have determined via experiment for Algorithm 2 are given in Table 3.

4.4 Building the TRGSelect Graph

To build the TRGSelect graph, memory references in the profiling window are scanned sequentially and each of these memory references is attributed to some profiled object. Then, the access patterns with respect to other objects in the window are used to add appropriate edges (or increase edge-weights) in the TRGSelect graph, with the help of the following data structures:

1. set O_{TRG}: objects of a given executable, which is also the set of vertices of TRGSelect graph
2. set E_{TRG}: edges of the TRGSelect graph
3. queue TRGQueue: A FIFO queue which records a finite history of object access patterns in the profile

Ideally, TRGQueue (the reference history window) should be able to grow without any bound so that all interleavings are accurately reflected in TRGSelect. However, maintaining such an accurate history is space and time-prohibitive, and also quite unnecessary for the following reason. An object, after being brought into the cache, does not stay there indefinitely – it typically gets evicted after a while due to a conflict or capacity miss. Thus, if consecutive accesses to an object are so far apart as to not appear in a large window, the particular interleavings not recorded are less important (that is, it would be very difficult

```
 1: if number of edges is TRGSelect > trigger_value then
 2:     low_cutoff ← Λ percentile of all edge weights
 3:     high_cutoff ← Υ percentile of all edge weights
 4:     for all edges E in TRGSelect graph do
 5:         if E is marked as 'spurious' and its weight < high_cutoff then
 6:             delete E
 7:         end if
 8:     end for
 9:     for all edges E in TRGSelect graph do
10:         if weight of E < low_cutoff then
11:             mark E as 'spurious'
12:         else
13:             mark E as 'important'
14:         end if
15:     end for
16: end if
17: if number of edges is TRGSelect > max_trg_size then
18:     aggressive_cutoff ← Θ percentile of all edge weights
19:     for all edges E in TRGSelect graph do
20:         if weight of E < aggressive_cutoff then
21:             delete E
22:         end if
23:     end for
24: end if
25: trigger_value ← number of edges in TRGSelect + trigger_delta
```

Algorithm 2. Edge Filtering for a Particular Epoch

Table 3. Parameters for Edge Filtering

Parameter	Value
initial trigger_value	5×10^6
trigger_delta	10^6
max_trg_size	12×10^6
Λ	30
Υ	40
Θ	30

to remove all interleavings and keep the object in the cache over a long time period, anyway). We have observed that we can trim TRGQueue after its size exceeds twice the targeted cache size without affecting the quality of placement. Algorithm 3 sketches the steps involved in building the TRGSelect graph.

4.5 Placement Algorithm

For independent data placement, the cache blocks are partitioned into *native* and *foreign* sets. If we know the application is going to be executed on an SMT processor with k contexts, the top $\frac{1}{k}$ cache blocks are marked as *native*, and

```
 1: $O_{TRG} \leftarrow \Phi$
 2: $E_{TRG} \leftarrow \Phi$
 3: add the stack object to $O_{TRG}$
 4: add the constant and global objects to $O_{TRG}$ by scanning symbol-table
 5: add the heap objects to $O_{TRG}$ by scanning the memory-allocation calls
 6: repeat
 7:     scan the next memory reference $m_r$
 8:     find object $o$ such that $m_r$ accesses $o$ and $o \in O_{TRG}$
 9:     if $o$ is not the tail of TRGQueue then
10:         enqueue $o$ to TRGQueue
11:         object $p \leftarrow$ second-last object in TRGQueue
12:         while $p \neq$ NULL or $p \neq o$ do
13:             if edge$(o, p) \in E_{TRG}$ then
14:                 edge-weight[edge$(o, p)$] $\leftarrow$ edge-weight[edge$(o, p)$] $+1$
15:             else
16:                 $E_{TRG} \leftarrow E_{TRG} \cup$ edge$(o, p)$
17:                 edge-weight[edge$(o, p)$] $\leftarrow 1$
18:             end if
19:             $p \leftarrow$ predecessor of $p$ in TRGQueue
20:         end while
21:         if size of all objects in TRGQueue exceeds threshold $S_{TRGQ}$ then
22:             prune TRGQueue
23:         end if
24:         if size of $E_{TRG}$ exceeds threshold $S_{ETRG}$ then
25:             prune $E_{TRG}$ {see Algorithm 2}
26:         end if
27:     end if
28: until there are no more memory references to scan
29:
30: prune $O_{TRG}$ {see Algorithm 1}
```

Algorithm 3. Building the TRGSelect Graph

other cache blocks are marked as *foreign*. For any valid placement of an object in a native block, we define an associated cost, which is the sum of the costs for each chunk placed in the contiguous cache blocks. The cost of a chunk is the edge weight (interleaving factor) between that chunk and all chunks of other objects already placed in that cache block (see algorithm 4).

If the cache block is marked as foreign, a bias is added to the overall cost to force the algorithm to only place an object or part of an object in the foreign section if there is no good placement in the native. The bias for an object is set to be λ times the maximum edge weight between a chunk belonging to this object and any other chunk in the TRGSelect graph. If an object faces high resistance (thus signifying a high probability of conflict) with the objects already placed in the native cache block, it might be (fully or partially) placed in the foreign cache blocks. Varying this bias allows a tradeoff between combined cache performance, and uncompromised cache performance when running alone.

```
1: cost ← 0
2: for all cache block C that is going to be occupied by this object do
3:    let p be the chunk of this object to be placed in C
4:    for all object-chunk pair q already placed in C do
5:       cost ← cost + edge weight between p and q in TRGSelect graph
6:    end for
7: end for
8: return cost
```

Algorithm 4. Finding Cost of a Placement

Our basic placement heuristic is to order the objects and then place them each, in that order, into the cache where they incur minimal cost. Since some objects are fundamentally different in nature and size from others, we came up with a set of specialized placement strategies, each targeting one particular type of object. Specifically, we will separately consider constant objects, small global objects, important global objects, and heap objects.

An object which resides in the code segment is defined as a constant object. Constant objects are placed in their default location (altering the text segment might have adverse effects on the instruction cache). However, when other objects are placed in cache, their temporal relationship with the constant objects is taken into consideration.

Small global objects are handled differently than larger objects, allowing us to transform potential conflicts into cache prefetch opportunities. A statically allocated object which resides in the data segment is defined as a global object. Furthermore, a global object is classified as *small* if its size is less than three-fourths of the block size. As in [1], we try to cluster the small global objects that have heavily-weighted edges in the TRGSelect graph and place them in the same cache block. Accessing any of the objects in the cluster will prefetch the others, avoiding costly cache misses in the near future. Small global objects are clustered greedily, starting with the pair of objects with the highest edge weight between them.

After a cluster has been formed, nodes representing individual objects in the cluster are coalesced into a single node (in the TRGSelect graph). The cluster will be assigned a starting location along with other non-small objects in the next phase of the placement algorithm.

Next, we place the global objects. Our greedy placement algorithm is sensitive to the order in which the objects are placed. By experimentation, we have found the following approach to be effective. We build a TRGPlace graph from the TRGSelect graph, where chunks of individual objects are merged together into a single node (edge weights are adjusted accordingly). Next, the most heavily weighted edge is taken from the TRGPlace graph. The two objects connected by that edge are placed in the cache, and marked as placed; however, recall that the actual placement still uses the TRGSelect graph, which tracks accesses to the individual chunks. Thus, two objects with a heavy edge between them may still overlap in the cache, if only some chunks of those objects have interleaving access pattern.

In each subsequent iteration of the algorithm, an unplaced object is chosen which maximizes the sum of TRGPlace edge-weights between itself and the objects that have been already placed. In case of a tie, the object with a higher reference count is given preference.

Unimportant global objects are placed so as to fill holes in the address space created by the allocation of the important global objects. Placement of important global objects usually creates large *holes* (a contiguous section in the address space where no object has been placed) in the data segment. When placing an unimportant object, we scan the data segment and place the object in the first available free region big enough to accommodate it.

Heap objects also reside in the data segment, however they are dynamically created and destroyed at runtime using malloc and free calls. Specifying a placement for heap objects is more difficult because a profiled heap object might not be created, or might have different memory requirements in a later execution of the same application with different input. Thus, we determine the placement assuming the object is the same size, but only indicate to our custom malloc the location of the first block of the desired mapping. The object gets placed there, even if the size differs from the profiled run.

Our customized memory allocation/deallocation routines are closely based on the FastFit algorithm [28]. Every memory request of less than 4 KB in size is rounded to the next power of two. For every power of two from 16 to 4096, there is a corresponding linked list of memory blocks. When malloc receives an allocation request, it tries to satisfy it from the corresponding linked list. If no free block is available in the corresponding linked list, or the request is for more than 4 KB of memory, then memory is allocated from a *wilderness chunk* using the traditional FirstFit algorithm [29].

During execution, our customized malloc first computes the HeapTag for the requested heap object. If the HeapTag matches any of the recorded HeapTags for which a customized allocation should be performed, malloc returns a suitably aligned address. When the newly created heap object is brought in the cache, it occupies the blocks specified by the placement algorithm.

4.6   Independent Placement Results

The effects of data placement by IND on miss rate and weighted speedup are shown in Figure 3 and Figure 4, respectively. The Baseline series shows data cache miss rate without any type of placement optimization. CCDP shows the miss rate if traditional CCDP is performed on each of the applications. Since CCDP ignores inter-thread conflicts, for four workloads CCDP actually increases the miss rate over Baseline. LG2ACC shows the miss rate if L1 data cache is implemented as a *Double access local-global split cache* [19]. Split caches are designed to reduce conflicts in a multithreaded workload, though in our experiments the split cache was not overly effective. The final three series (IND-30, IND-40, IND-50) show the effect of co-ordinated data placement with λ (the placement bias) set to 0.30, 0.40 and 0.50 respectively. The figure shows that no single value of λ is universally better than others, though all of them yield

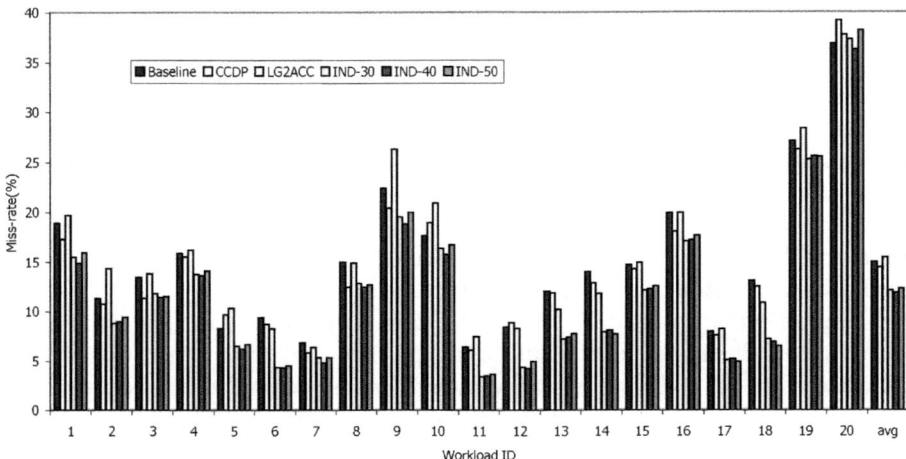

Fig. 3. Data Cache miss rate after Independent Placement (IND)

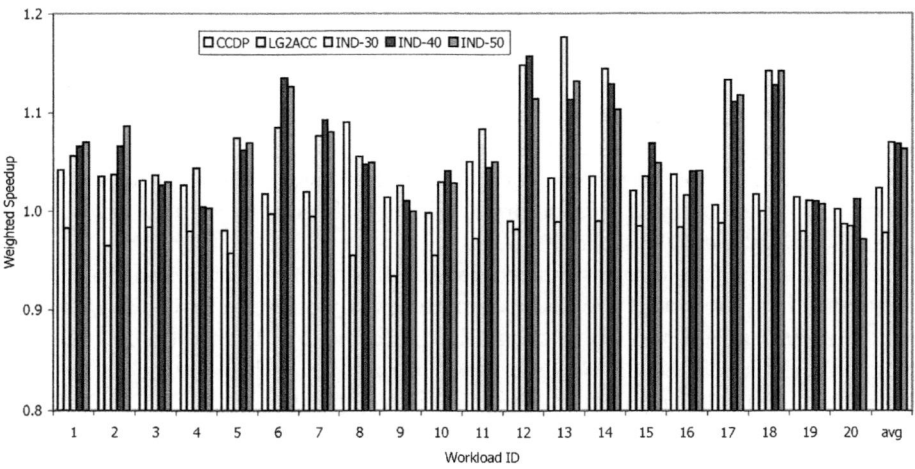

Fig. 4. Weighted Speedup after Independent Placement (IND)

improvement over traditional CCDP. For future work, it may be that setting
λ individually for each application, based on number and size of objects, for
example, will yield even better results.

A careful comparison of Figure 3 and Figure 1 shows that the effectiveness
of co-ordinated data placement is heavily correlated with the fraction of cache
misses that are caused by conflicts. On workloads like {*crafty eon*} (workload 6)
or {*gzip mesa*} (11), more than half of the cache misses are caused by conflicts,
and IND-30 reduces the miss rate by 54.0% and 46.8%, respectively. On the
other hand, only 6% of the cache misses in workload {*wupwise ammp*} (20) are
caused by conflicts, and IND-30 achieves only a 1% gain.

IND reduced overall miss rate by 19% on average, reduced total conflict misses by more than a factor of two, and achieved a 6.6% speedup. We also ran experiments with limited bandwidth to the L2 cache (where at most one pending L1 miss can be serviced in every two cycles), and in that case the performance tracked the miss rate gains more closely, achieving an average weighted speedup gain of 13.5%.

IND slightly increases intra-thread cache conflict (we still are applying cache-conscious layout, but the bias allows for some inefficiency from a single-thread standpoint). For example, the average miss rate of the applications, when run alone with no co-scheduled jobs increases from 12.9% to 14.3%, with λ set to 0.4. However, this result is heavily impacted by one application, *ammp* for which this mapping technique was largely ineffective due to the large number of heavily-accessed objects. If the algorithm was smart enough to just leave *ammp* alone, the average single-thread miss rate would be 13.8%. Unless we expect single-thread execution to be the common case, the much more significant impact on multithreaded miss rates makes this a good tradeoff.

5   Co-ordinated Data Placement

In many embedded or application-specific environments, programs that are going to be co-scheduled are known in advance. In such a scenario, it might be more beneficial to co-compile those applications and lay out their data objects in unison. This approach provides more accurate information about the temporal interleavings of objects to the layout engine.

Our coordinated placement algorithm (henceforth referred to as CORD) is similar in many ways to IND. However, in CORD the cache is not split into *native* and *foreign* blocks, and thus there is no concept of *biasing*. In CORD, the TRGSelect graph from all the applications are merged together and important objects from all the applications are assigned a placement in a single pass.

5.1   Merging of TRGSelect Graphs

The TRGSelect graph generated by executing the instrumented binary of an application captures the temporal relationships between the objects of that application. However, when two applications are co-scheduled on an SMT processor, objects from different execution contexts will vie for the same cache blocks in the shared cache. We have modeled inter-thread conflicts by merging the TRGSelect graphs of the individual applications. It is important to note that we profile each application separately to generate two graphs, which are then merged probabilistically. While we may have the ability to profile the two threads running together and their interactions, there is typically little reason to believe the same interactions would occur in another run. The exception would be if the two threads communicate at a very fine granularity, in which case it would be better to consider them a single parallel application.

Assigning temporal relationship weights between two objects from different applications requires modeling interactions that are much less deterministic than interactions between objects in the same thread. We thus use a probabilistic model to quantify expected interactions between objects in different threads.

Two simplifying assumptions have been made for estimating the inter-thread temporal edge weights, which make it easier to quantify the expected interactions between objects in separate threads. (1) The relative execution speeds of the two threads is known a priori. Relative execution speed of co-scheduled threads typically remains fairly constant unless one of the threads undergoes a phase change – which can be discovered via profiling. (2) Within its lifetime, an object is accessed in a regular pattern, i.e. if the lifetime of an object o is k cycles, and the total reference count of o is n, then o is accessed once every $\frac{k}{n}$ cycles. Few objects have very skewed access pattern so this assumption gives a reasonable estimate of the number of references made to an object in a particular interval.

We use these assumptions to estimate the interleavings between two objects (in different threads). From the first assumption, along with the known lifetimes of objects, we can calculate the likelihood that two objects have overlapping lifetimes (and the expected duration). From the second assumption, we can estimate the number of references made to those objects during the overlap. The number of interleavings cannot be more than twice the lesser of the two (estimated) reference counts. We apply a scaling factor to translate this worst-case estimate of the interleavings during an interval, into an expected number of interleavings. This scaling factor is determined experimentally. To understand the point of the scaling factor, if the two objects are being accessed at an equal rate by the two threads, but we always observe a run of two accesses from one thread before the other thread issues an access, the scaling factor would be 0.50. The steps required to merge two TRGSelect graphs into a single, unified graph is outlined in Algorithm 5.

In our experiments we have found it sufficient to only put temporal edges between *important* objects (i.e., objects not marked as unimportant) of each application, which eliminates edge explosion.

5.2   Coordinated Placement Results

The miss-rate impact and weighted speedup achieved by CORD is shown in Figures 5 and 6. The three series CORD-60, CORD-70 and CORD-80 represents the result of independent data placement with scaling factor set to 0.6, 0.7 and 0.8 respectively. The scaling factor represents the degree of interleaving we expect between memory accesses from different threads accessing the same cache set.

In most of the workloads, the speedup is somewhat more than that obtained from independent placement, thus confirming our hypothesis that being able to exploit more specific information about conflicting objects leads to better placement decisions. On the average CORD reduced miss rate by 26% and achieved 8.8% speedup. However, if one of these *optimized* applications is run alone (i.e. without its counterpart application) we do sacrifice single-thread performance slightly, but the effect is much less than the gain when co-scheduled. The amount of the single-thread loss depends somewhat on the scaling factor. The average Baseline miss rate was 12.9%. With coordinated placement, and a scaling factor

1: $O_{TRG,0} \leftarrow$ set of vertices in TRGSelect graph of application 0
2: $O_{TRG,1} \leftarrow$ set of vertices in TRGSelect graph of application 1
3: $E_{TRG,0} \leftarrow$ set of edges in TRGSelect graph of application 0
4: $E_{TRG,1} \leftarrow$ set of edges in TRGSelect graph of application 0
5:
6: $\{O_{TRG}$ and E_{TRG} are respectively the vertex and edge sets of the merged
   TRGSelect graph$\}$
7: $O_{TRG} \leftarrow O_{TRG,0} \cup O_{TRG,1}$
8: $E_{TRG} \leftarrow E_{TRG,0} \cup E_{TRG,1}$
9:
10: **for all** object $o \in O_{TRG,0}$ **do**
11:     **for all** object $p \in O_{TRG,1}$ **do**
12:         $LT_o \leftarrow$ life-time of o
13:         $R_o \leftarrow$ number of memory references to o
14:         $LT_p \leftarrow$ life-time of p
15:         $R_p \leftarrow$ number of memory references to p
16:         $LT_{o,p} \leftarrow$ overlapping life-time of o and p $\{$computed from LT_o, LT_p and
    relative rate of executions of two applications$\}$
17:         **if** $LT_{o,p} > 0$ **then**
18:             $R_o^n \leftarrow R_o \times \frac{LT_{o,p}}{LT_o}$
19:             $R_p^n \leftarrow R_p \times \frac{LT_{o,p}}{LT_p}$
20:             $E_{TRG} \leftarrow E_{TRG} \cup$ edge(o,p)
21:             edge-weight[edge$(o,p)] \leftarrow 2 \times min(R_o^n, R_p^n) \times s$ $\{s$ being the scaling factor$\}$
22:         **end if**
23:     **end for**
24: **end for**

Algorithm 5. Merging TRGSelect graphs

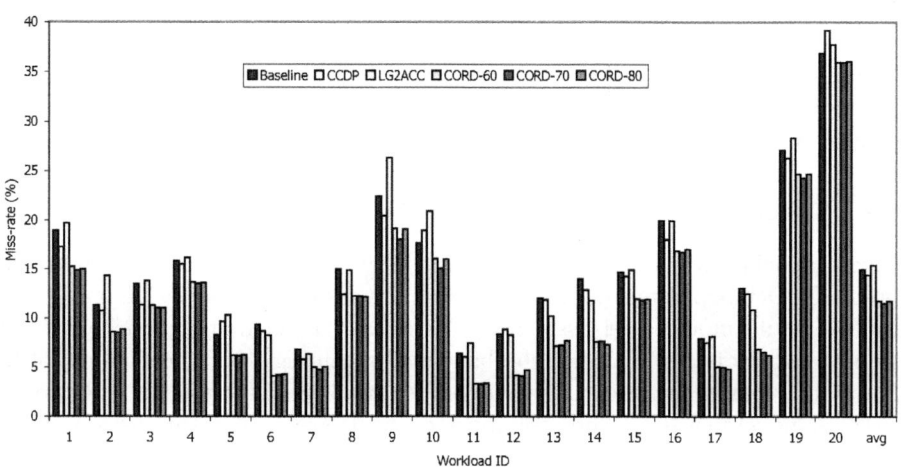

Fig. 5. Data Cache miss rate after Coordinated Placement (CORD)

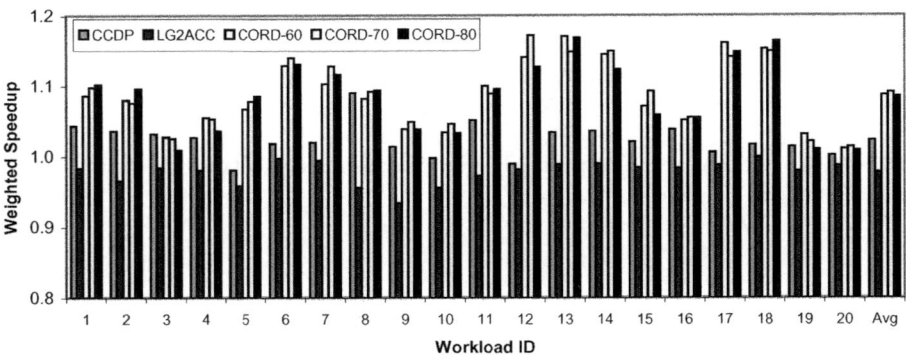

Fig. 6. Weighted Speedup after Coordinated Placement (CORD)

of 0.7, the average single-thread miss rate goes up to 13.1%, but when the scaling factor is 0.8, the miss rate actually becomes 12.7%.

We see in these figures, however, that overall the results are fairly insensitive to the scaling factor, which is closely tied to our estimates of relative execution speed of the two programs and the lifetimes of the objects. Thus, inexact estimates of any of these factors (expected rate of interleaving, relative execution rate, object lifetimes) should not have significant impact on the effectiveness of the technique.

6   Exploring Other Processor and Cache Configurations

Up to this point, we have demonstrated the effectiveness of our placement techniques for a single hardware configuration. We did extensive sensitivity analysis to understand how these techniques work as aspects of the architecture – such as cache sizes and organizations, cache latencies, and number of execution contexts in the processors – are modified. In this section we present and interpret the results of some of those experiments.

6.1   Effects of Cache Size and Associativity

Cache associativity is the most interesting alternative, in large part because proposed CCDP algorithms do not accommodate associative caches. The naïve approach would model a set-associative cache as a direct-mapped cache with the same number of sets. This has the benefit of retaining the correct model of line mapping – that is, two addresses that conflict in a 32 KB 2-way cache will also map to the same set in a 16 KB direct-mapped cache. However, this simplistic approach does not take into consideration false positives while enumerating conflicts, (i.e. this technique does not take into consideration the fact that k objects can share a single set in a k-way associative cache without causing any conflicts) and generally leads to sub-optimal object placement. The reason for the suboptimal placement is that the cost function is incorrect, and begins penalizing placements before they

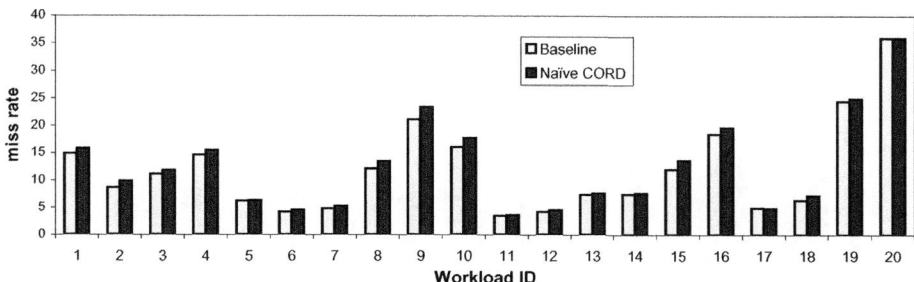

Fig. 7. Naïve Coordinated Data Placement with a Set-Associative Cache (32 KB, 2-way)

actually cause any misses. This can be particularly harmful for our independent placement (IND) algorithm, because a set-associative cache actually increases our ability to create unbalanced mappings – but only if the cost model allows us to.

But even in the case of coordinated placement, the incorrect cost function results in poor placement. This is shown in Figure 7, where we have modeled a 2-way 32 KB cache as a direct-mapped 16 KB cache, and the quality of the co-ordinated placement is actually consistently worse than the baseline placement.

For associative caches, any mapping function that used our `TRGSelect` graph would be an approximation, because we only capture 2-way conflicts. On the other hand, profiling and creating a hypergraph to capture more complex con-flicts would be computationally prohibitive. However, we found the following heuristic to work well when using our existing `TRGSelect` graph. We have ad-justed our default placement algorithm such that for a k-way set-associative cache, an object incurs placement cost only if is placed in a set where at least k objects have already been placed. This new policy tends to fill up every set in the associative cache to its *maximum capacity* before potentially conflicting objects are put in the set that already contains more than k objects.

Average miss-rate reductions and weighted speedups for the variety of bench-mark pairs is given in Figures 8 and 9 for different cache configurations. The split cache results (LG2ACC) are only shown for direct-mapped caches, because that technique is not applicable for set-associative caches. The results for set-associative caches, in particular, are indicative of the low incidence of conflict misses for these workloads. However, we do see that our techniques are effective – we eliminate the vast majority of remaining conflict misses. For a 16 KB, 2-way cache, we reduce total miss rate from 15.8% to 13.8%.

Although in some cases the performance gains are not high, they all still follow the trends we have seen so far. This is encouraging, since the low performance results are primarily the result of cache performance being good overall for those workloads. But because the trends remain the same, and we effectively reduce or nearly eliminate conflict misses in all cases, we have confidence that workloads that exhibit higher miss rates will be able to make good use of these techniques.

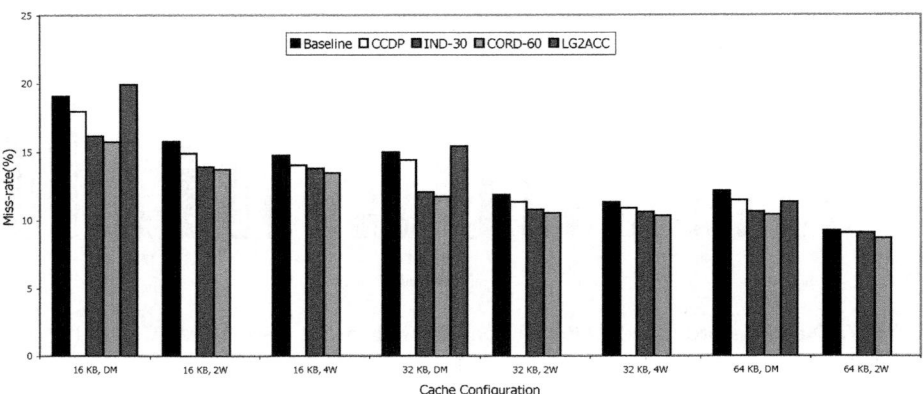

Fig. 8. Miss Rates for Different Cache Configurations. The set-associative results assume the new multithreaded set-associative cache placement algorithm.

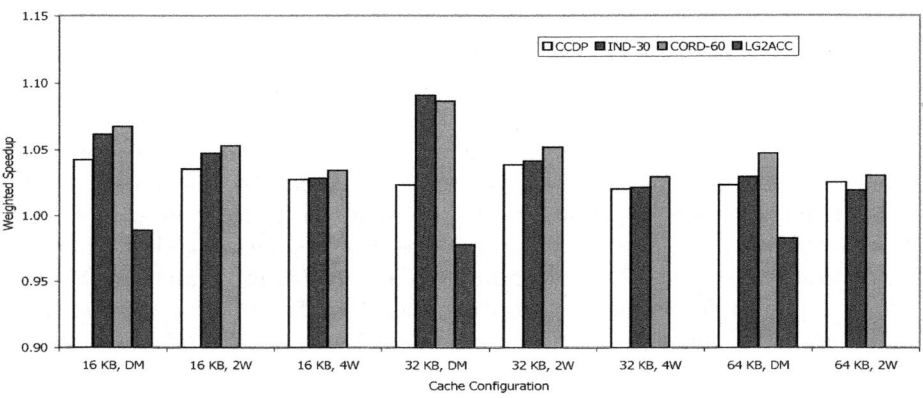

Fig. 9. Weighted Speedup for Different Cache Configurations

6.2   Increasing the Number of Execution Contexts

Our placement techniques were designed to adapt easily to processors having more than two execution contexts. For co-ordinated data placement of k applications, k TRGSelect graphs must be merged together before placement. Independent data placement requires the cache be partitioned into k regions, where each region contains the *hot* objects from one of the applications. Figure 10 and 11 shows the result of our placement techniques being applied to a four-threaded SMT processor.

For a 4-thread processor, IND-30 and CORD-60 reduced miss rates by 14% and 22% on the average; however, the actual weighted speedups were smaller (2.0% and 3.1% respectively), due to the SMT processors' ability to tolerate cache misses in a latency-limited configuration like the one we simulate. However, the more threads running on a core, the more likely we are to saturate memory bandwidth (both instruction execution rate and misses per instruction

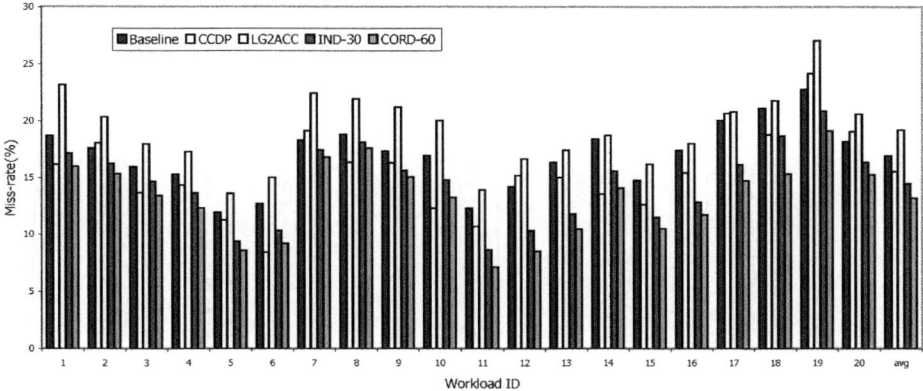

Fig. 10. Miss rate for a 4-context SMT processor

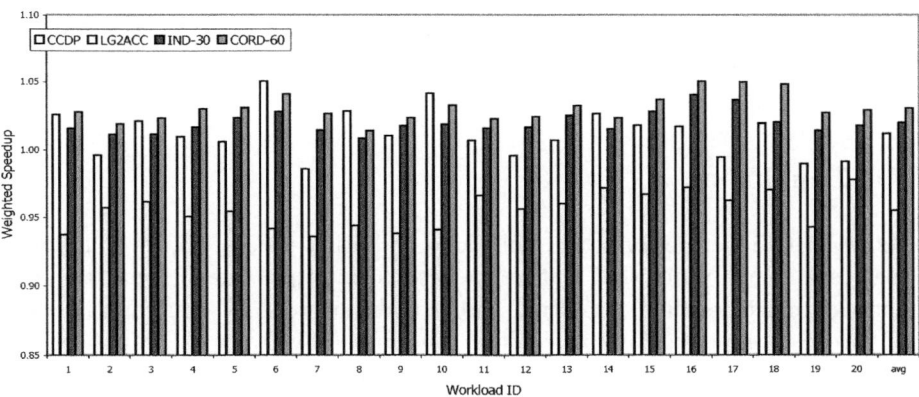

Fig. 11. Weighted Speedup for a 4-context SMT processor

go up significantly with more threads) – and in those scenarios the substantial reduction in miss rate would likely be translated directly into performance, as was demonstrated in the two-thread case. Moreover, there are other important advantages of reducing L1 miss rate, such as lowering net power dissipation.

6.3   Effects of Cache Miss Penalty

Up to this point we have assumed the L1 miss penalty (to the L2 cache) to be 15 cycles, which is a reasonable figure for current microprocessors. However, in future multi-core processors, pressure on L2 bandwidth and the overhead of cache-coherence protocols will result in higher L1 miss penalty. In figure 12, we plot the weighted speedup of co-ordinated and independent placement techniques for a range of L1 miss penalties. Not surprisingly, weighted speedup resulting from our placement algorithms increase monotonically with miss penalty. Thus, as we

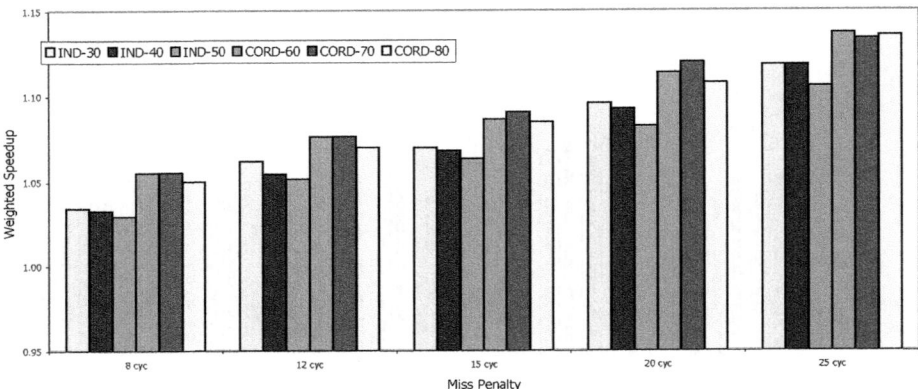

Fig. 12. Variation of Weighted Speedup with Miss Penalty

increasingly pack more contexts (cores and thread contexts) onto the die, while communication latencies across the die continue to increase, the importance of these techniques will only increase.

7   Conclusion

As we seek higher performance embedded and other processors, we will increasingly see architectures that feature caches and multiple thread contexts (either through multithreading or multiple cores), and thus we shall see greater incidence of threads competing for cache space. The more effectively each application is tuned to use the caches, the more interference we see between competing threads.

This paper demonstrates that it is possible to compile threads to share the data cache, to each thread's advantage. We specifically address two scenarios. Our first technique does not assume any prior knowledge of the threads which might be co-scheduled together, and hence is applicable to all general-purpose computing environments. Our second technique shows that when we do have more specific knowledge about which applications will run together, that knowledge can be exploited to enhance the quality of object placement even further. Our techniques demonstrated 26% improvement in miss rate and 9% improvement in performance, for a variety of workloads constructed from the SPEC2000 suite.

It is also shown that our placement techniques scale effectively across different hardware configurations, including various cache sizes, cache latencies, numbers of threads, and even set-associative caches.

Acknowledgments

This reasearch was supported in part by NSF Grant CCF-0541434 and Semiconductor Research Corporation Grant 2005-HJ-1313.

References

1. Calder, B., Krintz, C., John, S., Austin, T.: Cache-conscious data placement. In: Eighth International Conference on Architectural Support for Programming Languages and Operating Systems (1998)
2. Tullsen, D.M., Eggers, S., Levy, H.M.: Simultaneous multithreading: Maximizing on-chip parallelism. In: Proceedings of the 22nd Annual International Symposium on Computer Architecture (1995)
3. Tullsen, D.M., Eggers, S.J., Emer, J.S., Levy, H.M., Lo, J.L., Stamm, R.L.: Exploiting choice: Instruction fetch and issue on an implementable simultaneous multithreading processor. In: Proceedings of the 23rd Annual International Symposium on Computer Architecture (1996)
4. Li, Y., Brooks, D., Hu, Z., Skadron, K., Bose, P.: Understanding the energy efficiency of simultaneous multithreading. In: Intl Symposium on Low Power Electronics and Design (2004)
5. Seng, J., Tullsen, D., Cai, G.: Power-sensitive multithreaded architecture. In: International Conference on Computer Design (September 2000)
6. Kumar, R., Jouppi, N., Tullsen, D.M.: Conjoined-core chip multiprocessing. In: 37th International Symposium on Microarchitecture (December 2004)
7. Dolbeau, R., Seznec, A.: Cash: Revisiting hardware sharing in single-chip parallel processor. In: IRISA Report 1491 (November 2002)
8. Agarwal, A., Pudar, S.: Column-associative caches: A technique for reducing the miss rate of direct-mapped caches. In: International Symposium on Computer Architecture (1993)
9. Topham, N., González, A.: Randomized cache placement for eliminating conflicts. IEEE Transactions on Computer 48(2) (1999)
10. Seznec, A., Bodin, F.: Skewed-associative caches. In: International Conference on Parallel Architectures and Languages, pp. 305–316 (1993)
11. Lynch, W.L., Bray, B.K., Flynn, M.J.: The effect of page allocation on caches. In: 25th Annual International Symposium on Microarchitecture (1992)
12. Rivera, G., Tseng, C.W.: Data transformations for eliminating conflict misses. In: SIGPLAN Conference on Programming Language Design and Implementation, pp. 38–49 (1998)
13. Mueller, F.: Compiler support for software-based cache partitioning. In: Workshop on Languages, Compilers and Tools for Real-Time Systems, pp. 125–133 (1995)
14. Juan, T., Royo, D.: Dynamic cache splitting. In: XV International Confernce of the Chilean Computational Society (1995)
15. Bershad, B.N., Lee, D., Romer, T.H., Chen, J.B.: Avoiding conflict misses dynamically in large direct-mapped caches. In: Proceedings of the Sixth International Conference on Architectural Support for Programming Languages and Operating Systems, San Jose, CA, USA, October 5–7, pp. 158–170 (1994)
16. Sherwood, T., Calder, B., Emer, J.S.: Reducing cache misses using hardware and software page placement. In: International Conference on Supercomputing, pp. 155–164 (1999)
17. Nemirovsky, M., Yamamoto, W.: Quantitative study on data caches on a multistreamed architecture. In: Workshop on Multithreaded Execution, Architecture and Compilation (1998)
18. Hily, S., Seznec, A.: Standard memory hierarchy does not fit simultaneous multithreading. In: Proceedings of the Workshop on Multithreaded Execution Architecture and Compilation, with HPCA-4 (1998)

19. Jos, M.G.: Data caches for multithreaded processors. In: Workshop on Multi-threaded Execution, Architecture and Compilation (2000)
20. May, D., Irwin, J., Muller, H.L., Page, D.: Effective caching for multithreaded processors. In: Communicating Process Architectures, pp. 145–154. IOS Press, Amsterdam (2000)
21. Nikolopoulos, D.S.: Code and data transformations for improving shared cache performance on SMT processors. In: International Symposium on High Performance Computing, pp. 54–69 (2003)
22. Lopez, S., Dropsho, S., Albonesi, D.H., Garnica, O., Lanchares, J.: Dynamic capacity-speed tradeoffs in smt processor caches. In: Intl Conference on High Performance Embedded Architectures & Compilers (January 2007)
23. Kumar, R., Tullsen, D.M.: Compiling for instruction cache performance on a multithreaded architecture. In: 35th Annual International Symposium on Microarchitecture (2002)
24. Sarkar, S., Tullsen, D.M.: Compiler techniques for reducing data cache miss rate on a multithreaded architecture. In: Proceedings of the International Conference on High Performance Embedded Architectures and Compilers (2008)
25. Tullsen, D.M.: Simulation and modeling of a simultaneous multithreading processor. In: 22nd Annual Computer Measurement Group Conference (December 1996)
26. Tullsen, D.M., Brown, J.: Handling long-latency loads in a simultaneous multithreaded processor. In: 34th International Symposium on Microarchitecture (December 2001)
27. Srivastava, A., Eustace, A.: Atom: a system for building customized program analysis tools. SIGPLAN Notices 39, 528–539 (2004)
28. Grunwald, D., Zorn, B.G., Henderson, R.: Improving the cache locality of memory allocation. In: SIGPLAN Conference on Programming Language Design and Implementation (1993)
29. Robson, J.M.: Worst case fragmentation of first fit and best fit storage allocation strategies. The Computer Journal 20(3) (1977)

Improving Branch Prediction by Considering Affectors and Affectees Correlations

Yiannakis Sazeides[1], Andreas Moustakas[2,*],
Kypros Constantinides[2,*], and Marios Kleanthous[1]

[1] University of Cyprus, Nicosia, CYPRUS/HiPEAC
[2] University of Michigan, Ann Arbor, USA

Abstract. This work investigates the potential of *direction*-correlations to improve branch prediction. There are two types of *direction*-correlation: *affectors* and *affectees*. This work considers for the first time their implications at a basic level. These correlations are determined based on dataflow graph information and are used to select the subset of global branch history bits used for prediction. If this subset is small then *affectors* and *affectees* can be useful to cut down learning time, and reduce aliasing in prediction tables. This paper extends previous work explaining why and how correlation-based predictors work by analyzing the properties of *direction*-correlations. It also shows that branch history selected based on *direction*-correlations improves the accuracy of the limit and realistic conditional branch predictors, that won at the recent branch prediction contest, by up to 30% and 17% respectively. The findings in this paper call for the investigation of predictors that can efficiently learn correlations that may be non-consecutive (i.e. with holes between them) from long branch history.

1 Introduction

The ever growing demand for higher performance and technological constraints drive for many years the computer industry toward processors with higher clock rates and more recently to multiple cores per chip. Both of these approaches can improve performance but at the same time can increase the cycle latency to resolve an instruction, the former due to deeper pipelines and the latter due to inter-core contention for shared on-chip resources. Longer resolution latency renders highly accurate conditional branch prediction a necessity because branch instructions are very frequent in programs and need to be resolved as soon as they are fetched in a processor to ensure continuous instruction supply.

Today, after many years of branch prediction research and the two recent branch prediction championship contests [1,2], the accuracies of the state of the art predictors are high but far from perfect. For many benchmarks the O-GEHL and L-TAGE predictors[1] [3,4] have more than five misses per thousand

---

* The author contributed to this work while at the University of Cyprus.
[1] O-GEHL won the best practice award in the 2004 branch prediction contest and L-TAGE won the realistic track of the 2006 contest.

P. Stenström (Ed.): Transactions on HiPEAC III, LNCS 6590, pp. 69–88, 2011.

instructions. Such a rate of misprediction, depending on the average branch resolution latency and other execution overheads, can correspond to a substantial part of the total execution time of a program. A recent study shows that the misprediction overhead for an 8-way out-of-order processor using an 8KB O-GEHL predictor, for SPECINT CPU2000 benchmarks, can be up to 50% and on the average 17% of the execution time [5]. Consequently, we believe there is still a need to further improve prediction accuracy. The challenge is to determine how to achieve such an improvement.

In the seminal work by Evers et al. [6] it is shown that choosing more selectively the correlation information can be conducive for improving branch prediction. In particular, using an exhaustive search is determined for a gshare [7] predictor that only a few, not necessarily consecutive, of the most recent branches are sufficient to achieve best prediction accuracy. Furthermore, is demonstrated that a correlation may exist between branches that are far apart. The same work, introduces two reasons for why global history correlation exists between branches: *direction* and *in-path* correlation, and divides *direction*-correlations into *affectors* and *affectees*.[2] These various types of correlations can mainly be derived by considering the data and control flow properties of branches. These causes of correlation are only discussed qualitatively in [6] to explain what makes two-level branch predictors work, no measurements of their frequency or quantification of their importance are given.

The work by [6] motivated subsequent prediction research with goal the selective correlation from longer global history. One of the most notable is perceptron based prediction [9] that identifies, through training, the important history bits that a branch correlates on. The success of perceptron based prediction provides a partial justification for the claims by [6] for the importance of selective correlation. However, it was never established that the dominant perceptron correlations correspond to *direction* or *in-path* correlation and therefore remains uncertain if indeed such correlations are important or whether predictors exploit them efficiently.

One other interesting work by [8] investigated the usefulness of *affectors* branches, one of the types of *direction*-correlation introduced by [6] . In [8] the affector branches are selected dynamically from the global history using data dependence information and are used to train an overriding tagged predictor when a baseline predictor performs poorly. The experimental analysis, for specific microarchitectural configurations and baseline predictors, show that this idea can potentially improve both prediction accuracy and performance. This work also provides the first concrete evidence that the *direction*-correlation is an important information for prediction. However, [8] did not examine the importance of *affectees*.

In this paper we investigate the significance for improving branch prediction accuracy using the two types of *direction*-correlation: affectors and affectees.

---

[2] In [6] the two types of *direction*-correlations are defined but not named. In [8] they referred to them as affectors and forerunners. In this work, for symmetry we decided to name the forerunners as affectees.

Our analysis is done at a basic level because it does not consider implementation issues for detecting affectors and affectees correlations. The primary objectives of this paper is to establish the extent that state of the art predictors learn *direction*-correlations, and determine how precise the detection of *direction*-correlations needs to be for best accuracy. Our evaluation uses the two winning predictors of the limit and realistic track of the recent championship prediction [2] and considers their accuracy when they use the global history as is versus the global history packed [8] to "ignore" the positions with no *direction*-correlation.

Contributions
The key contributions and findings of this paper are:

- A framework that explains why some branches are more important than others to correlate on. The framework can be used to precisely determine these branches based on architectural properties without regard to implementation.
- An experimental analysis of the potential of *direction*-correlations to improve branch prediction accuracy.
- An investigation of the position and the number of *direction*-correlations reveals that their behavior varies across programs. Also, is very typical for programs to have branches with the number of correlations ranging from few branches to several hundreds. The correlations can be clustered together but also be very far apart, i.e. correlations may not be consecutive and can have holes between them. Affectees are found to be more frequent than affectors.
- Demonstrate that for best accuracy both affectors and affectees correlations are needed. Their use can provide accuracy improvements of up to 30% for the limit predictor, and 17% for the realistic predictor
- Show that it is crucial to include in branch history *direction*-correlations that are detectable by tracking dependences through memory.
- Establish a need to further study predictors that can learn correlation patterns with and without holes from long branch history.

The remaining of the paper is organized as follows. Section 2 defines what affectors and affectees correlations are and discusses parameters that influences the classification of a branch as correlating. Section 3 presents the experimental framework. Section 4 discusses the experimental results of this study and establishes the significance of affectors and affectees. Section 5 discusses related work. Finally, Section 6 concludes the paper and provides directions for future work.

2   Affectors and Affectees

This section defines what affector and affectee branches are and provides intuition as to why these are important branches to select for correlation. It also discusses how the treatment of memory dependences influence the classification of a branch as an affector or affectee of another branch. Finally, a discussion is presented on how this correlation information can be used for prediction. Part of this discussion is based on earlier work [6,8].

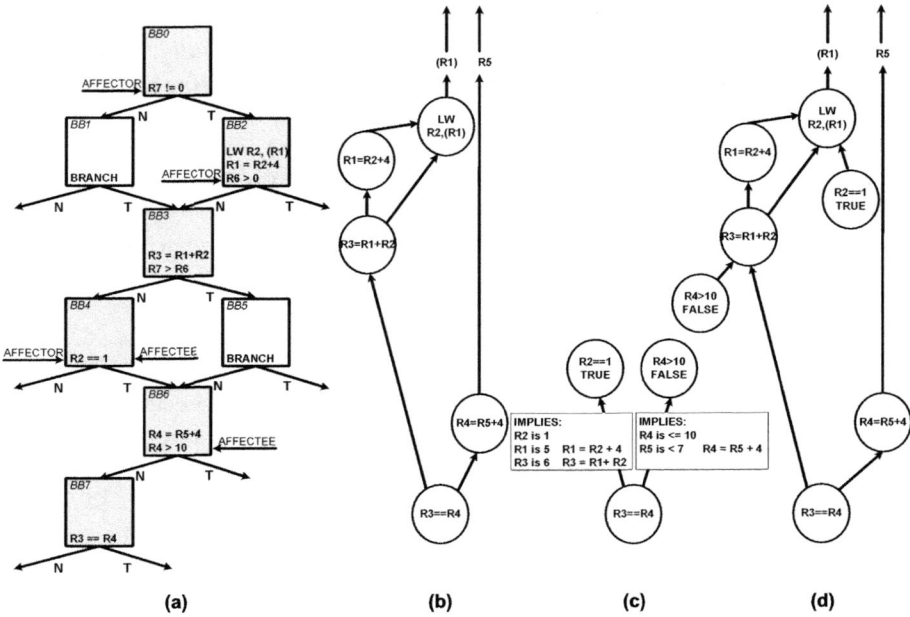

Fig. 1. (a) Example control flow graph, (b) affector graph, (c) affectee graph and (d) affector plus affectee graph

2.1 Definitions and Intuition

Affectors: A dynamic branch, A, is an affector for a subsequent dynamic branch, B, if the outcome of A affects information (data) used by the subsequent branch B. Affectors are illustrated using the example control flow graph in Fig. 1.a. Assume that the (predicted) program order follows the shaded basic-blocks and we need to predict the branch in the basic-block 7. The affector branches are all those branches that steer the control flow to the basic-blocks that contain instructions that the branch, in basic-block 7, has direct or indirect data dependence. In our example, these correspond to the branches in basic-blocks *BB0*, *BB2* and *BB4*. Effectively, the selected affector branches can be thought of as an encoding of the data flow graph leading to the branch to be predicted (this affector data flow graph is shown in Fig. 1.b). Predictors may benefit by learning affector correlations because when branches repeat with the same data flow graph they will likely go the same direction. Furthermore, affector correlations use a more concise branch history to capture the data flow graph leading to a branch and thus reduce learning time and table pressure for training a predictor.

Affectees: A dynamic branch, A, is affectee of a subsequent dynamic branch, B, if A is testing the outcome of an instruction C that can trace a data dependence to an instruction D in the data flow graph leading to B.[3] The direction of an affectee branch encodes, in a precise or imprecise manner, the values produced

---

[3] C and D can be the same instruction.

or yet to be produced by D and of other instructions in the data dependence graph from branch B to instruction D.

In the example in Fig. 1.a the branch in $BB7$ has two affectees, the branches in $BB4$ and $BB6$. More specifically, the branch $R2==1$ in $BB4$ is an affectee because it tests the outcome of the load instruction $LW\ R2,(R1)$, on which the branch $R3==R4$ in $BB7$ has an indirect data dependence (through the instructions $R3 = R1 + R2$ in $BB3$ and $R1 = R2 + 4$ in $BB2$). Since the direction of $R2==1$ is taken it implies that the test condition is true and consequently the value loaded from the load instruction $LW\ R2,(R1)$ is 1, the value produced by $R1 = R2 + 4$ is 5 and the result of $R3 = R1 + R2$ is 6. Therefore, in this case the direction of branch $R2==1$ in $BB4$ provides a precise encoding for the operand $R3$ of the branch $R3==R4$ in $BB7$. On the other hand, the false condition of the affectee branch $R4>10$ in $BB6$ is less precise and provides a range of possible values for the second operand $R4$ of the branch.

Essentially, affectees provide an encoding for values consumed or produced in the dataflow graph leading to the branch to be predicted. The affectee value encodings for the example in Fig. 1.a are shown in Fig. 1.c. Note that a branch can be both affector and affectee of another branch depending on its dependences. An example of such branch is $R2==1$ in $BB4$ in Fig. 1.a.

Combo: It is evident that the combination of affectors and affectees can be more powerful than either correlation alone since affectees can help differentiate between branches with the same data affector data flow graphs but different input values. Similarly, affectors can help distinguish between same affectee graphs that correspond to different affector graphs. The combined affector and affectee data flow graph of our running example is shown in Fig. 1.d.

Section 4 investigates how the above types of correlations affect branch prediction accuracy. We believe that existing predictor schemes are able to learn data flow graphs, as those shown in Fig. 1, but they do this inefficiently using more history bits than needed. Therefore, they may suffer from cold effects and more table pressure/aliasing. Our analysis will establish how much room is there to improve them.

2.2   Memory Dependences

For accurate detection of the direction-correlations data dependences need to be tracked through memory. That way a branch that has a dependence to a load instruction can detect correlation to other branches through the memory dependence. Although, tracking dependences through memory may be important for developing a better understanding for the potential and properties of affectors and affectees correlations, it may be useful to know the extent that such precise knowledge is necessary. Thus may be interesting to determine how well predictors will work if direction-correlations detected through memory dependences are approximated or completely ignored.

We consider two approximations of memory dependences. The one tracks the dependence of address operands of a load instruction ignoring the dependence for the data. And the other does not consider any dependences past a load instruction, i.e. limiting a branch to correlations emanating from the most recent load instructions leading to the branch. These two approximations of memory dependences need to track register dependences whereas the precise scheme requires maintaining dependences between stores and load through memory. We will refer to the precise scheme of tracking dependences as *Memory*, and to the two approximations as *Address*, and *NoMemory*. In Section 4 we will compare the prediction accuracy of the various schemes to determine the importance of tracking accurately correlations through memory.

For the *Memory* scheme we found that is better to not include the address dependences of a load when a data dependence to a store is found (analysis not presented due to limited space). This is reasonable because the correlations of the data encode directly the information affecting the branch whereas the address correlations are indirect and possibly superfluous.

Recall that our algorithm for detecting direction-correlations does not consider implementation constraints. It is based on analysis of the dynamic data dependence graph of a program. The intention of this work is to establish if there is potential from using more selective correlation.

2.3   How to Use Affectors and Affectees for Prediction

Based on the findings of this paper one can attempt to design a predictor grounds-up that exploits the properties exhibited by affectors and affectees correlations. That is also our ultimate goal and hopefully this paper will serve as a stepping stone in that direction. This, however, may be a non-trivial effort and before engaging in such a task may be useful to know its potential.

Therefore, in this paper we decided to determine the potential of affectors and affectees using unmodified existing predictors. We simply feed these predictors with the complete global history and with the history selected using affectors and affectees and compare their prediction accuracy. If this analysis reveals that the selective correlations have consistently and substantially better accuracy then may be worthwhile to design a new predictor.

The only predictor design space option we have is how to represent the selected bits in the global history register. In [8] they were confronted with a similar problem and proposed the use of *zeroing* and *packing*. Zeroing means set a history bit to zero if it is not selected while branches retain their original position in the history register. Packing moves all the selected bits to the least significant part of the history register while other bits are set to zero. Therefore, in packing selected branches lose their original position but retain their order. Our experimental data (not shown due to space constraints) revealed that packing had on average the best accuracy and is the representation we used for the results reported in Section 4.

Our methodology for finding the potential of affectors and affectees may be suboptimal because it uses an existing predictor without considering the properties exhibited in the global history patterns after selection. Another possible limitation of our study has to do with our definition of affectors and affectees. Alternative definitions may lead to even more selective and accurate correlations. For instance by considering only affectees that trace dependences to load instructions. These and other limitations to be found may lead to increased potential and thus the findings of this study should be viewed as the potential under the assumptions and constraints used in the paper.

3   Experimental Framework

To determine the potential of affectors and affectees to increase branch prediction accuracy we used a functional simulation methodology using a simplescalar [10] derived simulator. A subset of SPEC2000 and three SPEC95 benchmarks, listed in Table 1, are used for our analysis. For the SPEC2000 benchmarks the early regions, of 10-100 million instructions, identified by sim-point [11] are used, whereas for SPEC95 complete runs of modified reference inputs are executed. Some SPEC2000 benchmarks are not included because they required large memory and/or long simulation time to track dependences, affectors and affectees. The selected SPEC95 benchmarks exhibit the higher misprediction rates with a 32KB L-Tage predictor among integer SPEC95 benchmarks.

Table 1. Benchmarks

SPECINT CPU2000	bzip200, crafty00, eon00, gap00, gcc00, gzip00, mcf00, perlbmk00, twolf00, vortex00, vpr00
SPECFP CPU2000	ammp00, equake00, fma3d00, galgel00, mesa00 mgrid00 sixtrack00, wupwise00
SPECINT CPU95	gcc95, go95, ijpeg95

Two predictors are used in the experimentation: a 32KB L-TAGE [12] predictor with maximum history length of 400 bits, and the GTL [4] predictor with 400 maximum history length for the GEHL component and 100000 maximum history length for the TAGE component.

For the experiments where selective correlation is used, the selection is applied to the 400 bit global history of the L-TAGE predictor and to the 400 bit history used to access the GEHL component of the GTL predictor. Selection was not used for the TAGE component of GTL because the memory required to track affectors and affectees for a 100000 global history were extremely large and beyond the memory capacities of todays servers.

The detection of affectors and affectees is done on-line using the dynamic data flow graph of a program. Unless stated otherwise, the default policy is to track correlations through memory dependences.[4]

---

[4] In the conference version of the paper [13] the term oracle was used to signify the precise tracking of memory dependences assumed for obtaining some of the results. The same assumption is used for this paper but the term is omitted to avoid confusion with an oracle off-line analysis for detecting affectors and affectees.

The algorithm used to determine affectors is the simple approximation proposed in [8]. A dynamic branch is an affector, of a branch to be predicted, if it is the last, in the dynamic program order, branch that executed before an instruction in the dataflow graph of the branch to be predicted.

The algorithm that detects affectees tracks the *sources* for each unique state, register or memory location, updated during a program's execution. Sources are the roots in the dynamic data dependence graph of each dynamic instruction. Sources are either dynamic instances of instructions with no inputs, like a move immediate, or locations with program data input, i.e. locations read but not updated by a program instruction. Each unique source contains a bit vector with n bits. Every time an instruction executes it computes the union of its input operand sources to produce the set of sources to be written in its destination. Every time a conditional branch executes all sources shift their bit vector by one.[5] Also, the sources of the branch set their least significant bit to indicate that this branch can trace a dependence to this source. The above imply that when bit i of a source is set then the ith most recent branch has a dependence to this source. To determine the affectees of a branch we determine the union of its operands sources and bitwise-or these sources bit vectors. All the positions that are set in the resultant bit vector correspond to the global branch history positions with a correlation.

4   Results

We present three sets of results, the first analyzes the properties of affectors and affectees, the second discusses the accuracy of the GTL predictor, and the third shows the accuracy of the L-TAGE predictor.

4.1   Characterization of Affectors and Affectees

Fig. 2 and 3 show the cumulative distribution of dynamic branches according to the number of affector and affectee correlations they have. The number of correlations can not exceed 400 since we consider only correlations from the 400 most recent branches. We decided to analyze the behavior for the 400 most recent branches since the two predictors used in the study use a 400 entry global branch history register.

The results reveal that branches usually have much fewer affectors than affectees. For most benchmarks 80% of the branches have at most 30 affectors. According to the definition of affectors, this means that the computation that determines the outcome of a branch can be found in less than 30 out of the most recent 400 basic blocks preceded by a conditional branch. The outlier is *gcc00* where many branches have large number of affectors. The data about affectees

---

[5] A key optimization is to not shift all sources every time a branch executes but only the sources of the branch. The shift amount is determined based on the distance in branches between the current branch instruction and the last branch that updated the particular source.

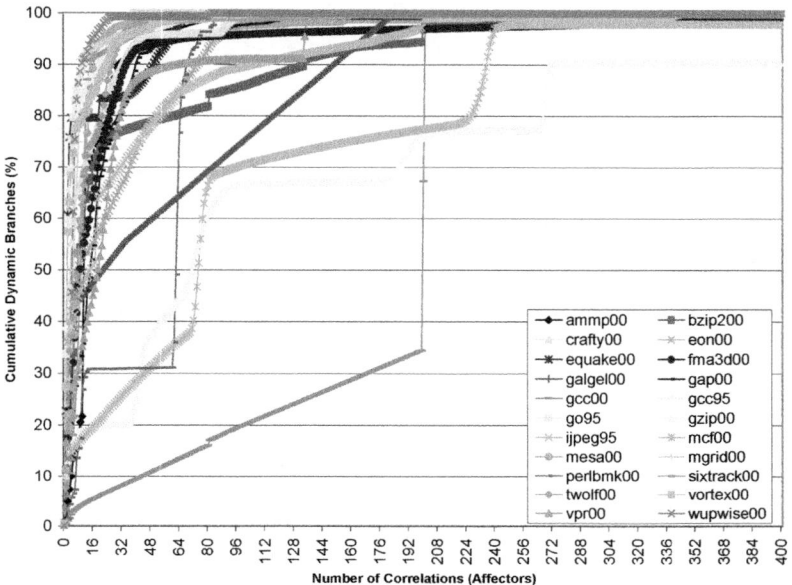

Fig. 2. Affectors distribution

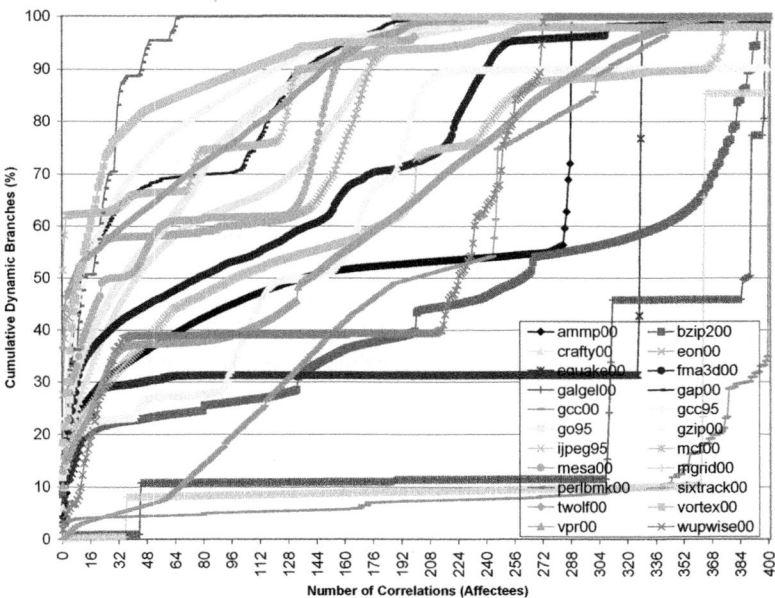

Fig. 3. Affectees distribution

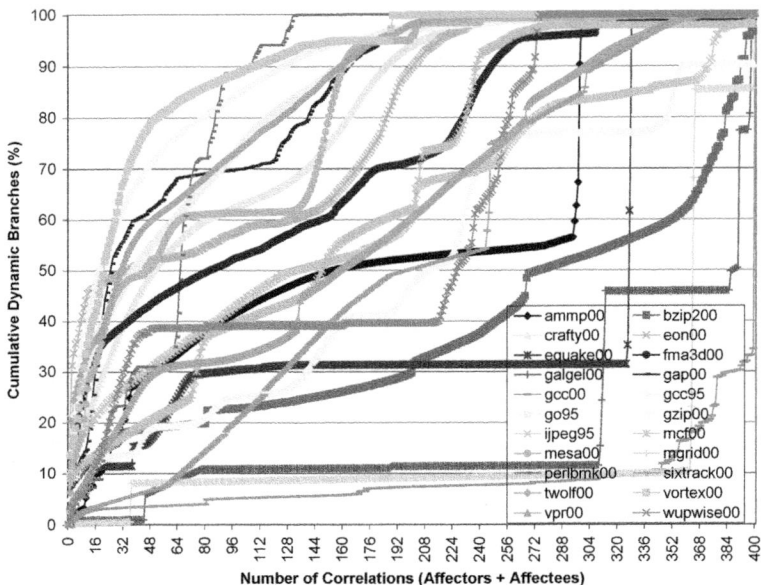

Fig. 4. Combined Affectors and Affectees distribution

correlations show clearly that for most programs 50% of the branches have 30 or more affectees. This means that a branch frequently checks information that directly or indirectly has been tested by at least 30 other out of the 400 most recent branches. The data also show few benchmarks, *bzip00, galgel00, gcc00,* and *mgrid00*, to have 300 or more affectee correlations.

The above observations suggest that the dynamic dataflow graphs of branch instructions are usually small and shallow (implied by the small number of affectors), and branches often share part of their dynamic data flow graphs with other branches (indicated by the large number of affectees).

The graph in Fig. 4 shows the distribution of the branches when we consider both affectors and affectees correlations. Overall, the data show that there are more correlations when we consider affectors and affectees in combination (compare Fig. 4 against Fig. 2 and 3). Nonetheless, the results for *ALL* benchmarks reveal that there are many branches that have much less than maximum number correlations. Therefore, if: (a) affectors and affectees are the dominant types of correlation that predictors need to learn, and (b) existing predictors are unable to use only the relevant part of history, then these data suggest that there may be room for improving prediction.

In Fig. 5 we attempt to give more insight by presenting the dominant patterns of correlation when we consider the combination of affectors and affectees. The figure shows for six benchmarks, *twolf00, bzip00, ammp00, crafty00, perlbmk00* and *equake00* what are the most frequent 1000 patterns of correlations. To help the reader we present these top patterns sorted from top to bottom according to the oldest position with a correlation (i.e. the most recent correlation position is

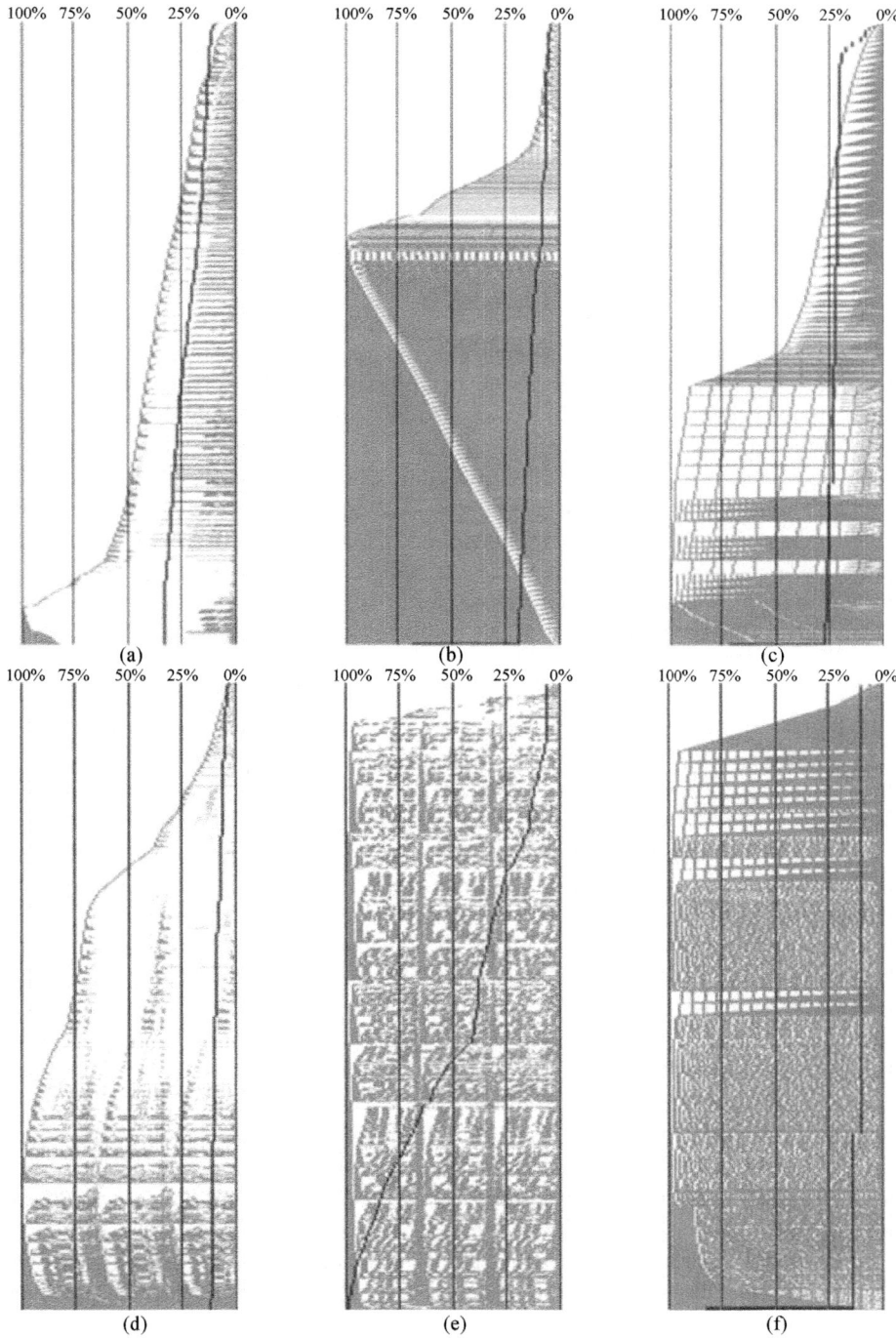

Fig. 5. Most frequent correlation patterns for (a) twolf00, (b) bzip00, (c) ammp00, (d) crafty00, (e) perlbmk00, and (f) equake00

Table 2. Representative Benchmarks for Correlation Patterns

Benchmark	Representative of Benchmarks
twolf00	vpr00, gcc95 and go95
bzip00	gcc00, gzip00, mcf00 and ijpeg95
ammp00	galgel00, mgrid00 and sixtrack00
crafty00	mesa00
perlbmk00	eon00, fma3d00, gap00, vortex00 and wupwise00
equake00	-

to the right). The curve that cut-across each graph represents from top to bottom the cumulative branch distribution of the patterns. This line is not reaching 100% since we only display the top 1000 patterns. A given pattern has a gray and white part representing the bit positions with and without correlations. To help the reader we present patterns with 100 positions where each position corresponds to 4 bits (a position is set to one if any of its corresponding four bits is set). These six graphs are representative of the remaining benchmarks we considered in this paper as shown in Table 2. Benchmark *equake00* has a unique behavior with very few dominant correlations patterns. For the following discussion we define the length of a correlation pattern to be the oldest position with a correlation.

One of the main observation from these data is that branch correlations are not always consecutive, there are *holes* between correlated branches. These holes can be of any size and a given correlation pattern can have one or more holes. The hole behavior varies across benchmarks, for *twolf00 and crafty00* like benchmarks is dominant whereas for *bzip00* like benchmarks they occur less frequently. Within a benchmark there can be both sparse and dense patterns.

More specifically, the results indicate that virtually always correlation patterns include at least few of the most recent branches (for each benchmark almost all patterns have at the right end - most recent branches - few positions set). Also, it is observed across almost all benchmarks that for a given correlation length the pattern with all positions set is very frequent. However, for *twolf00* like benchmarks many patterns have correlations that occur at the beginning and at the end of the pattern with all the branches in the middle being uncorrelated. Benchmark *crafty00* exhibits similar behavior with *twolf00* except that some correlations may exist in the middle. Another remark for *bzip00, ammp00* and *equake00* like benchmarks, is that they have many branches with correlations distributed over all 100 positions (bottom pattern in Fig. 5 for *bzip00, ammp00* and *equake00* accounts for over 40% of the patterns). Finally, *perlbmk00* like benchmarks are distinct because of few but often long correlation patterns.

Provided it is important to predict by learning precisely the above correlations, the results suggest that there is a need for predictors that can learn efficiently patterns with holes.

Another key observation from Fig. 5 is that correlation patterns occur usually across all history lengths. These underlines the need for predictors to be capable of predicting with variable history length. The distribution of patterns according

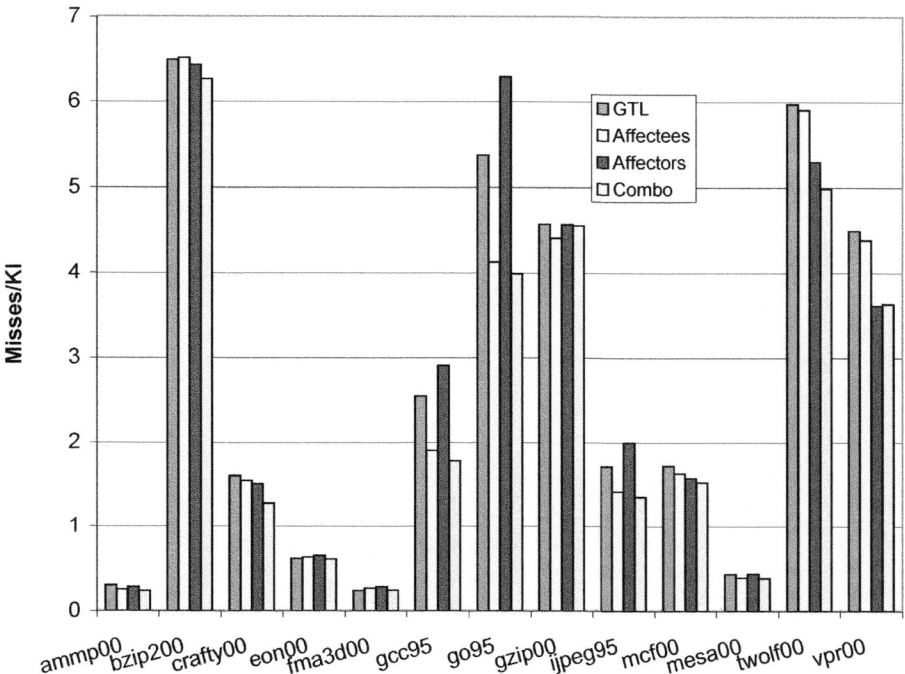

Fig. 6. GTL accuracy with selective correlation

to length is similar to the distribution in Fig. 4. Assuming is important to learn precisely the correlation patterns, the exponential like cumulative distributions of correlation lengths, for most benchmarks, suggests that most prediction resources should be devoted to capture correlations with short history length and incrementally use less resources for longer correlations. This observation clearly supports the use of geometric history length predictors [14].

The above observations may represent a call for predictors that can handle both geometric history length and holes. As far as we know no such predictor exists today. In the next section we attempt to establish the potential of such a predictor using two existing geometric history length predictors that are accessed with selected history, with holes, using affectors and affectees correlations. In the remaining paper we only present data for the benchmarks that exhibited at least 0.25 misses per one thousand instructions. The other benchmarks displayed minimal sensitivity to the predictor used and for the sake of graph clarity are omitted.

4.2 GTL Results

Fig. 6 shows the accuracy of the GTL predictor when accessed with full global history, only with affectors correlations, only with affectees, and with the combination of affectors and affectees. The data show that the combination of affectors

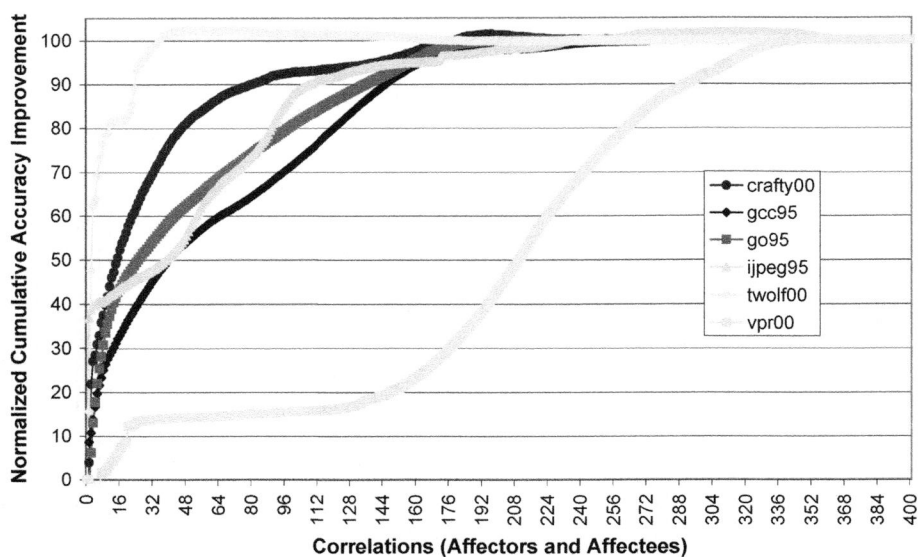

Fig. 7. Number of Correlations vs. Accuracy Improvement

and affectees provides the best performance. It is always the same or better than GTL and almost always better than each correlation separately. The exception are *gzip00* and *vpr00* where the combination does slightly worse than using only affectees and affectors respectively. This can happen when the one type of correlation is sufficient to capture the program behavior and the use of additional information is detrimental. The improvement provided by combining affectors and affectees is substantial for several benchmarks. In particular, for *crafty00, gcc95, go95, ijpeg95, twolf00, and vpr00* it ranges from 15% to 30%. The data clearly support the claim by [6] that *direction*-correlation is one of the basic types of correlations in programs that predictors need to capture. For the remaining paper we present results for experiments that combine affectors and affectees since they provide the best overall accuracy.

Fig. 7 shows the normalized cumulative improvement in prediction accuracy when using affectors and affectees over GTL as a function of the number of correlations. This is shown only for the benchmarks that experienced the largest accuracy improvement when using affectors and affectees. To illustrate how to interpret the graph consider *crafty00*. The *Combo* configuration in Fig. 6 reduces mispredictions of crafty by 20%. The data in Fig. 7 indicate that 90% of this improvement is due to correlations patterns that include less than 75 affectors and affectees. In general, the data in Fig. 7 reveal that most of the improvement from selective correlation is due to better prediction accuracy for the branches that have fewer than 100 branch correlations. This may indicate that the GTL predictor may be slow to learn or using more table resources than necessary for such branches. For all benchmarks there is little improvement for branches with over 300 correlations. This may suggest that the more bits in a correlation

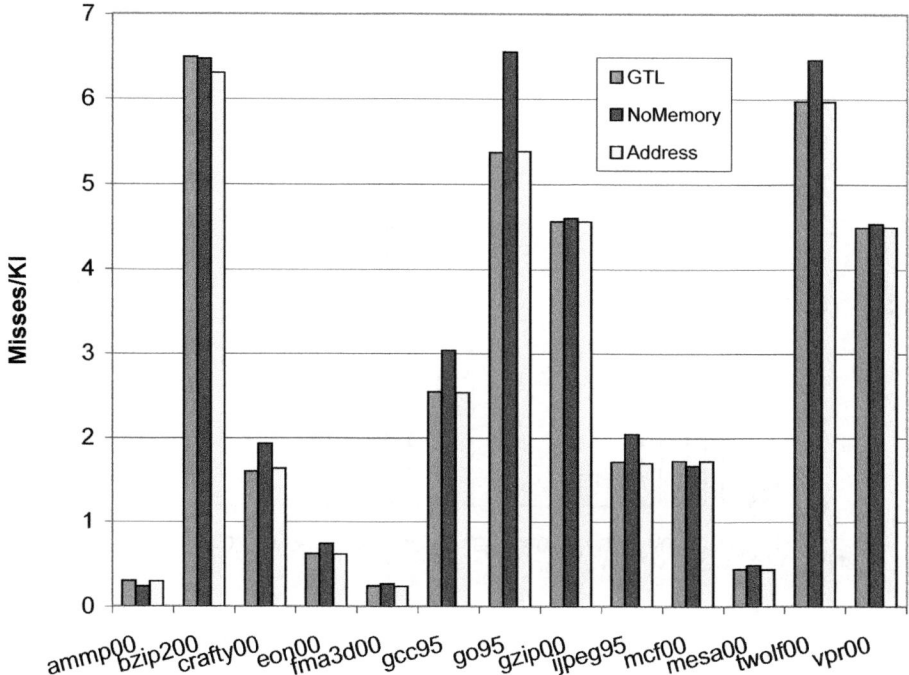

Fig. 8. Significance of Memory Dependences

pattern the closer the resemblance to the global history register and thus little room for improvement from selective correlation.

Fig. 8 shows the prediction accuracy when we combine affectors and affectees but with no correlations through memory. For each benchmark we present three results, the GTL predictor with full history, the affectors and affectees with no correlations past load instructions (NoMemory), and with correlations past load instructions using their address dependences (Address). The data show that there is very little improvement to gain when we do not consider correlations through memory dependences. The data indicate that an approximation of memory dependences using addresses dependences offers very little improvement. This underlines that important correlations from the data predecessors of load instructions are needed for improved accuracy.

The data show that selective correlation using the combination of affectors and affectees can provide substantial improvement in prediction accuracy. The results also show that correlations past memory instructions are important and that address dependences provide a poor approximations of the data dependence correlations. Overall, we believe the data suggest that may be worthwhile investigating the development of a predictor that is capable of learning correlations from long history with holes. These conclusions are true for GTL an unrealistically large predictor that demonstrate that the improvements are not mere accident but due to basic enhancements in the prediction process. However, we

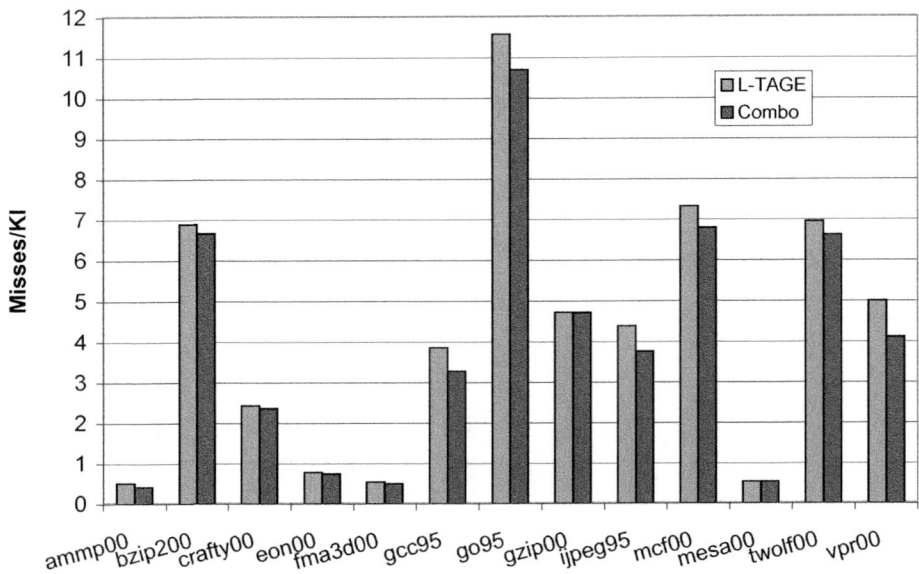

Fig. 9. L-TAGE accuracy with selective correlation

are interested to know if these observations hold for a realistic predictor. Next we consider selective correlation for a 32KB L-TAGE predictor.

4.3   L-TAGE Results

Fig. 9 shows the prediction accuracy for a 32KB L-TAGE when accessed using the complete global history (L-TAGE) and with selective history using the combination of affectors and affectees (Combo). The results show that selective correlation with affectors and affectees can also improve the accuracy of the L-TAGE predictor at a realistic size. The amount of improvement is significant for several benchmarks. In particular, for *gcc95, ijpeg95, and vpr00* is above 15% (for vpr 17%). We believe that these improvements call for the design of a predictor that can exploit *direction*-correlations.

The amount of improvements for L-TAGE are smaller as compared to GTL. However, one should recall that GTL is a completely different predictor not simply a bigger L-TAGE predictor. We also performed analysis of the importance of correlations through memory and the data suggest, similarly to GTL, that it is necessary to include such correlations for better accuracy.

5   Related Work

Since Smith [15] proposed the first dynamic table based branch predictor, innovation in the field of prediction has been sporadic but steady. Some of the key milestones are: correlation-based prediction [16] that exploits the global and or local correlation between branches, hybrid prediction [7] that combines different predictors to capture distinct branch behavior, variable history length [17] that adjusts the amount of global history used depending on program behavior, the use of perceptrons [9] to learn correlations from long history, geometric history length prediction [14] that employs different history lengths that follow a geometric series to index the various tables of a predictor, and partial tagging [18] of predictor table entries to better manage their allocation and deallocation. The above innovations have one main theme in common: the correlation information used to predict a branch is becoming increasingly more selective. This facilitates both faster predictor training time and less destructive aliasing. Our paper extends this line of work and shows that there is room for further improvement if we could select correlations with holes out of long history.

The importance for selective correlation is first established in the work by Evers et al. [6]. In that paper it is shown that a predictor that selectively correlates on few bits from the global history register can outperform a predictor that correlates on the entire global history register. The paper argues that the improvement is due to a reduction in the number of correlation patterns that need to learned which leads to faster training and less aliasing. However, the findings in [6] are based on an off-line oracle analysis. Fern et al. [19] proposed a possibly implementable on-line predictor based on the principles of dynamic decision trees capable of learning and correlating on a subset of history bits. An initial evaluation of this predictor revealed comparable performance to equal sized *Gap* [16] and *Pap* [16] predictors.

A return-history-stack [20] is a method that can introduce holes in the branch history. In broad terms, a return history stack pushes in a stack the branch history register on a call and recovers it on a return, thus introducing holes in the history. A return history stack is shown to be useful for a trace predictor [20] and offers modest improvements for a direction branch predictor [21]. This suggests that there are many cases where branches executed in a function are often no significant to correlate on for the branches that execute after the function return.

In two recently organized branch prediction championships [1,2] researchers established the state of the art in branch prediction. In 2006, the L-TAGE global history predictor [12] was the winner for a 32KB budget. L-TAGE is a multi-table predictor with partial tagging and geometric history lengths that also includes a loop predictor. In the 2006 championship limit contest the GTL predictor [4] provided the best accuracy. GTL combines GEHL [14] and L-TAGE predictors using a meta-predictor. The GEHL global history predictor [14] employs multiple components indexed with geometric history length. Our paper uses the L-TAGE and GTL predictors to examine our ideas to ensure that observations made are not accidental but based on basic principles. The use of longer history is central to these two predictors and the analysis in this paper confirmed the need and usefulness for learning geometrically longer history correlations.

Several previous paper explored the idea of improving prediction by encoding the data flow graphs leading to instructions to be predicted. They use information from instructions in the data flow graph [22,23,24,25,26], such as opcodes, immediate values, and register names, to train a predictor. Effectively these papers are implementing variations of predictors that correlate on affector branches. In [26], they consider using the live in values of the dataflow graphs when they become available and in [23] they examined the possibility of predicting such values. The inclusion of actual or predicted live-in values is analogous to the correlation on affectee branches of such values, since the predicted or actual outcome of affectee branches represents an encoding of the live-in values.

Mahlke and Natarajan [27] performed profiling analysis to determine simple correlation functions between register values and branch outcomes. Instructions are inserted in the code by the compiler to dynamically compute the branch direction according to the derived functions. In our view, this work also attempts to implement a variation of affectees correlation since the functions supply analogous information to what can be provided by affectee branches.

6 Conclusions and Future Work

In this paper we investigate the potential of selective correlation using affectors and affectees branches to improve branch prediction. Experimental analysis of affectors and affectees revealed that many branches have few correlations and often the correlations have holes between them. Prediction using selective correlation, based on affectors and affectees, is shown to have significant potential to improve accuracy for a both a limit and a realistic predictor. The analysis also shows that correlations past memory instruction are needed for best accuracy. Overall, our study suggests that may be worthwhile to consider the design of a realistic predictor that can exploit the properties exhibited by affectors and affectees correlation patterns by learning correlations with and without holes from long history.

A possible venue for future work is to train the tables of TAGE like predictors, that contain multiple prediction tables, with branch history with holes. The challenge is to decide what are going to be the holes in the branch history since different benchmarks have different hole patterns. To design efficiently such scheme it may be useful to first investigate and determine what is the relation between dynamic program properties and holes.

One other direction of work is to focus on difficult to predict branches and investigate their correlation patterns with increasingly longer history. Such an analysis will reveal the importance of selective correlation to distant correlations.

Another possible direction of future work, is to investigate which affectors and affectees are more important. A decision-tree based approach [5,19] can be used to establish such classification. Such an analysis can be useful for better understanding and hopefully further reduce the correlations required for best prediction.

Finally, the approach proposed in this paper can be applied to static branch prediction, and to other types of predictors, such as value and dependence predictors.

Acknowledgments. This work is partially supported by an Intel research grant and the University of Cyprus. Yiannakis Sazeides would like to thank Ronny Ronen, Roni Rosner, Avi Mendelson, Pierre Michaud, Hans Vandierendonck and Veerle Desmet for their encouragement and feedback on earlier versions of this work. The authors like also to thank the anonymous reviewers for their constructive critique and suggestions that helped improve the presentation of this manuscript.

References

1. Wilkerson, C., Stark, J.: Introduction to JILP's Special Edition for Finalists of the Championship Branch Prediction (CBP1) Competition. Journal of Instruction-Level Parallelism 7 (2005)
2. Jiménez, D.A.: The Second Championship Branch Prediction Competition. Journal of Instruction-Level Parallelism 9 (2007)
3. Seznec, A.: Genesis of the O-GEHL Branch Predictor. Journal of Instruction-Level Parallelism 7 (2005)
4. Seznec, A.: The Idealistic GTL Predictor. Journal of Instruction-Level Parallelism 9 (2007)
5. Desmet, V.: On the Systematic Design of Cost-Effective Branch Prediction. PhD Thesis, University of Ghent, Belgium (2006)
6. Evers, M., Patel, S.J., Chappel, R.S., Patt, Y.N.: An Analysis of Correlation and Predictability: What Makes Two-Level Branch Predictors Work. In: 25th International Symposium on Computer Architecture (June 1998)
7. McFarling, S.: Combining Branch Predictors. Technical Report DEC WRL TN-36, Digital Western Research Laboratory (June 1993)
8. Thomas, R., Franklin, M., Wilkerson, C., Stark, J.: Improving Branch Prediction by Dynamic Dataflow-based Identification of Correlated Branches from a Large Global History. In: 30th International Symposium on Computer Architecture, pp. 314–323 (June 2003)
9. Jimenez, D.A., Lin, C.: Dynamic Branch Prediction with Perceptrons. In: 7th International Symposium on High Performance Computer Architecture (February 2001)
10. Burger, D., Austin, T.M., Bennett, S.: Evaluating Future Microprocessors: The SimpleScalar Tool Set. Technical Report CS-TR-96-1308, University of Wisconsin-Madison (July 1996)
11. Perelman, E., Hamerly, G., Biesbrouck, M.V., Sherwood, T., Calder, B.: Using SimPoint for Accurate and Efficient Simulation. In: International Conference on Measurement and Modeling of Computer Systems (2003)
12. Seznec, A.: The L-TAGE Branch Predictor. Journal of Instruction-Level Parallelism 9 (2007)
13. Sazeides, Y., Moustakas, A., Constantinides, K., Kleanthous, M.: The Significance of Affectors and Affectees Correlations for Branch Predicion. In: International Conference on High Performance Embedded Architectures and Compilers, pp. 243–257 (January 2008)
14. Seznec, A.: Analysis of the O-GEometric History Length branch predictor. In: 32nd International Symposium on Computer Architecture (2005)
15. Smith, J.E.: A Study of Branch Prediction Strategies. In: 8th International Symposium on Computer Architecture, pp. 135–148 (May 1981)

16. Yeh, T.Y., Patt, Y.N.: Two-Level Adaptive Branch Prediction. In: 24th International Symposium on Microarchitecture, pp. 51–61 (November 1991)
17. Juan, T., Sanjeevan, S., Navarro, J.J.: Dynamic History-Length Fitting: A third level of adaptivity for branch prediction. In: 25th International Symposium on Computer Architecture, pp. 155–166 (June 1998)
18. Michaud, P.: A PPM-like, Tag-based Predictor. Journal of Instruction-Level Parallelism 7 (2005)
19. Fern, A., Givan, R., Falsafi, B., Vijaykumar, T.N.: Dynamic feature selection for hardware prediction. Journal of Systems Architecture 52(4), 213–234 (2006)
20. Jacobson, Q., Rottenberg, E., Smith, J.E.: Path-Based Next Trace Prediction. In: 30th International Symposium on Microarchitecture, pp. 14–23 (December 1997)
21. Gao, F., Sair, S.: Exploiting Intra-function Correlation with the Global History. In: Hämäläinen, T.D., Pimentel, A.D., Takala, J., Vassiliadis, S. (eds.) SAMOS 2005. LNCS, vol. 3553, pp. 172–181. Springer, Heidelberg (2005)
22. Farcy, A., Temam, O., Espasa, R., Juan, T.: Dataflow analysis of branch mispredictions and its application to early resolution of branch outcomes. In: 31st International Symposium on Microarchitecture, pp. 59–68 (December 1998)
23. Thomas, R., Franklin, M.: Using Dataflow Based Context for Accurate Value Prediction. In: 2001 International Conference on Parallel Architectures and Compilation Techniques, pp. 107–117 (September 2001)
24. Sazeides, Y.: Dependence Based Value Prediction. Technical Report CS-TR-02-00, University of Cyprus (February 2002)
25. Constantinides, K., Sazeides, Y.: A Hardware Based Method for Dynamically Detecting Instruction Isomorphism and its Application to Branch Prediction. In: 2nd Value Prediction Workshop (2004)
26. Chen, L., Dropsho, S., Albonesi, D.H.: Dynamic Data Dependence Tracking and its Application to Branch Prediction. In: 9th International Symposium on High Performance Computer Architecture, pp. 65–76 (February 2003)
27. Mahlke, S., Natarajan, B.: Compiler Synthesized Dynamic Branch Prediction. In: 29th International Symposium on Microarchitecture, pp. 153–164 (December 1996)

Eighth MEDEA Workshop
(Selected Papers)

Eighth MEDEA Workshop

Sandro Bartolini[1,*], Pierfrancesco Foglia[2,*], and Cosimo Antonia Prete[2,*]

[1] Department of Information Engineering, University of Siena, Siena, Italy
`bartolini@dii.unisi.it`
[2] Department of Information Engineering, University of Pisa, Pisa, Italy
`foglia, prete@iet.unipi.it`

Members of the HiPEAC EU Network of Excellence

It is our pleasure to welcome you to this special section of Transactions on High-Performance Embedded Architectures and Compilers (HiPEAC), presenting selected papers from the 2007 edition of Medea Workshop. This workshop, held in conjunction with the PACT conference since 2000, has moved its topics of interest from decoupled architectures to memory hierarchy arguments, with emphasis on embedded and application-specific CMP systems.

In these years, due to the growth of wire delay and power consumption issues, the focus of research in high performance systems has shifted towards CMP architectures. As a consequence, also memory hierarchy research need to cope with open issues related to CMP systems design: homogeneous vs heterogeneous architectures, exploitation of parallelism to improve performance and hide memory latency, acting at hardware and/or software levels, techniques to reduce power consumption and coherence-related traffic. Furthermore, the memory wall problem must be reconsidered in the new scenario, adapting old solutions or developing new ones. The papers in this section demonstrate some of the hot topics in CMP systems design, with authors coming from both industry and academia. We hope that you find these papers interesting in their insights, and informative in the details provided.

The first paper in this issue, "Exploring the Architecture of a Stream Register-Based Snoop Filter" by Blumrich et al., aims at reducing the negative effects of coherence-related traffic on performance and power in homogeneous CMP systems. This is achieved by proposing a combination of snoop filters and a small number of ad-hoc stream registers. The authors evaluate different filtering approaches, analyzing the effects of their parameters, and figure-out the most suitable filter combination. The proposed scheme demonstrates to eliminate 94%-99% of the unnecessary snoop requests (addresses that are not in cache) in case of Splash-2 benchmarks.

Clustered architectures represent one of the solutions to face out wire delay limits in conventional super-scalar architectures. To improve ILP, big reorder buffers are requested, but such big structures increase power consumption and are detrimental for performance due to wire delay. In "CROB: Implementing a Large Instruction Window though Compression", Latorre et al. propose a novel reorder buffer architecture, CROB (compressed ROB), that compresses ROB entries giving the illusion of having

---

* Guest Editors Transactions on HiPEAC.

P. Stenström (Ed.): Transactions on HiPEAC III, LNCS 6590, pp. 91–92, 2011.
© Springer-Verlag Berlin Heidelberg 2011

a larger ROB, without paying the associated implementation costs. Results show an average speed-up of 20% for a 128-entry ROB.

CMP cores usually adopt large last level caches to hide memory latency. Such caches may be private or shared among cores, but both solutions may be not adequate due to the different "memory pressures" exercised by the different cores. Besides, large caches can waste energy when execution phases of the running applications do not have a big working-set to accommodate. Mechanisms for dynamic management of cache allocation to cores and dynamic activation of cache portions can help solving both problems. The paper "Power-Aware Dynamic Cache Partitioning for CMPs" by Kotera et al. propose a power-aware cache management algorithm which employs power-gating and cache partitioning. It can be tuned to favor maximum power reduction, sacrificing some performance, or to reduce power while maintaining the same performance output. Dynamic tracking of cache locality is used both for allocation of cache ways to cores and for power control with negligible hardware implementation overhead. The proposed mechanism reduces energy consumption by 20%, while maintaining the same performance level, and up to 54% sacrificing 13% of performance.

Heterogeneous architectures are an interesting alternative to homogeneous CMP systems, but require significant programming effort to optimize the available computational power to the behavior of the application, and to hide memory latency. The paper "Parallelization Schemes for Memory Optimization on the Cell Processor: A Case Study on the Harris Corner Detector" by Saidani et al. evaluates various parallelization schemes driven by the application domain and by the underlying Cell architecture, in the case of Harris algorithm for detecting interesting points of an image. The authors highlight the impact of DMA transfers, SPE synchronizations and the effect of chaining techniques. The achieved performance are compared to conventional cache-based CMP systems.

Taken as a whole, the articles in this special issue illustrate some of the active topics in the domain of memory hierarchy research for CMP systems. We hope you enjoy reading them, and that you learn something from each, as we did. Big thanks go to Per Stenström, the editor-in-chief of these transactions, and to the people who made this special issue possible: the peer-reviewers and Roberto Giorgi, co-organizer of Medea workshop with us and our friend and collaborator in many research activities.

Exploring the Architecture of a Stream Register-Based Snoop Filter

Matthias Blumrich, Valentina Salapura, and Alan Gara

IBM Thomas J. Watson Research Center
Yorktown Heights, NY, USA

Abstract. Multi-core processors have become mainstream; they provide parallelism with relatively low complexity. As true on-chip symmetric multiprocessors evolve, coherence traffic between cores is becoming problematic, both in terms of performance and power. The negative effects of coherence (snoop) traffic can be significantly mitigated through the use of snoop filtering. The idea is to shield each cache with a device that can eliminate snoop requests for addresses that are known not to be in the cache. This improves performance significantly for caches that cannot perform normal load and snoop lookups simultaneously. In addition, the reduction of snoop lookups yields power savings. This paper describes Stream Register snoop filtering, which captures the spatial locality of multiple memory reference streams in a small number of registers. We propose a snoop filter that combines Stream Registers with "snoop caching", a mechanism that captures the temporal locality of frequently-accessed addresses. Simulations of SPLASH-2 benchmarks on a 4-core multiprocessor illustrate tradeoffs and strengths of these two techniques. We show that their combination is most effective, eliminating 94% - 99% of all snoop requests using only a small number of stream registers and snoop cache lines.

1 Introduction

As single-core performance becomes increasingly hard to improve, and marginal costs are growing, both in terms of complexity and power/performance inefficiency [1], the use of multi-core solutions to improve throughput in multi-threaded workloads has become increasingly attractive [2].

Unlike designs which target single-thread solutions with degrading power/performance efficiency, suitably scalable parallel workloads show little or no degradation in efficiency while delivering significant increases in performance through the use of multithreaded workloads. Using parallelism at the processor level also aligns with the limits of future technologies. Although performance growth has been driven by technologically-enabled increases in processor operating frequency for the past 20 years, it is increasingly hard to obtain with new technologies. One of the main reasons is the impact of wire delays as feature sizes are shrunk [3], requiring increasingly more sophisticated microarchitectures.

While faster transistors and wires are increasingly hard to obtain, the application of Dennard's CMOS scaling theory [4] is continuing to deliver improvements in density. Thus, multi-core solutions are based on a commercially viable exploitation of modern CMOS fabrication processes.

P. Stenström (Ed.): Transactions on HiPEAC III, LNCS 6590, pp. 93–114, 2011.

Several multi-core solutions have been introduced over the past few years, such as the IBM POWER4 and POWER5 servers, the IBM Blue Gene/P system [5], the Intel Quad Core processors [6], and the Cell Broadband Architecture [7]. Indeed, multi-core is now a well-established trend. A major challenge in the implementation of chip multiprocessors is providing a suitable memory subsystem and on-chip interconnect that combines low average access latency with high bandwidth.

As the number of processors per chip rises, the coherence traffic per processor consequently increases. One solution to reducing the cost of coherence is to manage it in software; a solution adopted by both the Blue Gene/L [8] and Cell system architectures. In Blue Gene/L, software managed coherence is achieved by using one of two software abstraction models: virtual node mode, wherein each processor is a separate node in the Blue Gene/L-optimized MPI implementation, or coprocessor mode, where one processor is a dedicated computational node and a second processor provides I/O and system management functions. In the Cell Broadband Architecture, coherent DMA and the SPU-local store provide the necessary memory abstractions for building high-performance systems. Although software-managed coherence offers an attractive solution to achieving low-complexity memory architectures, it requires advanced compilation technologies and careful application tuning. While this is acceptable for high-end application-specific systems, providing low-complexity, coherent memory is an attractive solution for a wider range of systems.

To reduce the complexity of implementing coherence in chip multiprocessors, two component costs must be addressed:

– The bottleneck of a bus-based snoop implementation, which must be arbitrated between a high number of nodes.
– The cost of providing snoop ports to each processor's cache, or the cost of maintaining a central directory.

In this paper we have investigated the use of coherence request filtering (or snoop filtering) in a point-to-point coherence network to address these costs. The basic idea is to provide a mechanism which will significantly reduce the interference of coherence requests with processor operations without incurring costs of chip area, memory latency, or complexity inherent in existing hardware coherency support.

The contributions of this work include (1) a novel, highly efficient, point-to-point snoop filter architecture filtering in excess of 98% of all snoop requests, (2) significant reduction of area over a solution that duplicates cache directories to provide separate snoop directories, (3) an architecture to exploit the cache replacement policy to periodically re-train the snoop filters, increasing filtering effectiveness from an average of 30% to an average of 90% for the workloads studied, and (4) evaluation of the proposed architecture, including variations of several key parameters.

This paper is organized as follows. We begin with related work in Section 2. Then Section 3 describes the snoop filter architecture, and Section 4 gives a detailed description of stream registers. The simulation environment and methodology are presented in Section 5, followed by experimental results and analysis in Section 6. Finally, Section 7 concludes.

2   Related Work

In prior art, JETTY [9] is a snoop filter that combines two complementary filtering methods. The JETTY paper defines a characterization of filters as "include" or "exclude". An include filter tracks what *is* contained in a cache (or caches) while an exclude filter tracks what *is not*. The exclude filter consists of a cache of recently invalidated lines. A snoop that hits in the exclude filter is guaranteed not to be in the cache, so it can be filtered. The JETTY include filter captures a superset of a cache's contents. A snoop that hits in the include filter may be in the cache and should not be filtered. The include filter is like a simple bloom filter with direct-map hash functions applied to sub-fields of the address.

The JETTY paper makes an argument for snoop filtering as a means for power savings. However, our work was primarily motivated by the need to filter useless snoops that reduce performance. We also considered chip area and power consumption as significant constraints, causing us to look beyond the simple and accurate method of duplicating the cache tags as a filter. Because our simulation methodology and system organization differ considerably from the JETTY study, it is difficult to compare performance results. However, we simulated many of the same applications using the same problem sizes.

Several coherent network switches contain snoop filters that block unnecessary coherence requests from ever leaving a node. One such example is the Scalability Port Switch of the Intel E8870 chipset [10]. In this case, the snoop filter tracks the state of all cache lines within a 4-processor node for a system with up to four such nodes. Kant [11] modeled a similar system architecture with such a snoop filter. This architecture is also described in the Azusa system [12], which is based on Intel Itanium processors and may use an Intel chipset.

In [13], a HyperTransport network switch for use with AMD Opteron processors is described. The snoop filtering technique is basically the same as that of the E8870, including the fact that 4-processor nodes are supported.

A similar but more tightly-coupled architecture is evaluated in [14], where a single memory controller switch connects multiple multi-processor nodes and contains a snoop filter. The filter prevents unnecessary snoop requests between the nodes, and several variants are studied.

Snoop filters in tightly-coupled multiprocessors, such as chip multiprocessors (CMPs), can be located at each processor in order to squash unnecessary snoops without changing the overall coherence scheme. Ekman et. al. [15] describe a CMP architecture with Page Sharing Tables, which are exclude filters at the granularity of memory pages rather than cache lines. This architecture is a bit more involved in that the Page Sharing Tables coordinate to track page sharing rather than just presence.

The idea of preventing remote snoop requests from being broadcast can also be applied at the chip level as described in [16]. In this work, snoop filters keep track of memory regions, which can be quite large, and block remote snoops for memory that is known not to be shared.

3   Snoop Filter Architecture

In symmetric multiprocessor (SMP) architectures, coherency snoop requests represent a significant fraction of all cache accesses, but only a small fraction of snoop requests are actually found in any of the remote caches [9,17]. This is particularly true of supercomputing applications where data partitioning and data blocking have been performed to increase locality of reference and optimize overall compute performance. As a result, embedded cores with single-ported caches suffer significant performance loss due to unnecessary snooping because their caches are unavailable during snooping.

While data reference locality may make a coherence implementation seem unnecessary, there is a fine line between being able to prove that there is no data sharing at all, and the statistical observation that almost all data references are local. The former is a program correctness statement, the latter is a performance statement. Thus, providing an efficient snoop filtering implementation that can filter the vast majority of non-shared data traffic without burdening the cache bandwidth of every processor in the system provides a significant performance improvement over traditional cache-coherent systems. Snoop filtering and cache coherence also offer advantages over programs operating on fully disjoint data sets without hardware coherence by simplifying application porting and tuning – it no longer becomes necessary to eliminate all remote references under all circumstances, but most remote references for most situations, leading to increased programmer productivity by letting programmers focus on the common case.

This motivated us to introduce a simple hardware device that filters out incoming snoop requests, reducing the number of actual snoop requests presented to the cache, thus increasing performance and reducing power consumption. A snoop filter is associated with each of the four processors and is located outside the L1 cache. To make a snoop filter a viable implementation choice, it has to meet several requirements:

- Functional correctness – the filter cannot filter requests for data which are locally cached.
- Effectiveness – the filter should filter out a large fraction of received snoop requests.
- Design efficiency – the filter should be small and power-efficient.

In theory, a perfect snoop filter can be created by duplicating the cache tag directory and using it to determine exactly which snoops should be forwarded to the cache. However, this approach generally does not meet the design efficiency requirement because of practical limitations. In particular, the cache tag store is a highly optimized and integrated component that cannot easily be extracted, and a custom-designed equivalent with the same performance requires a large investment of time and expertise to complete. Furthermore, this paper will show that a highly-effective filter can be implemented in a fraction of the area needed for duplicate cache tags.

Ideally, a snoop filter will operate at the (typically lower) memory nest frequency to reduce power dissipation and design complexity. Lower frequency and reduced latch count reduces the number of state transitions and load on clock nets, which are the major contributors to power dissipation. Operating the snoop filter at a lower frequency simplifies the design, as transactions have to be less heavily pipelined, eliminating a variety of bypass conditions which have to be validated and tested. It also simplifies timing closure.

In some sense, a snoop filter trades off power consumed by cache lookups with power consumed by the filter. However, there is an additional overall energy reduction because the processor performance benefit resulting from reduced snoop interference causes applications to complete sooner. Therefore, energy, measured as power consumed in time, is reduced.

In this work, we only consider a write-through L1 cache, where data integrity between the processors is maintained with a cache coherence protocol based on snoop invalidates. Thus, every time a processor issues a store, snoop invalidate messages are generated at all other processors, and no other coherence messages are required. This approach could be extended to write-back coherence protocols, where both read and write snoops generally require responses from remote caches. At each remote cache, the snoop filter would quickly determine whether the snooped address was not present, and if so, immediately send the response without the need to snoop the cache.

3.1 Point-to-Point Snoop Filter Interconnection

Previous work on snoop filters has only considered bus based systems. In such systems, all cache controllers snoop a shared bus to determine whether they have a copy of every requested data block. A simple and common-place coherence protocol that utilizes snooping is "write-invalidate".

In a write-invalidate protocol, each write causes all copies of the written line to be invalidated in all other caches. If two or more processors attempt to write the same data simultaneously, only one of them wins the race, causing the other processors' copies to be invalidated. The use of the shared bus enforces write serialization.

For every write bus transaction, all cache controllers have to check their cache address tags (a.k.a. snoop) independently to see if they are caching the written line. With the increasing number of processors on a bus, snooping activity increases as well. Unnecessary coherency requests degrade performance of the system, especially impacting the supercomputing applications where only a small fraction of snoop requests are actually found in any of the remote caches.

In [9], several proposals for reducing snoop requests using snoop filters are described. While reducing the number of snoop requests presented to a cache up to about 70%, the performance of the systems are still limited because of the interconnect architecture and lack of support for multi-porting. The architecture described is based on a shared system bus, which establishes a common event ordering across the system. While such global time ordering is desirable to simplify the filter architecture, it limits the possible system configurations to those with a single, shared bus. Alas, such systems are known to be limited in scalability due to contention for the single global resource. In addition, global buses tend to be slow, due to the high load of multiple components attached to them, and inefficient to place in CMPs.

Thus, in a highly-optimized, high-bandwidth system, it is desirable to provide alternate interconnect architectures, such as star or point-to-point. These are advantageous, as they only have a single sender and transmitter, thereby reducing the load, allowing the use of high speed protocols, and simplifying floor planning in CMPs. Using point-to-point interconnects also allows several transmissions to be in-progress simultaneously, thereby increasing the data transfer parallelism and overall data throughput.

Another limitation of the bus-based architecture is the inability to perform snoop filtering on several requests simultaneously, because simultaneous snoop requests from several processors have to be serialized by the bus. Allowing the processing of several snoop requests concurrently provides a significant increase in the number of requests that can be handled at any one time, and thus increases overall system performance. However, this increased data throughput means that snoop filters for such interconnects must be designed to accommodate multiple requests simultaneously.

In this paper, we opt for a system incorporating snoop filters to increase overall performance and power efficiency without limiting the system design options to a common bus. We have designed a snoop filter architecture supporting systems using point-to-point connections that allows each processor's snoop filter to filter requests from multiple memory writers concurrently. Our high-performance snoop filter is implemented in a pipelined fashion to enable high system clock speeds. Figure 1 illustrates our approach.

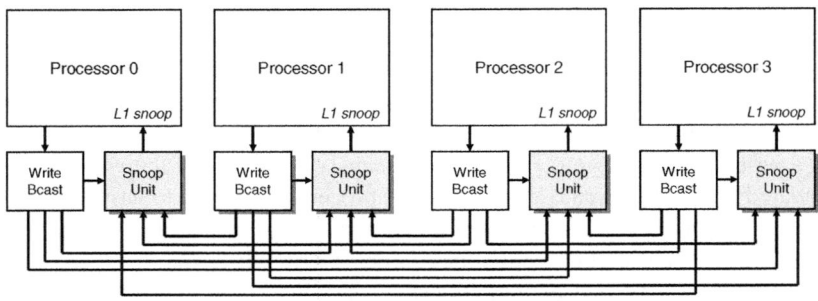

Fig. 1. Chip multiprocessor using snoop filters and a point-to-point interconnection architecture. All writes are broadcast by each processor to all remote caches for invalidation.

To take advantage of the point-to-point architecture and allow for concurrent filtering of multiple snoop requests, we implement a separate snoop filter block, or "port filter", for each interconnect port. Thus, coherency requests of all ports are processed concurrently, and a small fraction of all requests are forwarded to the processor. For example, each snoop filter in Figure 1 would have three separate port filters, each of which handles requests from one remote processor.

As the number of processors in a CMP scales up, the interconnect naturally transitions from point-to-point to a network-on-chip (NoC). At those scales, coherence protocols are likely to be based on directories, where filtering effectively takes place at the source. Therefore, our system architecture is most obviously applicable to CMPs of modest scale [18].

It should be noted that the snoop filters are basically transparent with respect to the behavior of the point-to-point interconnect. This interconnect poses particular design challenges, such as ordering between snoop invalidates, that exist regardless of the presence of snoop filters. In this study, we assumed a consistency protocol that is not sensitive to the order of invalidations coming from different processors. When necessary, a global synchronization would be used to enforce completion of all snoops.

3.2 Snoop Filter Variants

Early on, we decided to include multiple filter units which implement various filtering algorithms in each port filter block. The motivation for this decision was to capture various characteristics of the memory references because some filtering units best capture time locality of memory references, whereas others capture reference streams. We will show in this paper that the combination of filtering algorithms achieves the highest snoop filtering rate, reducing the number of snoop requests up to 99%.

We have explored a number of snoop filter variants, but have selected the combination of a stream register based filter and a snoop cache. The snoop cache is essentially a Vector-Exclusive-JETTY [9]. It filters snoops using an algorithm which is based on the temporal locality property of snoop requests, meaning that if a single snoop request for a particular location was made, it is probable that another request to the same location will be made soon. This filter unit records a subset of memory blocks that are *not* cached.

The stream registers use an orthogonal filtering technique, exploiting the regularity of memory accesses. They record a superset of blocks that *are* cached. Results of both filter units are considered in a combined filtering decision. If either one of the filtering units decides that a snoop request should be discarded, then it is discarded.

The snoop cache filter unit keeps a record of memory references which are guaranteed not to be in the cache. These blocks have been snooped recently (thus invalidated in the cache) and are still not cached (i.e. they were not loaded into the cache since invalidation). The snoop cache filter unit contains a small array of address tags. An entry is created for each snoop request. A subsequent request for the same block will hit in the snoop cache, and be filtered. If the block is loaded in the processor cache, the corresponding entry is removed from the snoop cache, and any new coherency request to the same block will miss in the snoop cache and be forwarded to the processor cache. There is one dedicated snoop cache filter unit for each remote memory writer (processor, DMA, etc.) to allow for concurrent filtering of multiple coherency requests, thus increasing system performance.

A single snoop cache contains M snoop cache lines, each consisting of an address tag field, and a valid line vector. The address tag field is typically not the same as the address tag of the L1 data cache, but is reduced by the number of bits used for encoding a valid line vector. The valid line vector is a bit-vector that records the presence of individual, consecutive lines within an aligned block. Thus, N least significant bits from the address are decoded to a valid line vector with 2^N bits, where each bit of the vector effectively utilizes the remainder of the stored address, significantly increasing the snoop cache capacity efficiently. In the extreme case when N is zero, the whole entry in the snoop cache represents only one L1 data cache line, and the valid line vector has only one bit, corresponding to a "valid" bit.

4   Stream Registers

The stream register filter unit was introduced in [19]. Unlike the snoop cache that keeps track of what *is not* in the cache, the stream register filter keeps track of what *is* in the cache (i.e. it is an include filter). More precisely, the stream registers keep track of at

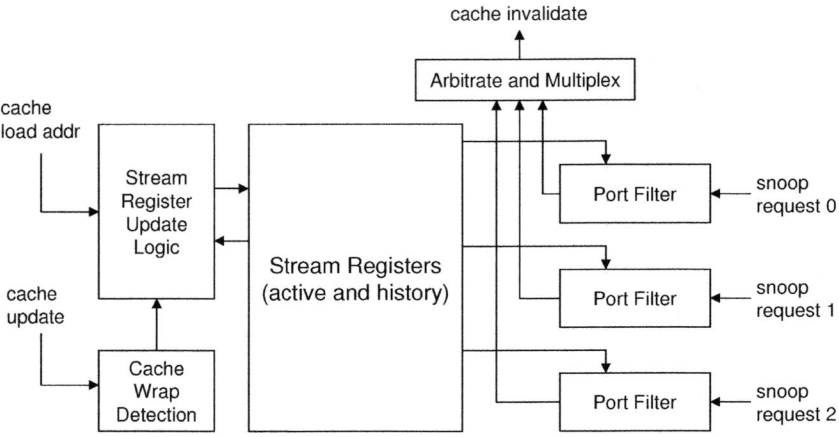

Fig. 2. Architecture of a snoop filter using stream registers. There are three port filters in order to handle snoop requests from all remote processors simultaneously.

least the lines that are in the cache, but may assume that some lines are cached which are not actually there. However, forwarding some unnecessary snoop requests to the cache does not affect correctness. The stream registers capture address streams, so they are advantageous for applications where too many spatially-distributed references overflow the snoop cache filter units.

The stream register filter unit consists of two sets of stream registers and masks (active and history sets), port filter logic, cache wrap detection logic, and stream register update logic, as illustrated in Figure 2. The stream registers and masks keep track of data which were recently loaded into the cache of the processor. One active stream register is updated every time the cache loads a new line, which is presented to the Stream Register Update Logic with appropriate control signals. A particular register is chosen for update based upon the current stream register state and the address of the new line being loaded into the cache.

Every remote snoop (snoop requests 0-2) is checked against the stream registers to see if it might be in the cache or not. This check can be performed in parallel because stream register lookups never change the state of the registers. Therefore, our architecture includes a port filter for each remote processor (or other snoop source such as DMA). Figure 2 shows three Port Filters. Snoop requests coming from one of the remote processors are checked in one of the Port Filters. Each arriving snoop requests address is compared with the state of the stream registers to determine if the snoop request could possibly be in the cache. In parallel, it is checked against a snoop cache, one of which exists in each Port Filter. If either the stream register or snoop cache lookup determine that the address is *not* in the L1 cache, then it is filtered out. Otherwise the request is forwarded to the Arbitration and Multiplexing interface and on to the cache. The Arbitrate and Multiplex logic shares the snoop interface of the cache between the Port Filters and queues unfiltered snoop requests, allowing for the maximum snoop request rate.

A stream register actually consists of a pair of registers (the base and the mask) and a valid bit. The base register keeps track of address bits that are common to all of the cache lines represented by the stream register, while the corresponding mask register keeps track of which bits these are. For example, if considering an address space of 2^{32} bytes with a cache line size of 32 bytes, a cache line load address is 27 bits in length, and the base and mask registers of the stream registers are also 27 bits in length.

Initially, the valid bit is set to zero, indicating that the stream register is not in use, and the contents of the base and mask registers are irrelevant. When the first cache line load address is added to this stream register, the valid bit is set to one, the base register is set to the line address, and all the bits of the mask register are set to one, indicating that all of the bits in the base register are significant. That is, an address that matches the address stored in the base register exactly is considered to be in the cache, while an address differing in any bit or bits is not.

At some point, another cache line load address will be added to this stream register. The new address is compared to the base register AND-ed with the mask register to determine which significant bits are different, and the mask register is then updated so that the differing bit positions become zeros in the mask. These zeros indicate that the corresponding bits of the base register are "don't-care", or can be assumed to take any value (zero or one). Therefore, these bits are no longer significant during comparisons to the stream register.

As an example, suppose the first two cache line load addresses are $0x1708fb1$ and $0x1708fb2$ (hexadecimal values). Then the contents of the stream register after these loads is:

Step 0: Base = $0x1708fb1$, Mask = $0x7ffffff$
Step 1: Base = $0x1708fb2$, Mask = $0x7fffffc$

As the second address and the base register differed in the two least significant bits, those bits are cleared in the mask register. At this point, the stream register indicates that the addresses $0x1708fb0$, $0x1708fb1$, $0x1708fb2$, and $0x1708fb3$ can all be in the cache because it can no longer distinguish the two least significant bits.

Every cache line load address is added to exactly one of the multiple stream registers. Therefore, the collection of stream registers represents the complete cache state. The decision of which active register to update is made by the register update logic. In order to capture streams, we want addresses separated by the same stride to be added to the same stream register. We say that such addresses have an affinity for one another. We considered two policies for determining affinity and selecting which stream register to update:

- choose the stream register with minimal Hamming distance from the line load address (i.e. the stream register which will result in the minimum number of mask register bits changing to zero).
- choose the stream register where the most upper bits of the base register match those of the line load address.

Either mechanism guarantees that all addresses presented to the stream registers will be included within them.

Another issue is when to choose a new register instead of one that already contains a stream. We do this by assigning an "empty affinity" to unused registers and then including them in the update selection process. So when using the Hamming distance policy, for example, an empty register is chosen if the empty affinity is less than the affinity calculated for all used registers.

Over time, as cache line load addresses are added to the stream registers, they become less and less accurate in terms of their knowledge of what is actually in the cache. Every mask bit that becomes zero increases the number of cache lines that the corresponding stream register specifies as being in the cache, reducing the effectiveness of the stream register filtering. In the limit, the mask register becomes all zeros and every possible address is included in the register and considered to be in the cache.

Loss of accuracy is a disadvantage common to every snoop filtering technique that uses much less storage than the cache tag array. Snoop registers are specifically intended to remain accurate for strided streams, but they will not fare well with random addresses. To overcome the progressive loss of accuracy, the stream register snoop filter includes a mechanism for resetting the registers back to their initial condition. As there is no efficient way to remove an address from the stream registers and guarantee correctness, the filter clears the registers whenever the cache has been completely replaced, and they begin accumulating addresses anew. We call this complete replacement (relative to some initial state) a "cache wrap". The cache wrap detection logic monitors cache updates and determines when all of the cache lines present in the initial state have been overwritten. To do this, information must be provided by the L1 cache, either in the form of individual replacement notifications, or as a single event indicating that a wrap has occurred.

At that point, all of the stream registers are copied to a second "history" set of registers and masks and the "active" stream registers are all cleared to begin accumulating cache line load addresses anew. In addition, the state of the cache at the time of the wrap becomes the new initial state for the purpose of detecting the next cache wrap. The stream registers in the history set are never updated. However, they are treated the same as the active set by the Port Filters when deciding whether a snoop address could be in the cache. Their purpose is to make up for the fact that individual cache sets wrap at different times, but never survive two cache wraps.

The stream registers exploit periodic cache wrapping in order to refresh, and they rely upon knowing when the wraps occur. The second requirement is not difficult to implement, but does require a modified cache that either indicates all replacements, or tracks them from some point in time and indicates when all lines have been replaced.

Periodic cache wrapping is not guaranteed, but occurs frequently in practice. Caches with a round-robin replacement policy, such as those of the IBM PowerPC cores used in the Blue Gene/L and Blue Gene/P supercomputers, wrap relatively frequently. Specific wrapping behavior is a function of replacement policy and workload behavior. In either case, it is statistically possible that wrapping occurs infrequently, or never (i.e. a particular cache set is seldom or never used), but this pathological situation is not a threat to correctness. If this is a serious concern, then the stream register architecture could be extended to include a full cache invalidation and stream register reset when no wrap occurs for a long period of time.

5   Experimental Methodology

The experiments in this paper represent our top-down approach of validating the stream register ideas and showing that stream registers are effective for a broad range of applications. Our methodology trades detail for the ability to process huge traces of several applications. We feel that this is the best approach because the order of memory accesses is the critical factor in determining snoop filter effectiveness. That is, the order of a snoop request for some address relative to a snoop filter acquiring that address is what determines whether the filter rejects the address or not. Other papers (such as JETTY [9]) relate filter effectiveness to performance gain and power reduction. For example, the JETTY paper estimates that L2 cache snooping alone accounts for 33% of the total power of a typical 4-way SMP.

For our experiments, we used several applications from the publicly-available SPLASH-2 [20] benchmark suite. These are well known benchmarks containing shared-memory applications that have driven much research on memory system architectures and cache-coherence protocols. We have chosen to use these publicly-available codes because they are good representatives for a wide range of scientific applications, which is where we expect to see the most significant impact of CMPs. We have run the kernels (LU, FFT, Cholesky, and Radix), and some of the applications (Barnes, Ocean, Raytrace, and Fmm).

For each of the benchmarks chosen, we have simulated a full, four-processor application run and collected the entire L1 data cache miss sequence to determine coherence snoop requests. Table 1 shows the benchmarks used, the total number of accesses to memory, and the average percentage of misses in the L1 caches. Whereas the hit rate in the local cache of a processor is high, the percentage of hits in the caches of all other processors (we refer to such processors as "remote") is very low.

Table 1 shows that across all benchmarks virtually all coherency snoop requests will miss in the remote caches, this representing the total coherency snoop filter opportunity. Such small hit rates are due to the relatively small (32KB) first-level caches and highlight the importance of snoop filtering for CMP cache coherence, particularly when maintained between L1 caches. Although few snoops hit, the ones that do are essential and the ones that do not should be filtered. We also list the total number of snoop requests generated by all four processors collectively (i.e. the total number of writes).

We used a custom simulator written with Augmint [21] to collect the memory access traces. Augmint is a public-domain, execution-driven, multiprocessor simulation environment for Intel x86 architectures, running UNIX or Windows. Augmint does not include a memory backend, thus requiring users to develop one from scratch. We modeled the L1 data caches of four PowerPC 440 processors [22] and an ideal memory system below that (since we were only concerned with the order of accesses and their effect on snoop filtering rates). Then we collected a trace of all memory references, including the source processor and address.

We developed a custom back-end simulator to process the traces and produce the results in this paper. Because we wanted to measure the relative effectiveness of snoop filters over very long traces, we were not concerned with cycle accuracy. We were only concerned with the order of accesses and their effect upon the snoop filters and caches. Therefore, the trace entries are processed in order, and they have an instant, atomic

Table 1. SPLASH-2 benchmark characteristics. The low remote cache hit rate shows that almost all invalidation snoops are useless and can be eliminated.

Benchmark	Input parameters	Accesses to memory	Local cache hit rate	Remote cache hit rate	Total coherency accesses
Barnes	16K particles	1,602,120,476	99.73%	0.00047%	1,968,916,971
FFT	256K points	58,481,113	97.12%	0.0000057%	52,627,671
LU	512 matrix	202,643,933	99.24%	0.0000088%	204,434,958
Ocean	258 x 258 ocean	310,234,016	93.36%	0.03%	143,647,839
Cholesky	tk15.O	678,266,460	99.43%	0.00043%	614,572,560
FMM	16K particles	2,084,764,684	99.76%	0.00016%	2,976,937,884
Radix	10M keys	2,716,061,135	99.48%	0.00068%	3,491,931,132
Raytrace	car	404,977,091	98.43%	0.018%	358,731,051

effect upon the simulated caches and snoop filters. This simplification allowed us to compare many different alternative architectures, while exposing the significant trends. As a result, however, we could not measure execution times.

The back-end simulator models the private L1 data caches and snoop filters of four processors. We model the cache of the PowerPC 440 embedded processor, which is the building block for the Blue Gene/L supercomputer [8]. Each cache is 32KB in size and has a line size of 32 bytes. The caches are organized as 16 sets, each of which has 64 ways and utilizes a round-robin replacement policy.

While such high associativity may seem extreme, it is important to note that associativity is a characteristic that improves cache accuracy at the potential cost of cycle time. Overall, the gain in accuracy from high associativity can compensate for ever-increasing memory latencies, especially in a CMP where the overall performance is not as closely coupled to the cycle time as it is in a uniprocessor. Round-robin replacement is a viable, perhaps necessary, choice for a highly-associative cache because of its implementation simplicity (compared to LRU). Because we were only concerned with the order of accesses and their effect on snoop filtering rates, we did not model the memory system below the L1 caches.

The back-end simulator responds to loads and stores as follows:

- LOAD: Update the local cache. Then update the stream registers (insert the load address) and the snoop caches (delete the load address) of the local snoop filter.
- STORE: Update the local cache. Then update the three remote snoop filters, which includes a lookup to see if the snoop resulting from the store should be filtered, and a snoop cache update if it is not. Finally, propagate snoop invalidations to all remote caches for which the snoop request was not filtered.

6   Experiments and Simulation Results

We are interested in exploring the snoop filter design space to find the best compromise that yields a good filtering rate. We studied the impact of several design parameters. For stream registers, we considered their number, the replacement policy, and the empty affinity. For the snoop cache, we considered the number of entries and the size of the valid line vector. The goal is to eliminate as many unnecessary coherence requests as possible, thus improving performance and reducing power dissipation. We also analyze the impact of using both snoop filter units together to exploit their combined strength, and explore several configurations to identify the optimal design point.

6.1 Stream Register Size

In order to determine the optimal number of stream registers, we have varied their number exponentially from 4 to 32, as shown in Figure 3. Not surprisingly, our experiments show that more stream registers filter a higher percentage of coherence snoop requests. But even when using only eight stream registers, we filter more than 90% of all snoop requests for three benchmark applications.

We observed that the effect of increasing the number of stream registers is not linear with respect to the snoop filter rate. Choosing only four stream registers is clearly a bad policy. For the SPLASH-2 benchmarks, selecting 8 or 16 stream registers seems to be the best compromise, whereas 32 stream registers (which doubles the area compared to 16 stream registers) only increases the snoop filter rate significantly for one benchmark.

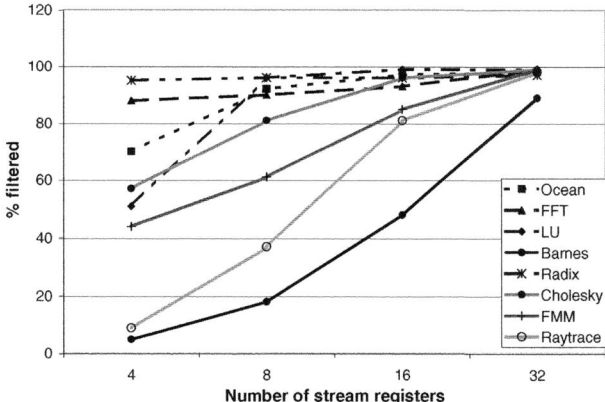

Fig. 3. Stream register filter behavior. Percentage of snoops filtered as the number of stream registers is increased.

6.2 Stream Register Update Policy

As previously described, every cache line load address is added to exactly one stream register. The register selected for update depends on the stream register update policy and the empty affinity value. We have evaluated two different selection policies:

– minimal Hamming distance, and
– most matching upper bits (MMUB).

For the minimal Hamming distance selection policy, we calculate the Hamming distance between each new load address and all stored values in the stream registers combined with their paired masks so that only relevant bits (i.e. bits that are 1 in the mask)

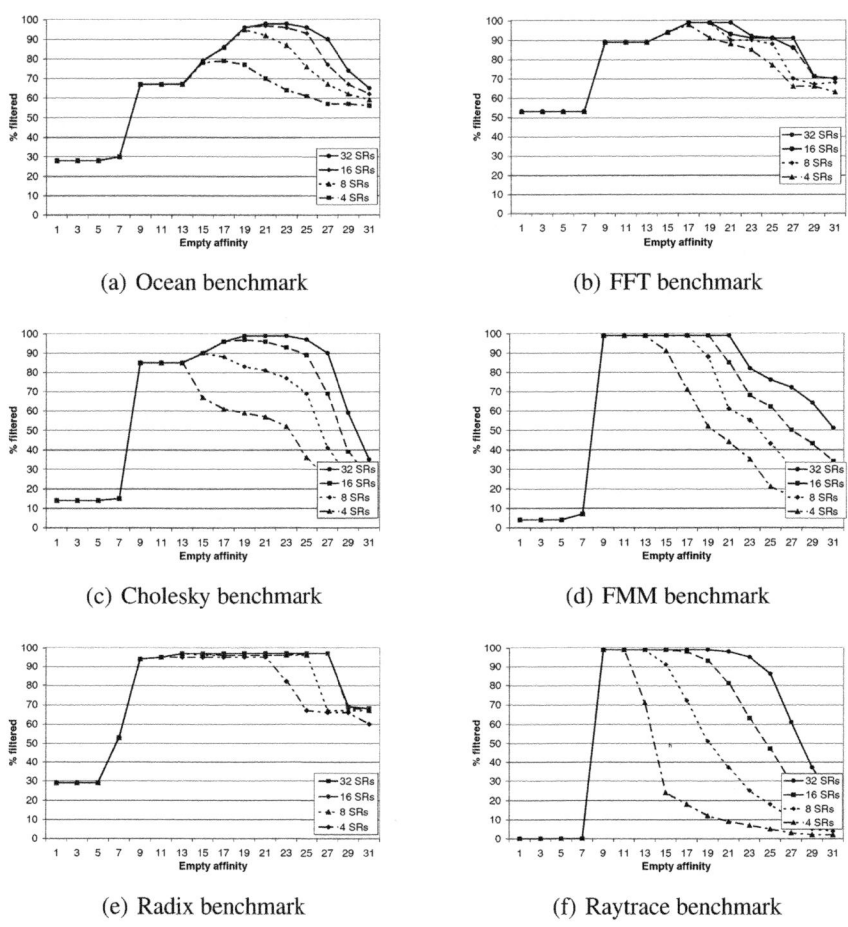

(a) Ocean benchmark

(b) FFT benchmark

(c) Cholesky benchmark

(d) FMM benchmark

(e) Radix benchmark

(f) Raytrace benchmark

Fig. 4. Percentage of snoops filtered as the empty affinity and number of stream registers is varied using the MMUB update policy

are considered. The affinity is the number of mask register bits that will be changed to 0, and the stream register with the minimum affinity is selected for update. In the MMUB update policy, we choose the stream register where the largest number of relevant upper bits match those of the line load address.

In our evaluation of stream register update policies, we have also varied the empty affinity value. As discussed in Section 4, empty affinity is the default threshold value assigned to an empty register. Figures 4(a) to 4(f) show the effect of varying the empty affinity for various stream register sizes using the MMUB update policy. If the empty affinity is set too low, empty stream registers are used to establish new streams even for memory accesses belonging to the same stream. As a result, the filter rate of the stream registers will be very low because few streams are captured. Similarly, setting the empty affinity value too high causes streams to share registers and obliterate each others mask bits, resulting in a low filter rate. When the empty affinity is increased to more than 13, it starts to play a role in the filter rate, depending on the number of stream registers. For filters having a higher number of stream registers, a higher affinity value is advantageous because it allows for more sensitive stream determination. For configurations with a smaller number of stream registers, a lower affinity allows for the most effective stream discrimination. Overall, the optimal empty affinity value is about 19 for eight stream registers, and about 23 for 32 stream registers.

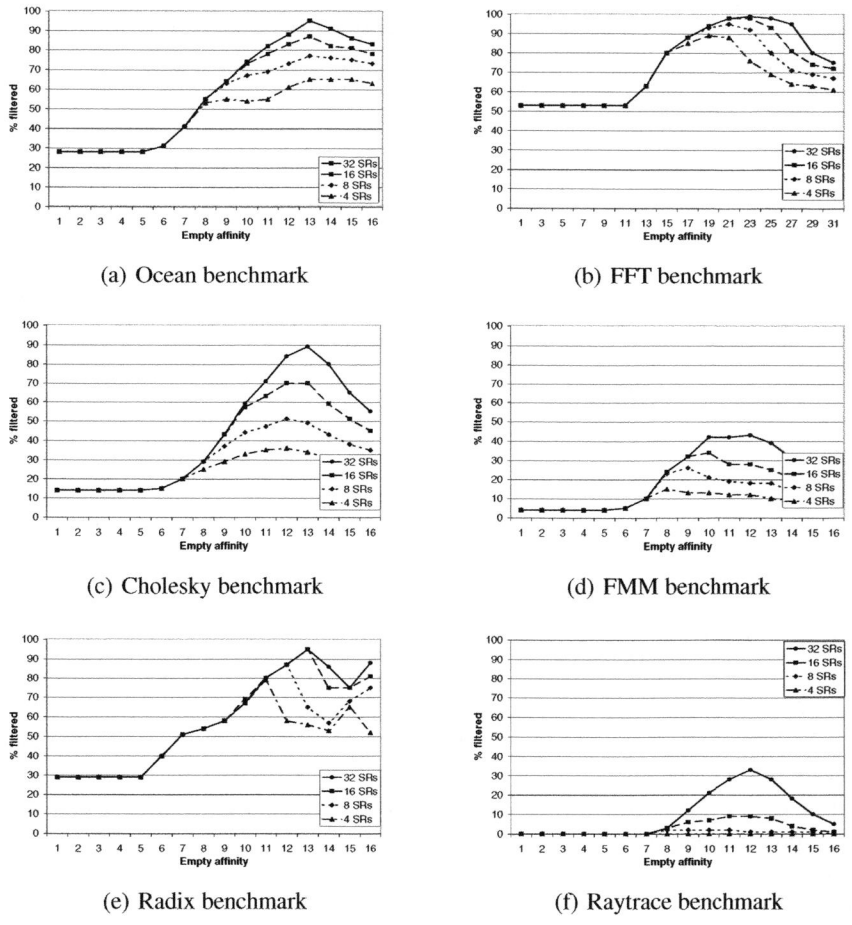

(a) Ocean benchmark

(b) FFT benchmark

(c) Cholesky benchmark

(d) FMM benchmark

(e) Radix benchmark

(f) Raytrace benchmark

Fig. 5. Percentage of snoops filtered as the empty affinity and number of stream registers is varied using the minimum Hamming distance update policy

Figure 5 shows the effect of varying the empty affinity for various stream register sizes using the minimum Hamming distance update policy. Similar to the MMUB update policy, setting the empty affinity too low or too high causes the filter rate of the stream registers to be low. The optimal empty affinity number is between 19 and 25, depending on the number of stream registers in the filter and the application's memory access pattern.

Across all applications, the sensitivity of the filter rate to the empty affinity value seem to be less for the MMUB update policy when compared with the minimum Hamming distance policy. In addition, for some applications - like Raytrace and FMM - the MMUB update policy significantly outperforms the Hamming distance policy. While MMUB achieves almost 100% filtering for these applications, the Hamming distance policy reaches less than 40%, even for the largest configurations.

The MMUB policy has the advantage of ignoring low-order address bits when establishing streams. The minimum Hamming distance policy results in well-correlated addresses that differ in their low-order address bits being mapped to different stream registers, thereby causing a kind of pollution which limits effectiveness.

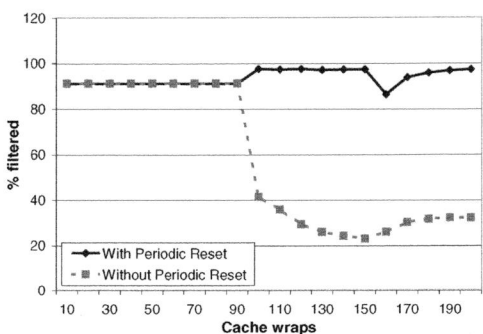

Fig. 6. Effectiveness of stream registers when implementing cache wrap for the FFT benchmark

6.3   Stream Register Clearing

As described in Section 4, the stream registers need to be cleared periodically in order to track changes in programs' L1 cache contents. The need for this is illustrated in Figure 6, which shows average, cumulative stream register effectiveness for a portion of the FFT benchmark running on a 4-processor CMP. During the course of the run, the caches wrapped 200 times.

Initially, the L1 working set is captured effectively by the stream registers and resetting provides no benefit. At around the 100th wrap, the working set changes, and the stream registers with reset can track the change. The stream registers without reset, however, forward many unnecessary snoops, causing their effectiveness to plummet. Although the stream registers without reset only become less accurate over time, the modest recovery in their effectiveness only indicates that the cache contents has changed in their favor.

6.4   Snoop Cache Size

In order to determine the optimal sizing for a snoop cache-based filter, we have varied two parameters: the number of lines, ranging from 4 to 64, and the number of bits used in the valid line vector, ranging from 1 to 64 (encoding 0 to 6 consecutive lines respectively). The results are illustrated in Figure 7 for several SPLASH-2 benchmarks.

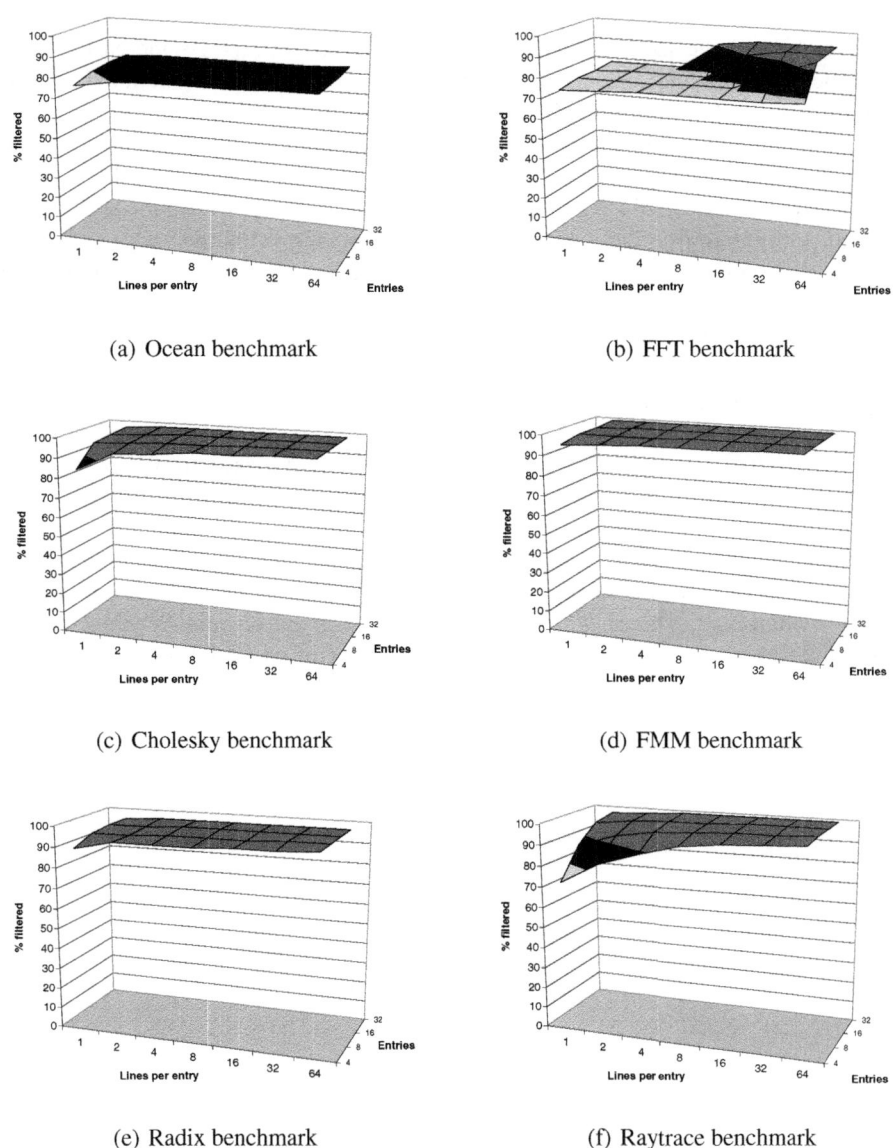

(a) Ocean benchmark

(b) FFT benchmark

(c) Cholesky benchmark

(d) FMM benchmark

(e) Radix benchmark

(f) Raytrace benchmark

Fig. 7. Snoop cache filter behavior. Percentage of snoops filtered as the number of entries and the number of lines per entry is varied.

Our experiments show that using filters with a greater number of snoop cache lines and/or a longer valid line vector are more effective at filtering snoop requests. But even for relatively small snoop caches having only 4 cache lines each, and with valid line vectors of 32 bits, we reach the snoop cache filter limit across the benchmark applications. The filter limit varies for various applications from 82% for Ocean to 99% for FMM.

We observe that for each application, depending of its memory access pattern, the shape of the cache size/valid vector line length surface differs. By increasing only the number of cache lines or only the length of the valid line vector, the maximum filtering possibility for a particular application can be reached. For example, Ocean (Figure 7(a)) reaches its maximum filtering rate of 83% for snoop cache filter units with almost minimal sizing, having only 4 cache lines and as little as 2-bit-long valid line vectors. Similarly, FMM (Figure 7(d)) reaches its filtering maximum of 99% with a small configurations of only 8 cache lines and 8-bit long valid line vectors.

On the contrary, the FFT benchmark reaches maximum filtering only for bigger configurations. As illustrated in Figure 7(b), at least 8 cache lines and 64-bit long valid line vectors are needed to reach the maximum filtering rate of 93%. The memory access pattern of FFT requires a higher number of cache lines because it has a high number of streams, and a higher number of bits in the valid line vector because these streams are longer.

The optimal snoop filter configuration achieves near maximum filtering across all benchmarks, requiring a minimal number of latches for its implementation. This translates directly to a minimal number of aggregated bits. The dependency on the number of bits required by each of the snoop cache sizes explored is illustrated in Figure 8.

We observe that the effect of increasing the number of cache lines and valid line vector length is not linear with respect to the area requirements. Whereas the snoop filtering rate varied symmetrically with the number of cache lines and the valid line vector length, the area requirement increases significantly when increasing the number of cache lines. Thus, snoop cache configurations with lower numbers of cache lines and longer valid line vectors are better design points. For the SPLASH-2 benchmarks, selecting 8 cache lines with 32- or 16-bit valid line vectors seems to be the best compromise.

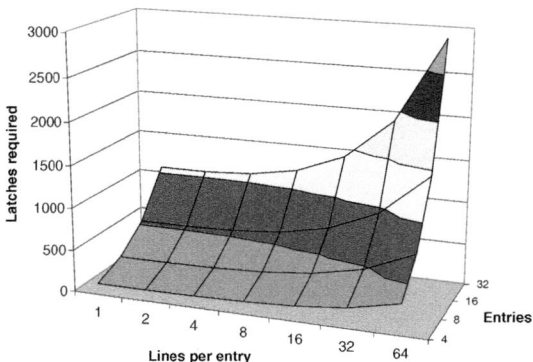

Fig. 8. Approximate number of latches required to implement a snoop filter unit with snoop caches, depending on the number of entries and the lines per entry

6.5   The Most Effective Combination

We have discussed and analyzed two snoop filters separately. As both filters cover different memory access patterns, the most effective filtering is achieved when putting the

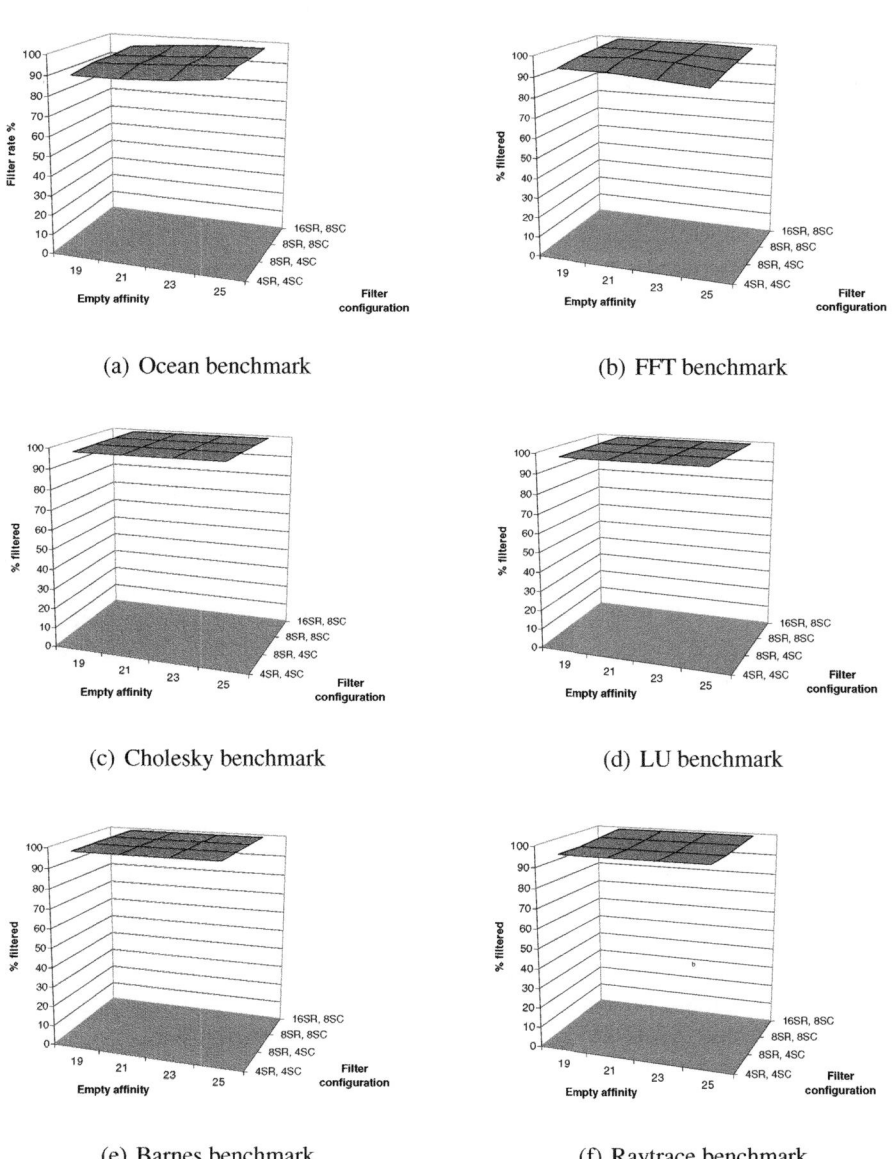

(a) Ocean benchmark

(b) FFT benchmark

(c) Cholesky benchmark

(d) LU benchmark

(e) Barnes benchmark

(f) Raytrace benchmark

Fig. 9. Combined filter behavior. Percentage of snoops filtered for several stream register and snoop cache configurations as the empty affinity is varied in its most effective range.

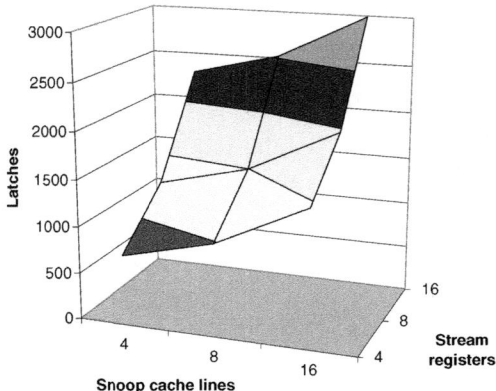

Fig. 10. Approximate number of latches required to implement a snoop filter unit with both snoop caches and stream registers, for several effective configurations

two filters together. We will show that using the combination of two filters, we can achieve high filtering rates even though each filter unit is quite small.

In order to determine the optimal sizing for our snoop filter, we have varied three parameters: the number of stream registers (4, 8, or 16), the number of snoop cache lines (4 or 8), and the empty affinity (in the most effective range from 19 to 25). We keep the snoop cache valid line vector at 32 bits in length. The results for several SPLASH-2 benchmarks are illustrated in Figures 9(a) to 9(f). Clearly, combining the two filtering techniques results in a highly effective combination across all of the benchmarks we studied.

Once again, we must consider the size of the combined filter in terms of latch count in order to determine the optimal configuration. Figure 10 shows how latch count varies with the number of stream registers and snoop cache lines for a valid line vector of 32 bits. The stream registers grow faster than the snoop caches, so the optimal configuration prefers larger snoop caches over more stream registers. The knee in the latch count and performance curves appears to be at 8 stream registers and 8 entries per snoop cache. By way of comparison, the L1 cache tags of the PowerPC 440 processor require more than an order of magnitude more latches.

7   Conclusion

With the emergence of commodity CMPs, we have entered the era of the SMP-on-a-chip. These high-performance systems will generate an enormous amount of shared memory traffic, so it will be important to eliminate as much of the useless inter-processor snooping as possible. In addition, power dissipation has become a major factor in chip density, so mechanisms to eliminate useless coherence actions will be important.

In this paper, we have described and evaluated a snoop filtering architecture that is appropriate for high-performance CMPs. Our architecture uses multiple, complementary filtering techniques and parallelizes the filters so that they can handle snoop requests from all remote processors simultaneously.

We have described stream register snoop filtering, which uses a small number of registers to capture strided access streams. We explored the stream register and snoop cache design spaces using the SPLASH-2 benchmarks together with a custom trace generator and simulator.

Finally, we developed a highly-effective snoop filter that combines stream registers with snoop caches, and experimentally evaluated this design. We show that the combined filter can be very small in size, yet effective over all of the benchmarks we studied.

Acknowledgements

This work has been supported and partially funded by Argonne National Laboratory and Lawrence Livermore National Laboratory on behalf of the United States Department of Energy under Subcontract No. B554331.

References

1. Srinivasan, V., Brooks, D., Gschwind, M., Bose, P., Zyuban, V., Strenski, P., Emma, P.: Optimizing pipelines for power and performance. In: Proceedings of the 35th Annual International Symposium on Microarchitecture, pp. 333–344. ACM/IEEE, Istanbul/Turkey (2002)
2. Salapura, V., et al.: Power and performance optimization at the system level. In: Proceedings of the 2nd International Conference on Computing Frontiers, pp. 125–132. ACM, Ischia (2005)
3. Gonzalez, R., Horowitz, M.: Energy dissipation in general purpose microprocessors. IEEE Journal of Solid State Circuits 31(9), 1277–1284 (1996)
4. Dennard, R., Gaensslen, F., Yu, H.-N., Rideout, V., Bassous, E., LeBlanc, A.: Design of ion-implanted MOSFETs with very small physical dimensions. IEEE Journal of Solid-State Circuits, 256–268 (1974)
5. IBM Blue Gene Team: Overview of the IBM Blue Gene/P project. IBM Journal of Research and Development 52(1/2) (January 2008)
6. Intel, Intel quad-core technology, http://www.intel.com/technology/quadcore
7. Gschwind, M., Hofstee, H.P., Flachs, B., Hopkins, M., Watanabe, Y., Yamazaki, T.: Synergistic processing in Cell's multicore architecture. IEEE Micro 26(2), 10–24 (2006)
8. Bright, A.A., Ellavsky, M.R., Gara, A., Haring, R.A., Kopcsay, G.V., Lembach, R.F., Marcella, J.A., Ohmacht, M., Salapura, V.: Creating the Blue Gene/L supercomputer from low power SoC ASICs. In: 2005 IEEE International Solid-State Circuits Conference on Digest of Technical Papers, pp. 188–189 (2005)
9. Moshovos, A., Memik, G., Falsafi, B., Choudhary, A.N.: JETTY: Filtering snoops for reduced energy consumption in SMP servers. In: Proceedings of the 7th International Symposium on High-Performance Computer Architecture, pp. 85–96 (2001)
10. Briggs, F., Chittor, S., Cheng, K.: Micro-architecture techniques in the Intel E8870 scalable memory controller. In: Proceedings of the 3rd Workshop on Memory Performance Issues, pp. 30–36 (June 2004)
11. Kant, K.: Estimation of invalidation and writeback rates in multiple processor systems, http://kkant.gamerspace.net/papers/inval.pdf
12. Aono, F., Kimura, M.: The Azusa 16-way Itanium server. IEEE Micro 20(5), 54–60 (2000)

13. Keltcher, C.N., McGrath, K.J., Ahmed, A., Conway, P.: The AMD opteron processor for multiprocessor servers. IEEE Micro 23(2), 66–76 (2003)
14. Chinthamani, S., Iyer, R.: Design and evaluation of snoop filters for web servers. In: Proceedings of the 2004 Symposium on Performance Evaluation of Computer Telecommunication Systems (July 2004)
15. Ekman, S., Dahlgren, F., Stenstrom, P.: TLB and snoop energy-reduction using virtual caches in low-power chip-multiprocessors. In: Proceedings of the 2002 International Symposium on Low Power Electronics and Design, pp. 243–246 (August 2002)
16. Moshovos, A.: Regionscout: Exploiting coarse grain sharing in snoop-based coherence. In: Proceedings of the 32nd Annual International Symposium on Computer Architecture, pp. 234–245 (June 2005)
17. Saldanha, C., Lipasti, M.: Power efficient cache coherence. In: Proceedings of the Workshop on Memory Performance Issues (June 2001)
18. Salapura, V., Blumrich, M., Gara, A.: Design and implementation of the Blue Gene/P snoop filter. In: Proceedings of the 14th International Symposium on High-Performance Computer Architecture, pp. 5–14 (February 2008)
19. Salapura, V., Blumrich, M., Gara, A.: Improving the accuracy of snoop filtering using stream registers. In: Proceedings of the 8th MEDEA Workshop, pp. 25–32 (September 2007)
20. Woo, S., Ohara, M., Torrie, E., Singh, J., Gupta, A.: The SPLASH-2 programs: Characterization and methodological considerations. In: Proceedings of the 22nd Annual International Symposium on Computer Architecture, pp. 24–36. ACM, New York (1995)
21. Nguyen, A.-T., Michael, M., Sharma, A., Torrellas, J.: The Augmint multiprocessor simulation toolkit for Intel x86 architectures. In: Proceedings of 1996 International Conference on Computer Design, pp. 486–490 (October 1996)
22. IBM, IBM PowerPC 440 product brief (July 2006), http://www-306.ibm.com/chips/techlib/techlib.nsf/products/PowerPC_440_Embedded_Core

CROB: Implementing a Large Instruction Window through Compression

Fernando Latorre, Grigorios Magklis, Jose González, Pedro Chaparro,
and Antonio González

Intel Barcelona Research Center, Intel Labs – UPC
{fernando.latorre,grigorios.magklis,pepe.gonzalez,
pedro.chaparro.monferrer,antonio.gonzalez}@intel.com

Abstract. Current processors require a large number of in-flight instructions in order to look for further parallelism and hide the increasing gap between memory latency and processor cycle time. These in-flight instructions are typically stored in centralized structures called reorder buffer (ROB), which is a centerpiece to handle precise exceptions and recover a safe state in the event of a branch misprediction. However, this structure is becoming so big that it is difficult to fit it in the power budget of future processors designs. In this paper we propose a novel ROB microarchitecture named CROB (Compressed ROB) that can compress ROB entries and therefore give the illusion of having a larger virtual ROB than the number of ROB entries. The performance study of CROB shows a tremendous benefit, with an average speedup of 20% and 12% for a 128-entry and 256-entry ROB respectively. For some benchmark categories such as SpecFP2000, speedup raise up to 30%.

1 Introduction

Modern out-of-order processors typically employ a reorder buffer (ROB) to retire instructions in program order [1]. In-order retirement enables precise bookkeeping of the architectural state, while making out-of-order execution transparent to the user. However, retiring instructions in program order increases the demand of some processor resources such as physical registers or the ROB entries themselves. The size of the ROB increases with every new processor generation. The reason is the continuously increasing difference between processor and memory speeds. Long-latency operations delay the instruction retirement and therefore the number of required in-flight instructions is augmented in order to keep the functional units busy. Besides, larger ROBs increase performance by exposing more instruction level parallelism.

Figure 1 shows the performance improvements obtained by increasing the ROB from 128 entries up to 1024 entries in a clustered microarchitecture. These numbers have been obtained by assuming an unbounded issue queue and physical register file to see the potential benefits of enlarging the ROB. As it can be seen, allowing just 128 in-flight instructions is an important limiting factor for performance. Nevertheless, it is not straightforward for the designers to implement larger ROBs because of power, area and cycle time constraints. As an example of the ROB size for a current processor, the Intel®Pentium® 4 supports up to 126 in-flight instructions [2].

P. Stenström (Ed.): Transactions on HiPEAC III, LNCS 6590, pp. 115–134, 2011.
© Springer-Verlag Berlin Heidelberg 2011

There are a number of proposals to overcome the limitation that the ROB imposes over the number of in-flight instructions [3][4][5].These techniques periodically checkpoint the processor state in order to support precise exceptions allowing ROB entries to be released out of program order, or even getting rid of the ROB. The authors have demonstrated great potential by using these checkpoint mechanisms as an alternative to the conventional ROBs. However, whenever either a misprediction or an exception arises a previous checkpoint must be restored and the instructions between the checkpoint and the offending instruction must be re-executed. This task and the periodic checkpoints that must be done increase the processor activity as well as the power dissipation of the processor.

In this paper we present a different approach to designing a reorder buffer that enables the processor to have many more instructions in-flight than the number of reorder buffer entries. This is achieved by introducing a level of indirection similar to the way that virtual memory pages are mapped to physical memory pages in modern operating systems. We propose that the Physical Reorder Buffer (PROB) of the processor (the traditional ROB) be divided into equally sized physical segments that are dynamically mapped to logical segments by a mapping table called the Logical Reorder Buffer (LROB). A physical segment is released (and allowed to be re-mapped) when all instructions kept in that segment are guaranteed to either atomically commit or atomically be squashed. Overall, the objective is to achieve high performance with a small reorder buffer with minimal extra activity. We refer to this novel design as *Compressed Reorder Buffer* (CROB).

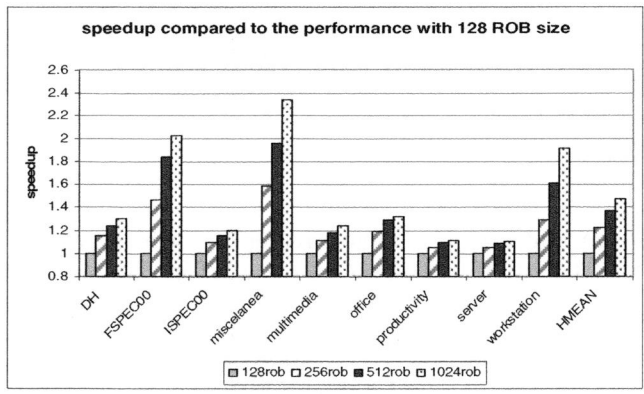

Fig. 1. Impact of the ROB size in a 2-clustered processor configuration with unbounded issue queue, unbounded registers and unbounded memory order buffer

2 Related Work

Some hardware resources such as issue queues, physical registers, memory order buffer and reorder buffer are cumbersome to enlarge [10]. On the other hand, it has been demonstrated that the processor performance is very dependent on the size of these components. Hence, many researchers have proposed alternative designs to better utilize these components. For instance, some previous work [6][7][8][9][10] propose splitting the back-end engine into multiple processing units called clusters. Moreover, decreasing the power consumption and the complexity of the issue queue [12][13][16][11][15][14][24] and the register file [17][18][20][19] has been widely addressed in the literature.

In [3], the authors propose a novel architecture named Cherry where ROB entries and physical registers are recycled as soon as the instructions are considered safe (all previous branches have been computed and all the previous loads have been issued), instead of waiting until the instruction commits. The main important difference between the proposal of this paper and Cherry, is that CROB does not require extra checkpointing. Another advantage of CROB is that ROB entries can be released earlier because it is not constrained by memory replay traps or branch mispredictions as opposed to Cherry. By contrast, the early register release scheme detailed in [3] is likely to be more effective than the one implemented on top of CROB. The proposals in [4] and [5] also rely on checkpointing.

Checkpointing has important overheads as described in [24] so that the number of instructions between checkpoints has to be quite large to reduce the cost of creating them. However, in the event of a branch misprediction, exception or memory replay, the instructions between the latest checkpoint and the offending instruction must be re-executed, which incurs in extra power dissipation. CROB does not require re-executions at all.

In summary, we propose a scheme that increases the number of in-flight instructions and does not require re-execution of instructions nor checkpointing. On the other hand, CROB could take advantage of some orthogonal techniques proposed in [3][4] such as the management of the memory order buffer or the early register release as well as the instruction group formation in [23]. These enhancements however are not considered in this paper.

3   Description of the Architecture

The evaluation of the CROB has been done on top of a state-of-the-art clustered processor. Nevertheless, the CROB can be used in any architecture as long as it has a ROB that does not store speculative register results. We believe clustered architectures are a good design for future processors because it allows building wide machines while controlling complexity. But, in order to keep wide machines busy we need to have a lot of instructions in flight, which means that bigger reorder buffers are required.

The baseline architecture is similar to the one proposed in [6]. A block diagram is shown in Figure 1. It consists of a monolithic front-end in charge of fetching, decoding and renaming instructions and a clustered back-end. This front-end fetches x86 macro-instructions and translates them into micro-operations that are stored in the trace cache. The main components in the front-end are the trace cache (TC) where micro-operations are stored, the instruction TLB (not shown in the figure), the branch predictor (BP), and the Macro Instruction Translation Engine (MITE) that translates macro-instructions into micro-operations before storing them into the TC. It also implements the instruction decoding, steering and renaming logic. The MROM is in charge of decoding complex macro-operations like string moves. A detailed description of these components can be found in [2].

Decoded instructions are steered to one of the two clusters for execution following the dependence- and workload-based algorithm described in [6]. Inter-cluster communication is performed via copy instructions that are generated on-demand by the rename logic. Every cluster includes an issue queue and three register files (integer, floating point and SSE). Once an instruction leaves the issue queue, it reads its source operands either from the register files or the bypass logic and executes in one of the functional units of the cluster. Finally, a shared memory order buffer and memory hierarchy is used to process store and load operations.

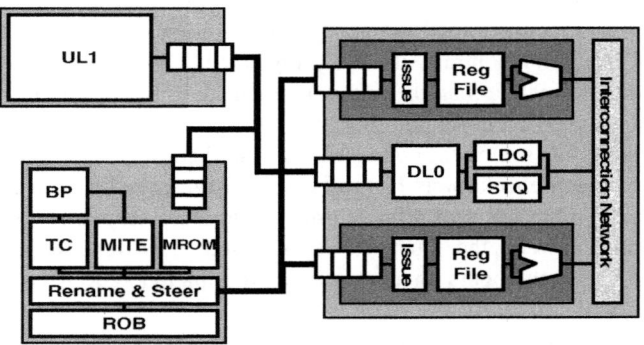

Fig. 2. Baseline architecture

4   ROB Implementation

Conventional *ROB* implementations are managed like FIFO queues where the entries are allocated at renaming and released at commit. However, from the time where an instruction finishes execution until the time it either commits or is squashed, the corresponding *ROB* entry is not used at all.

The proposed *ROB* is based on the observation that it is quite common to find sequences of consecutive instructions that have been executed but cannot be committed (because of an older instruction that has not finished yet). Figure 3 shows the larger pool of consecutive executed instructions found in the event of *ROB* full for the different categories. As it can be seen in Figure 3, almost 90% of the cycles that the ROB is full there are chunks of more than 8 consecutive completed instructions on average. Furthermore, scenarios where chunks of more than 16 or even 32 completed instructions are found represent 80% and 73% of the cycles respectively. Besides, the probability of finding chunks of consecutive completed instructions is very dependent on the application. For instance, whereas there are chunks of more than 32 executed instructions in 90% of the cycles for *FP* workloads, chunks of this size (or larger) are only found in 65% of the cycles for *server* applications.

Consecutive executed instructions can be managed as an atomic block if all of them are free of exceptions because all the branches in between have been computed (and the prediction validated to be correct). Hence, all these instructions are either in the correct path and therefore they will eventually be committed or in a wrong path and will all be squashed. A key observation is that the information required to either

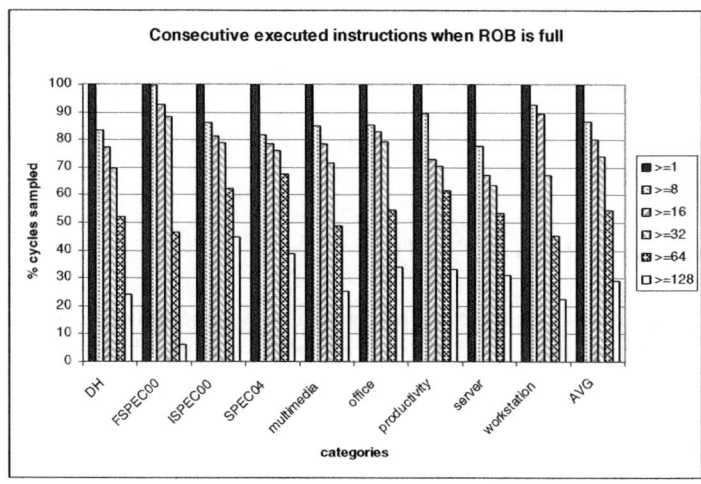

Fig. 3. Percentage of cycles that we can find at least one sequence of consecutive completed instructions larger than 1, 8, 16, 32, 64 and 128 (shown by the different bars) when a ROB with 256 entries is full

Pdest	Instruction
10	AX = LD(@AX)
20	BX = CX+AX
30	CX=CX+AX
35	DX = DX-CX
40	SI = LD(@AX)
41	DI=CX+AX

Sequence 1

Pdest	Instruction
42	AX = BX-CX
44	BX = LD(@AX)
47	CX=CX+AX
80	AX = BX-CX
85	BX = LD(@AX)
90	CX=CX+AX

Sequence 2

Pdest	Instruction
95	BX = BX-CX
1	DX = LD(@BX)
5	SI=SI+DI
9	AX = BX-CX
11	BX = LD(@AX)
14	DX=CX+AX

Sequence 3

Fig. 4. Example of physical registers that can be early released using a CROB. Pdest field shows the physical register allocated by the instruction. Instruction field shows the instruction that uses the entry.

commit or squash a whole chunk of instructions can be stored in a compressed manner using a small number of bits outside the *ROB*. Hence, the entries where these instructions reside can be released.

Besides, it is possible to take advantage of the atomicity of these sequences of executed instructions to implement a simple early register release mechanism. Assume a logical register (rX) that is mapped to two physical registers by two different instructions (pA and pB, in this program order) inside a given sequence of executed instructions. In this case, the first physical register (pA) is guaranteed not to be needed by any other instruction and can be released without waiting until the second instruction commits. In other words, all physical mappings created and re-defined inside a sequence can be released once all the instructions are completed. Therefore, conversely to other previous work, this early register release is non speculative [22][5]. Figure 4 shows an example where some physical registers can be released earlier.

Assuming sequence 1 is older than sequence 2 and sequence 3, instructions from sequences 2 and 3 will not release any register until instructions from segment 1 have committed in a processor with a traditional ROB. However, if all the instructions in sequence 2 have finished and they are free of exceptions then registers shaded in the figure could be released because it is guaranteed that they won't be used any more. The same applies to sequence 3.

5   Compressed ROB (CROB)

In this section we describe the main hardware components involved in the implementation of this technique as well as the way these structures behave in typical situations: instruction allocation, retirement, exceptions and branch mispredictions.

5.1   Hardware Components

The implementation of the compressed reorder buffer is described below and a block diagram is shown in Figure 5.

Physical Reorder Buffer (PROB)

This structure is an extension of a typical *Reorder Buffer (ROB)*–a FIFO structure implemented as a circular buffer with a head and a tail pointer. The *PROB* is divided into N equal segments ($N > 1$), each one having W entries. Moreover, the *PROB* has a head and tail pointer that point to the oldest and youngest instruction in-flight respectively.

Conversely to what happen with other processor out-of-order designs like the processors based on the Alpha ISA, the x86 architectures like the Intel processors deal with complex CISC operations (macro-operations) that are difficult to manipulate by an out-of-order engine. Therefore, as commented in section 3, the front-end cracks these macro-operations into as many micro-operations as needed in order to keep the semantics of the original CISC operation. These micro-operations (aka uops) may comprise one destination operand and two sources as conventional RISC instruction set architectures. This translation of macro-operations into uops has significant implications in the design of common *ROB*s and therefore in the design of the *PROB*. As an example, *PROB* entries are allocated per uop so that a macro-operation may comprise multiple *PROB* entries. Moreover, since the processor must provide precise exceptions at the macro-operation level it is not possible to commit any ROB entry belonging to a macro-operation until all uops comprising the x86 instruction have executed and they are free of exceptions. Once all uops of the macro-operation have correctly completed execution the *PROB* entries of the macro-operation can be retired in order in as many cycles as needed. Since we cannot reclaim any *PROB* entry until the whole macro-operation has completed we could only execute macro-operations with a number of uops lower or equal than the number of *PROB* entries. However, the definition of the x86 instruction set architecture solves this problem by allowing very complex macro-operations like string moves that may imply hundreds of uops to be partially committed. Therefore, interruptions that occur while these macro-operations are executed could be served by using and architectural state as if the macro-operation would have been half executed.

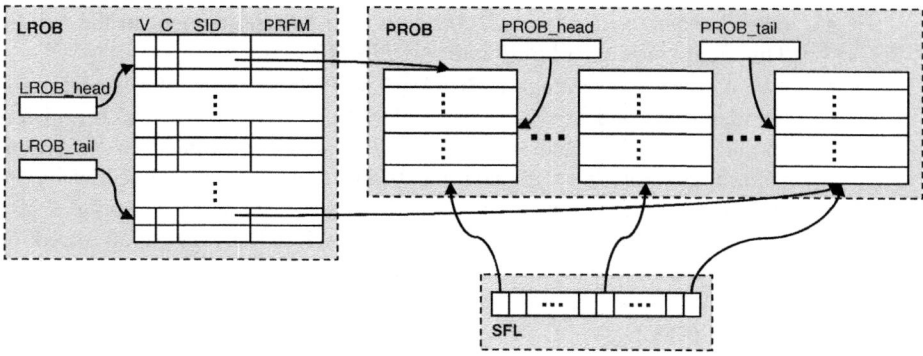

Fig. 5. CROB structure: Logical Reorder Buffer, Physical Reorder Buffer and Segment Free List

Every uop stores a *PROB* entry at the renaming stage including the following fields:

- Physical source register names (*PSRC1, PSRC2*) are the identifiers of the physical registers where the two source operands reside.
- Physical destination-register name (*PDST*) is the identifier of the physical register where the value produced by the uop (if any) will be stored.
- Logical destination-register name (*LDST*).
- Previous mapping of logical destination-register (*LASTMAP*) shows the physical register identifier where the previous instance of the same logical destination register in program order resides.
- Exception and control information. This information involves among other control bits: a bitmask describing the exception that the instruction should fire at commit time if any; bits to identify the beginning and the end of the macro-operation in order to perform the commit as commented above; and the outcome of the branch predictor in case of branches.

Logical Reorder Buffer (LROB)
The *LROB* must have a number of entries greater than the number of *PROB* segments. The goal of this structure is to keep the order in which the *PROB* segments were allocated. Thus, a new *LROB* entry is allocated every time a new *PROB* segment is allocated or reused. Note that the number of entries in this structure defines the maximum number of instructions the processor can have in-flight. This maximum number of in-flight instructions is equal to the number of *LROB* entries multiplied by the *PROB* segment size.

The *LROB* is a FIFO structure managed as a circular buffer. Apart from the *LROB* head and tail pointers (*LROB_head* and *LROB_tail*), the *LROB* manages the *PROB* head and tail pointers (*PROB_head* and *PROB_tail*), as will be described later. Each *LROB* entry requires the following fields:

- *Valid bit (V)* is set when the entry is in use.
- *Compressed bit (C)* indicates if the segment pointed by the *LROB* entry has been compressed.

- *PROB segment identifier (SID)* points to a *PROB* segment in the *PROB*. This field binds each *LROB* entry to a *PROB* segment.
- *Physical register free mask (PRFM).* The *PRFM* is a list of physical register identifiers and logical register identifiers. It indicates which registers should be de-allocated when the *PROB* segment pointed to by *SID* is committed. For those register identifiers that were not allocated by instructions in the segment the logical register they were mapping is also stored. This information is needed to rollback in the event of an exception as explained in the exception handling subsection.

Segment Free List (SFL)

The *SFL* indicates which *PROB* segments are currently unused. It is used every time the processor needs to allocate a new *PROB* segment and every time a *PROB* segment is released (de-allocated). It is implemented as a bit mask with as many bits as *PROB* segments (the i-th bit is set when the i-th *PROB* segment is available).

5.2 Hardware Behavior

The *CROB* is based on a segmented *ROB* structure as commented before where segments are allocated and released on demand. In this section we present the main actions that take place in the *CROB* during the execution of an application. It works very similar to a conventional *ROB*.

Segment Allocation

When new instructions are allocated[1] new entries in the *PROB* are needed. If the current *PROB* segment holding the youngest instructions (pointed by *LROB_tail*) has room for the new instructions, the allocation procedure involves simply incrementing the *PROB_tail* pointer. If the current *PROB* segment is full, a free *PROB* segment is obtained from the *SFL*. If there are no *PROB* segments available the allocation stalls; otherwise a *LROB* entry is allocated by increasing *LROB_tail*. The *SID* field of the new *LROB* entry points to the new *PROB* segment returned by *SFL* and the *PRFM* field is reset. The *PROB* segment is then removed from the *SFL*. When the *PROB_tail* reaches the end of a segment, the *LROB* is checked to find the next *PROB* segment in logical sequence and *PROB_tail* is updated to point to the first entry of that segment.

Every time a new instruction is allocated, the physical register free mask (*PRFM*) of the associated *LROB* entry is updated with the new instruction's *LASTMAP PROB* field. Moreover, if *LASTMAP* was not previously allocated by an instruction in the segment, the logical register is also written in the *PRFM*.

Segment Release

When a *PROB* segment is full and all the instructions of the *PROB* segment have finished execution without any exception the segment is released and the *C* bit is set to true. Segment release implies adding the *PROB* segment identifier to the *SFL* so that it becomes available for re-use.

---

[1] We use the term *instruction allocation* to refer to the action of dispatching a decoded and renamed instruction to the ROB and the issue queue.

Segment Retirement

Instructions from the "head" *PROB* segment (pointed to by *LROB_head*) are committed in the conventional way if the segment has not been released: each instruction frees the register designated by *LASTMAP* and *PROB_head* is incremented. When *PROB_head* reaches the end of the current *PROB* segment the following actions take place: (a) the *LROB_head* is updated to point to the next *PROB* segment in *logical sequence* (i.e. the *PROB* segment holding the oldest instructions), and the *LROB* entry is freed, (b) the *PROB_head* is updated to point to the first entry of the new *PROB* segment "head", and (c) the released *PROB* segment is added to the *SFL*. If the whole *PROB* segment can be committed, the following actions must be taken: (a) the *PRFM* is walked in order to de-allocate the physical registers released by the instructions in the segment, (b) the *LROB_head* is updated as above, (c) the *PROB_head* is updated as above, (d) the *PROB* segment is added to the *SFL*.

Branch Misprediction Recovery

During allocation of a conditional branch instruction, a copy of the *PRFM* entry of the current segment is saved along with a copy of the processor's Free List. If the branch is mispredicted the Free List and the *PRFM* are copied back in order to restore the correct logical to physical register mappings.

Exceptions handling

Exceptions rarely occur so slow mechanisms can be implemented with no impact on performance. Hence, *CROB* relies on traversing the *ROB* to handle exceptions. *ROB* can be traversed either backwards (rollback) or forward (having an architectural *RAT*). We chose rollback because an architectural *RAT* would have to be updated by every committed instruction; on the other hand, rollback only requires updating the speculative *RAT* at the event of an exception. When an exception occurs, rollback is performed as in a conventional *ROB* for those segments that have not been compressed. For the rest of segments *LROB* is accessed. *LROB* stores the previous mappings of the logical registers overwritten in the segment (*PRFM*). Note that the compression algorithm guarantees that exceptions never occur inside a compressed segment. Therefore, when a compressed segment is reached by the rollback mechanism, this segment is atomically traversed. Thus, *LROB* must only store the mappings that registers overwritten in the segment had before entering the segment. Thus, the number of entries in that structure is the minimum between the number of logical registers and the size of the *PROB* segments. In our case we need between 4 and 16 entries.

ROB wrapping

Traditional reorder buffers are implemented using a circular buffer structure. However, in the face of segment compression it is impossible to maintain correct segment order using the *LROB* structure if we allow each segment to be used as a circular buffer. The reason is that in such a case we could have two uncompressed logical segments mapped to the same physical segment. Therefore, in our proposed implementation a *PROB* segment cannot be used as a circular buffer. Assume entries in a *PROB* segment are numbered from *0* to *W-1*. Our design requires that *PROB_head* ≥ *PROB_tail* if they both point inside the same *PROB* segment. This means that in some cases we may not be able to allocate instructions although there are free entries in the *CROB*. Assume the case where all *N PROB* segments are in use (with logical order of segments same as physical). If *PROB_head* is in the last entry *(W-1)* of last segment *(N-1)*, it cannot wrap around to *PROB* segment 0, even if it has free entries in it (since *PROB_tail* points to this segment). Nevertheless, the number of entries unused by this reason is minimal.

6 Early Register Release

Early register release can be easily included into the segment release mechanism. It is an optional feature that enhances performance but it is not necessary for the correct operation of the *Compressed Reorder Buffer*. Note that our early register release proposal only releases registers that are guaranteed not to be needed any more. Therefore, neither an extra recovery mechanism is required nor costly (in terms of power and complexity) extra speculation is incurred. We present two different alternatives to implement the early register release mechanism.

Option A. Early Release via the *PROB*

In this implementation the *PROB* has an extra one-bit field *(EARLY)* for each entry that indicates whether the physical register identified by *LASTMAP* should be released when the *PROB* segment is released (*i.e.*, early) or should wait until the segment commits. Moreover, all renaming table entries are augmented with a single-bit field *(WRITTEN)* that indicates whether the current mapping has been established by an instruction in the current segment (the *WRITTEN* fields of all renaming table entries are set to zero whenever we allocate a new segment). When a new instruction redefines a logical register, the corresponding *WRITTEN* bit (before processing the instruction) is copied to the *EARLY* bit of the *PROB* entry of this instruction. At segment release time, the *PROB* segment is scanned and all entries with the *EARLY* bit set will update the processor's Free List to release the corresponding registers.

Option B. Early Release via the *LROB*

This implementation uses the same structure of renaming table as the above scheme but the early release information is kept in the *LROB* instead. Each *LROB* entry is extended with an *Early Release Mask* (ERM) field (with as many entries as number of slots in the segment). The *ERM* works similarly to the *PRFM*, but specifying which physical registers are to be released early (at segment release as opposed to segment commit time). As above, an instruction gets the early release information from the renaming table. If the register can be released early (*WRITTEN* is set), then the corresponding bit in *ERM* is set. If the register cannot be released early, then the corresponding bit in *PRFM* is set. At segment release time (a) the *ERM* is walked and all indicated registers are released, and (b) the *ERM* is reset. At commit time the *Free List* is updated by walking the *PRFM* and the *ERM*.

7   Experimental Results

This section first describes our simulation methodology and then presents the evaluation of the CROB and the early register release. Since CROB can be implemented with or without the early register release proposal we evaluate both separately. We present results for both an ideal configuration to show the potential and a realistic configuration.

Table 1. Benchmarks

Category	Description/Examples
DH	Digital Home algorithms
FSPEC00	Floating Point benchmarks from SPEC2K
ISPEC00	Integer benchmarks from SPEC2K
Multimedia	Mpeg, speech recognition
Office	Power Point, Excel
Productivity	Sysmarks2K
Server	TPC traces
Workstation	CAD, rendering
Miscellanea	Games and matrix algorithms

7.1   Simulation Methodology

The experiments have been conducted by using an in-house simulator that models the microarchitecture described in Section 3. The simulator is trace-driven but traces hold enough information to faithfully simulate wrong path execution. In a nutshell, the trace contains the state of the memory and the registers before the captured sequence of code started. It also includes a dictionary with the static instructions needed to execute the trace and the number of dynamic instructions retired before we found an interrupt (DMA, etc) in the captured trace. Then, the simulator uses the memory state to execute the instruction pointed by the IP pointer, executes it and updates the memory and register state accordingly. Instructions in wrong path are executed as any other instruction but the register and memory state are eventually recovered. Finally, interrupts are triggered as soon as the number of retired instructions matches with the one specified in the trace file. Our pool of benchmarks comprises 72 traces classified in 9 main categories (8 traces per category) based on their characteristics as shown in Table 1. The processor baseline configuration is described in Table 2.

7.2   Potential Benefit of CROB

The size of a segment is a trade-off between performance improvement and hardware overhead. Enlarging the segment size reduces the CROB cost because the number of

ROB slices is smaller. By contrast, implementing small ROB segments increases the chances of compressing a segment and therefore, achieves higher performance.

In this section, the potential of compressing the ROB is first studied. The goal is to evaluate the impact of the ROB compression for different number of segments and ROB sizes. For this initial potential study, an unbounded register file, issue queue and memory order buffer are assumed, to isolate the effect of ROB compression. Figure 6 shows the potential performance benefits in an architecture limited by the ROB size. Configurations with 128, 256, 512 and 1024 ROB entries are considered. *No CROB*

Table 2. Baseline processor configuration

Parameter	Value	Parameter	Value
Fetch width	6	Commit width	6
Misprediction pipeline length	14	ROB size	128-1024
Indirect branch predictor entries	4096	Gshare entries	32K
ITLB entries	1024	ITLB assoc.	8
Trace Cache size	32K micro-ops	Issue rate per cluster	4 + 2 for ld/st
Issue queue size per cluster	32	MOB	128
Int. registers per cluster	64-256	FP registers per cluster	64-256
SSE registers per cluster	64-256	DTLB entries	1024
DTLB assoc	8	L1 ports	1 read/ 1 write
L1 assoc	2	L1 size	32KBytes
L1 hit latency	1 cycle	L2 assoc	8
L2 size	4MB	L2 hit latency	12 cycles
Point to Point Links	2	Point to Point latency	1 cycle
Data buses (between L1 and L2)	2	Memory Latency	275 cycles

shows the speedup obtained by just enlarging a traditional ROB. *CROB 4 entries, 8 entries* and *16 entries* show the speedups of a CROB with segments of 4, 8 and 16 entries respectively. All speedups are relative to a conventional ROB with 128 entries.

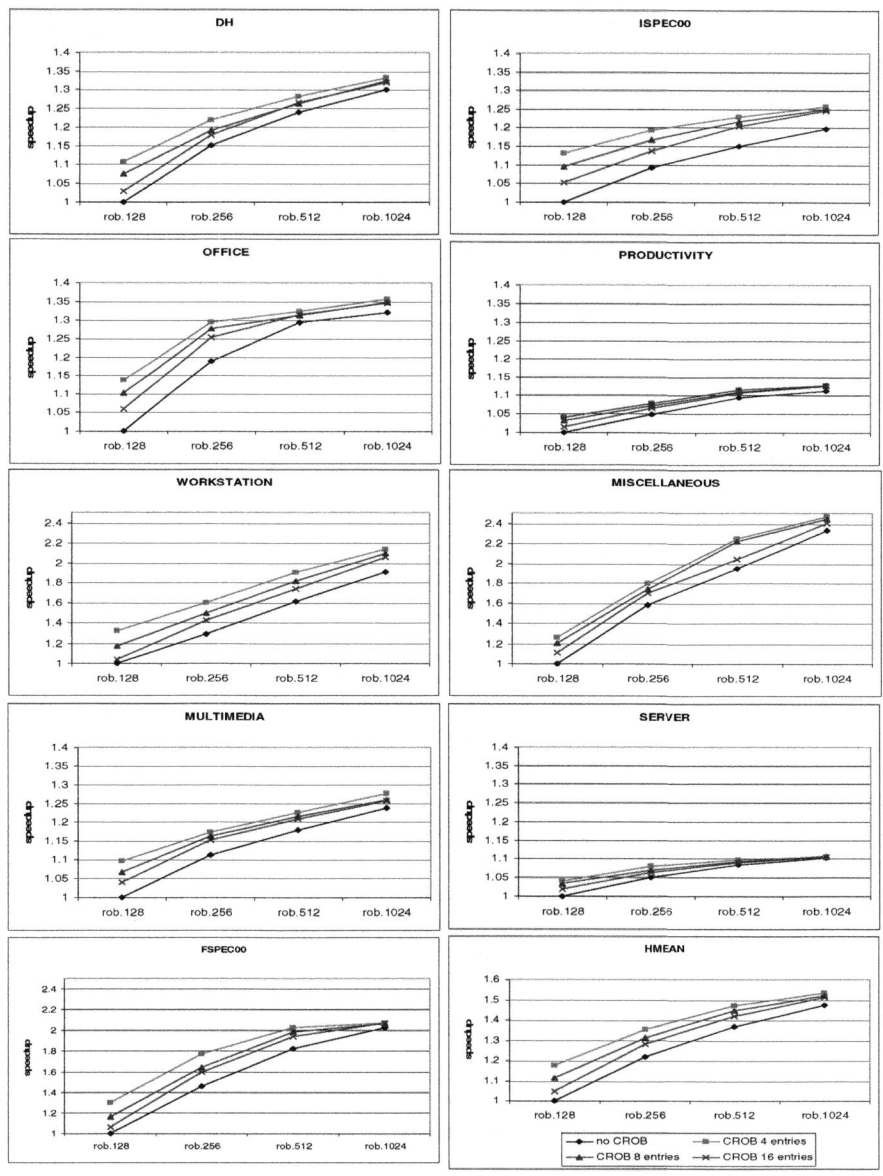

Fig. 6. CROB speedups for 4, 8 and 16 entries per segment and ROB size from 128 to 1024.Note that the Y-scale differs among charts.

All the workloads benefit from enlarging the ROB as it can be seen in Figure 6. However, two main groups of categories can be differentiated. The first group comprises *DH, ISPEC00, multimedia, office, productivity* and *server*. The performance curve for these groups flattens out at around 1024 ROB entries. There are two main reasons why these applications do not benefit from larger ROBs: on the one hand, some programs such as ISPEC contain a significant number of branch mispredictions; on the other hand, some benchmarks such as server are extremely memory bounded. These applications have many chains of dependent instructions that consume values from loads that miss in cache. *CROB* performance is always better than the traditional ROB for all the configurations and categories as shown in Figure 6. *CROB* with 4 entries per segment typically performs about the same as a conventional ROB with twice its size. *CROB* improves performance by 20% on average for 128 ROB entries, 12% for 256 entries and 9% for 512 entries. For *FSPEC00*, the average speedup is 30% for 128 ROB entries, and 23% for 256 ROB entries. Nevertheless, implementing 4-entry segments is challenging because it may require allocating instructions in more than one segment for those cycles where more than 4 instructions are renamed. For the remainder of this paper, we assume that instructions renamed and dispatched in a given cycle must be in the same segment; otherwise an additional cycle is needed. We have experimentally observed that the effect of this constraint on performance is negligible for 8-entry and 16-entry segments.

It can be seen that the larger the segments the more difficult to find candidates to be compressed, and the lower the benefit. This is explained by several reasons. On the one hand, by enlarging the segments, their number is reduced, as well as the probability of having a segment with all its instructions executed. Moreover, free entries of the oldest segment (the one pointed by LROB_head) cannot be reused until the whole segment is free. In spite of this, the benefits obtained by CROB with larger segment sizes are still very important. The average speedup for 8- and 16-entry segments is 10% and 5% respectively for a ROB with 128 entries. The average speedup is 8.5% and 6.5% respectively for a 256-entry ROB. Categories such as *miscellanea* get very high speedups even with large segments. These benchmarks achieve 20% and 10% average speedup for 8 entries and 16 entries per segment respectively and a ROB of 128 entries (18% and 14% respectively for 256 ROB size).

Finally, it can be seen that the potential of the *CROB* is very limited for configurations with ROB size greater than 1024 in all the categories but *workstation* because the ROB is not a bottleneck any more.

7.3 Early Register Release

Another advantage of the *CROB* implementation is that it enables techniques to perform non-speculative early register release, as described in Section 4.

In this section the potential performance improvements of early register release based on CROB is evaluated. For this potential study, a processor with unbounded issue queue, memory order buffer and ROB is assumed to isolate the impact of this register release by using different segment sizes. Note that for the experiments of this section, only registers are released early, as opposed to the whole ROB segment. Figure 7 shows the average performance for the different categories normalized to the performance obtained without early register release for a processor with 128 registers.

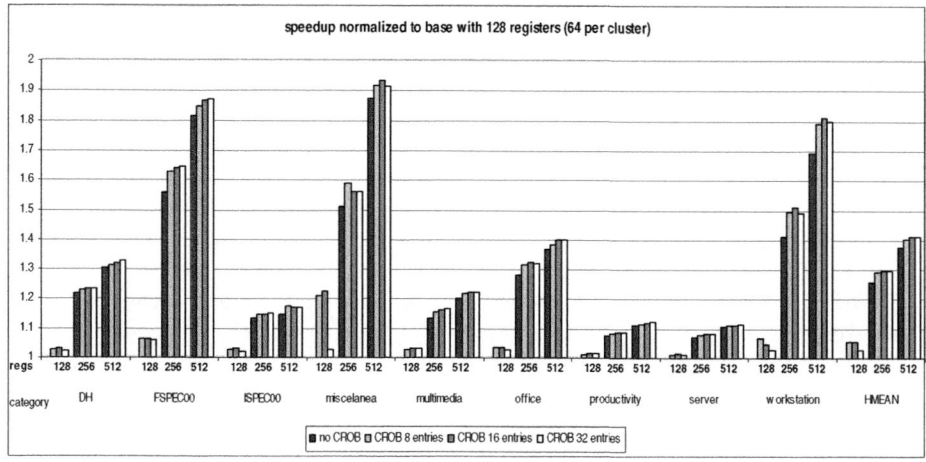

Fig. 7. Potential study of early register release based on CROB

No CROB stands for the baseline processor whereas *CROB 8, 16* and *32* entries refer to the early register release with segments of *8, 16* and *32* entries respectively. Configurations with *128, 256* and *512* registers are considered.

We can observe in Figure 7 that the configurations with either 8 or 16 entries per segment have the highest potential. For 128 registers, early register release improves performance by around 5% for all categories but *miscellanea*, for which the average speedup is 20%. On average, the performance benefits are 5% for 128 registers, 4% for 256 and 2% for 512 registers.

The moderate benefits of early register release are due to the fact that it needs large segments in order to increase the number of physical registers that can be early released. However, the larger the segment size, the lower the probability of finding a segment with all its instructions executed. Therefore, the segment size is a trade-off between the probability of finding a fully executed segment and the probability of finding registers eligible to be released inside the segment.

Finally, the number of available physical registers is an important factor in the effectiveness of this technique. As it can be seen in Figure 7, the average performance improvement for 128 registers in *Workstation with 16 entries* is 5% whereas for 256 it grows up to 7%, and goes down to 1% for 512 registers. The reason is that limiting the number of physical registers limits the number of in-flight instructions which in turn reduces the number of segments full of executed instructions. On the other hand, when the number of physical registers is very large, the register file is not a limiting factor any more and the performance benefits are very small. Intermediate design points where registers are neither scarce nor abundant are the scenario where this technique performs the best.

7.4 Putting It All Together

The previous section showed an analysis of the potential performance of CROB. The study assumed that physical registers, issue queues and memory order buffer were large enough to satisfy the applications requirements. In this section, we evaluate the behavior of CROB under a realistic processor configuration where memory order buffer, physical registers and issue queues are also constraining performance. We assume a clustered processor with the configuration shown in Table 2 with 256 registers (128 per cluster).

Figure 8 shows the performance improvement for a realistic configuration with 128, 256 and 512 ROB entries (both compressed and non-compressed). Each bar shows the speedup with respect to a baseline with a non-compressed ROB of 128 entries. For each configuration, results are presented for the baseline, non-compressed ROB (*no CROB*) and for the proposed compressed ROB with different segments sizes (*CROB.16*, *CROB.8* and *CROB.4* stand for CROB with 16, 8 and 4 entries per segment respectively).

We can first observe that increasing the ROB size from 256 to 512 entries results in very small performance improvement on average (2.5%). However, there are some applications whose performance is more sensitive to the ROB size, such *FSPEC00*. For these applications, increasing the ROB size from 256 to 512 entries provides a performance increase of 7%.

When CROB is enabled, the performance of a 256-entry CROB with 8 entries per segment is the same as that of a 512-entry non-compressed ROB for all the categories (including *FSPEC00*). For 128-entry ROB, CROB clearly outperforms the conventional one, providing a speedup of 15% and 10% with 4 entries and 8 entries per segment respectively. Besides, we can see average performance improvements of up to 28% and 16% in categories with high ROB demand such as *FSPEC00*. Benefits are reduced to 5% improvement with 16 entries per segment, although for some benchmarks such as *workstation* they are still significant (12% average speedup).

We have also evaluated the benefits of the proposed early register release scheme when implemented on top of ROB compression. We found that the gain across all benchmarks was negligible for a 256 ROB size, and it achieved a 1.5% average

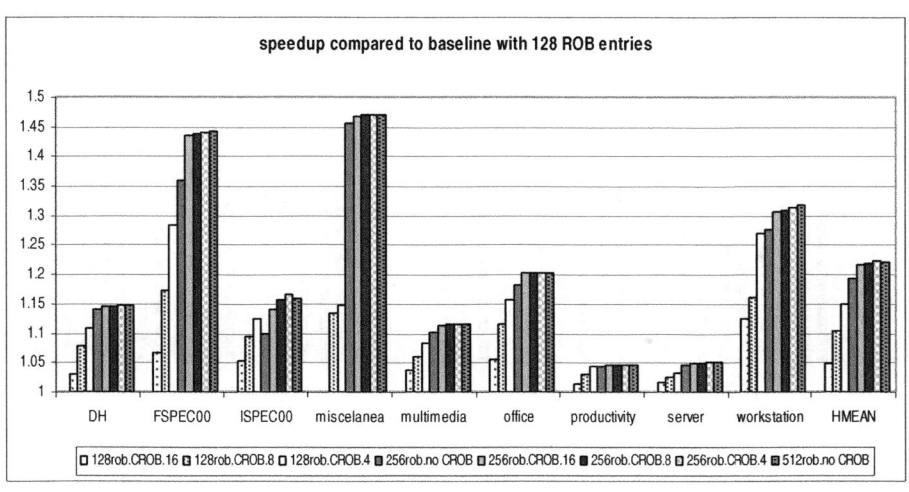

Fig. 8. Speedup of CROB with 16, 8 and 4 entries per segment

improvement for *FSPEC00 benchmark suite*, where a very high register pressure is observed. The reason is that 256 registers are usually enough to allocate the destination registers of all in-flight instructions (up to 256). Note that the maximum number of registers required at any point in time would be given by the ROB size, plus the number of architectural registers, plus some extra registers due to replicated values in clusters.

The number of *LROB* entries required to reach similar performance to an unbounded *LROB* has also been explored. For this evaluation we have chosen a configuration with 128 ROB entries and another with 256 ROB entries. Both configurations have been evaluated assuming 16 segments (8 entries per segment for the configuration of 128 and 16 entries per segment for the one with 256).

Figure 9 shows the performance obtained when using 32, 48 and 64 *LROB* entries normalized to the performance when the *LROB* is unbounded. As it can be seen, *ISPEC* is the most affected category when the *LROB* size is limited. However, this category is only affected when the ROB has 128 entries. In general, 48 *LROB* entries are enough to obtain the maximum benefit from the *CROB* in both configurations. However, this *LROB* size may be lowered to 32 entries without getting important performance drops (less than 0.5% on average).

Finally, the ROB structure represents a significant part of the area and power for microprocessors with large instructions windows. Parts of the ROB required multi-ported random access – not FIFO (e.g. completion flag, exception flags, target address of branches, instruction IP, etc.). As an example of the benefits of the CROB compared to a conventional ROB, we compare in Table 3 the area, access latency and energy per access of a 512-entry ROB and a CROB with 256 entries in the PROB and 48 entries in the LROB. Both configurations have about the same performance and are especially useful for applications that require large ROBs like the FSPEC00 category. The estimates have been computed using CACTI v3.0 [21] with some modifications to allow the modeling of such structures As it can be seen, CROB has a faster access time (which may not be useful if the ROB access is not in the critical path). However, an area reduction of 27% constitutes a very significant decrease in the area devoted to the ROB. Furthermore, the energy per ROB access is decreased by 19%.

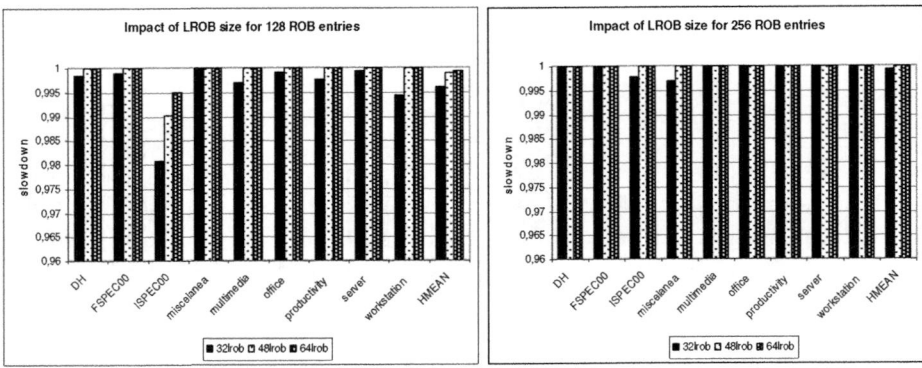

Fig. 9. Impact of the LROB size in the processor performance. Both ROB configurations (128 and 256 ROB size) implement 16 segments.

Table 3. CROB (PROB + LROB) vs banked conventional ROB

Latency	30% faster
Area	27% less area
Energy per access	16% energy reduction

8 Conclusions

Enlarging the ROB enables the exploitation of further ILP by allowing a larger number of in-flight instructions. However, this structure does not scale with ease and, increasing its size may negatively affect the processor power dissipation, area and cycle time. In this paper, we propose a new ROB design named CROB where each ROB segment is released as soon as all the instructions stored in it behave as an atomic unit. The proposed scheme does not need any type of speculation nor replay mechanism. Conversely to other previous proposals, CROB does not increase the number of instructions to be re-executed in the event of either branch mispredictions or exceptions, and thus it does not incur in this extra energy cost.

The potential study of CROB has shown an important speedup of 20% on average for a ROB of 128 entries and 12% for a ROB size of 256. For some benchmark categories such as *FSPEC00*, the speedup reaches up to 30% and 23% respectively. These statistics show what could be achieved by using smart techniques to implement very large register files, memory order buffers and issue queues, as can be found elsewhere in the literature. For a realistic configuration with a conventional register file, memory order buffer and issue queue, the benefits are somewhat lower but still very significant (15% on average and 28% for *FSPEC00*). Finally, the early register release has shown an average potential speedup of 5% and up to 20% for *miscellanea* workloads.

Acknowledgments

This work has been partially supported by the Spanish Ministry of Education and Science under grants TIN2004-03702 and TIN2007-61763 and Feder Funds.

References

1. Smith, J., Pleszkun, A.R.: Implementing precise interrupts in pipelined processors. IEEE Transactions on Computers 37(5), 562–573 (1988)
2. Hinton, G., Sager, D., Upton, M., Boggs, D., Carmean, D., Kyker, A., Roussel, P.: The Microarchitecture of the Pentium® 4 Processor. Intel Technology Journal (February 2001)
3. Martinez, J.F., Renau, J., Huang, M.C., Prvulovic, M., Cherry, T.J.: Checkpointed Early Recycling in Out-of-order Microprocessors. In: Proceedings of International Symposium on Microarchitecture (November 2002)
4. Akkary, H., Rajwar, R., Srinivasan, S.T.: Checkpoint Processing and Recovery: Towards Scalable Large Instruction Window Processors. In: Proceedings of International Symposium on Microarchitecture, pp. 423–434 (December 2003)
5. Cristal, A., Santana, O., Valero, M.: Toward Kilo-instruction Processors. ACM Transactions on Architecture and Code Optimization 1(4), 389–417 (2004)
6. Canal, R., Parcerisa, J.M., González, A.: Dynamic Cluster Assignment Mechanisms. In: Proceedings of International Symposium on High Performance Computer Architectures (2000)
7. Balasubramonian, R., Dwarkadas, S., Albonesi, D.: Dynamically Managing the Communication-Parallelism Trade-off in Future Clustered Processors. In: Proceedings of the Annual International Symposium on Computer Architecture (June 2003)
8. Baniasadi, A., Moshovos, A.: Instruction Distribution Heuristics for Quad-Cluster, Dynamically-Schedule, Superscalar Processors. In: Proceedings of International Symposium on Microarchitecture (December 2000)
9. Aggarwal, A., Franklin, M.: An Empirical Study of the Scalability Aspects of Instruction Distribution Algorithms for Clustered Processors. In: Proceedings of ISPASS (2001)
10. Palacharla, S., Jouppi, N.P., Smith, J.E.: Complexity-effective Superscalar Processors. In: Proceedings of the Annual International Symposium on Computer Architecture, pp. 210–218 (June 1997)
11. Brown, M.D., Stark, J., Patt, Y.N.: Select-free instruction scheduling logic. In: Proceedings of International Symposium on Microarchitecture, pp. 204–213 (December 2001)
12. Buyuktosunoglu, A., Bose, P., Cook, P.W., Schuster, S.E.: Tradeoffs in Power-Efficient Issue Queue Design. In: Proceedings of International Conference on Parallel Architectures and Compilation Techniques (November 2000)
13. Folegnani, D., Gonzalez, A.: Energy-Effective Issue Logic. In: Proceedings ACM/IEEE 27th Intl. Symposium Computer Architecture, pp. 230–239 (June 2001)
14. Fields, B., Rubin, S., Bodik, R.: Focusing Processor Policies via Critical-Path Prediction. In: Proceedings 28th annual Intl. Symposium on Computer Architecture, pp. 74–85 (2001)
15. Lebeck, R., Li, T., Rotenberg, E., Koppanalil, J., Patwardhan, J.: A Large, Fast Instruction Window for Tolerating Cache Misses. In: Proceedings ACM/IEEE 29th Intl. Symposium on Computer Architecture, pp. 59–70 (June 2002)
16. Ponomarev, D., Kucuk, G., Ghose, K.: Reducing Power Requirements of Instruction Scheduling Through Dynamic Allocation of Multiple Datapath Resources. In: Proceedings 34th ACM/IEEE International Symposium on Microarchitecture, pp. 90–101 (2001)

17. Capitanio, A., Dutt, N., Nicolau, A.: Partitioned Register Files for VLIWs: A Preliminary Analysis of Trade-offs. In: Proceedings of the International Symposium on Microarchitecture, pp. 292–300 (December 1992)
18. Wallace, S., Bagherzadeh, N.: A Scalable Register File Architecture for Dynamically Scheduled Processors. In: Proceedings of International Conference on Parallel Architectures and Compilation Techniques, pp. 179–184 (1996)
19. Gonzalez, A., Gonzalez, J., Valero, M.: Virtual-Physical Registers. In: Proceedings of International Symposium on High-Performance Computer Architectures, pp. 175–184 (February 1998)
20. Cruz, J.-L., Gonzalez, A., Valero, M., Topham, N.: Multiple-Banked Register File Architectures. In: Proceedings of International Symposium on Computer Architecture, pp. 316–325 (June 2000)
21. Shivakumar, P., Jouppi, N.P.: CACTI 3.0: An Integrated Cache Timing, Power, and Area Model. WRL Research Report 2001/2 (August 2001)
22. Ergin, O., Balkan, D., Ponomarev, D., Ghose, K.: Increasing Processor Performance Through Early Register Release. In: Proceedings of 22nd International Conference on Computer Design, pp. 480–487 (October 2004)

23. `http://www-03.ibm.com/servers/eserver/pseries/hardware/whitepapers/power4.html`
24. Raasch, S.E., Binkert, N.L., Reinhardt, S.K.: A Scalable Instruction Queue Design Using Dependence Chains. In: Proceedings of 29th Annual Int'l Symp. on Computer Architecture, pp. 318–329 (May 2002)
25. Moshovos, A.: Checkpointing Alternatives for High Performance, Power-AwareProcessors. In: Proceedings of the IEEE Intl' Symposium on Low Power Electronic Devices and Design (August 2003)

Power-Aware Dynamic Cache Partitioning for CMPs

Isao Kotera[1], Kenta Abe[1], Ryusuke Egawa[2],
Hiroyuki Takizawa[1], and Hiroaki Kobayashi[2]

[1] Graduate School of Information Sciences, Tohoku University
Sendai, 980-8578, Japan
{isao@sc.,abeken@sc.,tacky@}isc.tohoku.ac.jp
[2] Cyberscience Center, Tohoku Universeity
Sendai, 980-8578, Japan
{egawa,koba}@isc.tohoku.ac.jp

Abstract. Cache partitioning and power-gating schemes are major research topics to achieve a high-performance and low-power shared cache for next generation chip multiprocessors(CMPs). We propose a power-aware cache partitioning mechanism, which is a scheme to realize both low power and high performance using power-gating and cache partitioning at the same time. The proposed cache mechanism is composed of a way-allocation function and power control function; each function works based on the cache locality assessment. The performance evaluation results show that the proposed cache mechanism with a performance-oriented parameter setting can reduce energy consumption by 20% while keeping the performance, and the mechanism with an energy-oriented parameter setting can reduce 54% energy consumption with a performance degradation of 13%. The hardware implementation results indicate that the delay and area overheads to control the proposed mechanism are negligible, and therefore hardly affect both the entire chip design and performance.

1   Introduction

Recently, as CMOS technology advances, the number of available on-chip transistors for microprocessors has been exponentially increasing. So far, this has been the driving force for improving performance of microprocessors. However, it is difficult to keep the exponential performance improvement by technology scaling, due to an increase in the power dissipation, the limitation of increasing the clock frequency and the limitation of instruction-level parallelism[1]. A Chip Multiprocessor(CMP) is a promising architecture to effectively utilize a large amount of hardware budget on a chip and to enhance the performance by using thread-level parallelism[2].

To realize high performance CMP, on-chip shared cache mechanisms play the key role. However, a large shared cache faces two severe problems. One is that resource sharing among cores degrades the CMP performance. The other

P. Stenström (Ed.): Transactions on HiPEAC III, LNCS 6590, pp. 135–153, 2011.
© Springer-Verlag Berlin Heidelberg 2011

problem is that its large area leads to high power dissipation. The performance degradation problem is caused by conflicts on shared resources among cores. Cores generally share an L2 cache in a CMP. Cores can virtually use a large size cache by cache sharing, and threads in an application can share data via the shared cache. However, such a shared cache causes performance degradation if there are many cache access conflicts among cores. One solution to this problem is to increase the cache size. However, this approach leads to an increase in power consumption and an inefficient use of a large cache for most applications.

Suh et al. have first investigated the dynamic partitioning of a shared cache[3] to solve the performance degradation problem. They described a *marginal gain*-based cache partitioning algorithm and a low-overhead control scheme. Chandra et al. have also studied the performance impact of L2 cache sharing by threads on a CMP architecture, and proposed three models in order to accurately predict the performance using the stack distance and circular sequence profile of each thread[4,5]. The utility-based cache partitioning[6] proposed by Qureshi et al. achieves a high performance benefit with a low-overhead hardware configuration. In addition, they described that their partitioning algorithm has a higher scalability. However, these studies have not discussed the power consumption well.

On the other hand, the power dissipation due to driving a vast amount of hardware on a chip is becoming a critical problem in high-performance microprocessor design. Especially, static power consumption due to leakage current will become more dominant in the total power dissipation, as the gate width becomes smaller[7,8]. According to the International Technology Roadmap for Semiconductors[9], leakage power is expected to dominate more than 80% of the total power[10]. Therefore, computer architects have to consider static power consumption to realize power-aware computing[11].

Several approaches to reductions in static power consumption of a cache have been proposed. The mechanism of selective cache ways[12] provides functionality to turn off power supply to cache ways for reducing dynamic energy and is controlled by a performance metric given by users. The control is based on the result of application profiling. Powell et al. have proposed the DRI i-cache[13,14], which is an integrated architectural approach that turns off power supply to a part of cache sets for reduction of cache leakage. In addition, they provided the gated-Vdd transistor for circuit-level supply-voltage gating. However, the DRI i-cache can be applied only to an L1 instruction cache, which is based on a direct-mapped or low-associative cache with a small area. In order to reduce static power consumption, we have to consider not only an L1 instruction cache but also L1 data and a lower-level (L2, L3) caches, which occupy a larger fraction of the chip area. Furthermore, the DRI i-cache employed a coarse-grain resizing mechanism by changing the number of index bits. Therefore, it is difficult to finely adapt its size to the program requirement. To reduce leakage current, the cache decay mechanism[15] shuts off the power supply to invalidate cache lines in a way. It causes the performance degradation, since sleeping lines do not hold data. The drowsy cache[16] has been proposed to cover the drawback of the cache decay. It keeps supplying minimum power necessary to hold data to each line in the sleep mode, even though it has a large overhead due to the high complexity of its power-gating circuits. Those three approaches considered only the cache of a single-core processor, and hence a novel mechanism with power-aware control as well as effective partitioning for shared caches is highly desired for CMP design.

In this paper, we propose a power-aware cache partitioning mechanism for the shared cache in order to solve the problems of the performance degradation and the power dissipation in CMPs, focusing on the CMP architecture organized by two cores and a high-associativity shared cache. The proposed cache mechanism, which is an extension of the way-adaptable cache[17], has two functions: a way-allocation function for cache partitioning and a power control function for power-aware computing. The way-allocation function allocates ways of a set-associative cache to each core based on their contributions to the effective performance; each core can use the allocated ways as its private memory space as with the L1 cache. Ways are allocated to each core in proportion to the degree of locality. As a result, the L2 cache is shared among cores without conflicts, and hence the mechanism allows each core to exclusively use an appropriately-sized cache area. The function also helps to find out less needed cache ways, which hardly contribute to the performance. The power control function is applied to the way-adaptable cache to conserve the power dissipation by disabling these less needed ways. We evaluate the performance of the proposed mechanism in terms of three metrics. First, we use the weighted speedup to assess the performance improvement by the proposed way-allocation function. Then, the cache energy consumption is evaluated to show the power saving capability of the proposed power-aware cache partitioning mechanism. Finally, the hardware overhead to implement the control unit of the proposed mechanism is evaluated.

The rest of this paper is organized as follows. We first discuss the locality assessment in program execution in Section 2. In Section 3, we describe details on our proposed cache-partitioning and power-aware cache mechanism under some assumptions. In particular, we discuss our way-allocation and power control functions. Section 4 shows the performance evaluation of the proposed mechanism. Section 5 concludes the paper with some future work.

2   Locality Assessment

We discuss the locality assessment of memory reference for way-allocation and power control functions of the L2 shared cache for CMPs. We first review the stack distance profiling[4] that can assess the temporal locality of reference. Let C_1, C_2, ..., C_A, and $C_{>A}$ be $A + 1$ counters for an A-way set-associative cache with the LRU replacement policy. Here, C_i counts the number of accesses to the i-th line in the LRU stack. Therefore, the counters C_1 and C_A are used to count the numbers of accessed MRU (Most Recently Used) and LRU lines, respectively. $C_{>A}$ is used to count the number of cache misses.

Figure 1 shows examples of the stack distance profiling. The histogram of C_i obtained by the stack distance profiling can be used to distinguish two kinds of characteristic cache reference behaviors. In the case of a smaller working set

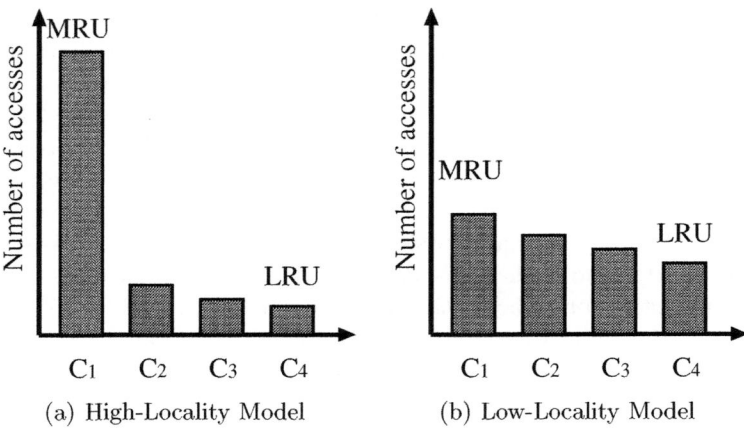

Fig. 1. Stack Distance Profiling

size, the cache accesses tend to concentrate on C_1 as shown in Figure 1(a). In the case of a larger working set, a distribution of cache accesses becomes flatter as shown in Figure 1(b). The locality can be represented by the ratio of an LRU count to an MRU count, using the stack distance profiling.

We define the following metric D to approximately assess the locality of a program[17].

$$D = \frac{LRU\,count}{MRU\,count}. \tag{1}$$

Here, $LRU\,count$ and $MRU\,count$ mean the numbers of LRU and MRU lines referenced in a certain period of cache accesses, respectively. Thus, if a program executed on a core has low-locality, D of the program becomes large. On the other hand, if it has high-locality, D becomes small.

3   Cache Control Mechanism

3.1   Assumptions

We propose a power-aware cache partitioning mechanism under the following assumptions.

- Two cores sharing an L2 unified cache on a chip configure a building block for CMPs. Each core has L1 private data/instruction caches.
- The L2 shared cache is a large, highly-associative on-chip cache, in which the supply voltage to each way can be shut off independently for power control using the power-gating circuits. Each core can access each way exclusively; the cache includes a mechanism that permits a core to access a way. In addition, we introduce an access monitoring unit to the L2 cache. This unit can count the numbers of misses and accesses to MRU and LRU lines.

- Our cache counts the number of accesses to LRU lines for data replacement based on the true-LRU policy.
- Co-scheduled threads on different cores are spawned from different applications. Therefore, they do not share any memory space. So, each core executes a different application in our evaluations. However, our cache can work as a conventional shared cache to access the shred data on the cache among co-scheduled threads spawned from the same application. Our mechanism assumes that the operating system, which manages the thread scheduling, is responsible for switching the partitioning mode and the conventional sharing mode. Both context switch and thread migration between cores are also not considered in this paper.

3.2   Mechanism Overview

We propose a power-aware cache partitioning mechanism under the above assumptions. Figure 2 shows the basic concept of the proposed cache mechanism. Each way is allocated to one of two cores. A virtual partition defined as the boundary between two areas, each allocated to one core, dynamically moves over the L2 cache during execution. Some ways are activated according to locality of memory reference in each area, and the other ways are inactivated for power saving. Each core can access allocated and activated ways only.

Figure 3 shows a control flow graph for an L2 cache shared with two cores. The first step is cache access sampling to obtain statistics used in calculation

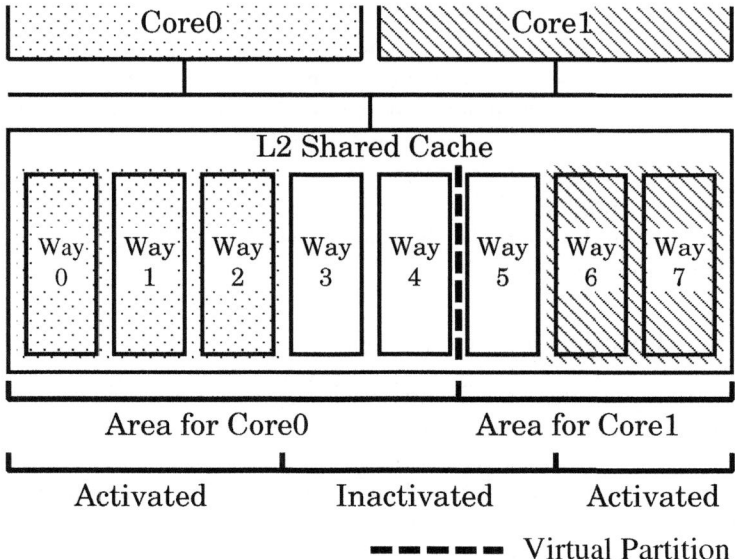

Fig. 2. Basic concept of way-allocation and power control (in the case of 2 cores with an L2 shared 8-way cache)

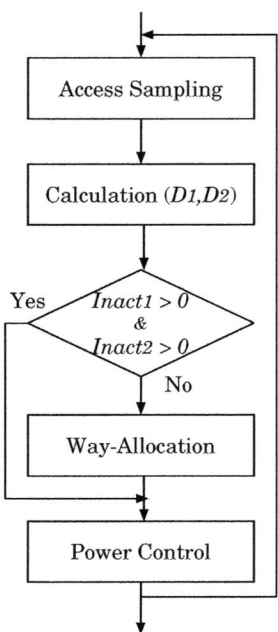

Fig. 3. Control flow graph

of D. This step is carried out at fixed intervals, e.g., every 100,000 L2 accesses. Our mechanism has a way-allocation function and a power control function. The former function decides which ways each core can use, and the latter decides how many ways are inactivated for power saving. In the case where both of the two cores have one or more inactivated ways, the way-allocation function is not performed, because way-allocation in such a situation does not decrease conflicts at all but causes a certain overhead.

The cache can randomly select a cache way to be reallocated or inactivated. Before inactivation, the data on the selected way are written back to the main memory for data coherency.

3.3   Way-Allocation Function

The way-allocation function allocates each way of a set-associative cache to a core; each core can use the allocated ways as its private memory space like the L1 cache.

We propose an allocation method that considers the cache reference locality using D. Here, we assume that the number of ways required by a program is proportional to the degree of the locality. After calculating D_i from the number of cache accesses of core $i(i = 0, 1)$, the following inequality is used to determine whether the number of ways allocated to core i should be increased or decreased.

$$\text{If } D_j > D_k \quad \begin{cases} Alloc_j \mathrel{+}= 1 \\ Alloc_k \mathrel{-}= 1. \end{cases} \tag{2}$$

Here, $Alloc_i$ is the number of ways that are allocated to core i, and satisfies the following conditions.

$$Alloc_{all} = \sum Alloc_i, \tag{3}$$

where $Alloc_{all}$ denotes the cache associativity. If $D_0 = D_1$, way-allocation is not performed.

3.4   Power Control Function

The power control function used in the proposed cache mechanism is based on the way-adaptable cache control[17]. The number of activated ways increases so as to keep D_i between two thresholds to prevent unacceptable performance degradation.

To avoid iterating activation and inactivation of a way, we have to both locally and globally observe the behavior in memory accesses. For locally observing the behavior, D defined by Equation (1) is again employed. On the other hand, for globally observing its local behavior, we adopt an n-bit state machine.

Observation of Local Behavior. To quantify the absolute magnitude of local demands for cache resources, D is compared with two thresholds, t_1 and t_2 ($t_1 < t_2$). If D, which is obtained in execution of a program on a core, is larger than t_2, the program can be considered to have low locality and hence to need many ways. In this situation, our mechanism outputs a signal inc (up-sizing request) to increase the number of activated ways. On the other hand, it gives a signal dec (down-sizing request) to decrease the number of activated ways if D is smaller than t_1. If D is between t_1 and t_2, our mechanism outputs a signal $keep$ to keep the current configuration. Our mechanism tends to output dec if both t_1 and t_2 are relatively large. On the contrary, it tends to output inc if both t_1 and t_2 are relatively small. Thus smaller thresholds make our mechanism performance-oriented, and larger ones make it energy-oriented. As a result, we can adjust the control policy from a performance-oriented configuration to an energy-oriented one.

Observation of Global Behavior. Comparison of D with the two thresholds gives the cache resizing requests: inc, dec, or $keep$. Activation and inactivation of a ways are basically controlled based on cache resizing demands obtained by local behavior observation. However, in the case of highly-irregular and unstable cache accesses, observation of only local behavior leads to iterations of activation and inactivation in a short period. This causes an increase in cache control overheads and cache misses. Thus, the power control should be done conservatively during highly-irregular and unstable situations. To this end, we incorporate an n-bit state machine into the power control function, in order to reflect a global behavior in the cache access, resulting in stable power control. The state machine

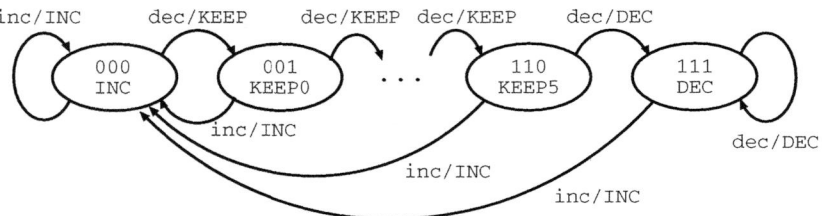

Fig. 4. The 3-bit State Machine

judges that the requests are strong if the same resizing demands continue for a certain period. Only if the request is considered strong, the mechanism resizes the activated area. In addition, we have to be conservative about decreasing the cache size, because it may cause severe performance degradation. Therefore, we use an asymmetric n-bit state machine.

Figure 4 shows a state transition diagram of an asymmetric 3-bit state machine. When *inc* is given to the state machine, it outputs the cache up-sizing control signal *INC* and then always transits to State 000 from any state. However, in the case of *dec* given, the machine works conservatively to generate the down-sizing signal *DEC*. Before moving into State 111 for generating the *DEC* signal, the machine transits to intermediate states form 001 to 110 to judge the continuity of the down-sizing requests. During these states, it outputs *KEEP* to keep the current cache configuration. After continuing *dec* requests, the machine outputs the *DEC* signal for down-sizing and then transits to State 111.

This state machine can prevent responding to temporary disturbances, and further make inactivation conservative to minimize the performance degradation induced by shortage of activated ways. Because the asymmetric machine realizes the cache resizing control so as to react quickly to up-sizing requests and slowly to down-sizing requests, it can minimize performance degradation.

4   Performance Evaluation

4.1   Methodology

We developed a cycle accurate simulator based on the M5 microprocessor architectural simulator tools[18] and the CACTI version 4.2 cache access time, cycle time, area, leakage, and dynamic power models[19] for the architectural function simulation. For the experiments, we examine a CMP of two Alpha-based cores with an L2 shared cache. The parameters used in the simulation are listed in Table 1. We simulate the first 500 million instructions using the reference input set. The sampling span of the proposed cache is 100,000 L2 cache accesses.

We use 15 workloads that consist of combinations of six benchmarks. Table 2 shows the benchmarks selected from the SPEC CPU2006 suite[20] for performance evaluation. Each core runs one independent benchmark program. In order to evaluate our proposal fairly, we select various benchmarks based on

Table 1. Simulation parameters

Parameter	Value
fetch width	8 insts
decode width	8 insts
issue width	8 insts
commit width	8 insts
Inst. queue	64 insts
LSQ size	32 entries
L1 Icache	32kB, 2-way, 32B-line, 1 cycle latency
L1 Dcache	32kB, 2-way, 32B-line, 1 cycle latency
L2 shared cache	1024kB, 32-way, 64B-line, 14 cycle latency
main memory	100 cycle latency
Frequency	1GHz
Technology	70nm
Vdd	0.9V

Table 2. Benchmark programs

Name	Function	Utility
gcc	C Compiler	High
bzip2	Compression	High
dealII	Finite Element Analysis	Sat
sjeng	Artificial Intelligence: chess	Sat
mcf	Combinatorial Optimization	Low
cactusADM(cactus)	General Relativity	Low

their cache resource utility graphs[6]. The utility graphs of the benchmark programs are shown in Figure 5. These graphs indicate their performance in IPC as a function of the number of activated ways. Based on the resource utility graphs, we classify the benchmarks into three groups: *high-utility* (High), *saturating utility*(Sat) and *low-utility* (Low). The applications that have *high-utility* benefit from an increase in activated ways (e.g. gcc, bzip2). These applications have a lower access locality as shown in Figure 1(b). The applications with *saturating utility* have a smaller working set than the applications with *high-utility*; giving more than eight ways dose not significantly improve their performance (e.g. dealII, sjeng). The applications that have *low-utility* do not benefit significantly from an increase in activated ways (e.g. mcf, cactusADM). These applications have a higher access locality as shown in Figure 1(a). We select two applications from each group. Table 2 shows the selected benchmarks and their utilities.

We evaluate our cache with the *weighted speedup* and its energy consumption. The weighted speedup is used as a metric for quantifying the performance of parallel processing, in which multiple applications execute in parallel on different cores. Let $SingleIPC_i$ be the IPC of the i-th application when it is executed on a single core and can exclusively use the entire resource of the CMP, and IPC_i be the IPC of an application when running with another application on the CMP. The weighted speedup is given by:

$$Weighted\ Speedup = \sum \left(\frac{IPC_i}{SingleIPC_i} \right). \tag{4}$$

With the information from M5 and CACTI, the cache energy consumption is calculated as follows:

$$E_{total} = E_d + E_s, \tag{5}$$

$$E_d = \int \left(E_{d\_data\_array} \times \frac{W_{active}}{W_{total}} \times A_{L2} \right) dt + E_{d\_data\_other} + E_{d\_tag}, \tag{6}$$

$$E_s = \int \left(P_{s\_data\_array} \times \frac{W_{active}}{W_{total}} \right) dt + E_{s\_data\_other} + E_{s\_tag}, \tag{7}$$

where,

$E_{d\_data\_array}$ = dynamic energy consumed at bit lines in a data array when all ways are activated,

$P_{s\_data\_array}$ = static power consumed at word lines when all ways are activated,

W_{active} = the number of activated ways,

W_{total} = the total number of ways in the L2 cache,

A_{L2} = the number of L2 cache accesses,

$E_{d\_data\_other}$ = the dynamic energy consumption at the other elements in a data array,

E_{d_tag} = the dynamic energy consumption at the others,

$E_{s\_data\_other}$ = the static energy consumption at the other elements in a data array, and

E_{s_tag} = the static energy consumption at the others.

The total cache energy consumption, E_{total}, is the sum of E_d and E_s that are the dynamic energy consumption for transistor switching and the static energy consumption due to leakage current, respectively. We also estimate E_d and E_s from the product of the array energy consumption and the proportion of the activated area.

4.2   Evaluation of Way-Allocation Function

To evaluate just our way-allocation function, we compare the performance of the way-allocation function with three caches: the utility-based partitioning[6] (*Utility-Based*) which is representative of current partitioning schemes, Half-and-Half which is a static equal partitioning between two cores, and the non-partitioning cache (*CONV*).

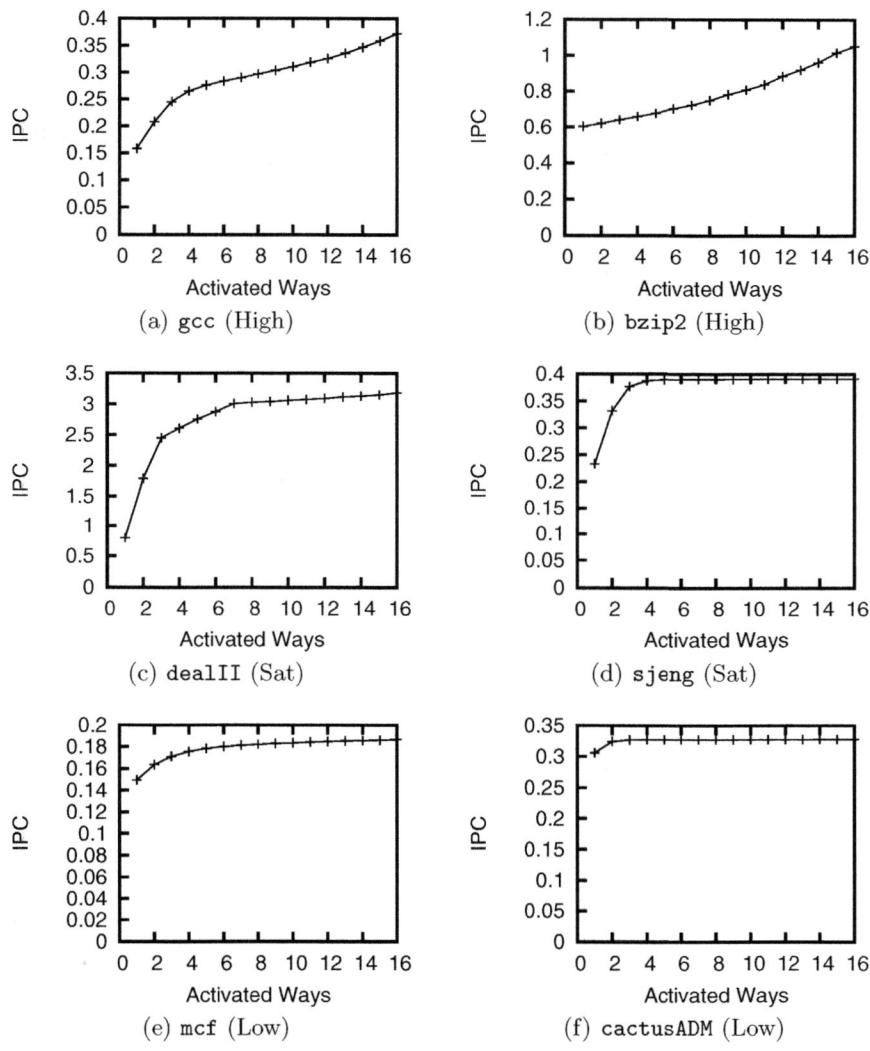

Fig. 5. Activated Ways vs. IPC

Figure 6 shows the evaluation results of the proposed way-allocation function. The horizontal axis in Figure 6 shows the combination of the benchmarks. The vertical axis shows the weighted speedups of CMPs. The bars labeled AVERAGE indicate the geometric means of weighed-speedups of each cache mechanism for individual benchmarks.

The weighted speedup of the proposed way-allocation always exceeds one; it outperforms the conventional cache for every combination listed in Figure 6. It improves by 2% on average. Therefore, it is obvious that the proposed cache mechanism can reduce cache conflicts, compared to the conventional one.

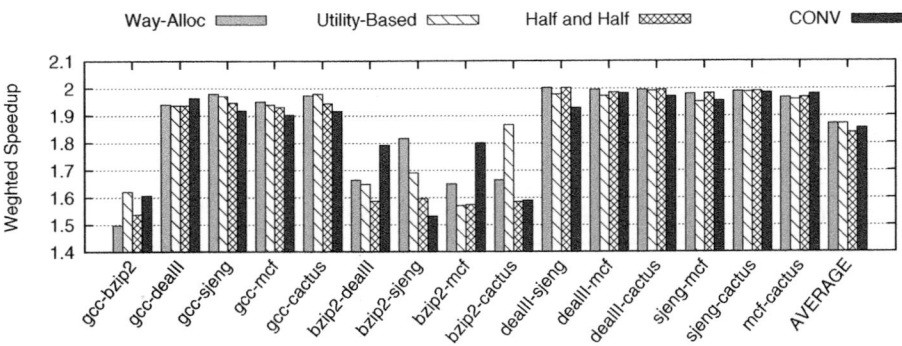

Fig. 6. Performance of Way-Allocation

As a result, the way-allocation based on locality assessment can prevent the performance degradation.

The weighted speedups of our cache and *Utility-Based* are the same as or more than that of *Half and Half* in almost all workloads. The static and equal partitioning cannot achieve the performance improvement. Therefore, the results indicate that the cache partitioning with the adaptive mechanism is beneficial. Moreover, the results also indicate that our way-allocation has a performance comparable to the utility-based cache partitioning scheme. In addition, our scheme can save the power consumption, while keeping a certain level performance by adding the power control function.

The weighted speedup obtained by the proposed cache mechanism outperforms the conventional cache for almost all combinations without `bzip2`. Especially, the speedup improves in every combinations with `sjeng`. Therefore, it is obvious that the way-allocation function of our cache is adequate for execution of the applications including the higher cache access locality: saturating or low utility. The validity of our locality assessment model are confirmed by these results.

Every benchmark pair including `bzip2` leads to either significant performance improvement or degradation. As the utility of `bzip2` does not saturate, its performance improves in proportion to the number of activated ways as shown in Figure 5(b). Therefore, it is difficult to define the appropriate position of the virtual partition. A solution to this problem remains as our future work.

4.3   Evaluation of Way-Allocation with Power Control

Performance and Power Consumption. The proposed cache mechanism is evaluated in terms of the average number of activated ways and the weighted speedup of CMP. Three different $(t1, t2)$-threshold settings for power control, $(0.1, 0.5)$, $(0.01, 0.05)$ and $(0.001, 0.005)$ are examined. We use an asymmetric 3-bit state machine to observe the global behavior in memory accesses. We consider a write-back overhead that is needed to keep data coherency when ways are inactivated, but do not consider a overhead in power-gating for cache ways.

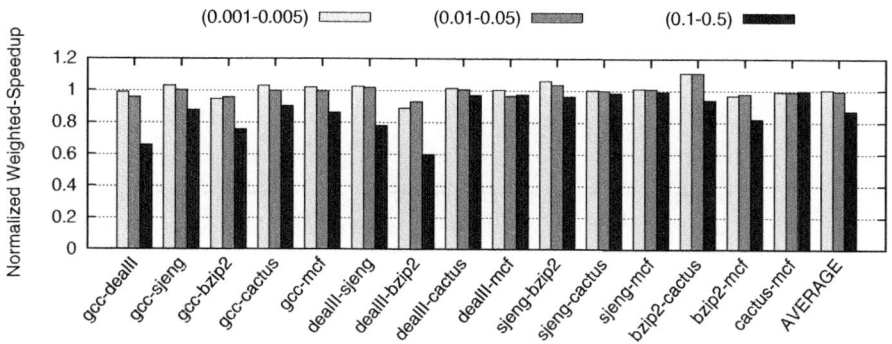

Fig. 7. Effects of t_1 and t_2 on Weighted Speedup

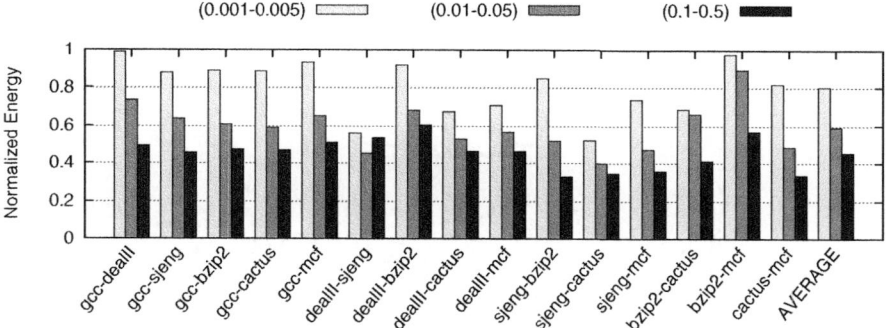

Fig. 8. Effects of t_1 and t_2 on Energy Consumption

Figures 7 and 8 show the weighted speedup and the energy consumption in all the benchmark combinations, respectively. The values of Figures 7 and 8 are normalized by the conventional cache. Figures 7 and 8 indicate that both of the weighted speedup and the energy consumption become their maximum values when the thresholds are $(0.001, 0.005)$ on almost all benchmark combinations. In contrast, when the thresholds are $(0.1, 0.5)$, both of them are their minimum values. When both benchmarks in the combinations have saturating or low utility (e.g. sjeng-cactus), the weighted speedup and the energy consumption are not sensitive to the configurations, and achieve high performance and low energy consumption. For example, in the case of a smaller threshold configuration $(0.001, 0.005)$ and the sjeng-cactus benchmarks, it can reduce 48% of the energy consumption while keeping the weighted speedup.

On average, the proposed cache can reduce energy consumption by 20% while keeping the performance, when the thresholds are smaller such as $(0.001, 0.005)$. On the other hand, in the case of larger thresholds such as $(0.1, 0.5)$, it can reduce a 55% energy consumption with a performance degradation of 13%. We have

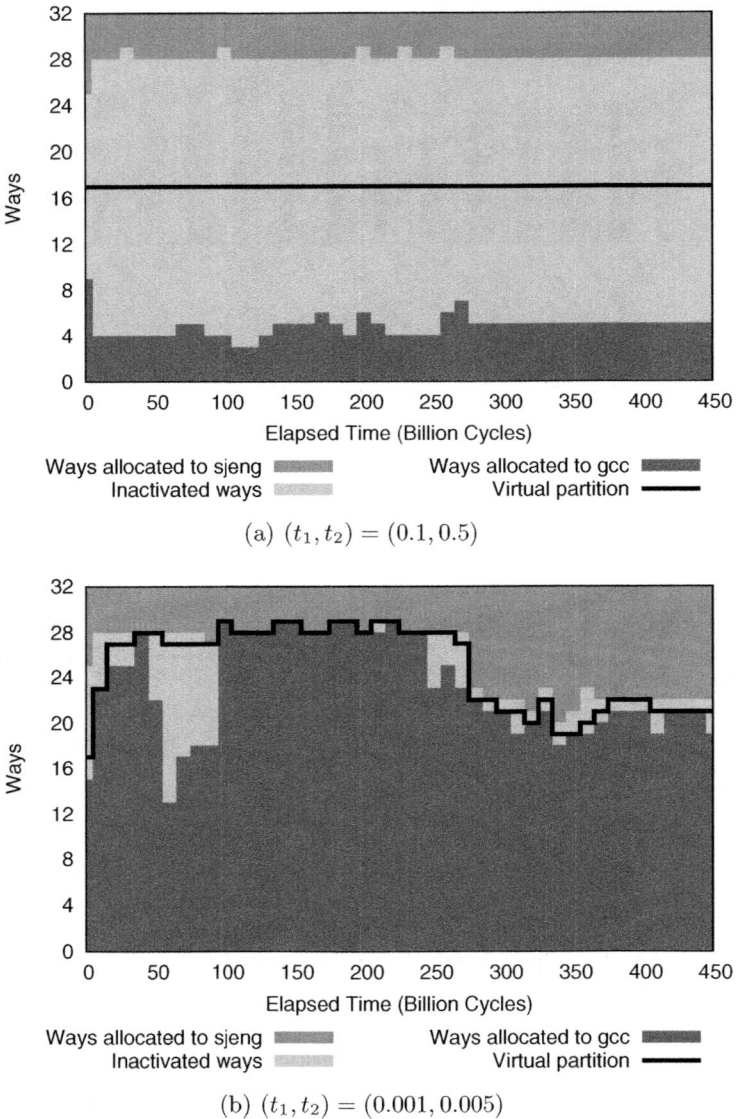

(a) $(t_1, t_2) = (0.1, 0.5)$

(b) $(t_1, t_2) = (0.001, 0.005)$

Fig. 9. Elapsed time vs. Allocated ways (gcc-sjeng)

confirmed that the values of the thresholds can decide the degree of the control policy between the performance-oriented and the energy-oriented configurations.

Figure 9 shows the dynamic behavior of the number of allocated and activated ways across time, when gcc and sjeng are executed in parallel. Most of the time, the allocation function is skipped, because most ways are inactivated for the energy-oriented configuration $(0.1, 0.5)$ as shown in Figure 9(a). The numbers of activated ways are not a significant difference between the cores. On the other

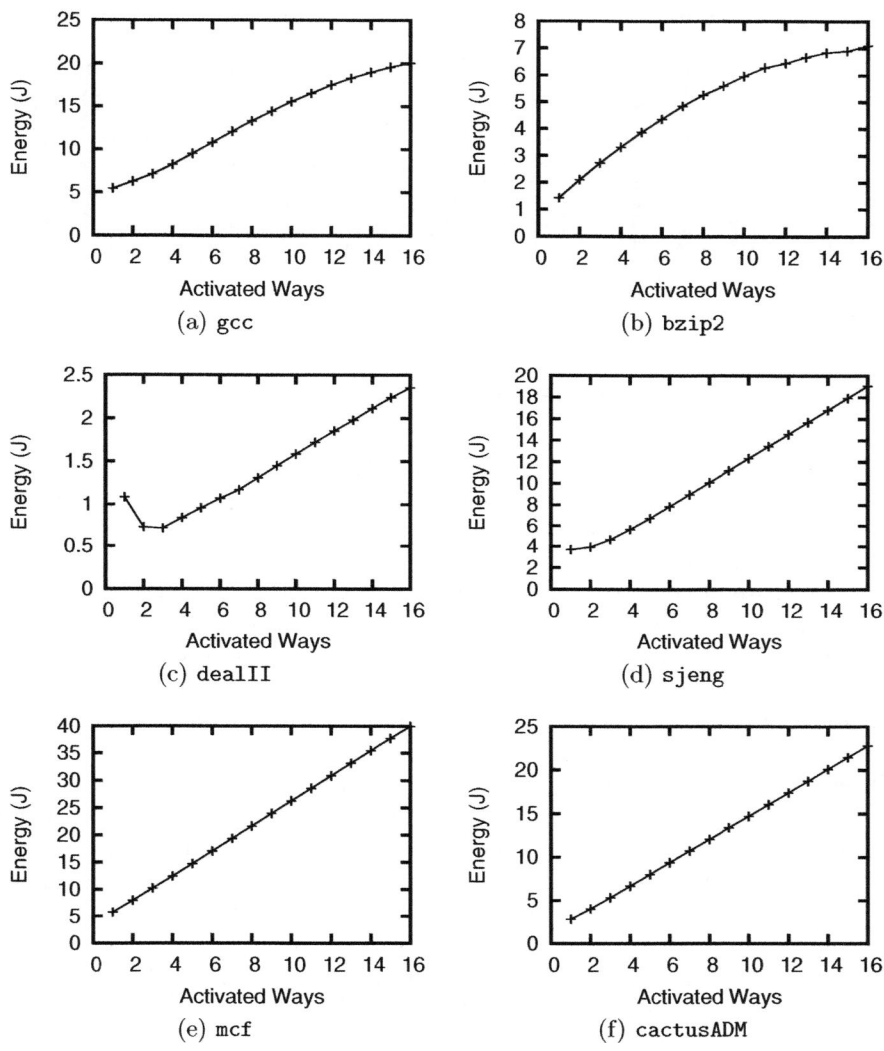

Fig. 10. Activated Ways vs. Energy Consumption

hand, with the performance-oriented configuration $(0.001, 0.005)$ as shown in Figure 9(b), almost all of ways are activated, and the way-allocation function effectively works. Especially, the activated ways of gcc increases significantly, because gcc have the lower access locality than sjeng. Therefore, our mechanism appropriately allocates cache ways, and controls the activated cache area based on the access locality.

In the cases of dealII-sjeng, the energy consumption is not minimum when thresholds are energy-oriented. This is because the execution time increases rapidly when the number of activated ways decreases. In fact, Figure 10 shows the energy consumptions of each benchmark with the number of activated ways. All but dealII show monotonic increase with the number of activated ways.

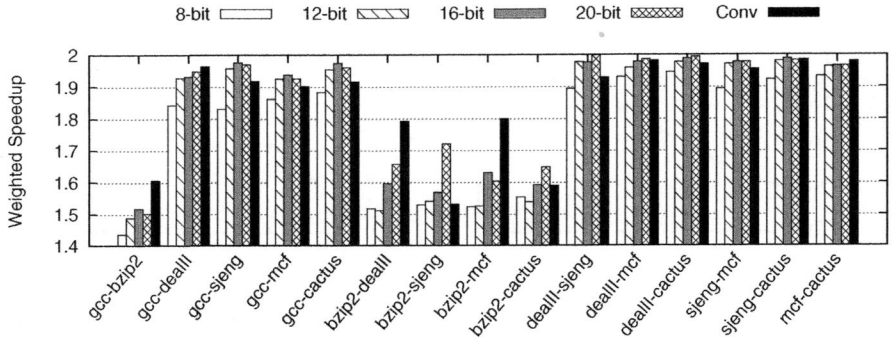

Fig. 11. Effects of Interval Length

However, in the case of combinations including dealII, the minimum energy consumption is achieved when three ways are activated. Therefore, our cache may not decrease the energy consumption on the energy-oriented configuration when the benchmarks like dealII are executed.

In the case of the combinations including bzip2 (e.g. gcc-bzip2), the maximum weighted speedup is achieved at medium thresholds $(0.01, 0.05)$. This is attributed to the fact that the benchmark has the high access utility and the large working set as shown in Figure 5. The behavior analysis of combinations including high utility applications will be discussed in our future work.

Effects of Sampling Intervals. The parameter N, which is the bit width of the sampling counter, defines the maximum sampling interval. Our control mechanism works after 2^N L2 cache accesses. When N is too small, the way-allocation and the power control are performed too often, resulting in an increase in the write-back overheads. On the other hand, the mechanism cannot control the number of ways on demand, when it is too large.

Figure 11 compares the weighted speedups of four interval configurations (N=8, 12, 16, 20; each sampling interval is 2^8, 2^{12}, 2^{16}, or 2^{20} L2 cache accesses.) and the conventional shared cache. We use the performance-oriented configuration $(t1, t2) = (0.001, 0.005)$. The results indicate that decrease in the number of bits of the counter leads to a performance degradation. The results of the 8-bit configuration fall below the conventional cache in all workloads. Moreover, each workload has its own optimal control interval. A majority of workloads reach their perk performances in the cases of 12-bit or 16-bit intervals. Hence, the control interval is an important parameter that decides the performance of our cache control mechanism.

4.4   Evaluation of Hardware Overhead

To evaluate hardware overheads of the proposed cache control mechanism, we design a circuit as shown in Figure 12. The designed circuit consists of two dividers (DIV), three comparators (D_COMP and T_COMP), and two state machines (STATE). Four configurations (N = 8, 12, 16, 20) were designed by Rohm 0.18 μm CMOS Technology, using Synopsys EDA tools.

Table 3 shows the design results of the four configurations. The delay time is enough small compared with the sampling interval; therefore, the delay of our mechanism hardly affects our way-allocation and power saving capability. Moreover, the circuit areas are extremely small compared with cache area. For comparison, we estimate the area of a 1MB 32-way cache by 0.18 μm CMOS Technology using CACTI [19]. Our proposed mechanism consumes only 0.1% of the cache memory area. The hardware overheads of our cache control mechanism, therefore, have an extremely small effect on the chip design.

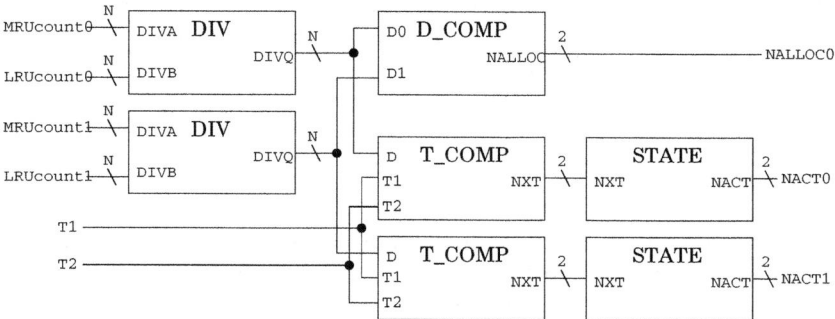

Fig. 12. Cache Control Block Diagram

Table 3. Hardware Overhead

	8-bit	12-bit	16-bit	20-bit
Delay (ns)	21.16	35.38	52.61	84.96
Area(μm^2)	27221	56314	92100	149831

5   Conclusions

This paper has proposed a power-aware cache partitioning mechanism for CMPs. We have defined a metric of cache reference locality based on the stack distance profiling. The mechanism has a way-allocation function and a power control function. The way-allocation function can decide the percentage of cache resources allocated to each core. The power control function decides the cache resources necessary for keeping the current performance. That is, the former is for a relative evaluation by comparing cores' demands for cache resources, and the latter is for an absolute evaluation by estimating the magnitude of the demand by each core.

The evaluation results show that although our cache mechanism and the utility-based scheme are comparable in the cache partitioning performance, our mechanism can save the power consumption. The evaluation results also show that the power control policy of our mechanism can be adjusted from a performance-oriented configuration to an energy-oriented one. The way-allocation cache with a performance-oriented parameter setting can reduce an energy consumption by 20%, while keeping the performance in comparison with a conventional one. On the other hand, the cache with a energy-oriented parameter setting can reduce 55% energy consumption with a performance degradation of 13%. Moreover, we have designed a control mechanism to evaluate hardware overheads. We have shown that our cache control hardware has an extremely small overhead and small effect on the chip design.

The experimental results also indicated that our mechanism does not work in some cases; there was a harmful effect on the performance for lower locality applications. In addition, our cache mechanism can only handle a unit of two cores and an L2 shared cache as a building block for CMPs. Addressing these limitations is the focus of our future work.

Acknowledgments

The authors would like to thank anonymous reviewers for their valuable comments. This research was partially supported by Grant-in-Aid for Scientific Research(B), the Ministry of Education, Culture, Sports, Science and Technology, No.18300011. This work is partially supported by VLSI Design and Education Center(VDEC), the University of Tokyo in collaboration with Synopsys, Inc.

References

1. Wall, D.W.: Limits of instruction-level parallelism. SIGARCH Comput. Archit. News 19(2), 176–188 (1991)
2. Nayfeh, B., Olukotun, K.: A single-chip multiprocessor. Computer 30(9), 79–85 (1997)
3. Suh, G.E., Rudolph, L., Devadas, S.: Dynamic partitioning of shared cache memory. Journal of Supercomputing 28(1), 7–26 (2004)
4. Chandra, D., Guo, F., Kim, S., Solihin, Y.: Predicting inter-thread cache contention on a chip multi-processor architecture. In: HPCA 2005: Proceedings of the 11th International Symposium on High-Performance Computer Architecture, Washington, DC, USA, pp. 340–351. IEEE Computer Society, Los Alamitos (2005)
5. Kim, S., Chandra, D., Solihin, Y.: Fair cache sharing and partitioning in a chip multiprocessor architecture. In: PACT 2004: the 13th International Conference on Parallel Architectures and Compilation Techniques, Washington, DC, USA, pp. 111–122. IEEE Computer Society, Los Alamitos (2004)
6. Qureshi, M.K., Patt, Y.N.: Utility-based cache partitioning: A low-overhead, high-performance, runtime mechanism to partition shared caches. In: MICRO 39: the 39th Annual IEEE/ACM International Symposium on Microarchitecture, Washington, DC, USA, pp. 423–432. IEEE Computer Society, Los Alamitos (2006)
7. Butts, J.A., Sohi, G.: A static power model for architects. In: MICRO-33: 33rd Annual IEEE/ACM International Symposium on Microarchitecture, pp. 191–201 (2000)

8. Kim, N., Austin, T., Blaauw, D., Mudge, T., Flautner, K., Hu, J., Irwin, M., Kandemir, M., Narayanan, V.: Leakage current: Moore's law meets static power. Computer 36(12), 68–75 (2003)
9. International technology roadmap for semiconductors, http://public.itrs.net
10. Meng, Y., Sherwood, T., Kastner, R.: Exploring the limits of leakage power reduction in caches. ACM Trans. Archit. Code Optim. 2(3), 221–246 (2005)
11. Stan, M., Skadron, K.: Power-aware computing. Computer 36(12), 35–38 (2003)
12. Albonesi, D.: Selective cache ways: on-demand cache resource allocation. In: MICRO-32: 32nd Annual International Symposium on Microarchitecture, pp. 248–259 (November 1999)
13. Powell, M., Yang, S.H., Falsafi, B., Roy, K., Vijaykumar, N.: Reducing leakage in a high-performance deep-submicron instruction cache. IEEE Transactions on Very Large Scale Integration (VLSI) Systems 9(1), 77–89 (2001)
14. Powell, M., Yang, S.H., Falsafi, B., Roy, K., Vijaykumar, T.N.: Gated-vdd: a circuit technique to reduce leakage in deep-submicron cache memories. In: ISLPED 2000: The 2000 International Symposium on Low Power Electronics and Design, pp. 90–95. ACM, New York (2000)
15. Kaxiras, S., Hu, Z., Martonosi, M.: Cache decay: exploiting generational behavior to reduce cache leakage power. In: 28th Annual International Symposium on Computer Architecture, June 30-July 4, pp. 240–251 (2001)
16. Flautner, K., Kim, N.S., Martin, S., Blaauw, D., Mudge, T.: Drowsy caches: simple techniques for reducing leakage power. In: 29th Annual International Symposium on Computer Architecture, May 25-29, pp. 148–157 (2002)
17. Kobayashi, H., Kotera, I., Takizawa, H.: Locality analysis to control dynamically way-adaptable caches. SIGARCH Comput. Archit. News 33(3), 25–32 (2005)
18. Binkert, N., Dreslinski, R., Hsu, L., Lim, K., Saidi, A., Reinhardt, S.: The m5 simulator: Modeling networked systems. IEEE Micro 26(4), 52–60 (2006)
19. Wilton, S., Jouppi, N.: Cacti: an enhanced cache access and cycle time model. IEEE Journal of Solid-State Circuits 31(5), 677–688 (1996)
20. The Standard Performance Evaluation Corporation, http://www.spec.org/

A Multithreaded Multicore System for Embedded Media Processing

Jan Hoogerbrugge and Andrei Terechko

NXP Semiconductors, Eindhoven, The Netherlands
{jan.hoogerbrugge,andrei.terechko}@nxp.com

Abstract. We describe a multicore system targeting media processing applications where the cores are multithreaded. The multithreaded cores use a new type of multithreading that we call Subset Static Interleaved (SSI) multithreading. SSI multithreading combines the advantages of blocked multithreading and a simple form of interleaved multithreading called static interleaved multithreading. SSI multithreading divides threads into foreground and background threads and performs static interleaving among the foreground threads. A foreground thread is swapped with a runnable background thread whenever the foreground thread is stalled. SSI multithreading achieves reduced operation latencies, memory latency tolerance, fast context switching, and compared to traditional dynamic interleaving, a relatively low design complexity of the register file.

We use a task scheduling unit (TSU) to dispatch tasks to the cores. The TSU is aware of the fact that the cores are multithreaded. This makes a more efficient mapping of tasks to cores possible by scheduling tasks on the least loaded cores.

We evaluate the system on an optimized Super HD H.264 decoder where the macroblock decoding and deblocking has been parallelized. The complexity of the H.264 standard and the high resolution makes this a challenging and performance demanding application. We achieve speedups of up to 17.7 times for 16 cores with four threads per core relative to a single-threaded single core. Furthermore, the proposed SSI multithreading achieves a speedup of 1.52 times relative to no multithreading, while blocked multithreading achieves only 1.38 times and a restricted form of interleaved multithreading achieves only 1.37 times speedup.

1 Introduction

Until recently multiprocessor systems where used for supercomputing and server applications, but with the introduction of single chip multiprocessors, called multicore, they are entering the personal computing market as well. Soon we will also see many examples of embedded computing where multicores are used to execute a single application. Note that although many embedded systems on chips contain several processor cores, an application (e.g. video decoding or channel decoding) typically runs only on one core.

P. Stenström (Ed.): Transactions on HiPEAC III, LNCS 6590, pp. 154–173, 2011.
© Springer-Verlag Berlin Heidelberg 2011

This paper describes a cache coherent multicore system targeting media processing in embedded applications. We evaluate the system with a parallelized H.264 video decoder on Super HD input streams (3840x2160 at 30 frames per second). The complexity of the H.264 standard and the high resolution makes this a challenging and performance demanding application. One of the novelties of the system is the multithreading of the cores. We apply a type of multithreading that we call Subset Static Interleaved (SSI) multithreading that tolerates memory latency, improves instruction level parallelism, and enables a cost-effective implementation of the register file. Another contribution of this paper is the task scheduling unit which knows about the utilization of each core. This makes it possible to make better scheduling decisions by trying to balance the load over the cores equally.

Our experimental multicore system is composed of TriMedia TM3270 VLIW [1] cores modified to support cache coherence and multithreading. TM3270 is designed for media processing (e.g. video decoding, audio decoding, graphics, and content analysis) and H.264 is one of the key applications for it. One TM3270 is capable to decode SD resolution H.264 in real-time. By instantiating multiple TM3270 cores and modifying them for multithreading we obtain a system which is capable to decode SHD resolution at a comparable clock frequency (+/- 400MHz). Notice that the resolution of SHD is 24 times higher than SD resolution.

The remainder of the paper is organized as follows. Section 2 categorizes multithreading and introduces the subset static interleaved multithreading. Section 3 describes the task scheduling unit (TSU) that balances the processing load over the multithreaded cores. Section 4 discusses the parallelization of the H.264 decoder which we will use for benchmarking purposes. Section 5 evaluates the performance of SSI multithreading compared to existing multithreading techniques. Furthermore we evaluate the effectiveness of the load balancing technique of the task scheduling unit. Section 6 discusses related work. Finally, Section 7 concludes the paper.

2 Multithreading

In a multithreaded core the execution data path is shared by multiple threads of control so that when a thread is not able to utilize the data path because of a stall or data dependences, the data path can be utilized by other threads. Each thread owns its own execution context consisting of a program counter and a register file. As memory latencies become longer and the data path provides more parallelism, it becomes harder to keep the wide issue data path utilized with one instruction stream, and therefore multithreading becomes more attractive.

2.1 Classification

Multithreaded cores can be classified based on whether the hardware is able to detect independent threads or the programmer is responsible for identifying independent threads [2]. The first class is called implicit multithreaded architectures which are still in an experimental stage. Explicit multithreaded architectures are much more mature and can be classified in three classes: blocked multithreading interleaved multithreading, and simultaneous multithreading [2].

- **Blocked multithreading**, also known as coarse-grain multithreading, executes instructions from a thread until it encounters a stall which takes more than a few cycles (see Figure 2a). A typical example is a cache miss where a processor stalls until data is fetched from memory. On such a stall the pipeline is flushed and restarted with instructions from another thread that is able to execute. This new thread is then executed until it also encounters a long stall.
- **Interleaved multithreading**, also known as fine-grain multithreading, dynamically selects every cycle another thread to enter the pipeline (see Figure 2b). Successive pipeline stages are therefore typically holding instructions from different threads. When a thread stalls on, for example, a cache miss, that thread is flushed from the pipeline and not selected anymore until the cache miss has been handled. A thread is flushed by canceling the instructions from it that come after the instruction that caused the stall.
- In the case of **simultaneous multithreading** (SMT), instructions from different threads might be present in the same pipeline stage simultaneously. This type of multithreading is typically applied for scalar ISAs in superscalar designs where multiple instructions streams are fed into an out-of-order execution pipeline [3]. However, it has also been attempted to apply this to VLIW ISAs where VLIW operations from different instructions are merged during execution [4,5].

In the sequel of the paper we refer to software threads as *tasks* or *software threads*, whereas hardware contexts in a multi-threaded core are termed *threads* or *hardware threads*.

2.2   Selection

When selecting a type of multithreading for an embedded VLIW mediaprocessor, interleaved multithreading seems to be most suitable candidate. Simultaneous multithreading is not attractive because of its high complexity that is necessary to merge the VLIW instructions. It is also the question how effectively VLIW instructions can be merged when the merging algorithm has to be kept simple. For example, if it is not allowed to issue the operations of one VLIW instruction into multiple cycles.

When comparing interleaved and blocked multithreading, the most attractive technique is interleaved multithreading. Because instructions from different threads are executed in an interleaved fashion, the operation latencies become shorter in terms of executed instructions from the same thread (not in terms of cycles). Shorter operation latencies make it easier to fill issue-slots of the VLIW instructions so that more instruction-level parallelism (ILP) can be exploited [6].

The register file complexity for interleaved multithreading is high. First we discuss a simplified version of dynamic interleaving, called static interleaving (SI),

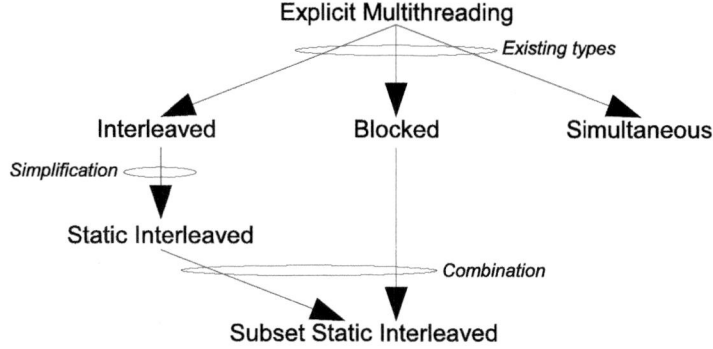

Fig. 1. Relations between described types of multithreading

in Subsection 2.3 We can combine this with blocked multithreading resulting in a technique we term Subset Static Interleaving (SSI), which we will introduce in Subsection 2.4. Subsection 2.5 describes a register file for SSI multithreading. Subsection 2.6 compares SI and blocked multithreading and motivates SSI multithreading as an interesting combination. Figure 1 shows how we arrive at SSI multithreading starting from existing techniques.

2.3   Static Interleaved Multithreading

The interleaving technique described so far is dynamic. The order in which the threads are selected to feed an instruction into the pipeline depends on their availability and is therefore dynamic. A less complex variant would be static interleaved (SI) multithreading, opposite to dynamic interleaved (DI) multithreading, where the order in which the threads are executed is fixed. In an N-way SI multithreaded core (a core with N threads), an instruction from thread i is executed in cycle $i \bmod N$ (see Figure 2c). A bubble is inserted into the pipeline when a thread is stalled. SI multithreading becomes even less complex relative to DI multithreading if all operation latencies in an N-way core are a multiple of N cycles. This can be achieved by inserting empty stages to increase the operation latency of a functional unit up to the next multiple of N cycles. The result is that all writes to the register file of a particular thread are happening in the same cycle modulo N. This means that write backs can be statically scheduled and we can use a simplified register file design as described in Section 2.5. Instead of inserting empty stages, one can also use the additional cycles to relax the timing of the operations or reduce the power consumption of an operation. An example of the latter is to replace a data cache with parallel tag and data access by a sequential design where only one way in the data array has to be accessed.

SI multithreading achieves the operation latency reduction that made (DI) interleaved multithreading attractive. If normally an operation takes C cycles to execute on a single threaded design, it will take $\lceil C/N \rceil$ cycles on an N-way SI multithreaded design. On the other hand, with respect to handling stalls due to cache misses it performs worse than DI multithreading. In DI multithreading the data path stays utilized on a stalling thread as long as there are other threads available for execution. However, with SI multithreading each stalling thread reduces the utilization by $1/N$ because bubbles are fed into the pipeline. Effectively, this means that N-way SI multithreading reduces both the operation latency as well as the memory latency[1] to serve a cache miss by a factor of N.

2.4   Subset Static Interleaved Multithreading

While blocked, simultaneous and DI multithreading potentially can reduce the effect of long stalls (e.g. cache misses) to zero memory latency cycles, SI multithreading is only able to reduce it by a factor of N. Subset static interleaved (SSI) multithreading improves this by having M foreground threads and $N - M$ background threads. SSI multithreading executes instructions from the M foreground threads in a cyclic fashion similar to what SI multithreading does for all N threads. In this case the operation latency reduction for SSI multithreading is a factor of M. Furthermore, for low complexity register file design, all operation latencies are assumed to be a multiple of M cycles. When a foreground thread stalls and a background thread is ready for execution, we exchange them so that the foreground thread becomes a background thread and vise versa. What we achieve is an operation latency reduction of M and full memory latency reduction as long as there are not more than $N - M$ threads stalled on cache misses. After that $1/N$th of the core becomes idle on the next stalled thread. Figure 2d illustrates the execution of SSI multithreading.

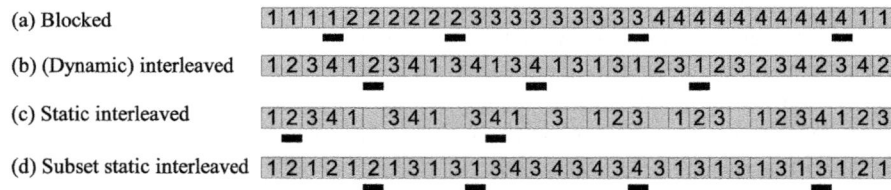

Fig. 2. Time lines for four types of multithreading with 4-way multithreading. Thread stalls are indicated by underlining the cycle. Pipeline bubbles are indicated by a blank box. For simplicity, bubbles due to context switches are not shown.

The number of foreground threads M is a parameter that we can chose between one and N. In the case of $M = 1$ it corresponds to blocked multithreading, while in the case of $M = N$ it corresponds to SI multithreading. Both blocked and SI multithreading has distinct advantages. Blocked multithreading better tolerates memory latency while SI multithreading reduces memory latency as

---

[1] With operation latency we mean the number of cycles it takes before the result of an operation becomes available for usage. The compiler uses these values to schedule the code. With memory latency we mean the number of cycles that the core stalls to handle a cache miss. This value is not used by the compiler.

well as operation latency. By choosing M between one and N we obtain a solution that performs better than the two extremes as shown by our experiments.

2.5   Register File Design

The register file is one of the most complex parts of wide-issue VLIW cores, which require a large number of ports and registers to feed multiple FUs with data. Processor cores for embedded systems often employ a RF (Register File) constructed of standard cells in contrast to many non-embedded processors with custom-layout RFs. Figure 3a shows the structure of a standard cell RF composed of write multiplexers, registers in flip-flops, and read multiplexers. Each register has a multiplexer tree at the input to select a value from one of the write ports. Furthermore, register's outputs are connected to multiplexers that select a register for each of the read ports.

Table 1. Maximum number of accessed contexts for the multithreading schemes

	SMT	Blocked	Dynamic Interleaved	Static Interleaved	SSI
reading	all	one	one	one	one
writing	all	one	all	one	one

An N-way multithreading core needs N times more registers. Let us consider access requirements of different multithreading schemes in Table 1. The *reading* row shows how many hardware threads can read source operands from their respective RFs each cycle. The *writing* row specifies how many hardware threads can write to their respective RFs each cycle. With N total threads in the cases of blocked and SI multithreading, as well as with N foreground threads in the case of SSI multithreading with all operation latencies being a multiple of N cycles, all reads from the same thread as well as all writes from the same cycle are happening in the same cycle modulo N. Thus, the Blocked and (Subset) Static Interleaved schemes each cycle read from only one register file and write to only one register file. This suggests that the read and write port multiplexer trees from Figure 3a can be shared by all the threads. Note, that the shared read and write multiplexers for multi-ported RFs often dominate implementation complexity. In fact, one can simply replace the register cell with multiple registers for different hardware contexts as shown in Figure 3b. The new multithreaded register cell consists of N regular registers and multiplexers around it that are controlled by the thread IDs of the reading and writing threads. Note, that the read (write) multiplexers in the multithreaded register cell are shared by all read (write) ports. This way, register file complexity for multithreaded schemes Blocked and (Subset) Static Interleaved can be limited. Our experimental layout exercises in CMOS 65nm technology indicate that the 4-way multithreaded RF designed as shown in Figure 3, is only 2.35 times larger than the single-threaded RF.

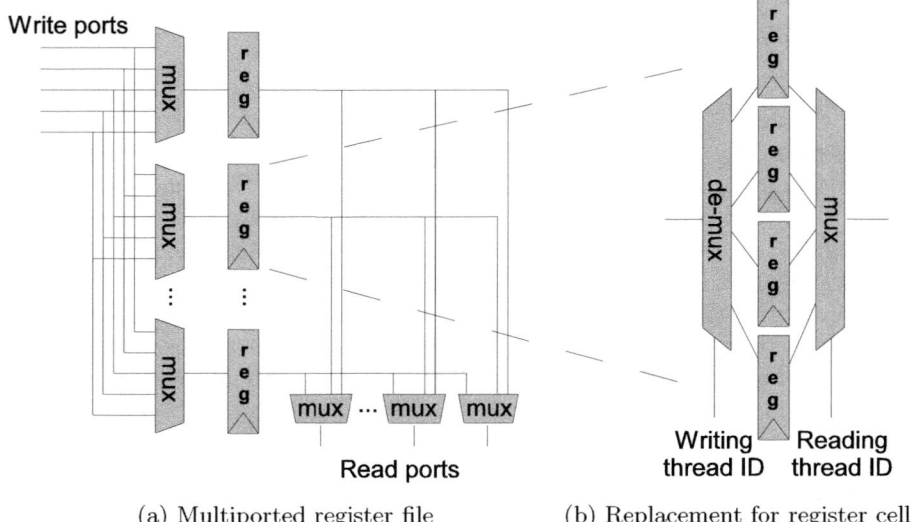

(a) Multiported register file   (b) Replacement for register cell

Fig. 3. Adapting the register file for multithreading. (a) Multi-ported register file for single threaded core. (b) Replacement for register cell to create a register file for a 4-way multithreaded core.

2.6 Multithreading Comparison

In order to understand the benefit of a combination between blocked and SI multithreading we should understand the advantages and disadvantages of both techniques.

1. The *single thread performance* of an N-way SI multithreaded core can be up to N times lower than the single threaded core, because an instruction from a thread is issued once every N cycles. Single thread performance is important when TLP is low.
2. N-way SI multithreading *reduces operation latency* by a factor of N which improves the ILP that can be exploited.
3. N-way SI multithreading *reduces memory latency* by a factor of N whereas blocked multithreading is able to reduce it to zero provided that at least one thread stays runnable.
4. N-way SI multithreading *needs N threads* to keep the core utilized, while blocked multithreading needs only one in the absence of stalls.
5. For blocked multithreading *the switch penalty* is determined by the pipeline stage where the switch is triggered. This stage and all earlier stages have to be flushed. For N-way SI multithreading only the stages holding instructions of the same thread have to be flushed, which is a factor of N lower, and therefore the switch penalty is also N times lower.

So both techniques have their merits and by selecting a proper value for the number of foreground threads for SSI multithreading we hope to maximize performance.

3   Task Scheduling

Our programming model relies on the programmer to extract parallelism from the application and define concurrent tasks. Besides the well-known Pthread API, the system can be programmed by short-running tasks that can be submitted and dispatched with low overhead. This makes fine-grain TLP possible. Submission of a task involves its registration in a shared pool of ready-to-execute tasks whereas dispatching allocates a task to a core and starts it up. The low overhead (+/- 15 cycles for submit and dispatch) is enabled by a hardware device, called the task scheduling unit (TSU), that is shared by the cores.

3.1   Task Scheduling Unit

Our task scheduling unit is based on the Carbon design [7]. It is basically a pool of tasks in a hardware structure to which task can be submitted and retrieved with special operations. This makes it an order of magnitude faster than an optimized software implementation would be. A task is typically a function pointer of the function that performs the task and arguments for it.

The TSU implements distributed task stealing, which also is used for software task pool implementations [8]. The TSU maintains a double-ended queue of tasks for every core in the system. Task submissions and retrievals are done on one side of the queue so that the order is first-in-last-out. Choosing the newest instead of the oldest is typically better for cache locality because the newest task often has data in common with the latest executed task. When a core wants to retrieve a task from its queue and finds it empty, it steals a task from a randomly chosen queue at the opposite side from which task are submitted, i.e., the oldest task in the queue.

Because the TSU has a finite capacity, it generates an interrupt when a queue gets nearly full. An interrupt handler will then spill tasks to an overflow area in memory. When later the queue gets nearly empty, again an interrupt is generated to copy back tasks from the overflow area.

3.2   Improvement for Multithreading

Whenever a software thread running on a core requests the TSU for a task and there is no task in any of the queues, the TSU blocks the requesting thread until a task becomes available. Then typically the longest blocked thread or a randomly selected blocked thread gets the task. In a multithreaded multi-core system this can easily lead to imbalance where, for example, some cores have only one runnable thread while others have all threads runnable. We can reduce such imbalance by making the TSU aware of the multithreaded cores. The heuristic,

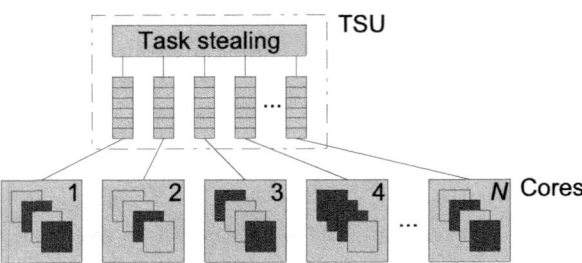

Fig. 4. Task scheduling unit. There is a queue in the TSU for every core. The cores have four threads shown as overlayed squares. Blocked threads are shown in dark color. Let us assume that core 1 submits a task to the TSU. In the case of the most-blocked heuristic, the task stealing module will sent this task to the queue for core 4 because this core has most threads blocked (3 threads).

which we call most-blocked-first, is to assign a task to a blocked hardware thread on a core which has the most threads blocked on the TSU, i.e., the least loaded core. This avoids much of the load imbalance problem.

Figure 4 shows a multicore system with a TSU. It illustrates that a submitted task will be allocated to core 4 because this core has the most threads blocked.

The improvement is relevant at the moments when there is insufficient task-level parallelism to keep all threads utilized. Handling of these moments efficiently is very important to obtain close to linear speedups.

4   Parallel H.264 Decoding

The H.264 / MPEG-4 Advanced Video Coding (AVC, part 10 of MPEG-4) standard for video compression can been seen as an improved successor of MPEG-2 and other parts of MPEG-4 [9,10]. It achieves a higher compression performance by more advanced coding techniques that are also much more compute intensive, and in particular, more control intensive. An example is sub-pixel motion compensation, which has 1/2 pixel resolution in MPEG2 and 1/4 pixel in H.264. The higher resolution makes motion compensation more expensive for H.264.

The high computational requirements make programmable implementations of H.264 decoding very challenging. While SD resolution (Standard Definition, 720×480) is possible on DSPs, HD (High Definition, 1920×1080) is only possible on high clock frequency cores or configurable cores [11], and SHD (Super HD, 3840×2160) is out of reach for single core programmable designs. Therefore, the only programmable solution appears to be a multicore one.

A H.264 decoding consists of three steps: entropy decoding, macroblock decoding, and deblocking. Entropy decoding translates the input bitstream into a sequence of encoded macroblocks. Macroblock decoding is the heart of the decoding process. It translates encoded macroblocks into pixel blocks of 16 times 16. Deblocking is a post pass filter that tries to remove artifacts in the output that are introduced due to block based compression. The decoded frames that are coming out of deblocking step are stored in memory and are used as reference in future frames.

4.1 Parallelization

Parallelization of H.264 decoding could be done by running the three decoding steps in parallel in a pipelined fashion. However, there is a feedback of reference frames from deblocking to macroblock decoding which limits parallelism. Therefore, we parallelized the three steps individually. Unfortunately, parallelization of entropy decoding for H.264 does not appear to be possible. Therefore, we still have to rely on dedicated hardware to do this in real-time for H.264 at SHD resolution. Fortunately, solutions for this exist. For example [12] describes a hardwired solution that needs 45MHz for HD resolution.

Parallelization of macroblock decoding and deblocking is very well possible and can be done in a similar manner [13]. We parallelized these two steps at the macroblock level by decoding macroblocks in parallel. Which macroblocks can be decoded in parallel is determined by dependences between macroblock that are described by the standard. Figure 5 shows these dependences. Macroblock decoding of block *current* in Figure 5 depends on blocks A, B, C, and D. Effectively, it depends on only two blocks C and D because these dependences cover the dependence on A and B as well. For deblocking, block *current* depends on B and D. We can decode/deblock macroblocks in parallel as long as we respect the dependences.

The parallelization is implemented by associating a reference counter with each macroblock. The value of the reference counter associated with macroblock M corresponds to the number of macroblocks on which M depends that have not been processed yet. This is a value between zero and two, where zero indicates that the macroblock is ready for processing. When a macroblock becomes ready for processing, a task is submitted to the TSU that performs the processing. Such a task does the actual processing, i.e. decoding or deblocking, and decrements reference counters to blocks on which the block depends afterward. Whenever a reference counter becomes zero, a task is submitted to the TSU to do the

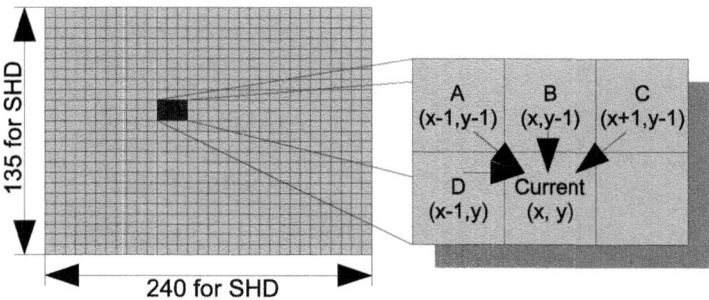

Fig. 5. Dependences between macroblocks

processing of the macroblock corresponding to it. The resulting parallel execution is a wave-front of macroblock processing from the top-left of the frame to the bottom-right. Parallelism ramps up in the beginning and ramps down at the end of a frame. In between the parallelism depends on the number of macroblocks on the wave-front, which is 120 at the peak for SHD for macroblock decoding and 135 for deblocking.

Note, that the scheduling of the decoding and deblocking tasks is dynamic. A static schedule would not be efficient as the execution time for each macroblock varies a lot.

4.2   Tail Submits

A task with task submits at the end of the task resembles a tail recursive function. Similar to recursive functions, we can replace a recursive task submit at the end of a task by a jump back to the beginning of the task. Figure 6 shows this optimization for macroblock processing in simplified pseudo code. In the original code, shown in Figure 6a, we see the actual decoding work followed by decrements of reference counters of macroblocks that depend on the just decoded macroblock. This has to be performed atomically to prevent inconsistencies. Depending on the outcome, up to two macroblocks become ready for processing, which are submitted to the task pool.

The optimized version of the code where tail submits have been replaced by jumps (goto's) to the beginning of the task is shown in Figure 6b. After decrementing the reference counters we determine how many macroblocks become

```
decode_mb(int x, int y)
{
    ... decoding (x, y) ...

    ready1 = atomic_decrement(...);
    ready2 = atomic_decrement(...);
    if(ready1)
        submit(decode_mb, x+1, y);
    if(ready2)
        submit(decode_mb, x-1, y+1);
}
```

```
decode_mb(int x, int y)
{
L:  ... decoding (x, y) ...

    ready1 = atomic_decrement(...);
    ready2 = atomic_decrement(...);
    if(ready1 && ready2) {
        submit(decode_mb, x-1, y+1);
        x += 1;
        goto L;
    } else if(ready1) {
        x += 1;
        goto L;
    } else if(ready2) {
        x -= 1; y += 1;
        goto L;
    }
}
```

(a) Original code   (b) After optimization

Fig. 6. Tail submits

ready for processing. If this is one macroblock, then we adjust the (x, y) position and jump back to the beginning of the task. If there are two ready macroblocks, we submit one and process the other one directly after that by jumping back to the beginning.

This optimization gives us two benefits. First, there is overhead involved in task submission and dispatching, which occurs less frequently after this optimization has been applied because one task performs the work for multiple macroblocks. Furthermore, there is task invariant code that can be moved out of the loop that is created by this optimization. The second benefit is more subtle. Because we have more control over the order in which the macroblocks are executed, we can obtain better data cache locality. This is achieved by executing macroblock (x+1, y) directly after (x, y) when possible and (x+1, y) instead of (x-1, y+1) when both are possible. Because the pixel lines of macroblocks (x, y) and (x+1, y) are adjacent in memory, many data that is needed for (x+1, y) is already in the data cache because it was necessary for (x, y). Therefore, more data will be reused.

5   Evaluation

5.1   Experimental Setup

Figure 7 shows the simulated architecture composed of multithreaded TriMedia cores, hardwired H.264 entropy decoder, TSU, synchronization unit, and shared memory. We used the following L1 data cache parameters values: 64KB size, 64B line size, 4 way set associative, fixed 40 cycles reload penalty, write back, MESI cache coherence, and allocate-on-write-miss policy [14]. The latencies, functional units, and issue-width (5 issue) are the same as the TM3270. We chose a fixed 40 cycle miss penalty reflecting a 40 cycle average miss latency. We do not model the shared L2 cache, L1 instruction caches and contention on interconnect and off-chip SDRAM memory. However, we believe that the high average miss latency represents the unmodelled parts in modern embedded systems on a chip.

For synchronization we modeled a synchronization unit that provides locks to implemented atomic operations. Among other purposes, they are necessary to perform atomic decrements on reference counters (see Section 4).

Our multithreading implements a priority scheme similar to the one of the IBM RS64 IV [15]. This scheme exchanges a foreground and background thread also when the former has a lower priority than the latter. One of the purposes of priorities is to reduce priority during the idle loop of the Pthread scheduler so that it does not consume resources when there are other threads that are executing useful code.

The H.264 decoder that we have parallelized and use for our experiments is optimized including extensive usage of intrinsics, and ILP exposing transformations.

We compiled the decoder with the TriMedia production compiler. For the runs with more than one foreground thread we compiled the application and the

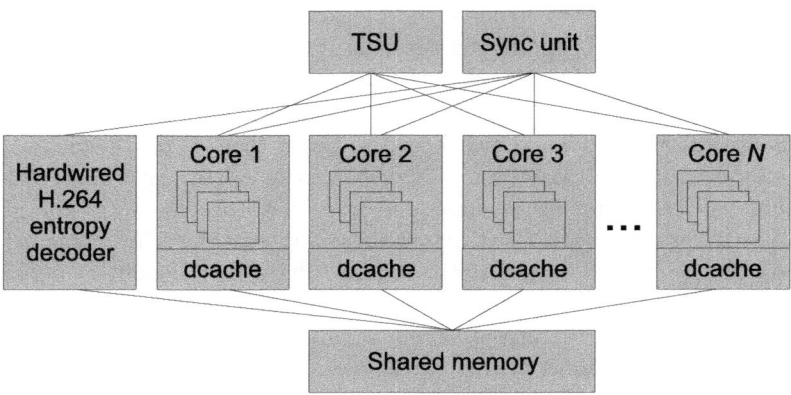

Fig. 7. Architecture of the simulated system

supporting libraries with reduced operation latencies and branch delay slots as described in Sectionsec-ssi.

5.2   Performance of SSI Multithreading

For evaluation of the described system and parallelized decoder, we use a video stream from the SVT High Definition Multi Format Test Set called 'CrowdRun'. We encoded this into a main profile H.264 bitstream. It resolution is 2160 × 3840, which is the closed to SHD (1920 × 3840) that we could find. Due to long simulation times, execution is restricted to 14 frames.

We vary the number of cores from 1 to 16 in powers of two. Furthermore, we experiment with 1 to 4 threads per core, and vary the number of foreground threads from one (blocked) to the number of threads (SI).

We evaluated two versions of the decoder, with and without the tail submit optimization (see Section 4.2), benchmarking different levels of manual optimization. As discussed in Section 4.2, the two versions differ in cache locality where the optimized version has a better locality.

Figures 8 to 11 show the outcome of our measurements where Figures 8 and 9 are for the tail submit optimized version and Figures 10 and 11 for the version without the optimization. Figures 8 and 10 show speedup relative to one single threaded core, while Figures 9 and 11 show the speedup relative to a single threaded system with the same number of cores, illustrating the performance advantage of multithreading.

It is important to note that the two versions of the H.264 decoder differ in execution time even on one single threaded core. The optimized version runs 1.31 times faster on one single threaded core. Hence, the baselines for Figures 8 and 10 are different. Results show speedups of up to 14.4 and 17.7 times for the optimized and non-optimized versions of the code, respectively. These numbers demonstrate the effectiveness of the H.264 decoder parallelization on our architecture.

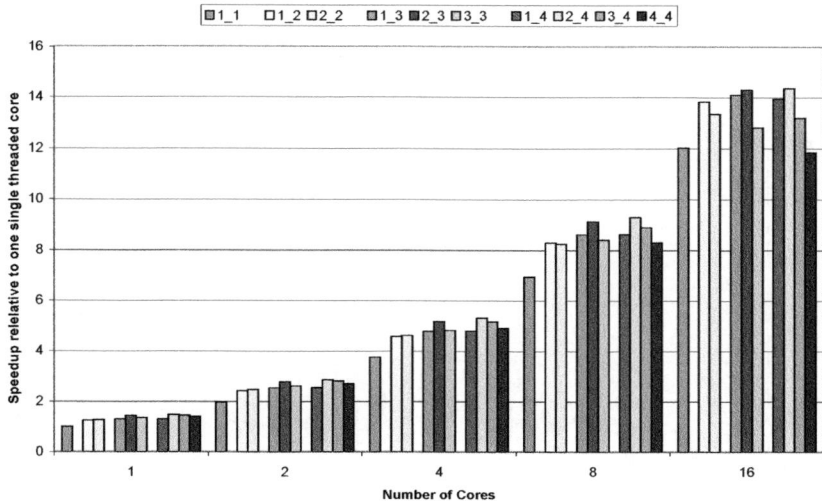

Fig. 8. Speedup for 1, 2, 4, 8, 16 cores relative to single threaded, single core. The bars are grouped in five groups; each group for a certain number of cores. The groups are further grouped in subgroups; each subgroup for a number of threads. The bars within a subgroup vary in the number of foreground threads. The bars are labeled F_T, where F is the number of foreground threads and T the total number of threads per core. Hence, blocked multithreading is at the left (1_N) and SI (N_N) multithreading at the right. Tail submits have been optimized.

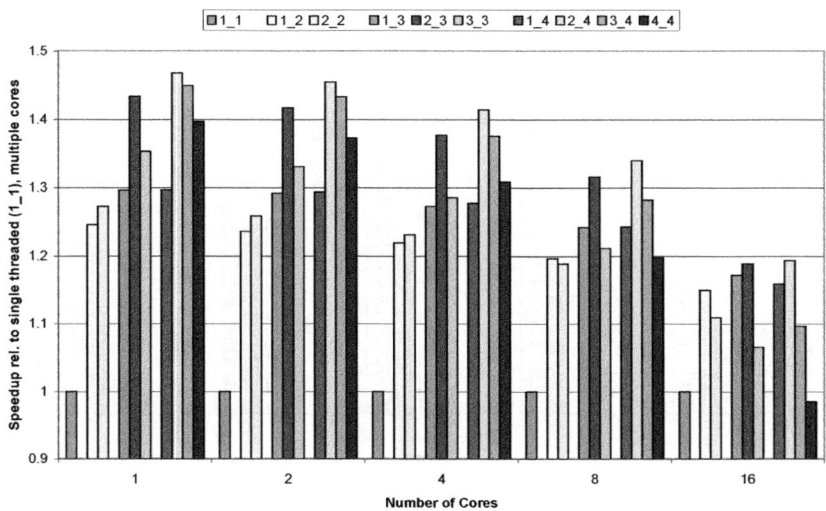

Fig. 9. The same as Figure 8 but speedup relative to single threaded multi-cores

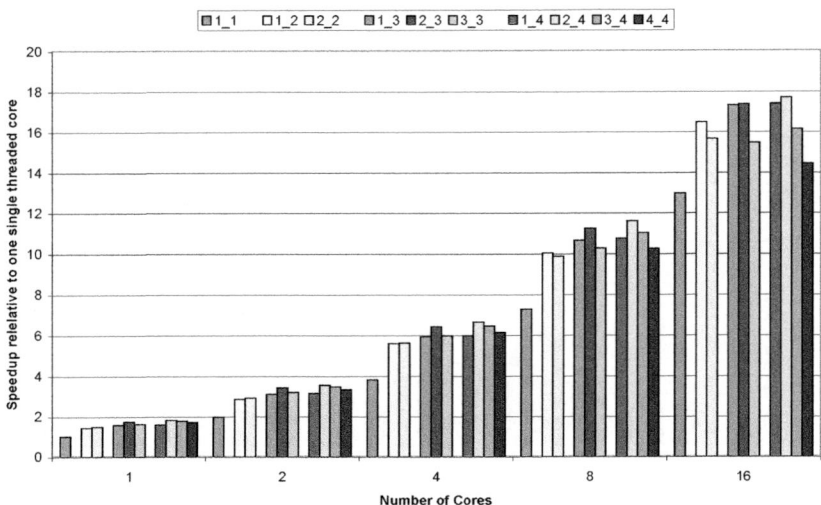

Fig. 10. The same as Figure 8 but without tail submit optimization. Note that Figure 8 has a different vertical scale. Also notice that although the speedup relative to one single threaded core is better than the version with the tail submit optimization, the absolute running times are longer.

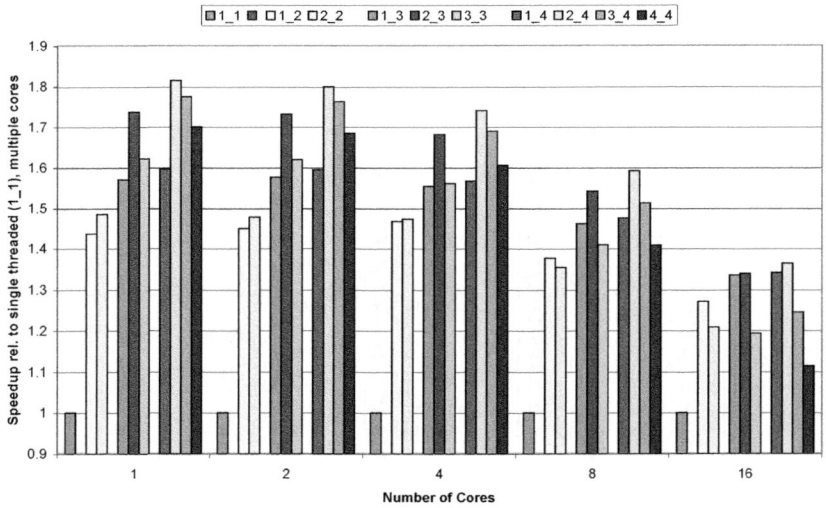

Fig. 11. The same as Figure 9 but without tail submit optimization. Note that Figure 9 has a different vertical scale.

Results also show that multithreading becomes less effective as the number of cores increases (see Figures 9 and 11). This is because the application does not provide sufficient parallelism for the hardware, which provides a TLP of 64 (for 16 cores and 4 threads per core).

The bars in Figures 8 to 11 are gathered in groups with the same number of cores and threads where the number of foreground threads vary from one (left, blocked) and all threads (right, SI). This shows that SSI multithreading (bar(s) in the middle) performs in all cases better than SI and blocked multithreading. The configuration with two foreground threads provides the best results. Averaged over 1 to 16 cores and the two versions of the code, the speedup of SSI multithreading relative to no multithreading is 1.52 times. SI multithreading and blocked multithreading achieve speedups of 1.37 and 1.38 times, respectively.

Comparing the two versions of the code, we see that multithreading is more effective on the version without the tail submit optimization than the version with. The speedups due to SSI multithreading for the first version are in the range of 1.36 to 1.81 while for the latter version it is 1.19 to 1.47. As discussed in Section 4.2, this can be explained by the data locality improvements of the tail submit optimization. This demonstrates the importance of employing optimized benchmarks, because non-optimized benchmarks exaggerate the performance benefit from multithreading.

It is also interesting to see that SI multithreading performs better than blocked multithreading with a low number of cores and becomes worse with a higher number of cores. As discussed in Section 2.6, SI needs more application TLP to keep hardware threads utilized. With more than eight cores the application is not able to provide sufficient TLP for SI multithreading. When the number of cores is low, though, the SI multithreading outperforms blocked multithreading due to reduced operation latencies.

5.3   Multithreading Aware Task Scheduling

In Section 3.2 we described how to make the TSU aware of the fact that the cores are multithreaded by means of the most-blocked-first heuristic. We argued that this is most important when the application utilizes less parallelism than the system provides. To evaluate this, we run the decoder on systems with 8 and 16 cores, 4 threads, and 1 to 4 foreground threads. We evaluate it on a SHD and HD streams. The latter has two times lower macroblock-level parallelism.

Table 2 shows the improvement of the most-blocked-first heuristic relative to selecting the longest blocked thread for a new task. It shows that the importance rises as the parallelism of the system increases ($8 \rightarrow 16$ cores) or the parallelism of the application decreases (SHD $\rightarrow$ HD). Results also show that multithreading aware task scheduling is more effective with fewer foreground threads. This is because threads get more cycles assigned to them on a partially loaded core if there are fewer foreground threads. The reason that there is still a slight speedup for SI multithreading is likely due to reduction in data cache sharing. Without caching effects, multithreading aware task scheduling should not be effective on SI multithreading.

Table 2. Speedups of the most-blocked-first heuristic

Cores	Stream	Speedup (%)			
		number of foreground threads			
		1 (blocked)	2 (SSI)	3 (SSI)	4 (SI)
8	HD	4.92	2.86	1.18	0.03
8	SHD	1.97	0.41	-0.23	0.14
16	HD	17.61	8.68	2.50	0.36
16	SDH	6.48	3.23	1.36	0.27

5.4   Discussion

The optimal number of foreground threads is application dependent. It depends on the importance of the items listed in Section 2.6 for a particular application. For the optimized H.264 decoder we found that two foreground threads is optimal for three and four threads. However we also experimented with SPLASH-2 benchmarks [16] that are not optimized for TM3270. For most of the SPLASH-2 benchmarks, the ILP on a single threaded core is low because floating point operation latencies are long and there are many memory references that the compiler can not disambiguate. Therefore, for most SPLASH-2 benchmarks the optimal number of foreground threads equals the number of threads, i.e., SI multithreading.

We can design cores such that the number of foreground threads is a run-time parameter. For example, we can construct a core with four threads where the number of foreground threads can be two or four. At run-time, the application can switch between the modes whenever it switches between parts of the application with different characteristics. These parts should be compiled (scheduled) with different operation latencies.

Real-time performance is typically very important for media processing applications. Although we did not experiment with it, multithreading might improve real-time performance because variation in the input data that translate in variation of memory access locality can be suppressed by the latency tolerance that multithreading provides.

6   Related Work

SSI multithreading is a combination of blocked multithreading and SI multithreading. With one foreground thread it corresponds to blocked multithreading and if all threads are foregrounds threads it is equivalent to SI multithreading.

Zuberek describes enhanced interleaved multithreading which is also a combination of blocked multithreading and SI multithreading [17]. He bases his performance analysis on Petri net models instead of executing application code. Moreover, Zuberek does not address implementation issues such as register file design.

Balanced multithreading, as proposed by Tune and et al., combines simultaneous multithreading and blocked multithreading in firmware so that long stalling threads are removed from the pipeline to free resources [18].

Examples of interleaved multithreaded machines are Horizon, MIT M-machine, Tera/Cray MTA, Denelcor HEP, Sun Niagara, Sandbridge Sandblaster [19], and MicroUnity MediaProcessor [20]. From what we know it appears that the MediaProcessor and the Sandblaster apply SI multithreading.

Van der Tol et al. pioneered parallel H.264 decoding [13]. They motivated parallelization at the macroblock level and described the dependences between macroblocks as well as the wave-front parallelism that results from it. In comparison with this work, van der Tol et al. do not report performance measurements, apply their work on HD streams, and do not use highly optimized code.

Ramadurai et al. describe a parallelized H.264 decoder for the Sandblaster multithreaded DSP [21]. They use intra macroblock parallelism for macroblock decoding, and, like [13] and our work, inter macroblock parallelism for deblocking. A disadvantage of intra macroblock parallelism is that it does not scale with the frame resolution. Ramadurai et al. do not report performance figures.

Parallelization of MPEG-2 decoding is easier to realize in comparison to H.264. An example of this is the work of Bilas et al. [22]. MPEG-2 has slices that can be decoded independently of at most one row of macroblocks. Furthermore, slices are easy to recognize in the bitstream by means of start codes. H.264 has the concept of independent slices as well but in the case of H.264 the slices could cover a whole frame, which would mean no parallelism.

7 Conclusions

We demonstrated the applicability of a multithreaded multicore for parallel H.264 decoding. The main contribution of this paper is the novel type of multithreading combining blocked multithreading and a restricted form of interleaved multithreading. This type, that we call subset static interleaved (SSI) multithreading, achieves reduced operation latencies, memory latency tolerance, fast context switching, and a relatively low design complexity of the register file. Results show a speedups of up to 17.7 times for 16 cores with four threads relative to a single core, single threaded system on a manually parallelized H.264 on a SHD bitstream. Furthermore, the proposed technique, SSI multithreading, achieves a speedup of 1.52 times relative to no multithreading, while blocked multithreading achieves 1.38 times and a restricted form of interleaved multithreading achieves 1.37 times speedup.

Furthermore, we use a task scheduling unit that is able to balance the load over the multithreaded cores. This improves performance in parts of the application where there is insufficient work for all threads. We observed the performance increase of 6.84% from the improvement of the task scheduling unit for multithreading. On an HD stream we measured speedups of up to 17.61%.

Future work includes optimization and benchmarking of other media applications (e.g., 2D to 3D conversion and frame-rate conversion), more accurate modeling, and RTL implementation to obtain accurate latency, area, and clock frequency figures. Furthermore, we would like to benchmark SSI multithreading against DI multithreading.

Acknowledgments. We would like to thank Arno Glim for providing the optimized H.264 decoder, Jan-Willem van de Waerdt for discussions, Chris Yen and Magnus Själander for back-end support in register file layout exercises.

References

1. van de Waerdt, J.W., Vassiliadis, S., Das, S., Mirolo, S., Yen, C., Zhong, B., Basto, C., van Itegem, J.P., Amirtharaj, D., Kalra, K., Rodriguez, P., van Antwerpen, H.: The TM3270 Media-Processor. In: MICRO 38: Proceedings of the 38th annual IEEE/ACM International Symposium on Microarchitecture, Washington, DC, USA, pp. 331–342. IEEE Computer Society, Los Alamitos (2005)
2. Ungerer, T., Robič, B., Šilc, J.: A Survey of Processors with Explicit Multithreading. ACM Comput. Surv. 35(1), 29–63 (2003)
3. Tullsen, D.M., Eggers, S.J., Levy, H.M.: Simultaneous Multithreading: Maximizing On-chip Parallelism. In: ISCA 1995: Proceedings of the 22nd Annual International Symposium on Computer Architecture, pp. 392–403. ACM Press, New York (1995)
4. Keckler, S.W., Dally, W.J.: Processor Coupling: Integrating Compile Time and Runtime Scheduling for Parallelism. In: ISCA 1992: Proceedings of the 19th Annual International Symposium on Computer Architecture, pp. 202–213. ACM Press, New York (1992)
5. Özer, E., Conte, T.M., Sharma, S.: Weld: A Multithreading Technique Towards Latency-Tolerant VLIW Processors. In: Monien, B., Prasanna, V.K., Vajapeyam, S. (eds.) HiPC 2001. LNCS, vol. 2228, pp. 1520–6149. Springer, Heidelberg (2001)
6. Jouppi, N.P., Wall, D.W.: Available Instruction-level Parallelism for Superscalar and Superpipelined Machines. In: ASPLOS-III: Proceedings of the Third International Conference on Architectural Support for Programming Languages and Operating Systems, pp. 272–282. ACM Press, New York (1989)
7. Kumar, S., Hughes, C.J., Nguyen, A.: Carbon: Architectural Support for Fine-grained Parallelism on Chip Multiprocessors. In: ISCA 2007: Proceedings of the 34th Annual International Symposium on Computer Architecture, pp. 162–173. ACM Press, New York (2007)
8. Blumofe, R.D., Joerg, C.F., Kuszmaul, B.C., Leiserson, C.E., Randall, K.H., Zhou, Y.: Cilk: An Efficient Multithreaded Runtime System. In: PPOPP 1995: Proceedings of the fifth ACM SIGPLAN Symposium on Principles and Practice of Parallel Programming, pp. 207–216. ACM Press, New York (1995)
9. Wiegand, T., Sullivan, G.J., Bjntegaard, G., Luthra, A.: Overview of the H.264/AVC Video Coding Standard. IEEE Trans. Circuits Syst. Video Techn. 13(7), 560–576 (2003)
10. Richardson, I.E.: H.264 and MPEG-4 Video Compresson. John Wiley and Sons, Chichester (2003)
11. Sci-Worx: MSVD-HD, Multi-Standard High Definition Video Decoder (2006), www.sci-worx.com

12. Chen, J.W., Lin, Y.L.: A High-Performance Hardwired CABAC Decoder. In: IEEE International Conference on Acoustics, Speech and Signal Processing, Santa Clara, California, United States, pp. 1520–6149 (2007)
13. van der Tol, E.B., Jaspers, E.G., Gelderblom, R.H.: Mapping of H.264 Decoding on a Multiprocessor Architecture. In: Image and Video Communications and Processing, Santa Clara, California, United States, pp. 707–718 (2003)
14. van de Waerdt, J.W., Vassiliadis, S., van Itegem, J.P., van Antwerpen, H.: The TM3270 Media-Processor Data Cache. In: Proceedings of the IEEE International Conference on Computer Design, pp. 334–341 (2005)
15. Borkenhagen, J., Eickemeyer, R., Kala, R., Kunkel, S.: A Multithreaded PowerPC Processor for Commercial Servers. IBM Journal of Research Development 44(6), 885–898 (2000)
16. Woo, S.C., Ohara, M., Torrie, E., Singh, J.P., Gupta, A.: The SPLASH-2 Programs: Characterization and Methodological Considerations. In: ISCA 1995: Proceedings of the 22nd Annual International Symposium on Computer Architecture, pp. 24–36. ACM Press, New York (1995)
17. Zuberek, W.M.: Performance Analysis of Enhanced Fine-Grain Multithreaded Distributed-Memory Systems. In: Proc. IEEE Conference on Systems, Man, and Cybernetics, Tucson, Arizona, United States, pp. 1101–1106 (2001)
18. Tune, E., Kumar, R., Tullsen, D.M., Calder, B.: Balanced Multithreading: Increasing Throughput via a Low Cost Multithreading Hierarchy. In: MICRO 37: Proceedings of the 37th annual IEEE/ACM International Symposium on Microarchitecture, Washington, DC, USA, pp. 183–194. IEEE Computer Society, Los Alamitos (2004)
19. Schulte, M., Glossner, J., Jinturkar, S., Moudgill, M., Mamidi, S., Vassiliadis, S.: A Low-Power Multithreaded Processor for Software Defined Radio. J. VLSI Signal Process. Syst. 43(2-3), 143–159 (2006)
20. Hansen, C.: MicroUnity's MediaProcessor Architecture. IEEE Micro 16(4), 34–41 (1996)
21. Ramadurai, V., Jinturkar, S., Moudgill, M., Glossner, J.: Multithreading H.264 Decoder on Sandblaster DSP. In: Proceedings at the 2005 Global Signal Processing Expo (GSPx) and International Signal Processing Conference (ISPC), Santa Clara, California (2005)
22. Bilas, A., Fritts, J., Singh, J.P.: Real-Time Parallel MPEG-2 Decoding in Software. In: IPPS 1997: Proceedings of the 11th International Symposium on Parallel Processing, Washington, DC, USA, pp. 197–203. IEEE Computer Society, Los Alamitos (1997)

Regular Papers

Parallelization Schemes for Memory Optimization on the Cell Processor: A Case Study on the Harris Corner Detector

Tarik Saidani, Lionel Lacassagne, Joel Falcou,
Claude Tadonki, and Samir Bouaziz

Institut d'Electronique Fondamentale
Université de Paris Sud
91405 Orsay Cedex
France

Abstract. The Cell processor is a typical example of a heterogeneous multiprocessor on-chip architecture that uses several levels of parallelism to deliver high performance. Reducing the gap between peak performance and effective performance is the challenge for software tool developers and the application developers. Image processing and media applications are typical "main stream" applications. We use the Harris algorithm for the detection of interest points in an image as a benchmark to compare the performance of several parallel schemes on a Cell processor. The impact of the DMA controlled data transfers and the synchronizations between SPEs explains the differences between the performance of the different parallelization schemes. The scalability of the architecture is modeled and evaluated.

1 Introduction

Image processing applications are generally composed of a set of basic operators. These components can be point to point operators or convolution kernels. Due to both computation and memory complexity, real-time execution of image processing algorithms has historically not been easily done efficiently. Multi-core processors family appeared to respond to an increasing demand of processing power that single-task scalar systems, which raised computing and energy efficiency problems, could not satisfy. Furthermore, computing and transfer workloads can be distributed on the multiple processing units to reduce the processing time, in particular for media processing application which are well suited for the multiple levels of parallelism provided by parallel architectures.

The Cell processor [16] is a good example of a heterogeneous multi-processor (Fig. 1). Composed of a 64-bit power processor element (PPE), eight specialized units called synergistic processors (SPE) and a high bandwidth bus called Element Interconnect Bus (EIB), that allows communications between the different components [9], The Cell is a heterogeneous, multi-core chip containing several levels of parallelism that can be exploited to reach high peak performances.

P. Stenström (Ed.): Transactions on HiPEAC III, LNCS 6590, pp. 177–200, 2011.

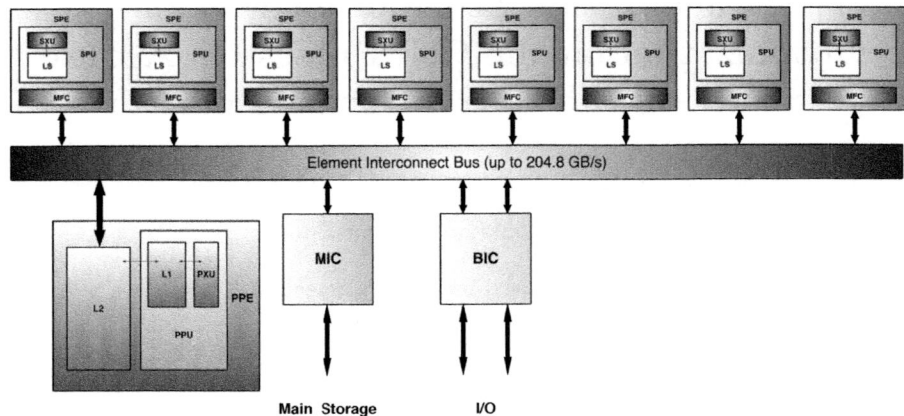

Fig. 1. Detailed view of the Cell Broadband Engine Architecture

Assuming a clock speed of 3.2 Ghz, the Cell processor has a theoretical peak performance of 204.8 GFlops/s in single precision. The EIB is composed of four 128-bit rings, each ring can handle up to three concurrent transfers. The theoretical peak bandwidth of the bus is 204.8 GBytes/s for internal transfers, when performing 8 simultaneous non-colliding 25.6 GB/s transfers (the Cell network topology allows only 8 transfers to be done in parallel without collision). The PPE unit is a traditional 64-bit PowerPC Processor with a vector multimedia extension (VMX aka Altivec). This Cell's main processor is in charge of running the OS, and coordinating the SPEs. Each SPE consists in a synergistic processor unit (SPU) and a Memory Flow Controller (MFC). The SPE holds a local storage (LS) of 256 KB, and a 128-bit SWAR (very close to Altivec) unit dedicated to high-performance data-intensive computation. The MFC holds a 1D DMA controller, that is in charge of transferring data from external devices to the local store, or writing back computation results to main memory. One of the main characteristics of the Cell processor is its distributed memory hierarchy. The main drawback of this kind of memory, is that the software must handle the limited size of the LS of each SPE, by issuing DMA transfers from or toward main storage (MS).

However, some specific programming aspects – namely Direct Memory Access (DMA) controlled transfers – makes it hard for developers to code and debug their applications quickly on the Cell processor. Therefore, it is necessary to develop software tools that can make the programming process less painful and the most suitable with the target architecture. Since the release of the first prototypes and simulator, there were several examples of application porting on the Cell BE, with various application domains like bio-informatics [19,18], graphics rendering [3] and other scientific computing kernels [20,7,15]. In [19] the authors adopted a progressive optimization strategy where a PPU version of the "Clustal W" applications was tuned so that the code matches the capabilities of the SPU cores. Various implementation strategies (MPI, OpenMP, SIMD) were tested and compared in [18] for a protein docking application, the influence of DMA transfers on performance was also discussed. On the other hand, various programming models was mapped on the Cell processor in the form of tools, programming languages and compilers [6,12,5,14]. In [5] the Cell BE is viewed as a shared memory SMP (Symetric Multi-Processor) where the compiler performs the task of distributing work over the SPEs via OpenMP parallelization directives and where data transfers to the local stores are handled implicitly using software caches. The CellSs[2] programming model is somewhat similar to OpenMP as it relies on code annotation to offload a part of the work to the SPEs except that it relies on a source to source C compiler and a locality-aware task scheduler optimizes data transfers at runtime. Message passing programming model is treated in [14]: applications are partitioned into MPI micro-tasks and a static scheduler performs the task of optimizing their execution on the parallel cores. Finally, the RapidMind [12] tool relies on a model where data transfers and computation kernels are completely decoupled so that optimizations like inter-kernel data access elimination and transfer/computation overlapping can be performed.

The goal of this paper is to evaluate the performance of some computation models relying on various communication and mapping strategies on the Cell BE processor for a representative image processing algorithm.

- The implementation and evaluation of several parallelization schemes for the Harris interest point detection algorithm are performed.
- The influence of DMA transfer size on the performance of each model is demonstrated.
- The impact of chaining technique to boost the performance on the Cell is exposed.
- A comparison between the Cell SPU unit and other cache-based SIMD extensions is provided.
- The scalability of the Cell processors is modeled and measured via efficiency and speedup metrics.

The paper is organized as follows. In Section 2, we describe our image processing algorithm: the Harris and Stephen corner detector. Section 3 describes the implementation models and their comparative performances. In Section 4 we model and evaluate the Cell scalability. Finally, we sum up our main contributions and discuss future work in Section 5.

2   The Harris Interest Point Detection Algorithm

Harris and Stephen [8] interest point detection algorithm is used in computer vision systems for feature extraction like motion detection, image matching, tracking, 3D reconstruction and object recognition. This algorithm was proposed to address the limitations of the Moravec corner detector [13] which was sensitive to noise and not rotationally invariant. A corner can be defined as the intersection of two edges when an interest point can be defined as a point which has a well defined position and can be robustly detected. Hence, the interest point can be a corner but also an isolated point of local intensity maximum or minimum, a line ending, or a point on a curve where the curvature is locally maximal.

2.1   Algorithm Description

Assuming image patches of dimensions $u \times v$ (in our case 3×3) in a grayscale 2-dimensional image I and shifting it by (x, y), the Harris operator is based on the estimation of local autocorrelation S for which the expression is:

$$S(x, y) = \sum_{u} \sum_{v} w(u, v) \left(I(u, v) - I(u - x, v - y) \right)^2 \tag{1}$$

By approximating S with a second order Taylor series expansion the Harris matrix M is given by:

$$M = \sum_{u} \sum_{v} w(u, v) \begin{bmatrix} I_x^2 & I_x I_y \\ I_x I_y & I_y^2 \end{bmatrix} \tag{2}$$

An interest point is characterized by a large variation of S in all directions of the vector (x, y). By analyzing the eigenvalues of M, this characterization can be expressed in the following way. Let λ_1, λ_2 be the eigenvalues on the matrix M:

1. If $\lambda_1 \approx 0$ and $\lambda_2 \approx 0$ then there are no features of interest at this pixel (x, y).
2. If $\lambda_1 \approx 0$ and λ_2 is some large positive value, then an edge is found.
3. If λ_1 and λ_2 are both large, distinct positive values, then a corner is found.

Harris and Stephens note that eigenvalues computation is expensive, since it requires the computation of a square root, and instead suggest the following algorithm:

1. For each pixel (x, y) in the image compute the autocorrelation matrix M:

$$M = \begin{bmatrix} S_{xx} & S_{xy} \\ S_{xy} & S_{yy} \end{bmatrix} ; \text{where:} S_{xx} = \left(\frac{\partial I}{\partial x} \right)^2 \otimes w, S_{yy} = \left(\frac{\partial I}{\partial y} \right)^2 \otimes w, S_{xy} = \left(\frac{\partial I}{\partial x} \frac{\partial I}{\partial y} \right) \otimes w \tag{3}$$

Where $\otimes$ is the convolution operator and w a Gaussian kernel.

2. Construct the coarsity map by calculating the coarsity measure $C(x, y)$ for each pixel (x, y), with k being a empirically determined constant:

$$C(x, y) = det(M) - k(trace(M))^2$$
$$det(M) = S_{xx} \cdot S_{yy} - S_{xy}^2$$
$$trace(M) = S_{xx} + S_{yy}$$

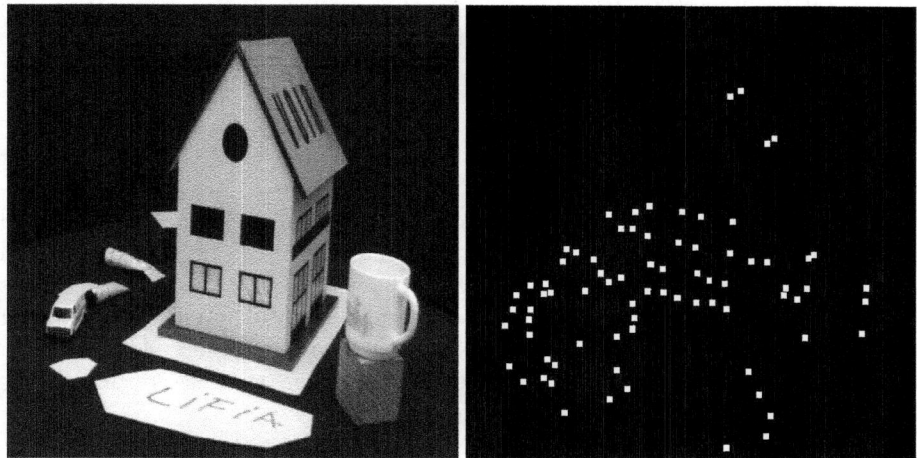

Fig. 2. Illustration of the interest point detection on a grayscale 512×512 image

An illustration of an input 512×512 grayscale image and a interest point detection on it are given in Fig. 2. To obtain this result, two additional steps are performed in order to extract visually appealing information from the dense coarsity matrix[1]. Those steps are:

1. Threshold the interest map by setting all $C(x, y)$ below a given threshold T to zero.
2. Local maxima are then extracted by filtering points which are greater than all the points in a 3×3 neighborhood.

2.2 Implementation Details

Grayscale 2-dimensional image pixels are typically 8-bit unsigned integers and the Harris algorithm output is in this case a 32-bit signed integer. However, because of the limitations of the Cell SPU ISA, and in order to guarantee a fair comparison between Altivec, SSE and Cell SPU, we chose the single precision floating point format for both input pixels and the output of the Harris operator. In our implementation of the Harris operator we divided the algorithm into four computation kernels: a Sobel operator representing the derivative in the horizontal and vertical directions, a multiplication operator, a Gaussian smoothing operator (w in Eq. 2) followed by a coarsity computation. In our implementation the k constant in Eq. 4 is fixed to 0 as it does not change the qualitative results. This leads to the data flow graph given in Fig. 3 which is representative of typical image processing algorithms as it includes convolution kernels and point to point operators and in which the Sobel operator convolution kernels (one for

---

[1] As those steps are merely cosmetic, we will not consider them as part of the algorithmic chain.

horizontal gradient $(GradX)$ and one for the vertical gradient $(GradY))$ and the Gauss smoothing kernel $Gauss$ are defined by :

$$GradX = \frac{1}{8} \begin{bmatrix} -1 & 0 & 1 \\ -2 & 0 & 2 \\ -1 & 0 & 1 \end{bmatrix} ; GradY = \frac{1}{8} \begin{bmatrix} -1 & -2 & -1 \\ 0 & 0 & 0 \\ 1 & 2 & 1 \end{bmatrix} ; Gauss = \frac{1}{16} \begin{bmatrix} 1 & 2 & 1 \\ 2 & 4 & 2 \\ 1 & 2 & 1 \end{bmatrix}$$

The convolution kernels computation consist in centering the kernel on a pixel and computing the cumulated sum of the point to point product of the kernel elements with the image patch surrounding the central pixel. Hence, the Harris algorithm can be considered as a memory bounded problem since this kind of operators are great bandwidth consumers as they consume more elements than they produce. For this reason we chose to perform memory access optimizations at several levels of the Cell processor memory hierarchy.

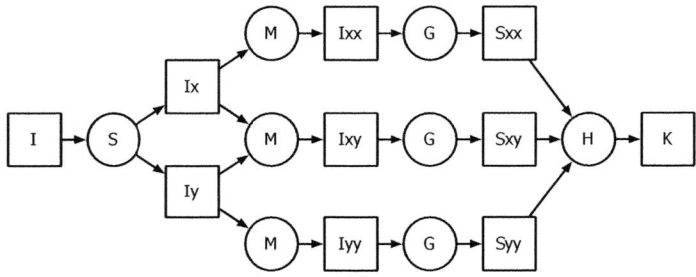

Fig. 3. Harris algorithm dataflow graph

3   Optimizations and Parallelization Strategies

Implementing a given image processing application on the Cell is not a trivial task as various level of optimization are available. We focus on two kind of optimizations : optimizations driven by the application domain and optimizations driven by the underlying architecture. We detail how those optimization techniques can be applied to the Harris algorithm and how they drive the parallelization strategy.

3.1   Signal Processing Optimization

The first optimizations to be applied are *Domain Specific*. Those optimizations include kernel separability, kernel overlapping and computation factorization.

Kernel Separability. In our case, we will take advantages of the fact that 2D convolution kernels used by the Gauss and Sobel operators are separable. A 2D convolution kernel is said to be separable if it can be expressed as the outer product of two vectors Eq. 4, 5 and 6).

$$Gauss = \frac{1}{16} \begin{bmatrix} 1 & 2 & 1 \\ 2 & 4 & 2 \\ 1 & 2 & 1 \end{bmatrix} = \frac{1}{16} \begin{bmatrix} 1 \\ 2 \\ 1 \end{bmatrix} * \begin{bmatrix} 1 & 2 & 1 \end{bmatrix} \tag{4}$$

$$Grad_X = \frac{1}{8} \begin{bmatrix} -1 & 0 & 1 \\ -2 & 0 & 2 \\ -1 & 0 & 1 \end{bmatrix} = \frac{1}{8} \begin{bmatrix} 1 \\ 2 \\ 1 \end{bmatrix} * \begin{bmatrix} -1 & 0 & +1 \end{bmatrix} \tag{5}$$

$$Grad_Y = \frac{1}{8} \begin{bmatrix} -1 & -2 & -1 \\ 0 & 0 & 0 \\ 1 & 2 & 1 \end{bmatrix} = \frac{1}{8} \begin{bmatrix} -1 \\ 0 \\ +1 \end{bmatrix} * \begin{bmatrix} 1 & 2 & 1 \end{bmatrix} \tag{6}$$

This reformulation reduces both the number of memory accesses and arithmetic complexity (see Table 1).

Convolution kernel overlapping. The second step is to take into account how kernels are applied. Due to overlapping (Fig. 4), there is only one new column of pixels to load from the memory at each iteration. Thanks to kernels separability, they are first applied column-wise by computing the vertical filtering. Temporary results are saved into registers and convolved with the horizontal filter. The typical loops transformation are *Register Rotation* and *Loop Unrolling* (an example is given in the next section). The *Register Rotation* is preferred because it does not increase the loop body and because no prolog neither epilogue are required.

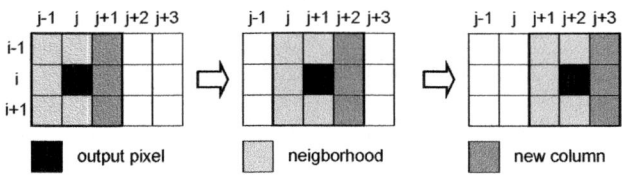

Fig. 4. Convolution kernel overlaping

Reduction and computation factorization. Once the 2D convolution kernels are split into two 1D convolution kernels and the kernel overlapping has been taken into account, *reduction* by column is applied to take advantage of the column reuse. Let us consider the convolution of the Gauss kernel[2] with a 3×4 pixels matrix (Eq. 7)[3].

---

[2] The same technique is also applied to the Sobel operator.
[3] Fractions have been removed to simplify the notation.

$$\begin{bmatrix} r_0 \ r_1 \end{bmatrix} = \begin{bmatrix} 1 & 2 & 1 \\ 2 & 4 & 2 \\ 1 & 2 & 1 \end{bmatrix} * \begin{bmatrix} a_0 & b_0 & c_0 & d_0 \\ a_1 & b_1 & c_1 & d_1 \\ a_2 & b_2 & c_2 & d_2 \end{bmatrix} \tag{7}$$

We have:

$$r_0 = \begin{bmatrix} 1 & 2 & 1 \end{bmatrix} * \left(\begin{bmatrix} 1 \\ 2 \\ 1 \end{bmatrix} * \begin{bmatrix} a_0 \\ a_1 \\ a_2 \end{bmatrix}, \begin{bmatrix} 1 \\ 2 \\ 1 \end{bmatrix} * \begin{bmatrix} b_0 \\ b_1 \\ b_2 \end{bmatrix}, \begin{bmatrix} 1 \\ 2 \\ 1 \end{bmatrix} * \begin{bmatrix} c_0 \\ c_1 \\ c_2 \end{bmatrix} \right) \tag{8}$$

Let r_a, r_b and r_c be the *reduced* registers by column:

$$r_a = \begin{bmatrix} 1 \\ 2 \\ 1 \end{bmatrix} * \begin{bmatrix} a_0 \\ a_1 \\ a_2 \end{bmatrix}, \quad r_b \begin{bmatrix} 1 \\ 2 \\ 1 \end{bmatrix} * \begin{bmatrix} b_0 \\ b_1 \\ b_2 \end{bmatrix}, \quad r_c \begin{bmatrix} 1 \\ 2 \\ 1 \end{bmatrix} * \begin{bmatrix} c_0 \\ c_1 \\ c_2 \end{bmatrix} \tag{9}$$

The output r_0 can be expressed as:

$$r_0 = \begin{bmatrix} 1 & 2 & 1 \end{bmatrix} * \begin{bmatrix} r_a & r_b & r_c \end{bmatrix} = r_a + 2r_b + r_c \tag{10}$$

In order to compute r_1, the first column is recycled by loading three data (column d: d_0, d_1, d_2), and applying the 1D kernel to get a new *reduced* register r_a (Eq. 11). Thus r_1 can benefit of the previous computations (Eq. 12).

$$r_a = \begin{bmatrix} 1 \\ 2 \\ 1 \end{bmatrix} * \begin{bmatrix} d_0 \\ d_1 \\ d_2 \end{bmatrix}, \tag{11}$$

$$r_1 = \begin{bmatrix} 1 & 2 & 1 \end{bmatrix} * \begin{bmatrix} r_b & r_c & r_a \end{bmatrix} = r_b + 2r_c + r_a \tag{12}$$

Each *reduced* register is used thrice, thus saving memory accesses and computations.

The arithmetic complexity of the Harris operators are given in table 1, where *Number* indicates the number of calls to each operator when no optimizations are performed and when kernel separability and overlapping are exploited. We notice that those simple optimizations reduce the global complexity by 46%.

Temporal Pipelining. In a *producer-consumer* point of view, there are actually two kind of operators in the Harris operator, each having a specific memory access pattern:

- point to point operators, like the Multiplication and the Coarsity operators, that consume a 1×1 data to produce a 1×1 data.
- 3×3 convolution kernels, like the Sobel gradients ($Grad_X$ and $Grad_Y$) and the Gauss smoother that consumes 3×3 data and produces a 1×1 data (Fig. 5).

Table 1. Arithmetic operator complexity with/without optmizations

Operator	Number	MUL	ADD	Total
Complexity without optimization				
Sobel	2	3	5	16
Mul	3	1	0	3
Gauss	3	6	8	42
Coarsity	1	2	1	3
Total	-	29	35	**64**
Complexity with optimizations				
Sobel	2	0	5	10
Mul	3	1	0	3
Gauss	3	0	6	18
Coarsity	1	2	1	3
Total	-	4	30	**34**

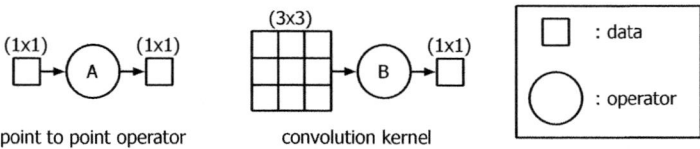

Fig. 5. Producer-consumer model: memory access pattern for point operator and convolution kernel

The *Temporal pipelining* optimization consists in chaining operators together by adapting their memory access patterns in order to remove the intermediate LOAD/STORE instructions.

Figure 6 sums up the various pipelining rules. In rule 1, the output pattern of the first operator already fit the input pattern. No pattern adaptation is required before removing the intermediate memory access. For rule 2 : there is nothing to do for pipelining a 3×3 convolution kernel with a point operator. But permuting point operator and convolution kernel (rule 3) requires unrolling the first operator in order to adapt the pattern. In that case the first operator should be unrolled thrice in both dimensions. The last rule is the pipelining of two 3×3 convolution kernels (rule 4). As for the third rule, the first operator should be unrolled 3×3 times. The big difference in that case is that the new input pattern is 5×5, that requires 25 registers just to hold the loaded data. One possible drawback of this pipelining is *spill code* if the compiler runs out of register. The last point about pipelining is to see the Sobel gradient operator as one operator instead of two: 3×3 points are loaded only one time but consumed twice to produce two points, one for $Grad_X$ and one for $Grad_Y$.

Benefits of Domain Specific Optimizations. The leading idea of all those optimizations is to reduce complexity. This can be done by both the reduction of

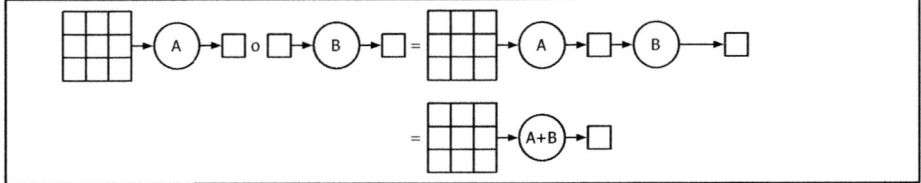

rule #1: point operator chained with point operator

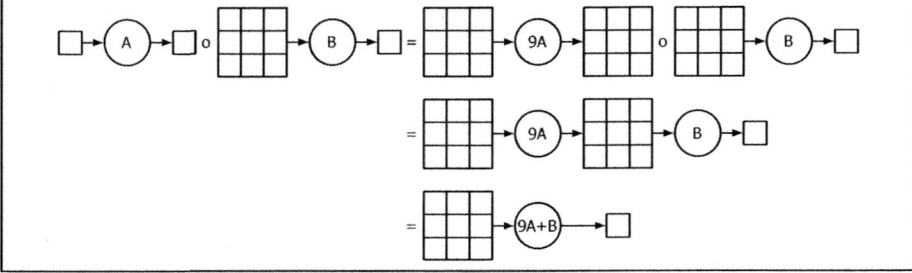

rule #2: convolution kernel chained with point operator

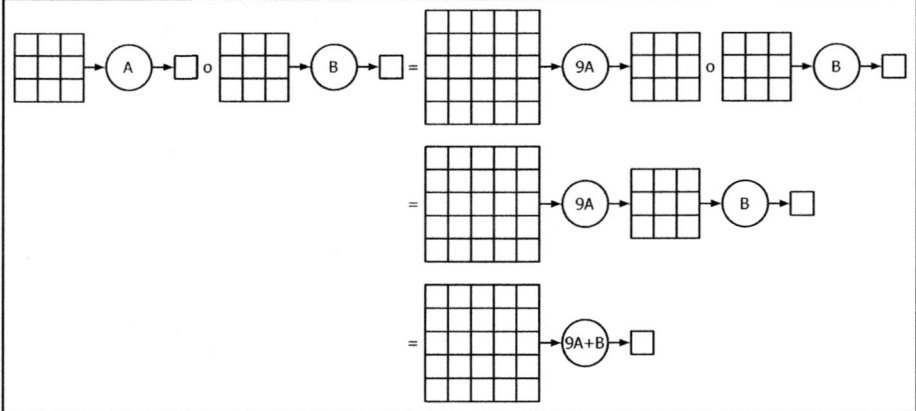

rule #3: point operator chained with convolution kernel

rule #4: convolution kernel chained with convolution kernel

Fig. 6. Pattern fitting pipelining rules

the number of computations per point (arithmetic transformation like reduction) and the amount of memory accesses (temporal pipelining).

By combining these two kind of optimizations, there are four versions of the Harris operator: the basic implementation of Harris with or without arithmetic optimizations, and the HalfPipe implementation of Harris with or without arithmetic optimizations. The HalfPipe optimization consists in applying rule #2 to

Table 2. Complexity of memory accesses pattern, with/without optimizations

Operator	Number	Input Pattern	Number	Output Pattern	Total
NoPipe version					
Sobel	2	3×3	2	1×1	20
Mul	3	1×1	3	1×1	6
Gauss	3	3×3	3	1×1	30
Coarsity	3	1×1	1	1×1	4
Total		51		9	**60**
NoPipe with Register Rotation and Reduction					
Sobel	1	3×1	2	1×1	5
Mul	2	1×1	3	1×1	5
Gauss	3	3×1	3	1×1	12
Coarsity	3	1×1	1	1×1	4
Total		17		9	**26**
HalfPipe version					
Sobel+Mul	1	3×3	3	1×1	12
Gauss+Coarsity	3	3×3	1	1×1	28
Total		36		4	**40**
HalfPipe version with Register Rotation and Reduction					
Sobel+Mul	1	3×1	3	1×1	6
Gauss+Coarsity	3	3×1	1	1×1	10
total		12		4	**16**
FullPipe version					
Sobel+Mul+Gauss+Coarsity	1	5×5	1	1×1	26
total		25		1	**26**
FullPipe version with Register Rotation and Reduction					
Sobel+Mul+Gauss+Coarsity	1	5×1	1	1×1	6
total		5		1	**6**

Harris: pipelining a convolution kernel with a point to point operator: Sobel is pipelined with Mul and Gauss is pipelined with Coarsity. Finally, one can remove too the normalization coefficients of Gauss and Sobel 1/16 and 1/8 that are usually used in image processing to normalize the output of these kernels to get the same magnitude as the input, but that is, in our case, useless as the threshold performed is relative to the maximum extracted value. The memory complexity of the operator is given in table 2 where *Number* indicates the number of *Input Pattern* and of *Output Pattern* of each operator.

3.2 DMA Related Optimizations

DMA transfers are the main issue when developing image processing applications on the Cell processor. The developer must care about certain considerations when performing data transfers from main storage to local stores, or between local stores. The first parameter to consider when transferring data to the SPE is the size of the transfers. We measured the bandwidth of data transfer size varying from 8 to 16384 bytes which is the maximum size that can be issued by a single DMA request for the Cell MFC. The data must be transferred by 16 KB chunks to have a full bandwidth on the EIB, smaller transfers are done with a reduced bandwidth (Tab. 3). The internal bus bandwidth is also related to the number of concurrent transfers, as that the EIB can handle up to 12 parallel transfers (3 per ring but only 8 without potential collision (as explained in section 3). The second parameter to consider is the physical proximity (aka SPE affinity), between SPEs when performing an inter-SPE transfers. This parameter can not be controlled by the user as the task of scheduling tasks on SPEs is done by the kernel scheduler. Finally, data being transfered must be contiguous in memory[4]. Those limitations have a big impact on the tiling strategy. As local store has only 256 KB to hold both code and data, large amounts of data being processed have to be split into *tiles* which size is compatible with the memory available on the SPEs and compatible with the maximal size of a DMA transfer.

Table 3. Aggregate bandwidth for inter-SPE DMA transfers with 8 SPE transferring concurrently on a QS20 Blade

Size (B)	Agg BW (GB/s)	Size (B)	Agg BW (GB/s)
8	0.92	512	47.92
16	1.86	1024	72.57
32	3.72	2048	86.48
64	7.42	4096	94.09
128	14.87	8192	97.72
256	27.37	16384	104.10

3.3   Parallel Implementations

In all the following figures, S refers to the Sobel operator, M to the multiplication, G to Gauss and H to Harris. The gray rectangles represents an SPE unit. The source image is divided into p regions of processing (RoPs), p being the number of available SPEs. Each Rop is then split into tiles. The operators consumes input tiles and produces output tiles. We assume that tile width equals RoP and image widths in order to avoid transfers of non contiguous memory regions.

Conventional SPMD. The conventional SPMD programming model (Fig. 7) equally divides the image into 8 RoPs, mapped on the SPEs (in the figure, only 4 SPEs are drawn to get a smaller figure, but 8 SPEs are actually used). All SPUs execute the same program/code.The PPU lets the SPUs run one operator on the whole image before proceeding with the next operator. For example, it will not issue the command for Multiplication operator until all the SPEs have finished

---

[4] Such DMA transfer are said to be mono-dimensional or *1D*.

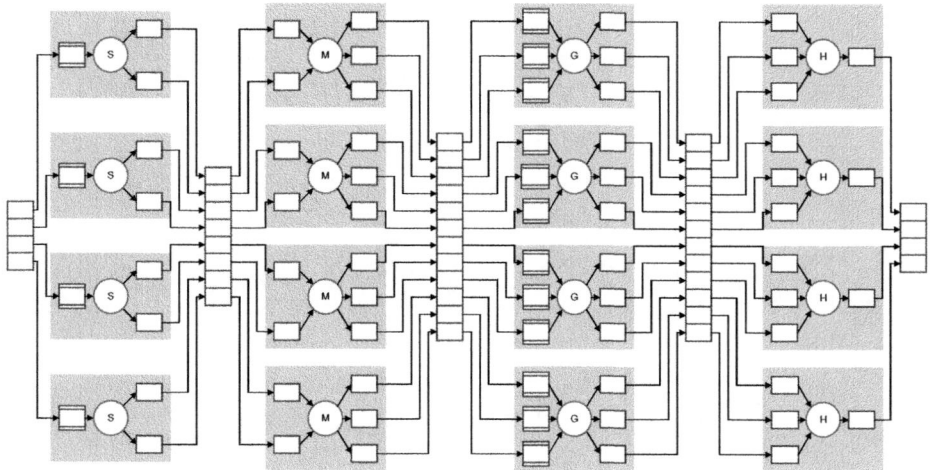

Fig. 7. Conventional SPMD model

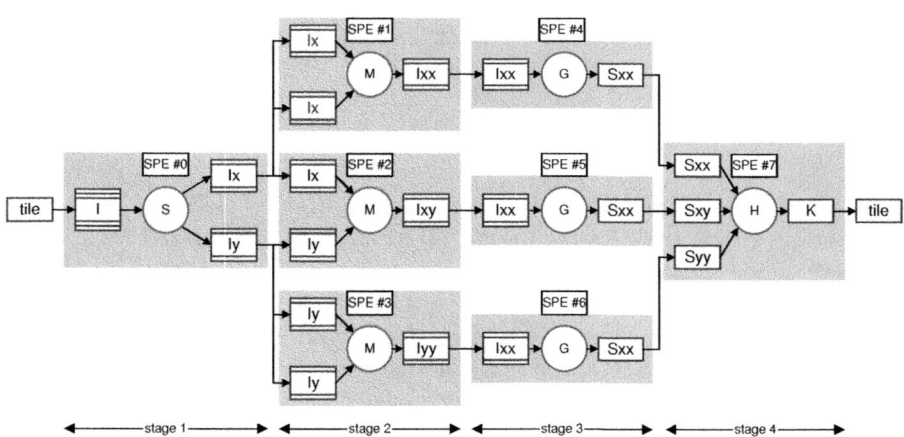

Fig. 8. Conventional pipeline model

performing the Sobel operator and the whole of the image has been transfered
back into the MS.

Conventional Pipeline. This implementation of the algorithm (Fig. 8) consists in mapping the graph in pipeline fashion, where the RoP consists in the
entire image. This way, we considerably serialize the algorithm, and maximize
the amount of transfers between SPEs. Assuming that most of the transfers are
performed serially, the contention rate on the bus is minimized. The transfers in
this version are characterized by top and bottom borders, added for the convolution kernels (neighborhood pixels). Left and right borders where removed by
performing registers rotation.

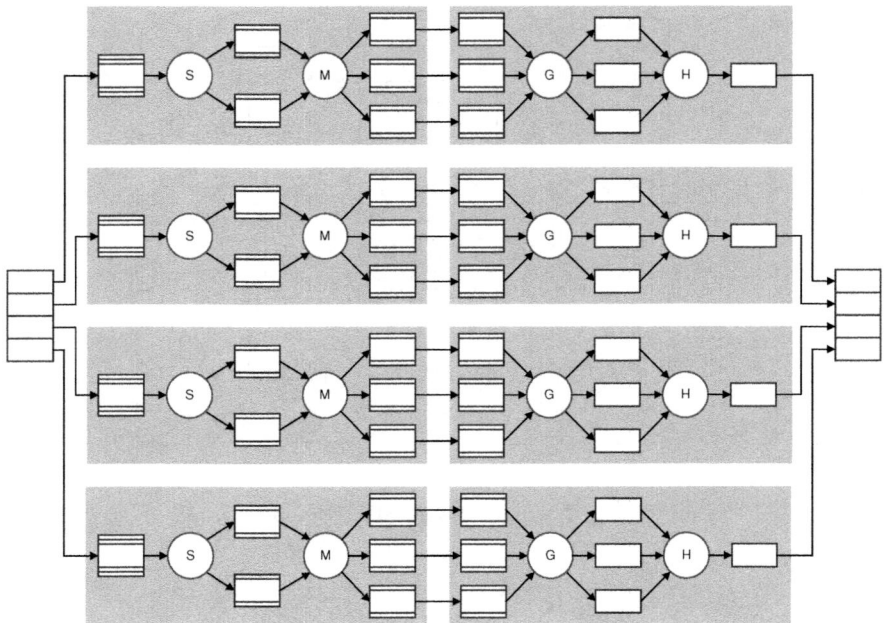

Fig. 9. Half chaining model on 2 SPEs

Half Chaining: 2 SPEs. In this version (Fig. 9), we merge two successive operators in pairs, the Sobel with the Multiplication, and Gauss with Harris. Thus, we divide the graph into two threads, that can be duplicated four times to fill in the entire set of SPEs. Unlike the previous version, and considering that there are four threads running concurrently in each step, the EIB bandwidth can be considerably affected because of the important amount of concurrent transfers.

Half Chaining + Half Pipeline. The difference that we can note here is that in opposition to the previous model, the Sobel and Mul operators are chained in order to avoid the time loss in LOAD and in STORE instructions residing between these two steps. Therefore, the number of cycles per pixel can be considerably improved since we know that the memory instruction latency equals 6 in the SPU [9].

Full Chaining + Half Pipeline: 1 SPE. By chaining all the operators into the same SPE, this implementation not only allows removing LOAD/STORE instructions between operators, but also improves the parallelism rate of the algorithm, since we can split the input image into 8 slices and use one SPU to perform all the operations.

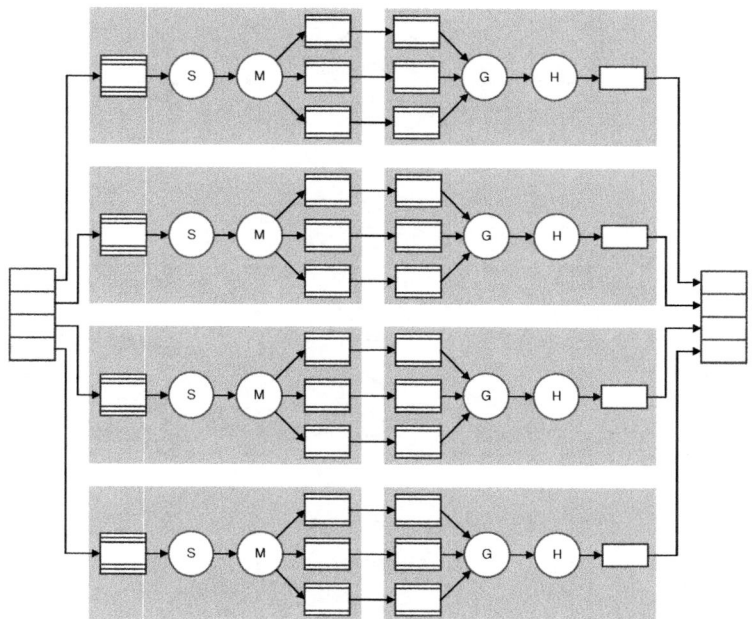

Fig. 10. Half chaining + half pipeline on 2 SPEs

3.4 Models Comparison

Fig. 12 gives the comparison between the different implementation models of the
Harris algorithm on the Cell processor. The first observation that can be made is
that the conventional pipeline version gives the worst performances, which was
expected: this version is deliberately serialized and does not fully exploit the
TLP (Thread Level Parallelism) offered by the target architecture. The other
observations match our expectations:

- Our memory optimization techniques improve global performances as the
  fastest implementation is the *Half pipeline+Full chaining* version where operators are pipelined and chained inside an SPE.
- The versions where inter-SPE transfers are used, have good performances as
  the *No pipeline+Half chaining* model runs faster than the *SPMD* model
  where data transits only on the external memory bus. In addition *Half
  pipeline+Half chaining* is almost as fast as the best version, which proves
  that inter-SPE bandwidth is comparable to local LOAD/STORE bandwidth.

3.5 Tile Size Influence

As stated in [11,10] the size of transfered data blocks has an influence on the
bandwidth on the EIB. In our application domain bandwidth performance is
critical for the overall performance of an algorithm since they are characterized

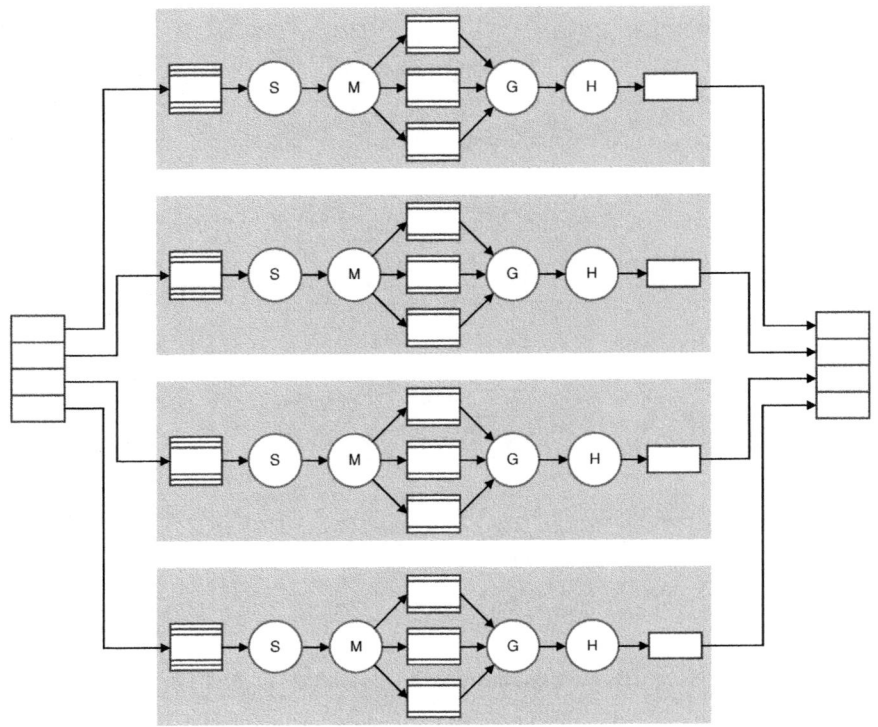

Fig. 11. Half chaining + half pipeline model on 1 SPE

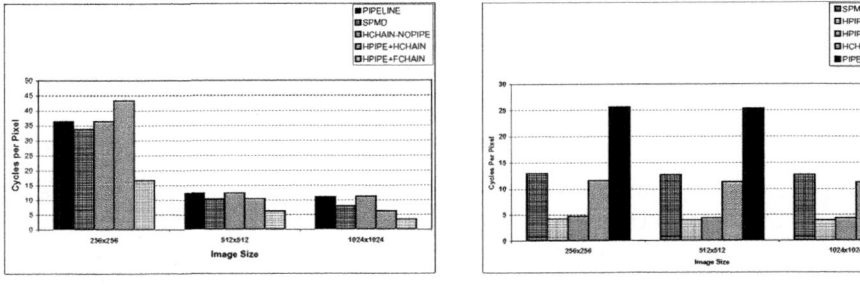

Fig. 12. Comparison benchmark for implementation models: The left figure shows results obtained in [17]

by a large transfer/computation ratio. Fig. 13 states that the best *cpp* is reached when transferring 16 KB tiles which can be explained as follows:

- 16 KB is the transfer size that guarantees a maximum bandwidth on the EIB.
- Big tile size reduces the amount of reloaded data when performing convolution kernels.

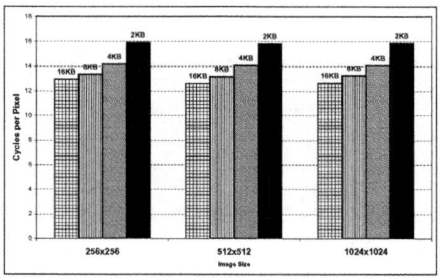 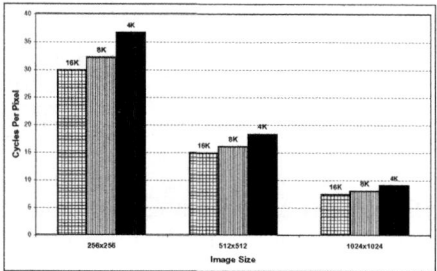

Fig. 13. Influence of transfer size on the performance, full pipeline model 1 SPU : The left figure shows results obtained in [17]

3.6   Performance Analysis

The comparison of global performance of the different implementation models is not sufficient to prove that memory optimizations are the main factor for performance improvement. In order to give a more accurate analysis, we performed time measurements at the SPU level where we evaluated the gain provided by merging computation kernels and performing inter-SPE communication. One can note that the *Conventional Pipeline* and *SPMD* models are not considered because their were implemented just to serve as a reference and can not be compared with the other models as it does not benefit of most of the optimizations techniques that we cited above.

Table 4 shows on the one hand the clock cycle count for the Halfchain version where two kernels are decoupled and an intermediate LOAD/STORE operations are required between them and on the other hand the Halfchain+Halfpipe version where the two kernels are merged (the **o** operator denotes the function composition (merging) operator) and the intermediate LOAD/STORE are removed. As we see in Tab. 4 the speedup provided by this code transformation reaches ×7.2.

The other optimization that we performed which consists in replacing inter-SPE DMA by local LOAD/STORE instructions aims to demonstrate the benefit of keeping data inside the local store as the maximum theoretical bandwidth is 51.6 GB/s for a LOAD/STORE in the LS and 25.6 GB/s for an inter-SPE GET/PUT DMA operation. One can note the the maximum bandwidth for LOAD/STORE in Tab. 5 computed assuming that there is 1 instruction issued each cycle (pipelined execution) for a clock frequency of 3.2 Ghz. The same assumption was made in [10] for the LS bandwidth measurement. On the other hand, we used the

Table 4. Operator fusion comparison

Model	Operator	Cycles Count	Speedup
Halfchain	Sobel+Mul+LOAD/STORE	119346	x
Halfchain	Gauss+Coarsity+LOAD/STORE	188630	x
Halfchain+Halfpipe	(Sobel o Mul)+LOAD/STORE	16539	7.2
Halfchain+Halfpipe	(Gauss o Coarsity)+LOAD/STORE	504309	3.5

Table 5. Average bandwidth comparison between models

Model	Communication Type	Average Bandwidth GB/s
Halfchain	inter-SPE DMA	6.95
Halfchain+Halfpipe	LOAD/STORE	51.6

IBM Performance Debugging Tool (PDT) to measure the average effective DMA bandwidth the result is given in Tab. 5. We observe that there is an order of magnitude between the two transfer rates which explains the difference in global performance between *Halfchain* and *Fullchain* versions. The measurements that we performed give a more precise view of the factors that influence the global performance of the different implementations. Merging computation kernels, reduces the memory complexity by maximizing the reuse of register to perform intermediate computations. However, this optimization should be used with care as there is a limited amount of available register to store intermediate results (128 for the SPU). On the other hand, keeping data in the local store whenever it is possible is a good practice as the LOAD/STORE bandwidth is higher than inter-SPE DMA bandwidth. This last optimization increases data locality and thus global performance but is limited by the available memory space (256 KB for the SPE local store).

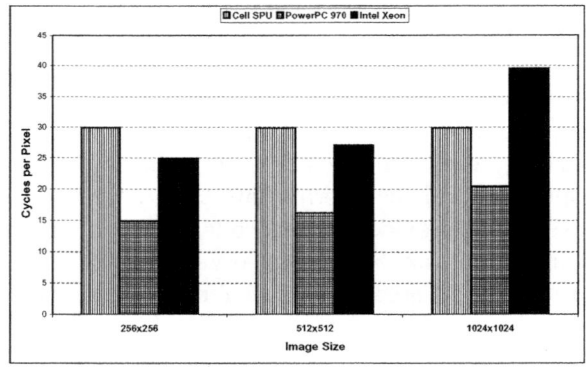

Fig. 14. Performance comparison between SPU, Intel Xeon and PowerPC 970

3.7 Comparison between the SPU and General Purpose Processors (GPP) with SIMD Extensions

Comparing Cell performance with GPP implementation is interesting as the main difference is the memory management DMA versus cache. Fig. 14 provides the *cpp* of Harris half-pipe version running on 1 thread on 1 core on a PowerPC 970 running at 2.5 Ghz and a Core2Duo Xeon 2.5 Ghz at , with Altivec or SSE SIMD instructions. We can note that GPPs become inefficient when data can not fit in the cache for large image size due to cache replacement policy. Besides, this phenomenon does not occur with DMA controlled transfers : the image size has no impact on performance. This last characteristic is very interesting for computer vision systems as the execution time can be predicted accurately and therefore the system can satisfy a real-time constraint.

3.8   Discussion on Benchmarking Methodology

There are several reasons that justify the difference in performance results obtained above and those in [17]:

1. Since we adopted a separated source compilation (one source for the PPU and one for the SPU), we were forced to change the compiler from IBM XLC (ppu-xlc, spu-xlc) to GCC (ppu-gcc, spu-gcc) as in the last release of the Cell SDK (3.0), the XLC compiler became exclusively single-source. This first point can explain the difference in global performance as some compiler optimizations can be performed by XLC and not by GCC and vice versa.
2. The second reason concerns measurement methodology. In the [17] we measured the cycles count in the PPE using the time base counter, with two versions of the code: the first one including computation and the overhead related to thread creation and synchronization and the other one without computation. Then we subtracted the second from the first to get the computation duration. These measures were performed over several runs, and the mean value was taken. However, data presented a great sensitivity to image size. In this paper we took a more representative case were we consider the input data coming from a continuous stream and we make the measure on the PPE with an additional outer loop in the SPEs to process more than one image. This leads to a thread overhead becoming negligible when compared to the pure processing time. As this time was subject to big variation in the [17] we chose this method to attenuate its effect.
3. The last reason is about the computation tiles. In [17], the tile size is fixed to $16K$ and its width w always equals the image width W but its height h varies with W, typically $h = \frac{16K}{w}$. As stated in [1] h has an influence on the amount of reloaded data for a tile (when h increases this amount decreases), we decided to adopt a new measurement methodology where we consider a $16K$ tile with h and and w being constants (in our case $h = 16$ and $w = 256$) in order to eliminate this perturbation. Hence, the *cpp* is less sensitive to image size, which is more coherent as the tile size is a constant whatever the image size is. Table 6 gives the percentages of reloaded data with different couples of (h, w). From these values, we conclude that the amount of reloaded data explains the great sensitivity to image size for the left histograms in Fig. 12 and Fig. 13.

4   Scalability Measure on the Cell Processor

In this section, we evaluate the scalability of the Cell processor by both measuring and modeling *Speedup* and *Efficiency* metrics. The measurements provide

Table 6. Illustration of the difference of the amount of reloaded data depending on the tile height for the Halfpipe+Halfchain model

Image Size $H \times W$	Tile Size $h \times w$	Total Reload Ratio %
256×256	16×256	11
512×512	8×512	20
1024×1024	4×1024	33

informations on how the Cell architecture scales to the Harris algorithms when varying the number of used SPUs. Modeling those metrics allows the prediction of scalability when considering future Cell generations with more accelerator units (SPUs).

Amdahl's Law. In the basic formulation of the Amdahl's law the execution time of any algorithm on a sequential machine is divided into two parts: the time to execute the pure sequential part of the code Seq_0 and the time to execute the part of the code that is parallelizable Par_0. For a machine containing p processors the execution time will have the following expression:

$$T(p) = Seq_0 + \frac{Par_0}{p} \tag{13}$$

Driscoll and Daasch Reformulation. The last formulation is not appropriate to predict performance on the Cell processor. The sequential portion of the code consisting in the cost of the thread creation, communications and synchronization of the threads. These parameters depend on the number of processors, namely they increase when the number of processors increases. The parallel portion of the code is also a function of p. These assumptions was made in [4] by Driscoll et al. We concluded after measurements that :

$$Seq(p) = a_s p + b_s \tag{14}$$

and

$$Par(p) = a_p p + b_p \tag{15}$$

Where a_s, b_s, a_p, b_p are constants that we measured in our experiments. This leads to the following expression of the execution time:

$$T(p) = a_s p + b_s + \frac{a_p p + b_p}{p} = a_s p + b_s + a_p + \frac{b_p}{p} \tag{16}$$

One of the main characteristics of parallel architectures that reflect there performance is their scalability. Scalability metrics show how the system adapt to a certain workload when increasing the number of processing units. *Efficiency* and *Speedup* are one of the basic metrics of scalability, they are defined by the following expressions:

$$E = \frac{T_s}{p T_p} \tag{17}$$

$$S = \frac{T_s}{T_p} \tag{18}$$

Where T_s is the execution time on one processor , p the number of processors and T_p is the execution time on p processors. If we replace T_p and T_s by the expression in Eq. 16 we find the following expression of the efficiency:

$$E = \frac{a_s + b_s + a_p + b_p}{a_s p^2 + (a_s + a_p)p + b_p} \tag{19}$$

This leads to an efficiency decreasing when p increases. The expression of the speedup is of the form :

$$S = \frac{(a_s + b_s + a_p + b_p)p}{a_s p^2 + (a_s + a_p)p + b_p} \tag{20}$$

Which is also a decreasing function of p. One must know that that the expressions above was evaluated when considering one input image for the algorithm.

When processing an image stream which is typically captured by a video camera, we can consider the cost of thread creation and synchronization ($Seq(p)$ in the formulas) negligible comparing to the parallel time (computation). We derive equations 21, 22 and 23 assuming that $Seq(p) = 0$

$$T(p) = \frac{Par(p)}{p} = a_p + \frac{b_p}{p} \tag{21}$$

$$E = \frac{a_p + b_p}{a_p p + b_p} \tag{22}$$

$$S = \frac{(a_p + b_p)p}{a_p p + b_p} \tag{23}$$

These expressions gives a speedup increasing with p until a saturation value of $(1 + \frac{b_p}{a_p})$ and an efficiency decreasing with p but slower than in the previous case. As we observe in Fig. 15 and Fig. 16 the measured scalability metrics matches our model as speedup increases with p and efficiency decreases with p. The measurements were performed with varying the number of used SPUs and the execution time one SPU served as the sequential time T_s ($T(p = 1)$).

From the experiments above we can conclude on how the Cell processor scales to our application which is a data-parallel/memory-bounded problem by making this two assertions:

- The current Cell processor with eight SPUs has a good scalability as the *Speedup* is close to the number of the working SPUs and *Efficiency* is close to 1.
- In the future releases of the Cell where there would be more SPUs, scalability will not be as good as we measured because an increasing number of cores leads to the decrease of *Efficiency* and thus to a saturating *Speedup*.

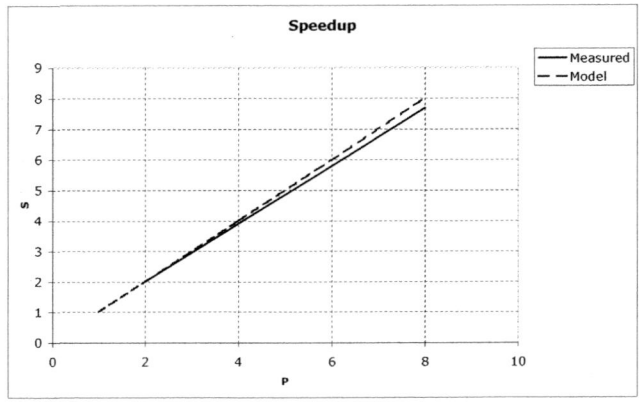

Fig. 15. Speedup measure for a stream of 1000 images of size1024 × 1024

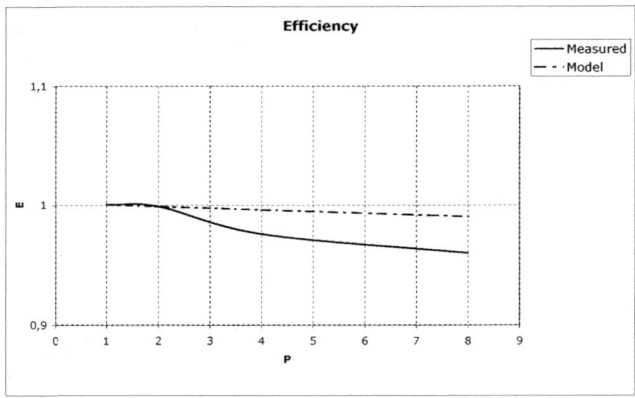

Fig. 16. Efficiency measure for a stream of 1000 images of size1024 × 1024

5   Conclusion and Future Work

In this paper, we investigated how a sample image processing algorithm - the Harris corner detector - can be efficiently implemented while taking into account the various architectural particularities of this processor. We explore, contrary to previous works, other models than the simple SPMD parallelization technique. We explored a variety of parallelization schemes that took advantage of the main architectural features of the Cell: a DMA based, distributed memory. The different optimization techniques, *Domain Specific* or those related to the Cell architectures were analyzed. By combining each step of our algorithm in various manners, we demonstrated that chaining and pipelining operators had a large impact on global performance of the application. Our schemes were benchmarked on the Harris corner detector because it features both point-to-point and convolution operations, making it a realistic sample of more complex image processing library. We also proposed a model of efficiency and scalability for the Cell processor in order to be able to predict performance of future releases of the machine with a greater number of SPEs. Future works includes: a deeper analysis of the relation between tiles shape and size and the overall algorithm performance. Other optimization techniques such as multi-buffering will be explored in the future.

References

1. 12th IEEE Real-Time and Embedded Technology and Applications Symposium (RTAS 2006), April 4-7. IEEE Computer Society, San Jose (2006)
2. Bellens, P., Perez, J.M., Badia, R.M., Labarta, J.: Cellss: a programming model for the cell be architecture. In: Proceedings of the ACM/IEEE Supercomputing Conference (2006)
3. Benthin, C., Wald, I., Scherbaum, M., Friedrich, H.: Ray tracing on the cell processor. In: IEEE Symposium on Interactive Ray Tracing (2006)
4. Driscoll, M.A., Daasch, W.R.: Accurate predictions of parallel program execution time. J. Parallel Distrib. Comput. 25(1), 16–30 (1995)
5. Eichenberger, A.E., O'Brien, J.K., O'Brien, K.M., Wu, P., Chen, T., Oden, P.H., Prener, D.A., Shepherd, J.C., So, B., Sura, Z., Wang, A., Zhang, T., Zhao, P., Gschwind, M.K., Archambault, R., Gao, Y., Koo, R.: Using advanced compiler technology to exploit the performance of the cell broadband engineTM architecture. IBM Syst. J. 45(1), 59–84 (2006)
6. Fatahalian, K., Knight, T.J., Houston, M.: Sequoia: Programming the memory hierarchy. In: Proceedings of the 2006 ACM/IEEE Conference on Supercomputing (2006)
7. Greene, J., Cooper., R.: A parallel 64k complex fft algorithm for the ibm/sony/toshiba cell broadband engine processor. In: Global Signal Processing Expo. (2005)
8. Harris, C., Stephens, M.: A combined corner and edge detector. In: 4th ALVEY Vision Conference (1988)
9. IBM. Cell Broadband Engine Programming Handbook. IBM, version 1.0 edn. (2006)
10. Ramirez, X., Jimenez-Gonzalez, A., Martorell, D.: Performance analysis of cell broadband engine for high memory bandwidth applications. In: Proceedings of the IEEE International Symposium on Performance Analysis of Systems & Software (2007)
11. Kistler, M., Perrone, M., Petrini, F.: Cell multiprocessor communication network: Built for Speed. IEEE Micro 26(3), 10–23 (2006)
12. McCool, M.D.: Data-parallel programming on the cell be and the gpu using the rapidmind development platform. In: GSPx Multicore Applications Conference (2006)
13. Moravec, H.: Obstacle avoidance and navigation in the real world by a seeing robot rover. In tech. report CMU-RI-TR-80-03, Robotics Institute, Carnegie Mellon University & doctoral dissertation, Stanford University (September 1980); Available as Stanford AIM-340, CS-80-813 and republished as a Carnegie Mellon University Robotics Institue Technical Report to increase availability

14. Ohara, M., Inoue, H., Sohda, Y., Komatsu, H., Nakatani, T.: Mpi microtask for programming the cell broadband enginetm processor. IBM Syst. J. 45(1), 85–102 (2006)
15. Petrini, F., Fossum, G., Fernandez, J., Varbanescu, A.L., Kistler, M., Perrone, M.: Multicore surprises: Lessons learned from optimizing sweep3d on the cell broadband engine. In: IEEE/ACM International Parallel and Distributed Processing Symposium (March 2007)
16. Pham, D.C., Aipperspach, T., Boerstler, D., Bolliger, M., Chaudhry, R., Cox, D., Harvey, P., Harvey, P.M., Hofstee, H.P., Johns, C., Kahle, J., Kameyama, A., Keaty, J., Masubuchi, Y., Pham, M., Pille, J., Posluszny, S., Riley, M., Stasiak, D.L., Suzuoki, M., Takahashi, O., Warnock, J., Weitzel, S., Wendel, D., Yazawa, K.: Overview of the architecture, circuit design, and physical implementation of a first-generation cell processor. IEEE Journal of Solid-State Circuits 41(1), 179–196 (2006)
17. Saidani, T., Piskorski, S., Lacassagne, L., Bouaziz, S.: Parallelization schemes for memory optimization on the cell processor: a case study of image processing algorithm. In: MEDEA 2007: Proceedings of the 2007 Workshop on MEmory Performance, pp. 9–16. ACM, New York (2007)
18. Servat, H., González-Alvarez, C., Aguilar, X., Cabrera-Benitez, D., Jiménez-González, D.: Drug design issues on the cell BE. In: Stenström, P., Dubois, M., Katevenis, M., Gupta, R., Ungerer, T. (eds.) HiPEAC 2007. LNCS, vol. 4917, pp. 176–190. Springer, Heidelberg (2008)
19. Vandierendonck, H., Rul, S., Questier, M., De Bosschere, K.: Experiences with parallelizing a bio-informatics program on the cell BE. In: Stenström, P., Dubois, M., Katevenis, M., Gupta, R., Ungerer, T. (eds.) HiPEAC 2007. LNCS, vol. 4917, pp. 161–175. Springer, Heidelberg (2008)
20. Williams, S., Shalf, J., Oliker, L., Kamil, S., Husbands, P., Yelick, K.: Scientific computing kernels on the cell processor. Int. J. Parallel Program. 35(3), 263–298 (2007)

Constructing Application-Specific Memory Hierarchies on FPGAs

Harald Devos[1], Jan Van Campenhout[1],
Ingrid Verbauwhede[2], and Dirk Stroobandt[1]

[1] Parallel Information Systems, ELIS-Dept., Ghent University,
Sint-Pietersnieuwstraat 41, B-9000 Gent, Belgium
{harald.devos,jan.vancampenhout,dirk.stroobandt}@elis.UGent.be
[2] Katholieke Universiteit Leuven, ESAT
Kasteelpark Arenberg 10, B-3001 Leuven-Heverlee, Belgium
Ingrid.Verbauwhede@esat.kuleuven.be

Abstract. The high performance potential of an FPGA is not fully exploited if a design suffers a memory bottleneck. Therefore, a memory hierarchy is needed to reuse data in on-chip buffer memories and minimize the number of accesses to off-chip memory. Buffer memories not only hide the external memory latency, but can also be used to remap data and augment the on-chip bandwidth through parallel access of multiple buffers. This paper discusses the differences and similarities of memory hierarchies on processor- and on FPGA-based systems and presents a step-by-step methodology to construct a memory hierarchy on an FPGA.

1 Introduction

FPGAs (Field Programmable Gate Arrays) offer a high computational power thanks to the massive parallelism available and the huge on-chip bandwidth. However, the total on-chip memory size is fairly small. Usually an off-chip memory is needed. The bandwidth to this external memory may become a bottleneck, especially for data-intensive applications, such as video coding and image processing. Typically, this memory is made in a technology, e.g., SDRAM, with an indeterministic latency and with a low bandwidth if transfers are not done in burst mode. This indeterministic latency may also be caused by the fact that the main memory is shared with other cores on the FPGA. To reduce the bandwidth requirements a memory hierarchy is needed. If frequently used data is stored in on-chip buffers, the off-chip memory accesses can be reduced and grouped into bursts.

Using multiple parallel accessible memory banks (Fig. 1(a)) increases the available off-chip memory bandwidth. On the other hand, using multiple on-chip buffers increases the on-chip memory bandwidth (Fig. 1(b)). If the reuse of buffered data is high enough, i.e. the transfers between external memory and on-chip buffers are within the bandwidth constraints, the latter solution is better since the accesses to on-chip memory are faster and more power efficient. If

P. Stenström (Ed.): Transactions on HiPEAC III, LNCS 6590, pp. 201–216, 2011.

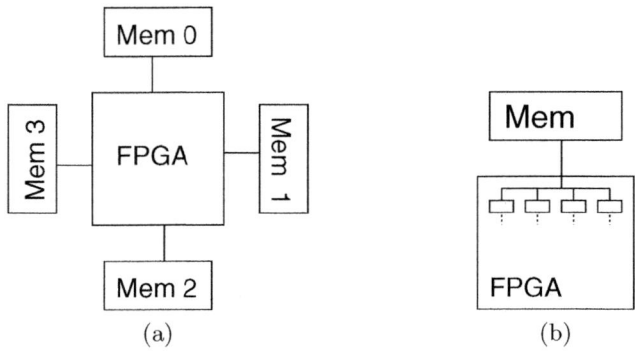

Fig. 1. Multiple memory banks (a). Single memory bank with multiple on-chip buffer memories (b).

the use of multiple external memory banks is unavoidable, a memory hierarchy for each bank should be considered and the memory access patterns should be optimized to use these hierarchies.

In processor-based systems a memory hierarchy consists of caches or scratch-pad memories [1]. This is a fixed memory hierarchy and the application code has to be optimized to optimally use this given memory structure, e.g., by doing loop transformations to increase the data locality, i.e. to bring accesses to the same or neighboring data elements closer together in time [2,3]. On an FPGA the designer has to construct the memory hierarchy using the available memory blocks. This offers the freedom to build an application-specific memory hierarchy, i.e. to also adjust the memory system to the application and not only the application to the memory hierarchy. An in-depth comparison between memory systems on processors and on FPGAs is presented in Sect. 2.

This paper does not focus on ways to improve the locality of data accesses or map data to memories. Instead, we focus on hardware implementation aspects of building a memory hierarchy and the impact of choices made by the way data is mapped onto buffers. The influence of address expressions on circuit complexity is studied in Sect. 3, which offers many optimization opportunities.

A step-by-step methodology is given to insert a memory hierarchy into a system (Sect. 4). As a case study an implementation of an Inverse Discrete Wavelet Transform (IDWT) will be extended with a memory hierarchy and integrated in a video decoder on an FPGA (Sect. 5).

2   Comparison of Memory Systems on Processors and on FPGAs

The target of using memory hierarchies is the same for processors and for ar-chitectures built on FPGAs: storing frequently used data in buffer memories close to the functional units to minimize the data access times. In both cases

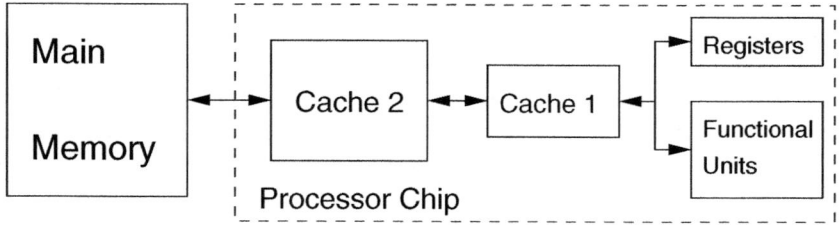

Fig. 2. Memory hierarchy on a typical processor

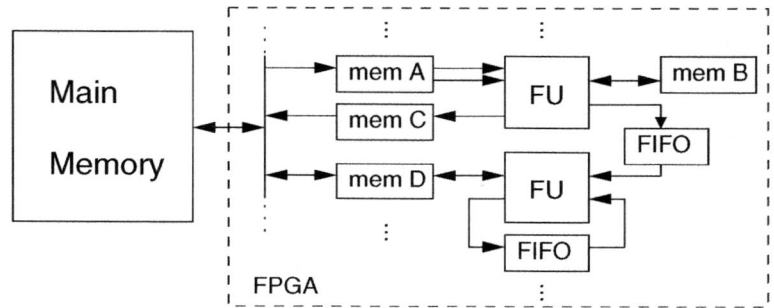

Fig. 3. Example memory hierarchy on an FPGA (FU = Functional Unit)

the application should be adjusted to benefit from such a memory system using techniques such as register promotion [4] or loop transformations [2,3] to improve the temporal and spatial locality. However, there are many differences caused by implementation aspects.

Processors have a fixed memory hierarchy consisting of a main memory, caches at several levels and one or more register files (Fig. 2). The sizes of all the memories are fixed and applications need to be adjusted to fit these sizes. Caches typically have a replacement policy so programmers should not care about explicit control of transfers between main memory and caches. A disadvantage is that the choice of data that is overwritten by newly fetched data is not always optimal for the given application. Scratch-pad memories may offer a better solution when the data accesses are known at compile time [1,5]. Prefetching [6] of data may hide external access times by overlapping them with computations. In cache-based systems a hash function is typically applied to the addresses which may cause irregular problem size / performance characteristics caused by (e.g. 64K) aliasing [7].

FPGAs have no standard memory hierarchy. They contain lots of memory blocks which have to be combined to build a custom memory system (e.g. Fig. 3). There are many similarities with scratch-pad memory based systems: user-defined explicit data transfers, burst transfers (cf. prefetch) between (external and internal) memories in parallel with computations, ...

However, there are also lots of differences: processors typically have a *vertical* memory hierarchy while on an FPGA the memory system can be made more *horizontally*, i.e. placing several memories next to each other on a certain level such that they can be accessed in parallel by the functional units. FIFOs and local memories may be used, next to registers, to store intermediate results of functional units and pass data between them. As such there is a tremendous on-chip bandwidth. If the intermediate data sets are too large, part of it has to be stored off-chip, passing through I/O buffers which aid in grouping the memory transfers into bursts.

Due to the limited size of memory blocks on FPGAs, larger buffer memories are constructed by combining multiple memory blocks (Fig. 4(a)). These memory blocks can also be accessed independently. This allows parallel accesses to the buffers which may reduce the execution time (number of clock cycles) (Fig. 4(b)). The usage of dual-port memories allows to transfer data between the main memory and the buffers in parallel with the operation of the functional unit, and to use different clock domains for both tasks. Also the fact that dual-port memories can have different word sizes at both ports can be exploited.

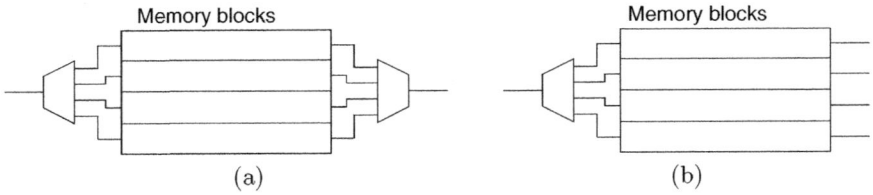

Fig. 4. Multiple memory blocks combined with (de)multiplexers to form larger buffers (a) can be accessed in parallel (b)

We can conclude that because of the similarities with scratch-pad based systems many of the optimizing transformations developed for processor-based systems also have to be applied for FPGA-based systems. For example, in the work of Hu et al. [3] the data sets used in each loop of a loop nest are determined and a data reuse analysis leads to the construction of a data reuse tree. Nodes of this tree representing data subsets (copy candidates) are then mapped to the scratch-pad memory according to the size constraints. This method could be extended to application-specific memory systems where different copy candidates may, e.g., be mapped to different memories with sizes fit to the size of the copy candidate (of course within resource constraints).

The additional benefits of custom-built memory systems need additional optimization techniques. Next to this, automation of the construction of a memory system is needed. A methodology for the construction of a memory hierarchy will be presented in Sect. 4.

Table 1. Influence of address expressions on circuit complexity for the Sobel Edge Detection on an Altera Stratix EP1S25F1020C5. LE = number of Logic elements, DSP = number of DSP blocks (9-bit equivalent), Mem bits = size of on-chip memory. Cycles and execution time (T) for an image of 320×320 pixels. A one cycle access time to external memory is assumed.

	Design	Address	LE	DSP	Mem bits	f(MHz)	Cycles	T(ms)
	1	C = port	766	7	0	76.52	915873	11.97
	2	C' = 512	675	0	0	112.45	915873	8.14
BA_c	3	C = port	733	0	0	114.27	916193	8.02
	4	C' = 512	668	0	0	112.64	916193	8.13
FIFOs	5	C = port	737	6	8192	87.46	714261	8.17
	6	C' = 512	636	0	8192	124.08	714261	5.76
FIFOs	7	C = port	701	0	8192	116.62	714580	6.13
BA_c	8	C' = 512	622	0	8192	113.66	714580	6.29

3   Influence of Address Complexity on Circuit Complexity

The way memory addresses are computed has an influence on the circuit complexity of an implementation. Consider for example an image processing system that reads a 2-dimensional array A. The typical way to store this array leads to address expressions with a multiplication:

$$\text{Address}\,(A(i,j)) = BA + i \times C + j \;,$$

with BA the base address and C the number of columns. If C is not a power of 2 or C is a parameter, which only receives a value during execution, this is an expensive operation. Without loss of generality we will further assume that $BA = 0$ (Fig. 5(a)).

A straight-forward simplification is to align all lines to a multiple of a power of 2. This is shown in Fig. 5(b), where C' is the smallest power of 2 for which $C' \geq C$, if C is known, or $C' \geq C_{\max}$ if C is a parameter with $C_{\max}$ as the maximal possible value. This leads to an increase of the memory size with a factor

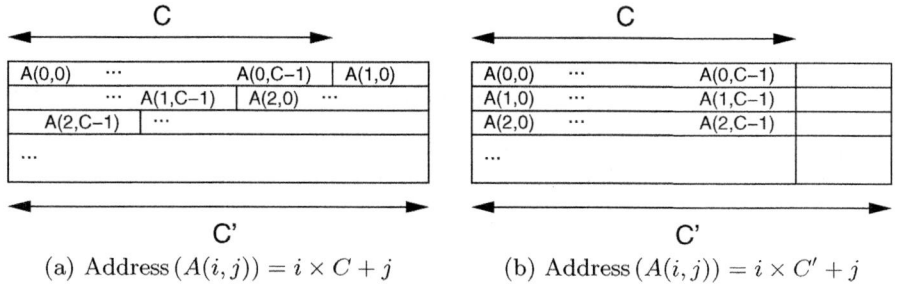

(a) Address $(A(i,j)) = i \times C + j$ (b) Address $(A(i,j)) = i \times C' + j$

Fig. 5. By inserting empty space into the memory, address expressions can be simplified

C'/C but simplifies the address calculation complexity.[1] Quantitative figures for an implementation of the Sobel Edge Detection algorithm can be found in Table 1. Since here the goal of the experiments is to study the influence of address expressions, no buffer memories are inserted yet and a one cycle access time to memory is assumed (as if the memory was on-chip). In design 1, DSP blocks are utilized to implement the multiplication which is eliminated by using C' in design 2.

If an image is processed row by row (with some reuses of the lines above and below) the expensive multiplication can also be eliminated by incrementing the row base address with the number of columns at each row iteration:

$$\text{Address}\,(A(i,j)) = \text{Address}\,(A(i_c + i_{os}, j)) = BA_c + i_{os} \times C + j \ ,$$

where i_c is the iterator pointing to the current row, and BA_c is the address of the first element of this row $(BA_c = i_c \times C)$. Since BA_c is augmented with C every row iteration, no multiplication is needed. i_{os} is a small constant used to access the surrounding rows. In the example of the Sobel Edge Detection $i_{os} \in \{-1, 0, 1\}$ which does also not need a multiplier. As in the previous paragraph C may be replaced with C'. The corresponding designs are found in Table 1, designs 3 and 4. Note that the designs using incremental address calculation (3 and 4) are faster than those not using it (1 and 2). However, this is not always the case. The designs 5–8 are similar to 1–4, but use two FIFO buffers to store the two previously accessed image rows. This reduces the number of external memory accesses with a factor 3 and changes the influence of the address computations. Now, the fastest design (6) does not use incremental address calculation.

Accesses to on-chip memory have to be fast since they limit the speed of the functional unit. Therefore, the address expressions for these accesses have to be kept simple. Address calculations for off-chip memory accesses can be spread over several clock cycles, since only one evaluation is needed for an entire burst transfer. The methods discussed above to simplify addresses for off-chip memory are also applicable for on-chip memory. Since until now we assumed a one-cycle access time as if on-chip memory was used, we expect similar performance improvements for on-chip address calculation. A difference is that multiple addresses off-chip will be mapped to the same buffer memory location.

Only a few lines can be stored in a buffer. If this number of lines R' is also set to a power of 2 and the mapping of lines of the image to lines of the buffer is done in a circular way the address becomes

$$\begin{aligned}\text{Address}\,(A(i,j)) &= (i \bmod R') \times C' + j \\ &= i(r - 1 \text{ downto } 0) \ \& \ j \ , \quad \text{with } R' = 2^r \ . \end{aligned} \quad (1)$$

As a result, only the least significant bits of i have to be generated. Note that the addition is in fact only a concatenation, denoted with "$\&$".

Using C' instead of C now sacrifices on-chip memory. In the introduction, the limited amount of on-chip memory was mentioned as the motivation for

---

[1] Note that when C is only known at execution time and $C_{\max}$ is a power of two (as is often the case) no extra memory is needed.

using buffer memories, At first sight sacrificing memory does not seem a good option. However, the scale differs with an order of magnitude. For a typical image processing application an entire image does not fit into the memory. The largest subset of an image that is worth storing on-chip is in the order of a few lines (e.g., corresponding to the data reuses of a sliding window operation), which can be stored easily in the FPGA RAM blocks. This leaves room to sacrifice some memory space as long as the reuse set (these few lines) can be stored. Saving memory to store more lines has little advantage[2] since the larger reuse set, i.e. one image, will never fit on chip.

These methods differ from the address optimization techniques used when targeting processor-based systems (cf. Sect. 6). For processors, modulo operations have to be avoided to save instruction cycles. On FPGAs modulo operations by powers of two reduce the area and increase the maximal clock speed, which cannot be altered on processors.

4   Step-by-Step Construction of a Memory Hierarchy

Many high-level synthesis tools generate one memory for each array in the input code. Also when building a design manually, it is easier to start the design process with multiple memories and only construct a memory hierarchy with one main memory later on. Therefore, we present a step-by-step design flow to transform a system with multiple memory banks, similar to the systems in Fig. 1(a) and 7(a), to a system with one external memory and on-chip buffers, similar to the systems in Fig. 1(b) and 7(c). Here, an overview of the flow is given. A detailed elaboration is found in the case study in Sect. 5.

1. On-chip memories are added to contain intermediate data sets that are small enough to fit in them. This includes techniques such as register promotion. If results produced by one operation are consumed by another operation in the same order, FIFO buffers can be used.
2. The address expressions are optimized as described in Sect. 3. At this point synthesis is faster than after the entire memory system is constructed. Now, all addresses point to external memory but later on most of them will access on-chip buffers.
3. Buffers are inserted between each external memory and the functional unit. The size is kept as large as the external memory itself so that no remapping of data and changes in address expressions are needed. In a later step the buffers will be reduced to actually fit on chip. A single copy transaction (for each memory/buffer pair) of all data to the buffer at the start of execution and a single transfer to the *external* memory at the end suffices for correct behavior. Separate I/O modules take care of these copy transactions. In the next step the transfers will be partitioned into smaller steps.

---

[2] Having the capacity to buffer more lines may be used, e.g., to enlarge the burst transfers or tolerate greater variance in the transactions to the external memory.

4. The two large copy operations are split into smaller prefetch and store operations, such that at each moment only a small amount of data in the buffers
   is alive (= transferred and still needed). Synchronization between the data
   transfers and the operation of the functional unit ensures correct behavior.
   For this the technique of Hu et al. [3] to extract copy candidates can be used.
5. The data in the buffers is remapped such that the buffers can be resized and
   fit in on-chip memories. A *hash function* (cf. caches) translates the indices
   of the arrays into the new address expressions. The I/O modules take care
   of translations between on- and off-chip addresses, similar to the *direct* and
   strided mapping supported by the Impulse memory controller [8].
6. If desired, buffer memories may be split into smaller memories to allow parallel access (Fig. 4) and reduce the clock cycle count.
7. The external memories are merged to form one main memory. Base addresses
   are added to the addresses used in the prefetch and store transfers. The I/O
   modules are all connected to the same memory. Arbitration between the
   transfers is needed to avoid conflicts.

By doing the transformations in small steps, errors can be detected more easily
and faster, since simulation is possible at any time. To increase the reusability, a
modular architecture is used. When transferring the design to another platform
only the I/O modules have to be adapted. By using hash functions instead of
simply adapting the address expressions, the data mappings can be changed in
an easier way, e.g., when a device upgrade offers the option to use more on-chip
memory. This does not result in an area overhead since bits not used by the hash
function will be optimized away by the synthesis tools (cf. (1)).

5 Case Study: System Integration of an IDWT

The 2-D Discrete Wavelet Transform (DWT) and its inverse (IDWT) are commonly used in image processing and compression applications, e.g., JPEG-2000.
They contain operations commonly used in many other image processing applications, such as sliding window operations (2-D FIR filter), up- and downsampling,

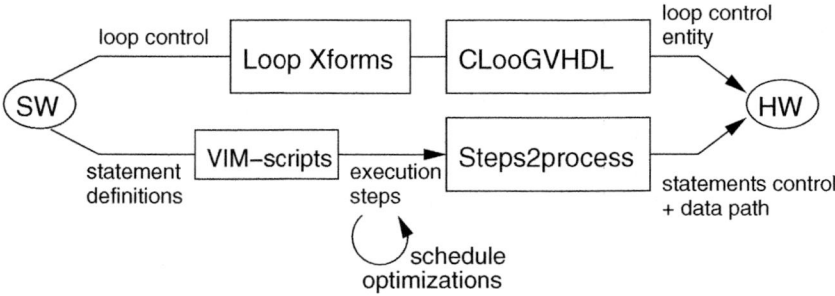

Fig. 6. Tool flow used to generate the IDWT implementation

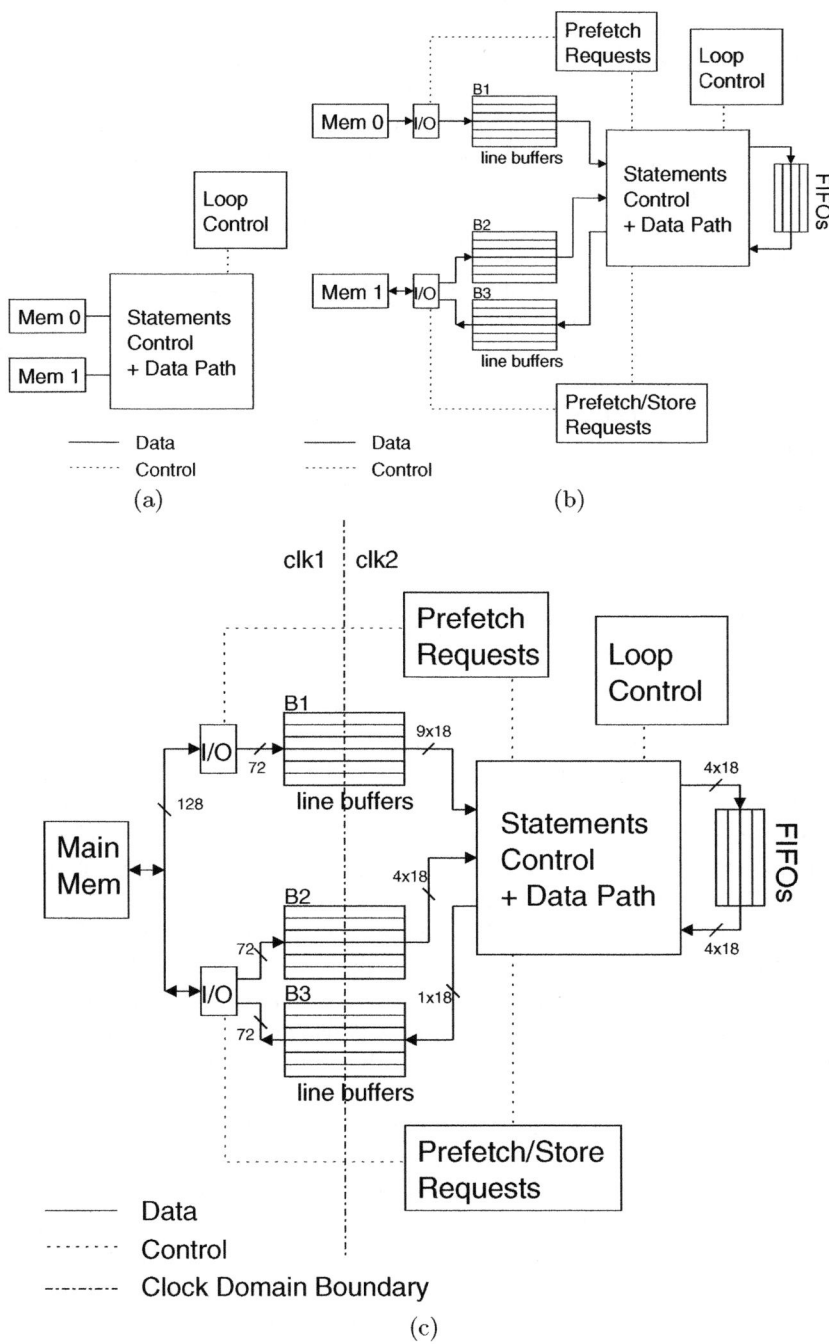

Fig. 7. Line-Based IDWT without memory hierarchy (a), after adding buffers (b), and after full system integration (c)

mirroring at the borders, ... Therefore, results similar to those reported in this section are expected for many other image processing applications.

We will start from a design without memory hierarchy, but with a data locality optimized by loop transformations. It has been semi-automatically generated using the design flow shown in Fig. 6 as described in [9] and summarized in this paragraph. A software implementation in C is split into statement definitions and the loop control structure. Loop transformations are applied on the latter using the URUK/WRaP-IT tool suite [10] to improve the spatial locality, resulting in a so-called line-based variant. With CLooGVHDL a loop control entity is generated. The statement definitions are translated to a VHDL syntax using VIM-scripts [11].[3] The scripts translate array accesses into memory accesses with a one-cycle access time. The result is a list of execution steps for each statement. On this, schedule optimizations are done (also integrated into the scripts). The *Steps2process* tool generates a finite state machine to execute the statements based on the schedule specifications. The architecture of the generated design is shown in Fig. 7(a) and synthesis results are found in Table 2.

The fact that software code equivalent to the hardware is available can be exploited for the construction of a memory hierarchy as shown below.

5.1   Adding New Hardware Structures

The design tools mentioned above will be reused for the extension of the architecture with a memory system. New hardware constructs are inserted one after another, iterating over the following steps:

First, C preprocessor macros that simulate the behavior of the new construct are written. For example, a *push* and a *pop* macro to write to and read from a FIFO buffer. In C this is simulated by accessing an array and incrementing a counter. A VHDL block that corresponds with the new type of construct is written. Procedures or functions that correspond to the functionality of the C macros are written. For a FIFO this is the instantiation of FIFO entities and writing the VHDL procedures *push_fifo* and *pop_fifo* that access such a structure. Next, the VIM-scripts are extended to replace the C macros with the corresponding VHDL procedure or function calls. This work only has to be done for the first FIFO (or other new kind of block). Additional FIFOs reuse these constructs.

After the equivalence of the C and VHDL constructs and the mapping from the first to the second are tested, the new C macro can be used in all C code, where desired. Finally, the generated VHDL is tested and the impact of the new hardware structure may be examined after synthesis. Where possible optimizations are done. For example, removing unused data structures or doing schedule optimizations. After the introduction of the FIFOs more data elements can be accessed in parallel, which allows to shorten the schedules. These optimizations can be included in the scripts.

---

[3] This is only a temporary solution. Plans are to integrate a C parser. This is only an implementation issue and does not influence the methodology.

This approach is similar to the way many high-level synthesis tools work. They extend C with macros that correspond to predefined hardware structures. Here, the difference is that new macros, not predefined by such tools, such as queues for prefetch requests, can be added and used with little effort.

5.2 Inserting Buffers

The extension of the design from Fig. 7(a) to (b) is done step-by-step following steps 1 through 6 listed in Sect. 4. For each new type of construct a flow as described in Sect. 5.1 is used.

1. Four FIFO buffers are inserted to transfer data from the vertical to the horizontal wavelet transformation. This halves the accesses to the *main* memories Mem 0 and Mem 1. Since the FIFO buffers can be accessed in parallel with the external memories the execution time is decreased (Table 2).
2. Since the dimensions of the input image are run-time parameters and $C_{\mathrm{max}} = 512$ we align al image lines to a multiple of 512. By using a function call for the address calculation the address expression can easily be modified afterwards.
3. Mem 0 is only used for input values so applying step 3 of our methodology is straight-forward, i.e., one copy transaction at the start of execution to a buffer as large as Mem 0. Mem 1 is used for intermediate results. It passes the result of one level of the wavelet transform to the next. Therefore, copy operations are needed at the beginning and end of the execution of each wavelet transformation level.
4. The copy operations are split into transactions of one line of an image or wavelet sub-band. A block transfer system copies data from the main memories to and from the buffers. A queue of prefetch and store requests is kept in the Prefetch(/Store) Requests entities. A new fetch request is added a few row iterations before the data is needed. Synchronization points are used to ensure that when a line in one of the buffers is accessed, all transfers between that line and the main memory are finished. Therefore, if the system is not bandwidth limited, only in the beginning time is spent waiting for data. A block transfer is specified by the source and target address and the amount of data to be copied.
5. The buffers with sizes equal to the original memories are reduced to the line buffers B1(16 lines), B2(8 lines) and B3(8 lines). The address expressions referring to the buffer memories are extended with modulo expressions.
6. The line buffers B1 and B2 are split into parallel accessible buffers of one line to increase the on-chip bandwidth (cf. Fig. 4). This results in a large reduction in the number of clock cycles as shown in Table 2. The design in Fig. 7(b) is reached.

For the Stratix S60 the clock speed is increased after adding the memory hierarchy, thanks to the simplification of the address expressions. The clock speed on the S25 is lowered due to congestion in the FPGA routing (area usage of almost 70%) but would be even worse without the address simplifications.

Table 2. Synthesis results of the IDWT with and without memory hierarchy. CIF resolution = 352 × 288 pixels. LE = Logic Elements. Results obtained with Altera QuartusII v6.1 for the Altera Stratix EP1S25F1020C5 (S25C5) and EP1S60F1020C6 (S60C6, lower speed grade). The number of cycles and frame rate assume a one cycle ($1/f_{max}$) access time to the main memories. With an SDRAM, this would be the performance when a cache running at f_{max} is used and no misses occur (i.e. the latency to the SDRAM is hidden, e.g., by prefetching). As a result this gives no measure of the performance improvement created by hiding the memory latency or reducing the number of off-chip accesses, but only of the improvement caused by the parallelism introduced by the memory system.

Archi-tecture	LE	Buf Mem (bit)	DSP bl. (#Mul)	Cycles (88 × 72)	f_{max} (MHz) S25C5	f_{max} (MHz) S60C6	Frames/s (CIF) S25C5	Frames/s (CIF) S60C6
Fig. 7(a)	10836	0	18 (9)	161037	50.12	43.40	19.71	17.07
"+FIFOs	10881	18432	18 (9)	148941	51.81	46.68	22.03	19.85
Fig. 7(b)	17350	297504	18 (9)	59240	47.22	45.60	50.50	48.77

5.3 Further Integration

Further integration work is needed to put the design on an Altera PCI Development Board with a Stratix EP1S60F1020C6 FPGA and 256 MiB of DDR SDRAM memory (from Fig. 7(b) to (c)).

The content of the two main memories is mapped onto the single DDR SDRAM memory (step 7). An Avalon switch fabric [12] connects the DDR core (memory controller) with the I/O blocks. These blocks take care of the conversion of local addresses, used within the IDWT, to addresses in the *global* memory space. Since the 18 bit word width, used until now, does not correspond to the 128 bit data ports of the DDR controller, the word size at the left side of the line buffers is set to $4 \times 18 = 72$ bit and converted to and from $4 \times 32 = 128$ bit using sign extension and truncation.

The Avalon fabric only supports burst transfers that are a multiple of 16 B (128 bit) long and start at an address that is a multiple of 16 B. Therefore, the lines in all wavelet sub-bands are aligned to a multiple of 128 bit in the main memory by letting each row start at a multiple of 512 pixels (1 pixel = 4B). This inserts more unused space than strictly needed, but memory space was not a problem in the DDR-memory and it simplifies address calculations, similar to the example in Fig. 5. A DMA controller (Direct Memory Access) drives the burst transfers [12].

To allow the memory controller and the wavelet transform to run at their maximal frequency, different clock domains are introduced. The dual-port memories offer a safe clock domain crossing for the data. For the control signals extra registers are inserted (brute-force synchronization).

Finally, other blocks are connected to the switch fabric to build the RESUME scalable wavelet-based video decoder described in [13]. It can decode

26.15 frames/s (clocking the DDR at 65 MHz, limited by the FPGA synthesis process). The IDWT on its own, clocked at 54 MHz (reached with other tool settings than for Table 2), can transform 53 frames/s.

Power and energy dissipation figures of the IDWT implementation described above and a fully manual design without locality optimizations are found in [14]. The reduction of off-chip memory accesses leads to a large reduction of the dissipated energy which compensates the increased on-chip dissipation due to the larger amount of logic (total energy saving of a factor 2.2).

The final circuit has become much larger than the original one (Table 2). A large part of this circuitry is used for multiplexers connecting the parallel buffers of one line with the parallel computational units. In fact these lines are accessed in a circular way and this could in principle be implemented using FIFOs, as was done for the Sobel Edge Detection (Table 1, designs 5–8). This would remove the multiplexers and many address calculations. In fact these FIFOs should have been introduced in step 1. The reason that this has not been done is because of the fact that there is an irregular behavior at the borders of each image or wavelet sub-band. There, mirroring is used to virtually extend the domain outside the borders which introduces an irregular memory access pattern. This hinders the use of FIFOs. The original program can be adapted to allow the use of FIFOs at these locations but this falls outside the scope of this paper and is left as future work.

6 Related Work

6.1 Address Expressions

A good data locality is needed to reuse data stored on-chip as much as possible. As mentioned above, loop transformations can improve this locality [15,2,3].

A side effect of loop transformations is that address expressions may become complex. Therefore, address optimization techniques have been developed. Many exploit the repetitive evaluation of these expressions in a loop and use differences of the terms of an expression to calculate the next value, similar to the usage of BA_c in Sect. 3 (Method of Difference). Sheldon et al. [16] present techniques to eliminate division and modulo operations, by inserting conditionals and using algebraic axioms and loop transformations. Most techniques optimize the evaluation of a given set of address expressions, possibly sharing logic among different address expressions [17]. Only a few remap data to simplify the address expressions [18,8]. Most methods are useful for both software and hardware implementations. A difference is that multiplications or modulo reductions with powers of 2 require shift operations on a processor but have no cost on an FPGA. Zissulescu et al. [19] focus on the generation of fast address calculation circuitry for FPGAs. They use number theory axioms and the method of difference to reduce the strength of the expressions but do not remap data to simplify them.

6.2 High-Level Synthesis Tools

In recent years many high-level synthesis (HLS) tools have been developed. Many of them extend a software programming language such as C with pragmas and macros to describe parallelism and the use of library constructs such as FIFOs.

Synfora PICO [20] does register promotion and tiling, but in order to further optimize the memory system the user has to insert FIFO constructs and pragmas to declare local memory.

NEC CyberWorkBench [21] has a user directive to specify if a 2-D array will be implemented with minimal size or with rows aligned to a power of two (cf. Sect. 3). The choice between the two is not made automatically.

Since sliding window operations are often used in image processing applications, several HLS tools focus on extracting such operations and mapping them on predefined architecture templates, e.g, SA-C [22] and ROCCC [23].

The Compaan/LAURA system converts an application into a Kahn-process network by automatically inserting FIFO buffers [24]. This could be used in the first step of our methodology. When a data set is not consumed in the order it is produced, reorder buffers are introduced. In the worst case these buffers may become too large to fit on chip. Loop transformations may be needed to avoid this.

A more extensive comparison of high-level synthesis tools with a focus on memory systems is found in Chapter 2 of [25].

We conclude that current HLS tools leave the design of the memory system to the designer but ease the construction of it by providing constructs to describe them at a higher level, or use predefined solutions for specific frequently used structures.

A common problem with HLS tools is the integration with user-built structures. This is done through communication by predefined (bus-)protocols which do not allow a tight integration or else the interaction should be described at a low level which removes the advantage of using HLS languages. An ideal high-level synthesis tool should offer tight integration with user-built blocks by allowing to extend the set of macros or pragmas such that references to custom blocks can be recognized and dealt with on a footing of equality with the library blocks provided by the tools. This was the reason of using VIM-scripts. They allow to extend the set of macros to tightly integrate new blocks, such as the prefetch queue. The disadvantage was that some extra work is needed which we will try to eliminate by extending our tool suite.

7 Conclusions and Future Work

Application-specific memory hierarchies offer advantages that general purpose cache systems or scratch-pad memories do not offer, such as simplification of address calculation hardware and the increase of parallelism through buffer partitioning.

This paper presented a methodology to transform a system using multiple memories step-by-step into a system with a memory hierarchy connected to an external memory with unpredictable access times. Using a modular design description increases the reusability. With a good choice of data mapping in the buffers, addresses can be simplified to optimize the performance, possibly at the cost of a higher memory usage.

For many of the code transformation steps that were done partially manually, techniques to fully automate them are already available. Future work consists of integrating them and extend them where needed in the context of FPGA-based design. Better synthesis results are expected if the original code is transformed towards the targeted memory system, e.g., to increase the number of FIFO buffers.

Acknowledgements

This research is supported by the I.W.T. grant 060068 and the F.W.O. grant G.0475.05. Ghent University is a member of the HiPEAC Network of Excellence.

References

1. Banakar, R., Steinke, S., Lee, B.-S., Balakrishnan, M., Marwedel, P.: Scratch-pad memory: design alternative for cache on-chip memory in embedded systems. In: CODES 2002: Proceedings of the Tenth International Symposium on Hardware/software Codesign, pp. 73–78. ACM Press, New York (2002)
2. McKinley, K.S., Carr, S., Tseng, C.-W.: Improving data locality with loop transformations. ACM Transactions on Programming Languages and Systems 18(4), 424–453 (1996)
3. Hu, Q., Kjeldsberg, P.G., Vandecappelle, A., Palkovic, M., Catthoor, F.: Incremental hierarchical memory size estimation for steering of loop transformations. ACM Transactions on Design Automation of Electronic Systems 12(4), 50 (2007)
4. Carribault, P., Cohen, A.: Applications of storage mapping optimization to register promotion. In: ICS 2004: Proceedings of the 18th Annual International Conference on Supercomputing, pp. 247–256. ACM Press, New York (2004)
5. Geelen, B., Brockmeyer, E., Durinck, B., Lafruit, G., Lauwereins, R.: Alleviating memory bottlenecks by software-controlled data transfers in a data-parallel wavelet transform on a multicore DSP. In: Proceedings 1st Annual IEEE BENELUX/DSP Valley Signal Processing Symposium - SPS-DARTS, pp. 143–146 (April 2005)
6. Vanderwiel, S.P., Lilja, D.J.: Data prefetch mechanisms. ACM Comput. Surv. 32(2), 174–199 (2000)
7. Shahbahrami, A., Juurlink, B., Vassiliadis, S.: Improving the memory behavior of vertical filtering in the discrete wavelet transform. In: CF 2006: Proceedings of the 3rd conference on Computing Frontiers, pp. 253–260. ACM Press, New York (May 2006)
8. Zhang, L., Fang, Z., Parker, M., Mathew, B.K., Schaelicke, L., Carter, J.B., Hsieh, W.C., McKee, S.A.: The Impulse memory controller. IEEE Transactions on Computers 50(11), 1117–1132 (2001)
9. Devos, H., Beyls, K.E., Christiaens, M., Van Campenhout, J., D'Hollander, E.H., Stroobandt, D.: Finding and applying loop transformations for generating optimized FPGA implementations. In: Stenström, P. (ed.) Transactions on High-Performance Embedded Architectures and Compilers I. LNCS, vol. 4050, pp. 159–178. Springer, Heidelberg (2007)

10. Girbal, S., Vasilache, N., Bastoul, C., Cohen, A., Parello, D., Sigler, M., Temam, O.: Semi-automatic composition of loop transformations for deep parallelism and memory hierarchies. Int. J. Parallel Program. 34(3), 261–317 (2006)
11. Oualline, S.: Vi IMproved (VIM). New Riders, Indianapolis (2001)
12. Eeckhaut, H., Christiaens, M., Stroobandt, D.: Improving external memory access for Avalon systems on programmable chips. In: FPL 2007, 17th International Conference on Field Programmable Logic and Applications (August 2007)
13. Eeckhaut, H., Devos, H., Lambert, P., De Schrijver, D., Van Lancker, W., Nollet, V., Avasare, P., Clerckx, T., Verdicchio, F., Christiaens, M., Schelkens, P., Van de Walle, R., Stroobandt, D.: Scalable, wavelet-based video: from server to hardware-accelerated client. IEEE Transactions on Multimedia 9(7), 1508–1519 (2007)
14. Devos, H., Hendrik, E., Christiaens, M., Stroobandt, D.: Energy scalability and the RESUME scalable video codec. In: Benini, L., Chang, N., Kremer, U., Probst, C.W. (eds.) Power-aware Computing Systems, Dagstuhl Seminar Proceedings, Dagstuhl, Germany, Internationales Begegnungs-und Forschungszentrum für Informatik (IBFI), Schloss Dagstuhl, Germany, vol. 07041 (January 2007), http://drops.dagstuhl.de/opus/volltexte/2007/1112
15. Wolf, M.E., Lam, M.S.: A data locality optimizing algorithm. In: PLDI 1991: Proceedings of the ACM SIGPLAN 1991 Conference on Programming Language Design and Implementation, pp. 30–44. ACM Press, New York (1991)
16. Sheldon, J., Lee, W., Greenwald, B., Amarasinghe, S.: Strength reduction of integer division and modulo operations. In: Dietz, H.G. (ed.) LCPC 2001. LNCS, vol. 2624, pp. 1–14. Springer, Heidelberg (2003)
17. Miranda, M.A., Catthoor, F.V., Janssen, M., De Man, H.J.: High-level address optimization and synthesis techniques for data-transfer-intensive applications. IEEE Transactions on Very Large Scale Integration (VLSI) Systems 6(4), 677–686 (1998)
18. Panda, P.R., Catthoor, F., Dutt, N.D., Danckaert, K., Brockmeyer, E., Kulkarni, C., Vandecappelle, A., Kjeldsberg, P.G.: Data and memory optimization techniques for embedded systems. ACM Transactions on Design Automation of Electronic Systems 6(2), 149–206 (2001)
19. Zissulescu, C., Kienhuis, B., Deprettere, E.: Expression synthesis in process networks generated by LAURA. In: 16th IEEE International Conference on Application-specific Systems, Architectures and Processors (ASAP), pp. 15–21 (July 2005)
20. Synfora: PICO technology white paper (v.10)
21. NEC: CyberWorkBench, http://www.necst.co.jp/product/cwb/english/
22. Bohm, W., Hammes, J., Draper, B., Chawathe, M., Ross, C., Rinker, R., Najjar, W.: Mapping a single assignment programming language to reconfigurable systems. Journal of Supercomputing 21(2), 117–130 (2002)
23. Guo, Z., Buyukkurt, B., Najjar, W., Vissers, K.: Optimized generation of datapath from C codes for FPGAs. In: DATE 2005: Proceedings of the Conference on Design, Automation and Test in Europe, pp. 112–117. IEEE Computer Society Press, Washington, DC (2005)
24. Verdoolaege, S., Nikolov, H.N., Stefanov, T.P.: Improved derivation of process networks. In: ODES-4: 4th Workshop on Optimizations for DSP and Embedded Systems (March 2006)
25. Devos, H.: Loop Transformations for the Optimized Generation of Reconfigurable Hardware. PhD thesis, Ghent University (February 2008)

First Workshop on Programmability Issues for Multi-core Computers (MULTIPROG)

autopin – Automated Optimization of Thread-to-Core Pinning on Multicore Systems

Tobias Klug, Michael Ott, Josef Weidendorfer, and Carsten Trinitis

Technische Universität München
Lehrstuhl für Rechnertechnik und Rechnerorganisation / Parallelrechnerarchitektur
(LRR/TUM)
Boltzmannstraße 3, 85748 Garching bei München
{klug,ottmi,weidendo,trinitic}@in.tum.de

Abstract. In this paper we present a framework for automatic detection and application of the best binding between threads of a running parallel application and processor cores in a shared memory system, by making use of hardware performance counters. This is especially important within the scope of multicore architectures with shared cache levels. We demonstrate that many applications from the SPEC OMP benchmark show quite sensitive runtime behavior depending on the thread/core binding used. In our tests, the proposed framework is able to find the best binding in nearly all cases. The proposed framework is intended to supplement job scheduling systems for better automatic exploitation of systems with multicore processors, as well as making programmers aware of this issue by providing measurement logs.

Keywords: Multicore, CMP, automatic performance optimization, hardware performance counters, CPU binding, thread placement.

1 Introduction

During recent years, a clear paradigm shift from increasing clock rates towards multicore chip-architectures (CMP) has taken place. Considering chip manufacturers' long-term objective of integrating 128 and more cores onto one die, there are several open issues with respect to programmability and scalability that have to be examined. In the past, a serial program could benefit from a new processor model simply because processors' clock frequencies were increased from current models to successors. Consequently, even standard applications ran faster without any need to modify a single line of source code. With energy efficiency as a new optimization goal, clock frequencies have to stay more or less stable, and additional performance gains are only obtainable by parallelism on the core level. In order to take advantage of existing and future multicore processor architectures, it is essential to develop parallel applications and to adapt existing serial applications accordingly. Otherwise, all but one core remain idle, and no performance gain can be achieved at all. Parallel programming is leaving the high performance computing (HPC) niche and establishing itself as a mainstream programming technique.

P. Stenström (Ed.): Transactions on HiPEAC III, LNCS 6590, pp. 219–235, 2011.

Asymmetric particularities of the memory subsystem are a big obstacle for runtime performance on shared memory machines, as they need to be taken care of explicitly. Non Uniform Memory Access (NUMA) architectures are a familiar example. A new type of asymmetric property comes with shared caches in multicore processors: The access history of one or multiple nearside cores can significantly influence the speed of memory accesses. While overlapping working sets in threads running on cores sharing a cache can reduce runtime, the non-existence of any overlapping usually degrades performance by cutting available cache space into half. Without sophisticated tools and detailed analysis, the programmer can only roughly assess the reason for acceleration or slowdown in the parallel code, let alone come up with optimization strategies for badly running code. This problem is expected to increase with the number of cores available on one chip[1], as in this case the need for complex on-chip interconnect and cache buffer hierarchies is evident.

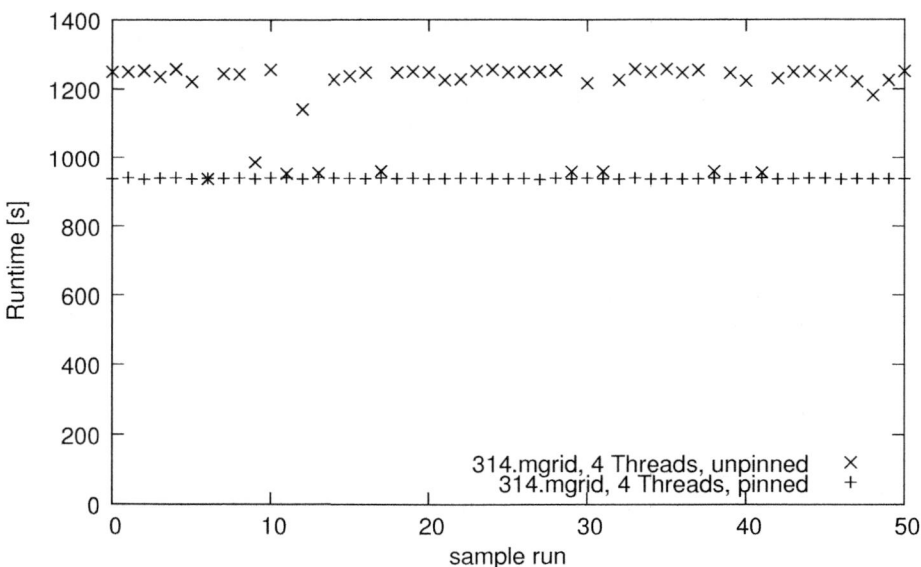

Fig. 1. Comparison of unpinned runs vs. runs under control of autopin. Four threads on the Caneland platform.

To overcome the issue with non-uniform memory subsystems, including the shared cache problem, we propose an automatic approach in this paper: While the application is running, the `autopin` tool checks a given set of fixed thread-to-core bindings (called *pinnings*) in order to find the pinning with optimal performance. In this study, we used `autopin` to find optimal pinnings for applications

---

[1] In the remainder of this work, the term chip will refer to a single physical processor chip which may consist of multiple processor cores plus cache. Hence, the term core will refer to a single x86 based physical processor unit.

in the SPEC OMP benchmark[2] on various multicore systems. We check pinnings where all cores are active as well as pinnings with a smaller number of threads than cores available on a given system. This is due to the fact that one core on a multicore processor can already fully exploit the available connection to main memory, thus slowing down any work on other cores on the same chip. In this case, it might be recommended to not use these cores for the parallel application. In addition, there exist applications that run with thread counts which do not match available core counts: Examples are parallel tree traversals or load balancing schemes generating/killing threads on the fly. The proposed framework is intended to supplement job scheduling systems for better automatic exploitation of systems with multicore processors, as well as making programmers aware of the given issue by providing measurement logs.

To illustrate this with an example, figure 1 shows runtimes for the SPEC OMP's 314.mgrid benchmark with four threads for 50 sample runs. The 314.mgrid benchmark will be explained in further detail in section 4. Without any control of the pinning, the operating system's scheduler decides on which cores the threads will run. As can be seen in figure 1, runtimes can vary significantly and are hard to predict. However, with the use of the autopin tool, optimal thread pinning ensures optimal performance as well as equally distributed runtimes over all sample runs.

2   Related Work

With the large amount of different computer systems available today, regarding available resources, from internode connection and memory subsystem parameters (e.g. cache sizes) to CPU features like superscalarity and vector units, it has always been difficult to come up with an algorithm implementation that optimally exploits these resources. A common approach is to use performance analysis tools such as GProf [1] or Intel VTune [2], and to adapt the code to a specific system. However, this approach is not always feasible: When software is run by a user on a site other than the development site, there usually will be an executable binary for a class of systems (as e.g. for commercial software). Often, the user can not even check if the application runs at optimal performance on his (expensive) system. To still allow for good exploitation, different approaches exist: Foremost, the best code optimization approaches are architecture independent, e.g. using algorithms with lower complexity. For caches, *cache oblivious algorithms* [3] use recursive splitting of data structures for blocking optimization, independent on cache size. Another approach is to check for hardware features at runtime (as in math libraries from vendors [4]) or at install time with an automated search for best parameters and according recompilation. This also includes a feedback compilation step as supported by most compilers (e.g. Intel Compiler Suite, PGI Compilers, GNU Compiler Collection), which can even adapt to a user's typical input data. A well known example for this strategy,

---

[2] http://www.spec.org/OMP

searching for best parameters for cache optimization, is the Atlas library [5]. Our automated search for best thread-to-core pinning takes a similar approach.

Documented hardware performance counters are built into every processor on the market today. Similar counters have always been present in processors to allow for internal correctness checks after production. The good news is that since quite some time these performance counters have been documented and can be used by various tools. Unfortunately, the amount of different events that can be measured varies from processor type to processor type (for example, see the manuals for Intel [6] or AMD [7] processors). This means that there is no standard (yet) that determines which performance counters have to be present in a processor. Recently, Intel has added a simple counter interface and a few specific events to its x86 architecture (for processors based on the Core microarchitecture). Typically, there are 2 or 4 counters available for a huge number of event types related to the processor pipeline, the cache subsystem, and the bus interface, thus allowing to check the utilization of resources. However, the semantics of events can be difficult to interpret, and often, detailed documentation is rare. Hardware Performance Counters are either used to read exact counts, or to derive statistical measurements. The most common commercial tool is VTune [2]. A library for multiple platforms and operating systems to read counters is PAPI [8]. For Linux, there is a statistical measurement tool called OProfile [9], available as part of the standard kernel. However, to get read access to counters, it is required to install a kernel patch (Perfctr), complicating the use significantly. Additionally, HP has started to work on another kernel patch called perfmon2 [10]. This patch initially existed for the Linux Itanium architecture only but now also provides support for latest Intel and AMD processors. Its user level parts (libpfm, pfmon) form the basis for autopin.

So far, the de facto standard shared memory API OpenMP [11] was mostly used on large shared memory architectures. With the new memory and cache hierarchies being introduced by multicore architectures, thread pinning becomes increasingly important for OpenMP programs with regard to scalability issues. [12] and [13] discuss operating system and compiler dependent calls to control pinning as well as page allocation on ccNUMA, CMP (chip multiprocessing), and CMT/SMT (chip multithreading/simultaneous multithreading) architectures running Linux or SOLARIS. Carrying out several OpenMP benchmarks, the authors conclude that affinity is especially important for OpenMP performance on ccNUMA machines, with OpenMP nesting still being difficult on those architectures. From the operating systems' point of view, SOLARIS and SunStudio provide better tools to deal with the problem, however, Linux is catching up. The authors also observe performance benefits through shared caches in multicore architectures.

In [14], the author argues that using multicore platforms effectively will be a key challenge for programmers in the future. The article discusses the challenges posed by multicore technology, reviews recent work on programming languages potentially interesting for multicore platforms, and gives an overview on on-going activities to extend compiler technology with regard to multicore programming, which also affects thread pinning.

3   The autopin Tool

As a proof-of-concept implementation of our framework for automated CPU pinning, we extended the **pfmon** utility from the perfmon2 package (see [10]) with the required functionality.

The cores to be used and the order in which the cores are assigned to the threads is specified by the user via an environment variable called SCHEDULE. Each position of this string-variable defines a mapping of a thread ID to a CPU core ID. For example, SCHEDULE=2367 would result in the first thread being pinned to core #2, the second thread to core #3, and so on. The user may pass several, comma-separated sets of scheduling mappings via this environment variable.

Upon creation, each new thread is enumerated and pinned to one specific CPU core using the sched_setaffinity() system call according to the first entry of the SCHEDULE variable. Pinning of the additional management thread created by Intel's OpenMP implementation is omitted. Hence, this thread is scheduled by the operating system.

If the user provided more than one scheduling mapping, the tool will probe each of these mappings for a certain time interval t. Probing is performed using the following algorithm:

1. Let the program initialize for i seconds.
2. Read the current timestamp ts_1 and value pc_1 of the performance counter for each thread.
3. Run the program for t seconds.
4. Read the current timestamp ts_2 and value pc_2 of the performance counter for each thread.
5. Calculate the performance rate $r_j = (pc_2 - pc_1)/(ts_2 - ts_1)$ for each thread j and the average performance rate r_{avg} over all threads.
6. If further mappings are left for probing, re-pin the threads according to the next pinning in the list, let the program "warm up" for w seconds, and return to 2.

The initialization step in 1. is required to avoid measuring potential sequential phases in the initial stage of the program [15].

The "warm up" time after each re-pinning is needed for the actual rescheduling of the threads and to refill the cache.

All parameters t, i, and w can be specified in the command line. Otherwise, the following default values (obtained by previous experiments) will be used: $t = 30$, $w = t/2$, and $i = w$.

The specific average performance rate r_{avg} of each scheduling mapping is written to the console. After all mappings have been probed, autopin displays the mapping which achieved the highest performance rate and re-pins the threads accordingly. The program then continues execution with this optimal pinning which will not be changed until the program terminates. Additionally, every t seconds the current performance rate is calculated and written to the console.

As non-optimal pinnings might be used in the beginning, a slight overhead is imposed during this phase. However, in most cases this overhead can be neglected, especially if t and w are small compared to total application runtime, see section 5 for detailed analysis.

The performance counter event which is used for the calculation of the performance rate can be specified by the user with the -e parameter. A list of events which are supported by libpfm for the used architecture can be retrieved by calling autopin -L.

As outlined in [16], thread migration on NUMA systems poses additional challenges: As accesses to non-local memory can decrease performance, not only the thread itself has to be migrated, but also its referenced memory pages. On operating systems which support next touch memory policy, pages are migrated automatically after thread repinning. The current stable Linux kernel only allows for manual page migration. However, there is a patch for the development branch which provides the required functionality [17]. autopin triggers automatic page migration as provided by this kernel patch.

4   Experimental Setup

This chapter describes the experimental setup that has been chosen in order to assess the performance of the autopin framework. First, the deployed benchmark suite SPEC OMP is described. After this, the hardware platforms that were used to perform the benchmark applications under control of autopin are specified. The last section deals with different CPU pinnings that were selected to be evaluated by autopin during the benchmark run.

4.1   Benchmark

SPEC OMP was used as a benchmark basis for autopin. It is an OpenMP benchmark suite for measuring performance of shared memory parallel systems consisting of eleven applications (see table 1), most of which are taken from the scientific area [18].

There are two different levels of workload for SPEC OMP: Medium and Large. All benchmark runs were executed with medium size, as the maximum number of cores used was 16, whereas runs with workload size large are intended to be used for large scale systems of 128 and more cores. In SPEC OMP all benchmark applications are provided in form of source code and have to be compiled with an appropriate compiler. For all hardware platforms described below, Intel Compiler Suite 9.1 was utilized.

4.2   Hardware Environment

Our testbed consists of several machines:

- One node with two Intel Clovertown processors. The Clovertown processor consists of four cores, while two cores have a shared Level 2 cache (4 MB),

Table 1. SPEC OMP benchmark applications

application name	description
310.wupwise	quantum chromodynamics
312.swim	shallow water modeling
314.mgrid	multi-grid solver in 3D potential field
316.applu	parabolic/elliptic partial differential equations
318.galgel	fluid dynamics analysis of oscillatory instability
320.equake	finite element simulation of earthquake modeling
324.apsi	weather prediction
326.gafort	genetic algorithm code
328.fma3d	finite-element crash simulation
330.art	neural network simulation of adaptive resonance theory
332.ammp	computational chemistry

respectively. Our system has 16 MB of cache in total, runs at a clock rate of 2.66 GHz and has 8 GB RAM, DDR2 667 MHz. The frontside bus has a clock rate of 1333 MHz.

Figure 2 demonstrates a schematical diagram of this machine, which will be referred to as Clovertown. The core numbers in the figure are corresponding to the logical processor id assigned by the Linux kernel. The drawing also illustrates which cores are sharing a cache (for instance core #0 and core #2). Whether two cores share a cache or not can be detected with the authors' false sharing benchmark [19].

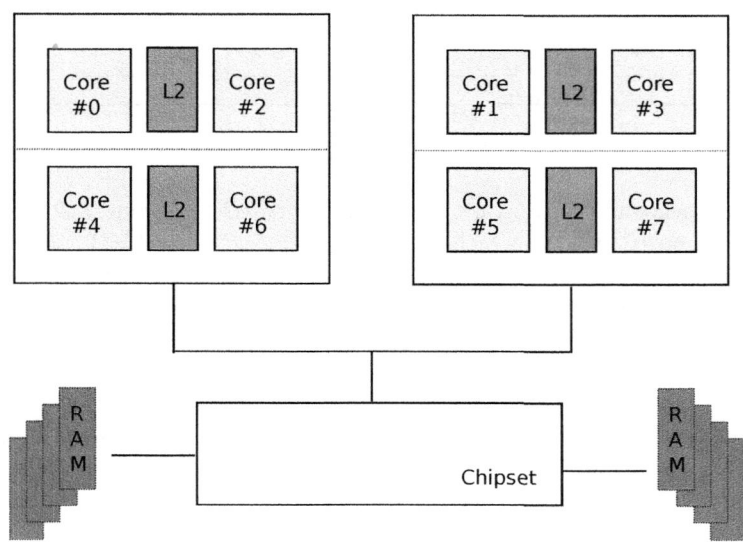

Fig. 2. Intel Clovertown System

– A system with four Intel Tigerton processors. The Tigerton processor consists of four cores, while two cores have a shared Level 2 cache (4 MB), respectively. There are four independent frontside buses (1066 MHz), so each CPU has a dedicated FSB. Each FSB is connected to the Chipset (Clarksboro) which has a 64 MB snoop filter. The memory controller can manage four fully buffered DIMM channels (see figure 3). Our system has 32 MB of cache in total, runs at a clock rate of 2.93 GHz and has 16 GB RAM (DDR2 667 MHz). This machine will be referred to as Caneland.

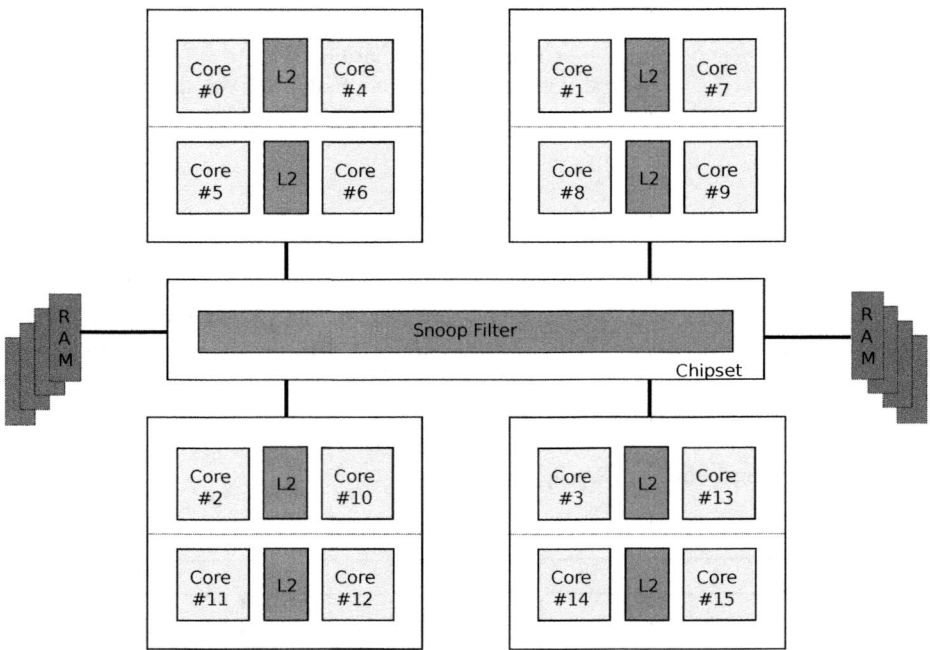

Fig. 3. Intel Caneland Platform

– A two socket machine, equipped with two AMD Opteron 2352. Each CPU has four cores, each of which has a L2 cache size of 512 KB. All cores on a chip are sharing a 2 MB L3 Cache. The four cores are running at a clock rate of 2.1 GHz. The system has 16 GB main memory, DDR2 667 MHz. In contrast to the two hardware platforms described above, this system represents a NUMA-Architecture. Each CPU has an integrated memory controller and can access local memory faster than remote memory. Access to remote memory takes place via HyperTransport (see figure 4). This machine will be referred to as Barcelona in the following sections.

4.3   Thread-to-Core Pinning

All benchmark applications were started with autopin monitoring the hardware counters INSTRUCTIONS_RETIRED on Intel architecture and accordingly

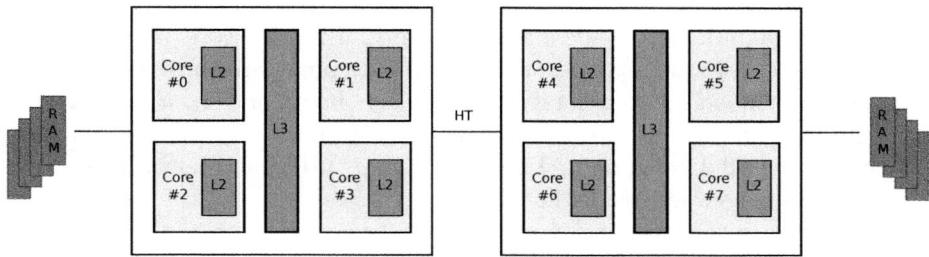

Fig. 4. AMD Barcelona System

RETIRED_INSTRUCTIONS on AMD architecture. As the deltas of the performance counters are divided by the measurement time interval, the measured metric represents the MIPS rate. For floating point intensive programs it might also be interesting to count the retired floating point instructions and calculate the FLOPS rate.

Table 2. Investigated CPU Pinnings for Different CPU Architectures. The first column shows the number of threads used, the second to fourth columns stand for the different thread-to-core pinnings.

#Threads	Caneland	Clovertown	Barcelona
1	1	4	1
2	1,2 1,7 1,8	2,6 4,5 4,6	4,5 2,6 4,6
4	1,7,8,9 1,8,2,11 5,8,11,14 8,9,11,12	4,5,6,7 2,3,6,7 1,3,5,7	2,6,3,7 4,6,5,7 1,3,5,7
8	1,7,8,9,2,10,11,12 4,6,7,9,10,12,13,15 5,6,8,9,11,12,14,15	0,1,2,3,4,5,6,7	0,1,2,3,4,5,6,7

We did not probe all possible pinnings, as most of them are redundant due to symmetries of the architectures:

- For the 1-thread runs we chose a core which is located on a different chip than core #0 as this one often is used for operating systems tasks and thus could disturb the benchmark.
- For runs with 2 threads we chose configurations on two different chips, on one chip with the 2 cores sharing the L2 cache (Intel only), and on one chip with both cores not sharing the cache.
- The measurements with 4 threads were carried out on 1 chip with all cores utilized, on 2 chips once with 2 cores not sharing the L2 cache and – where

applicable – once with 2 cores sharing the L2 cache. On the Caneland platform we additionally made a run on 4 chips, using one core per chip.

- On Clovertown and Barcelona 8 threads were pinned to the core IDs in the same order as they were forked (e.g. the 1st thread on core #0, the 2nd on core #1, and so on). On the Caneland platform we probed configurations exploiting all 4 cores on 2 chips, and 4 chips utilizing 2 cores each – once with shared cache once without.
- The 16-core runs on Caneland were conducted analogously to the 8-core runs on the Clovertown platform.

The detailed list of probed CPU pinnings can be found in table 2. In order to find the best and worst pinning, we made additional runs with `autopin` being called with one SCHEDULE-parameter only, so the CPU pinning stayed unchanged from start to finish. Such runs were performed for every pinning listed in table 2. So for example, on the Caneland platform for two threads there are the following CPU pinnings to investigate: (1,2), (1,7) and (1,8). Accordingly `autopin` was called with SCHEDULE=12,17,18. Additionally, autopin was called three times one after another with parameter SCHEDULE=12 for the first run, SCHEDULE=17 for the second run and SCHEDULE=18 for the last run. This way it is possible to double-check if `autopin` really found the perfect CPU pinning.

5   Results

5.1   Verification of the `autopin` Approach

As described in chapter 4, we used the SPEC OMP benchmark suite to evaluate the effectiveness of our approach. As this suite consists of 11 individual benchmark applications, presenting the runtimes for all benchmarks, architectures, and configurations (# of cores used, pinning to cores) would go beyond the scope of this paper. Therefore, we only discuss three of the benchmark applications in detail: 314.mgrid, 316.applu, and 332.ammp. For the remaining benchmarks we will only sum up our observations shortly.

In comparison with the measurements presented in [16], the slightly modified algorithm (extended by the initialization phase), in combination with page migration on NUMA architectures as described in section 3, is able to find optimal pinnings for almost all benchmarks on all three platforms: In nearly all cases a pinning with a total runtime not exceeding the perfect pinning's runtime by one per cent was found. Only on the Caneland platform, in two cases (312.swim and 332.ammp) a pinning with a total runtime of less than 5% above the perfect pinning's runtime was found. The experiments have been carried out using autopin's default parameters ($t = 30$, $w = t/2$, and $i = w$).

On all platforms, different CPU pinnings had only little effect on the total runtime of the benchmarks if only one core or all available cores were utilized. Note that this does not mean that one can neglect CPU pinning in these cases. Pinning is still important to prevent threads from moving from one core to another.

On the Clovertown platform, CPU pinning is most important for configurations with 2 cores. For 8 benchmarks, the difference in total runtime between the optimal and the worst configurations was over 20% (over 50% for 314 and 316). For the remaining three (324, 328, 332) it is in the range of 3-10%. For configurations with 4 utilized cores, pinning improved the total runtime between 1 and 7% and in one case (314) by 17%.

The Caneland platform is very sensitive to CPU pinning. Pinnings on two cores showed runtime differences in the range of 25-65% for 8 benchmarks out of 11. 324, 328, and 332 were in the range of 4-15%. The gap between the optimal and the worst pinning even increases for setups with 4 cores: only for 3 benchmarks (324, 328, 332) the difference was below 50%, 312 and 314 even showed differences over 100%. For 8 cores the runtime differences were widely distributed between 7 and 78%. Furthermore, for all benchmarks besides the usual suspects 324, 328, and 332, the best 4-core pinning showed better runtimes than the worst 8-core pinning. Utilizing all 16 cores improves runtime only slightly for most benchmarks. In fact, for 314 and 320, the optimal 4-core pinnings achieve better runtimes.

In general, the Barcelona platform seems to be more tolerant on wrong CPU pinnings. At least on 2-thread runs: runtime differences for the best and worst pinning were between 0.1 and 6.5%, except for 312 where the gap was 32%. On 4-thread configurations the pinning has a higher impact, though not as high as on the Caneland platform: for most benchmarks the runtimes differed between 1.5 and 28%, with 312 making an exception again by showing a gap of 58%.

For all data sets, the 2-core configurations which pinned the threads to cores on different chips showed the best runtimes. With 4 threads, it is best to pin them on cores which don't share a common cache on Intel Platforms. This is simply due to the fact, that with two cores sharing a common L2 cache, one core can utilize the whole 4MB L2 cache for one thread if the other one is idle. The same is true for 8-core configurations on Caneland. On the Barcelona it is best to distribute the threads equally to both chips. Being a NUMA architecture, this gives the highest aggregated memory bandwidth to all threads. Furthermore, as the L3 cache is shared between all cores on one chip, the available cache per thread is higher, if half of the cores are idling.

Figures 5, 7 and 9 show the total runtimes (in seconds) of the 314.mgrid benchmark on the Clovertown, Caneland and Barcelona platform utilizing 1, 2, 4, 8, and 16 (Caneland only) cores. For 1 core and 8 cores (16 on Caneland) we only show the runtime for one CPU pinning as different pinnings had only little effect on the total runtime in these cases. For the other core counts we show runtimes of the worst ("max") and the best ("optimal") pinning, as well as for the configuration autopin has proposed ("autopin") - which in all cases is identical to the optimal pinning. Note that on the Intel systems, utilizing more than 4 cores does not improve runtimes any further - even with perfect pinning. If the wrong pinning is chosen, the runtime can be worse than the runtime with perfect pinning on half the number of cores. This effect significantly influences performance on the Caneland platform: The worst 2- and 4-core setups are less

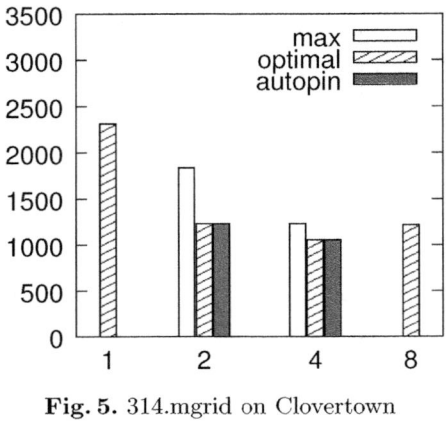

Fig. 5. 314.mgrid on Clovertown

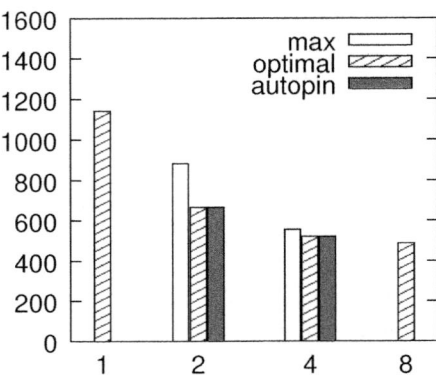

Fig. 6. 316.applu on Clovertown

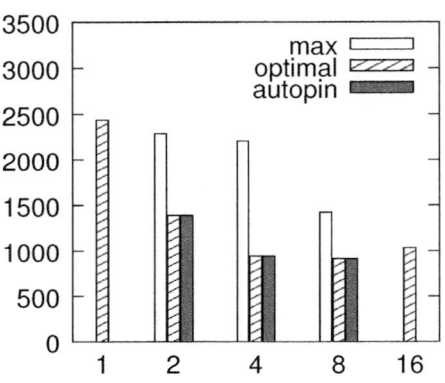

Fig. 7. 314.mgrid on Caneland

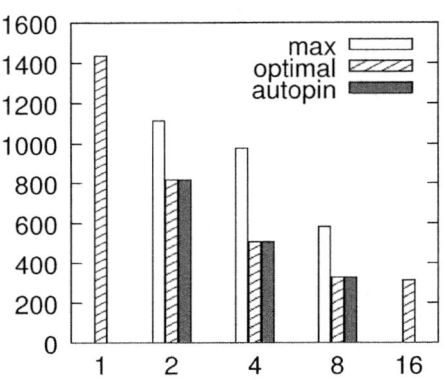

Fig. 8. 316.applu on Caneland

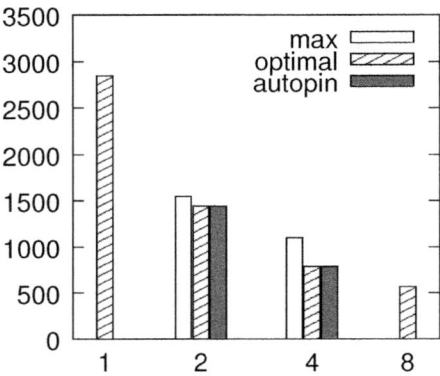

Fig. 9. 314.mgrid on Barcelona

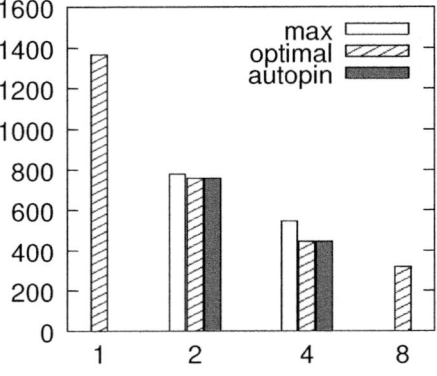

Fig. 10. 316.applu on Barcelona

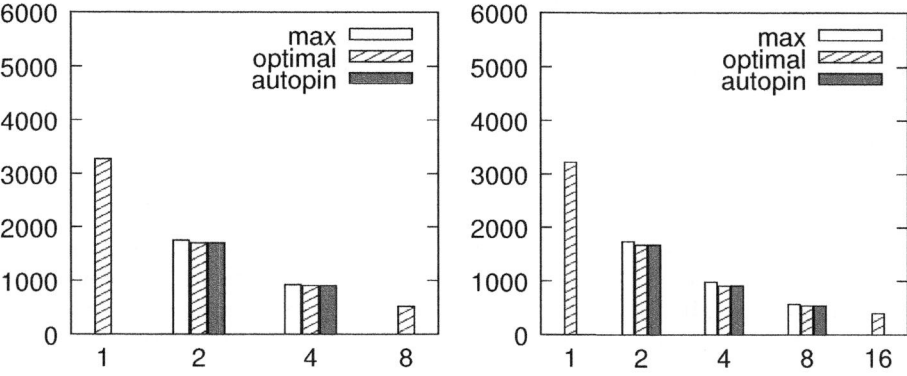

Fig. 11. 332.ammp on Clovertown   **Fig. 12.** 332.ammp on Caneland

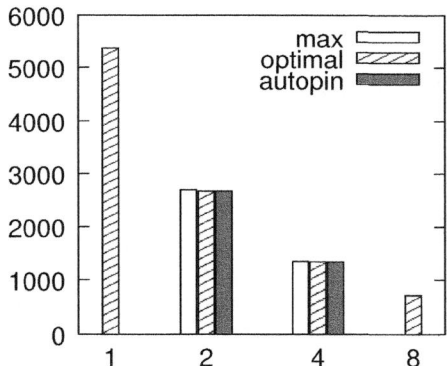

Fig. 13. 332.ammp on Barcelona

than 9% faster than the single-core setup. On Barcelona, wrong pinning does not show problems for 2 threads: the runtimes for both cases are within metering precision. For 4 cores the difference is approximately 20%. Furthermore, the scaling behavior on Barcelona is better than on Intel platforms: while the latter one can not benefit from more than 4 cores, the AMD system scales fine up to 8 cores. This leads to the fact that the total runtime for 8 Opteron cores is shorter than the runtime for 16 Tigerton cores. Given the fact that the single core runtime on the Opteron was 40% higher than on the Intel processors, this is remarkable.

Similar effects can be observed on the 316.applu benchmark (see figures 6, 8 and 10), especially on Caneland: Doubling the number of utilized CPU cores can slow down the computation if the wrong pinning is used. While this effect is weaker for the Clovertown, it still shows poor scaling performance. Again, using more than 4 cores does not improve performance at all. The Barcelona only shows runtime differences for the 4 core setup (44%). For optimal pinning, runtimes and scaling behavior is very similar to the Intel processors.

The 332.ammp benchmark draws a whole different picture as one can see on figures 11-13: Pinning of threads has almost no impact on the runtime and even on the Intel platforms we can see almost linear speedups up to 16 cores. We assume that this benchmark can run almost totally in cache and is therefore not limited by the memory bandwidth which is shared with the other cores.

5.2 Overhead Examination

As shown above, autopin was able to reliably detect optimal pinnings for nearly all benchmarks under consideration using the default parameters. However, to obtain maximum benefit for the user, the overhead imposed by autopin should be kept at a minimum level. This overhead is caused by the fact that during the different phases (initialization, warmup, and measurement) the application also runs with "slow" pinnings.

Hence, in order to find an optimal tradeoff between minimum overhead and reliable detection of optimal pinning, further experiments were carried out for different values of i, w, and t on the Barcelona and Clovertown platforms. These experiments showed that even for $i = 30s$, $w = 3s$, and $t = 10s$, optimal pinning is found for all benchmarks on the Clovertown platform. On the Barcelona

Table 3. autopin overhead on Clovertown: The first column shows the benchmark under consideration, the second column the number of threads, the third column the benchmark's total runtime with the fixed optimal pinning, the fourth column the total runtime under autopin probing several pinnings, the sixth column shows the difference between column three and four in per cent, the seventh column the total runtime with the slowest fixed pinning, and the last column shows the difference between column four and seven in per cent.

Benchmark	#Threads	Best Pinning [s]	autopin [s]	diff [%]	Worst Pinning [s]	diff [%]
310	2	655.12	659.27	0.63	785.95	19.22
310	4	484.53	486.94	0.5	656.02	34.72
312	2	932.41	949.13	1.79	1426.97	50.35
312	4	910.28	916.16	0.65	1388.78	51.59
314	2	1227.04	1231.28	0.35	1840.65	49.49
314	4	1058.51	1069.58	1.05	1779.32	66.36
316	2	656.73	667.29	1.61	882.99	32.32
316	4	522.95	528.57	1.07	787.69	49.02
320	2	287.24	295.01	2.71	379.63	28.68
320	4	253.64	258.25	1.82	350.08	35.56
324	2	572.85	574.82	0.34	604.66	5.19
324	4	313.63	314.83	0.38	345.05	9.6
328	2	1085.02	1090.55	0.51	1213.67	11.29
328	4	668.01	670.81	0.42	800.9	19.39
330	2	350.34	358.13	2.22	463.95	29.55
330	4	281.75	286.16	1.57	361.56	26.35
332	2	1755.84	1769.65	0.79	1795.86	1.48
332	4	941.98	941.57	-0.04	971.8	3.21

Table 4. `autopin` overhead on Barcelona. See caption of table 3 for an explanation of the table's columns.

Benchmark	#Threads	Best Pinning [s]	autopin [s]	diff [%]	Worst Pinning [s]	diff [%]
310	2	913.14	924.27	1.22	941.49	1.86
310	4	482.99	494.04	2.29	543.41	9.99
312	2	650.17	696.41	7.11	903.09	29.68
312	4	464.64	495.98	6.75	776.7	56.6
314	2	1440.37	1448.52	0.57	1545.21	6.68
314	4	784.52	793.36	1.13	1102.33	38.94
316	2	757.97	713.11	-5.92	779.39	9.29
316	4	445.45	420.22	-5.66	546.74	30.11
320	2	318.86	322.72	1.21	334.81	3.75
320	4	200.23	204.09	1.93	235.12	15.2
324	2	768.28	775.6	0.95	850.34	9.64
324	4	373.72	376.84	0.83	428.73	13.77
328	2	1064.43	1075.35	1.03	1125.79	4.69
328	4	571.38	599.47	4.92	655.09	9.28
330	2	567.76	569.73	0.35	573.98	0.75
330	4	297.51	299.4	0.64	306.17	2.26
332	2	2673.66	2697.62	0.9	2698.7	0.04
332	4	1334.3	1349.42	1.13	1343.9	-0.41

platform a slightly higher value of $w = 10s$ was required, which is necessary for page migration to take place.

Tables 3 and 4 show the total runtimes of the SPEC OMP benchmarks for the fixed optimal pinning, under `autopin` probing several pinnings, and for the fixed slowest pinning. Column five shows the relative runtime overhead in per cent imposed by `autopin`. On the Clovertown platform this overhead turns out to be below 3% in all cases. Running the application without `autopin` may cause runtimes up to 66% higher than those yielded by `autopin` in case the operating system's scheduler happens to choose the worst pinning as depicted in the last two columns. Due to the additional cost of memory page migration, the overhead on the Barcelona platform is slightly higher for memory intensive applications (up to 7.5%). Nevertheless, compared to the worst pinning, significant runtime improvements can be achieved. Interestingly, for the 316.applu benchmark the runtimes under `autopin` are even lower than the best fixed pinning. This might be due to the fact that this application prefers different pinnings in different program execution phases. See section 6 for a further discussion of this observation.

6 Conclusion and Outlook

In this paper we pinpointed the importance of correct CPU pinnings that account for both application characteristics as well as hardware properties. It is obvious that this topic will become even more crucial with future multicore processor architectures, which will have much more complicated on-chip interconnects with strongly varying access speeds. Remarkably, the best and worst pinnings for some applications yielded a runtime difference of more than 100 per cent.

Additionally, we presented the `autopin` framework, which allows to automatically determine the thread pinning best suited for a shared memory parallel program on a selected architecture. This is achieved by evaluating the performance of different pinnings by means of hardware performance counters. It has been shown that `autopin` reliably proposes optimal pinnings for the SPEC OMP benchmark on UMA as well as NUMA architectures.

Future versions of `autopin` can be improved in several ways. At the moment the user needs profound knowledge on the hardware infrastructure (i.e. how many cores are available on how many sockets, how many cores are on a chip, which cores do share caches, etc.) in order to choose a reasonable set of schedule mappings. To make the tool easier to use for people with no background in computer architecture, a mechanism could be implemented that automatically detects the hardware infrastructure and selects appropriate schedule mappings to be analyzed. A promising idea that goes one step further is to integrate parts of `autopin` into the scheduler of the Linux kernel.

In its current version, `autopin` starts with one pinning and switches to the next pinning after a specified time frame and so on. When no more pinnings to be tested are left, `autopin` re-pins to the best mapping found so far and uses this pinning until the program terminates. This behavior could be inappropriate for programs that have strongly varying execution phases. For example, a parallel program with four active threads might have a first phase in which it is memory bound. Within this phase, distributing threads over four different chips makes much more sense than putting all threads together onto one chip. Consider the next phase to be dominated by very fine grain communication with all relevant data being held in caches. This time the situation is vice versa, and pinning all threads onto one chip with four cores sharing a L3 cache would be most efficient. Taking these considerations into account, the idea is to adapt `autopin` to continuously monitor the application and restart the repinning process if the application's performance drops under a certain threshold.

Acknowledgements

The work presented in this paper has been carried out in the context of the Munich Multicore Initiative MMI[3]. The authors would like to thank Sun Microsystems and Intel Corporation, who kindly provided hardware platforms for our experiments.

References

1. Graham, S.L., Kessler, P.B., McKusick, M.K.: gprof: a Call Graph Execution Profiler. In: SIGPLAN Symposium on Compiler Construction, pp. 120–126 (1982)
2. Intel: VTune Performance Analyzer, http://www.intel.com/software/products/vtune

---

[3] http://mmi.in.tum.de

3. Frigo, M., Leiserson, C.E., Prokop, H., Ramachandran, S.: Cache-Oblivious Algorithms. In: FOCS 1999: Proceedings of the 40th Annual Symposium on Foundations of Computer Science, p. 285. IEEE Computer Society Press, Washington, DC (1999)
4. Intel: Math Kernel Library,
   http://developer.intel.com/software/products/mkl
5. Whaley, R.C., Dongarra, J.J.: Automatically Tuned Linear Algebra Software. Technical report (1997)
6. Intel Corporation: Intel 64 and IA-32 Architectures: Software Developer's Manual, Denver, CO, USA (2007)
7. Advanced Micro Devices: AMD64 Architecture Programmer's Manual. Number 24593 (2007)
8. Browne, S., Dongarra, J., Garner, N., London, K., Mucci, P.: A scalable cross-platform infrastructure for application performance tuning using hardware counters. In: Supercomputing 2000: Proceedings of the 2000 ACM/IEEE Conference on Supercomputing, Washington, DC, USA, p. 42. IEEE Computer Society, Los Alamitos (2000)
9. Levon, J.: OProfile manual, http://oprofile.sourceforge.net/doc/
10. Eranian, S.: The perfmon2 Interface Specification. Technical Report HPL-2004-200R1, Hewlett-Packard Laboratory (February 2005)
11. OpenMP.org: The OpenMP API specification for parallel programming,
    http://www.openmp.org/
12. Chapman, B., an Mey, D.: The Future of OpenMP in the Multi-Core Era. In: ParCo 2007: Proceedings of the International Conference on Parallel Computing: Architectures, Algorithms and Applications, pp. 571–572. IOS Press, Amsterdam (2008)
13. an Mey, D., Terboven, C.: Affinity Matters!, http://www.compunity.org/events/pastevents/parco07/AffinityMatters_DaM.pdf
14. Chapman, B.: The Multicore Programming Challenge. In: Xu, M., Zhan, Y.-W., Cao, J., Liu, Y. (eds.) APPT 2007. LNCS, vol. 4847, p. 3. Springer, Heidelberg (2007)
15. Fürlinger, K., Moore, S.: Continuous runtime profiling of openmp applications. In: Proceedings of the 2007 Conference on Parallel Computing (PARCO 2007), pp. 677–686 (September 2007)
16. Ott, M., Klug, T., Weidendorfer, J., Trinitis, C.: autopin - Automated Optimization of Thread-to-Core Pinning on Multicore Systems. In: Proceedings of 1st Workshop on Programmability Issues for Multi-Core Computers (MULTIPROG) (January 2008), http://www.lrr.in.tum.de/~ottmi/docs/multiprog08.pdf
17. Schermerhorn, L.T.: Automatic Page Migration for Linux - A Matter of Hygiene (January 2007); Talk at linux.conf.au 2007
18. Saito, H., Gaertner, G., Jones, W.B., Eigenmann, R., Iwashita, H., Lieberman, R., van Waveren, G.M., Whitney, B.: Large system performance of spec omp2001 benchmarks. In: Zima, H.P., Joe, K., Sato, M., Seo, Y., Shimasaki, M. (eds.) ISHPC 2002. LNCS, vol. 2327, pp. 370–379. Springer, Heidelberg (2002)
19. Weidendorfer, J., Ott, M., Klug, T., Trinitis, C.: Latencies of conflicting writes on contemporary multicore architectures. In: Malyshkin, V.E. (ed.) PaCT 2007. LNCS, vol. 4671, pp. 318–327. Springer, Heidelberg (2007)

Robust Adaptation to Available Parallelism in Transactional Memory Applications

Mohammad Ansari, Mikel Luján, Christos Kotselidis, Kim Jarvis,
Chris Kirkham, and Ian Watson

The University of Manchester
{ansari,kotselidis,jarvis,mikel,chris,watson}@cs.manchester.ac.uk

Abstract. Applications using transactional memory may exhibit fluctuating (dynamic) available parallelism, i.e. the maximum number of transactions that can be committed concurrently may change over time. Executing large numbers of transactions concurrently in phases with low available parallelism will waste processor resources in aborted transactions, while executing few transactions concurrently in phases with high available parallelism will degrade execution time by not fully exploiting the available parallelism. Three questions come to mind: (1) Are there such transactional applications? (2) How can such behaviour be exploited? and (3) How can available parallelism be measured or calculated efficiently? The contributions of this paper constitute the answers to these questions.

This paper presents a system, called transactional concurrency tuning, that adapts the number of transactions executing concurrently in response to dynamic available parallelism, in order to improve processor resource usage and execution time performance. Four algorithms, called controller models, that vary in response strength were presented in previous work and shown to maintain execution time similar to the best case non-tuned execution time, but improve resource usage significantly in benchmarks that exhibit dynamic available parallelism.

This paper presents an analysis of the four controller models' response characteristics to changes in dynamic available parallelism, and identifies weaknesses that reduce their general applicability. These limitations lead to the design of a fifth controller model, called P-only transactional concurrency tuning (PoCC). Evaluation of PoCC shows it improves upon performance and response characteristics of the first four controller models, making it a robust controller model suitable for general use.

1 Introduction

The future of processor architectures has been confirmed as multi-core [1,2,3], and mainstream processor manufacturers have all changed their product lineup. Multi-core processors set a new precedent for software developers: software will need to be multi-threaded to take advantage of future processor technology [4]. Furthermore, given that the number of cores is only likely to increase, the

P. Stenström (Ed.): Transactions on HiPEAC III, LNCS 6590, pp. 236–255, 2011.

parallelism in the software should be abundant to ensure it continues to improve performance on successive generations of multi-core processors.

Transactional Memory (TM) [5,6,7] is a programming abstraction that promises to simplify parallel programming by offering implicit synchronisation. Programmers using TM label as *transactions* those portions of code that access shared data, and the underlying TM ensures safe access. The TM implementation monitors the execution of transactions, and for any two transactions that have access conflicts the TM implementation will *abort* one, and let the other continue executing. A transaction *commits* if it does not have access conflicts, thus making its updates to shared data available to the rest of the application.

Figure 1 shows examples of fluctuating available parallelism patterns that transactional applications may exhibit during execution. We define available parallelism as *the maximum number of transactions that can be committed concurrently*, i.e. none aborting. Executing applications that have dynamic available parallelism with a fixed number of concurrent transactions can hurt performance and be resource inefficient. Executing large numbers of transactions concurrently in phases with low available parallelism a) wastes resources in the execution of aborted transactions, b) hurts performance by increasing the number of access conflicts that have to be resolved, and c) hurts performance and wastes resources when aborted transactions need to be rolled back. Similarly, executing too few transactions concurrently in phases with high available parallelism hurts execution time performance.

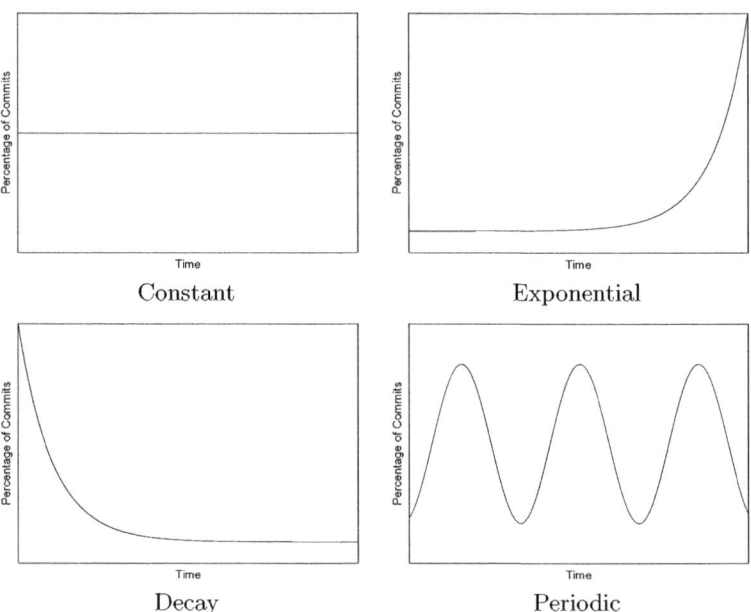

Fig. 1. Example patterns of available parallelism, expressed as a percentage of concurrently attempted transactions that commit

This paper studies a technique to take advantage of dynamic available parallelism. *Transactional concurrency tuning* dynamically adjusts the number of transactions executing concurrently with respect to the available parallelism, in order to improve execution time performance and resource usage efficiency. We identify *Transaction Commit Rate* (TCR), which is the percentage of committed transactions out of all executed transactions in a sample period, as a suitable lightweight, application-independent measure of available parallelism.

Four controller models that vary in their response strength to changes in available parallelism are implemented, and evaluated. Following an investigation of their response characteristics, a fifth controller model was implemented that combines the strengths of the four models and improves their response characteristics. Evaluations are performed using a synthetic benchmark, Lee-TM [8,9], and STAMP [10] applications Genome, KMeans, and Vacation, which have become popular [11,12,13,14,15,16] non-trivial benchmarks in TM research. Evaluation is carried out using DSTM2 [17], a software TM (STM) implementation.

The paper is organised as follows: Section 2 introduces transactional concurrency tuning and the controller models. Section 3 evaluates the controller models. Section 4 discusses the applicability and effectiveness of transactional concurrency tuning. Section 5 concludes the paper.

2   Transactional Concurrency Tuning

Transactional concurrency tuning has its origins in control theory, which is widely used in industrial processes to maintain system parameters at user-defined optima. Defining transactional concurrency tuning for TM using control theory terminology, the control objective is to maintain the *process variable* TCR at a *setPoint* desirable value, in spite of *unmeasured disturbance* from fluctuating available parallelism. TCR and *setPoint* are percentage values in the range 0–100%. The *setPoint* determines how conservative a controller model is towards resource usage efficiency. A high *setPoint*, e.g. 90%, causes a controller model to be quick to reduce threads when TCR decreases, but slow to adapt to a sudden large increase in TCR, and vice versa. Transactional concurrency tuning also has a parameter called *samplePeriod* over which the TCR is sampled in order to make a transactional concurrency tuning decision. The controller models set this parameter in different ways.

The *controller model output* is to modify the number of threads executing transactions in response to changes in TCR. In order to do this, a thread pool framework is implemented to execute transactions, and the controller model output changes the number of threads active in the thread pool. Each worker thread has its own work queue, as the traditional single work queue architecture can quickly become a bottleneck. The worker threads also implement work stealing [18] to reduce load imbalance. Application threads submit jobs to the thread pool, and submission can be either synchronous, i.e. the application thread waits until the transaction commits, or asynchronous, i.e. the application thread submits the job, but does not wait for the transaction to commit. Using only syn-

1. if `currentTime` − `lastSampleTime` < *samplePeriod*, goto Step 1;
2. `TCR` ← `numCommits` / `numTransactions` × 100;
3. Δthreads ← *controller model output*
4. `newThreads` ← `numCurrentThreads` + Δthreads;
5. Adjust `newThreads` such that *minThreads* ≤ `newThreads` ≤ *maxThreads*;
6. `numCurrentThreads` ← `newThreads`;
7. Set `lastSampleTime` ← `currentTime`, go to Step 1;

Fig. 2. Transactional concurrency tuning pseudocode, with modular controller model

chronous submission emulates the existing TM programming model, but asynchronous submission may improve exploitation of high available parallelism; if the number of worker threads is increased such that it is greater than the number of application threads, synchronous submission will not deliver enough jobs for all worker threads. Figure 2 illustrates how the transaction concurrency tuning system permits modular controller models, i.e. the policy for determining the *controller model output*.

2.1   Four Controller Models

This section introduces four controller models from the authors' previous work [19] that vary in their response strength to the difference in the measured value of the process variable and the *setPoint*. Preliminary experimental analysis found the controller models described below to have unstable controller model output using a single value for the *setPoint* (e.g. 70%) so a *setPointRange* (e.g. 50–80%) is selected.

SimpleAdjust is the simplest controller model, and increments the number of worker threads by one if the sampled TCR is above the upper *setPointRange* value, or vice versa. When the TCR is within *setPointRange*, no change is made.

ExponentialInterval extends SimpleAdjust aiming to improve response time to TCR changes. If a change to the number of worker threads is made then *samplePeriod* is halved, i.e. the next change, if necessary, will be made sooner. Conversely, *samplePeriod* is doubled if the number of worker threads is left unchanged. As before, the number of worker threads is only increased or decreased by one. A *samplePeriodRange* that restricts the *samplePeriod* must be defined.

ExponentialAdjust also extends SimpleAdjust aiming to improve response time to TCR changes. It calculates the adjustment to the number of worker threads based on the difference in sampled TCR and the *setPointRange*. The further the sampled TCR from the *setPointRange*, the greater the adjustment. The formula initially chooses to add or subtract one worker thread, and then doubles this value for every 10% the TCR is outside the *setPointRange*. For example, using a *setPointRange* of 50–60% and a sampled TCR of 82%, ExponentialAdjust calculates a TCR difference of 22%, and thus doubles the number of threads twice $(1 \rightarrow 2 \rightarrow 4)$ to add four worker threads.

ExponentialCombined is a combination of ExponentialInterval and Exponential-Adjust. ExponentialCombined has the sample interval adjustment of Exponential-Interval, and the variable worker thread adjustment of ExponentialAdjust, resulting in the most responsive controller model.

2.2   P-only Controller Model

This section begins by describing the fifth controller model, called P-only transactional concurrency tuning (PoCC), then goes on to discuss the features introduced to make it more general purpose than the four controller models described previously. Specifically, PoCC adds two enhancements: a proportional gain formula, and minimum transaction count filter. PoCC is based on a P-only controller model [20] and is presented as pseudocode in Figure 3.

1. If `numTransactions` $< minTransactions$, goto Step 1;
2. ΔTCR $\leftarrow$ TCR $- setPoint$;
3. If (`numCurrentThreads`$= 1$) & (TCR $> setPoint$);
   (a) then Δthreads $\leftarrow 1$;
   (b) else Δthreads $\leftarrow \Delta$TCR $\times$ `numCurrentThreads` $/ 100$
       (rounded to the closest integer);

Fig. 3. PoCC controller model pseudocode

In step 1, a new parameter *minTransactions* is added that acts as a filter against noisy TCR profiles such as in Figure 12. Such noisy samples may occur due to the average transaction's duration being longer than the *samplePeriod*. The four previous controller models, lacking PoCC's filter, absorbed noise by using a large *samplePeriod*, which was a trade-off of responsiveness for robustness. PoCC's filter allows it to be highly responsive, by using a short *samplePeriod*, but still be robust to noisy samples. Thus, in PoCC, *samplePeriod* is determined based on the overhead of executing the control system loop, and does not have to filter noisy samples.

The first four controller models used an absolute gain formula to calculate Δthreads, which led to a change in `numCurrentThreads` even if small ΔTCR values occurred. Such a response was disproportionate at low worker thread counts, e.g. an increase from 1 thread to 2 threads for a TCR only 1% higher than the `setPoint`. This unstable behaviour was controlled by using a *setPointRange*. However, over large worker thread counts, a *setPointRange* range results in poor responsiveness as it produces coarse-grain control. In step 3(b) PoCC uses a proportional gain formula (i.e., proportional to the number of current worker threads) that allows, in response to small ΔTCR, Δthreads to be zero at low worker thread counts, and fine-grain control at large worker thread counts. Thus, PoCC improves responsiveness, because its proportional gain formula allows it to use a *setPoint* rather than a *setPointRange*, and still result in stable behaviour at low worker thread counts.

3   Evaluation of the Controller Models

The evaluation is split into several sections: execution time, resource usage, transaction execution metrics, and finally an investigation of controller model response characteristics. The controller models are abbreviated to SA, EI, EA, EC, and PoCC, respectively.

Hereafter, *static execution* refers to execution with a fixed number of threads, and *dynamic execution* refers to execution under any controller model. All experiments use the thread pool to execute transactions. All benchmarks are executed using 1, 2, 4, and 8 *initial threads*. We use the term initial threads as dynamic execution may change the number of threads (between 1 and 8) at runtime. Experiments are executed five times, and the mean results reported. This paper restricts the number of worker threads in the thread pool to a maximum of 8, which is equal to the number of cores in the hardware platform used in the evaluations, and a minimum of 1. Unless specified, references to changing numbers of threads imply thread pool worker threads, and not application threads.

3.1   Controller Model Parameters

Through preliminary experimentation with LeeH (explained later in Section 3.3) the parameters of the first four controller models were set to: *samplePeriod* of 10 seconds, *setPointRange* of 50–80%, and *samplePeriodRange* of 4–60 seconds. PoCC's parameters are: *setPoint* of 70%, *minTransactions* of 100. Experimental evaluation found execution of the complete control loop took on average 2ms with PoCC, thus *samplePeriod* is set to 1 second for PoCC to make its overhead negligible.

3.2   Hardware and Software Platform

The platform used for the evaluation is a 4x dual core (8 core) AMD Opteron 2.4GHz system with 16GB RAM, openSUSE 10.1, and Java 1.6 64-bit using the parameters -Xms1024m -Xmx14000m.

DSTM2 is used with its default configuration of eager validation, visible readers, and shadow atomic factory. DSTM2 has been modified to maintain a thread pool as described earlier. DSTM2 supports a number of contention managers (CMs). In DSTM2, a CM is invoked by a transaction when it finds itself in conflict with another transaction. The CM decides which transaction should be aborted based on its policy. The CMs used in this paper are described briefly below, and for further details refer to [21,22,23].

Aggressive always aborts a conflicting enemy transaction.

Backoff gives the enemy transaction exponentially increasing amounts of time to commit, for a fixed number of iterations, before aborting it.

Karma assigns dynamic priorities to transactions based on the number of objects they have opened for reading, and aborts enemy transactions with lower priorities.

Eruption is similar to Karma, and assigns dynamic priorities to transactions based on the number of transactional objects they have opened for reading. Conflicting transactions with lower priorities add their priority to their opponent to increase the opponent's priority, and allow the opponent to abort its enemies, and 'erupt' through to commit stage.

Greedy aborts the younger of the conflicting transactions, unless the older one is suspended or waiting, in which case the older one is aborted.

Kindergarten makes transactions abort themselves when they meet a conflicting transaction for the first time, but then aborting the enemy transaction if it is encountered in a conflict a second time.

Polka combines Karma and Backoff by giving the enemy transaction exponentially increasing amounts of time to commit, for a number of iterations equal to the difference in the transactions' priorities, before aborting the enemy transaction.

Priority is a static priority-based manager, where the priority of a transaction is its start time, that immediately aborts lower priority transactions during conflicts.

3.3   Benchmarks

One synthetic and seven real, non-trivial benchmark configurations are used in this paper. The synthetic benchmark, StepChange, oscillates the TCR from 80% to 20% in steps of 20% every 20 seconds, and executes for a fixed 300 seconds. StepChange needs to be executed with the maximum 8 threads to allow its TCR oscillation to have impact, as it operates by controlling the number of threads executing committed or aborted transactions.

The non-trivial benchmarks used are Lee's routing algorithm [8], and the STAMP [10] benchmarks Genome, KMeans, and Vacation, from STAMP version 0.9.5, all ported to execute under DSTM2. All benchmarks, with the exception of Genome, are executed with high and low data contention configurations, as shown in Table 1. Lee's routing algorithm uses early release [24] for its low data contention configuration, which releases unnecessary data from a transaction's read set to reduce false conflicts. This requires application-specific knowledge to determine which data is unnecessary, and manual annotation of the code. In some other publications, e.g. [8], LeeH is referred to as Lee-TM-t, and LeeL is referred to as Lee-TM-ter. The input parameters for the benchmarks are those recommended by their respective providers. The average benchmark execution times are shown in Table 2, and dynamic available parallelism in Figure 4, both using the Priority contention manager.

Table 1. Benchmark configuration parameters used in the evaluation

Configuration Name	Application	Configuration
StepChange	StepChange	max_tcr:80, min_tcr:20, time:300, step_size:20, step_period:20,
Genome	Genome	gene_length:16384, segment_length:64, num_segments:4194304
KMeansL	KMeans low contention	clusters:40, threshold:0.00001, input_file:random10000_12
KMeansH	KMeans high contention	clusters:20, threshold:0.00001, input_file:random10000_12
VacL	Vacation low contention	relations:65536, percent_of_relations_queried:90, queries_per_transaction:4, number_of_transactions:4194304
VacH	Vacation high contention	relations:65536, percent_of_relations_queried:10, queries_per_transaction:8, number_of_transactions:4194304
LeeL	Lee-TM low contention	early_release:true, file:mainboard
LeeH	Lee-TM high contention	early_release:false, file:mainboard

Table 2. Average benchmark execution times in seconds, including one standard deviation, using the Priority contention manager

	Genome	KMeansH	KMeansL	LeeH	LeeL	VacH	VacL
1 thread	179±1.9	23.6±6.1	22.2±3.5	418±6.4	394± 4.0	524±9.4	475±3.7
2 threads	117±4.8	23.0±7.0	20.4±6.7	250±3.5	326±20.4	362±3.5	390±9.9
4 threads	88±2.9	21.3±3.4	17.7±3.3	162±2.1	280± 8.2	294±3.1	360±3.1
8 threads	83±9.1	27.6±7.8	16.4±4.5	115±4.1	285±14.2	291±3.0	381±9.7

The benchmarks have been modified to use the thread pool to execute transactions. Only KMeans partially uses synchronous job submission as part of each thread's code executes two transactions, the second of which needs a return value from the first. The remaining benchmarks use asynchronous job submission. Lee-TM and Vacation create all jobs during benchmark initialisation, which is excluded from the recorded execution time. Genome and KMeans create jobs dynamically, and thus include job creation time in the recorded execution time. Jobs are submitted in a round-robin manner to the multiple work queues.

3.4   Execution Time

Execution time results are presented in two parts. First, LeeH is investigated using all CMs, but only with the first four controller models. The motivation is to see if the effect on performance varies with the CM used. Second, the

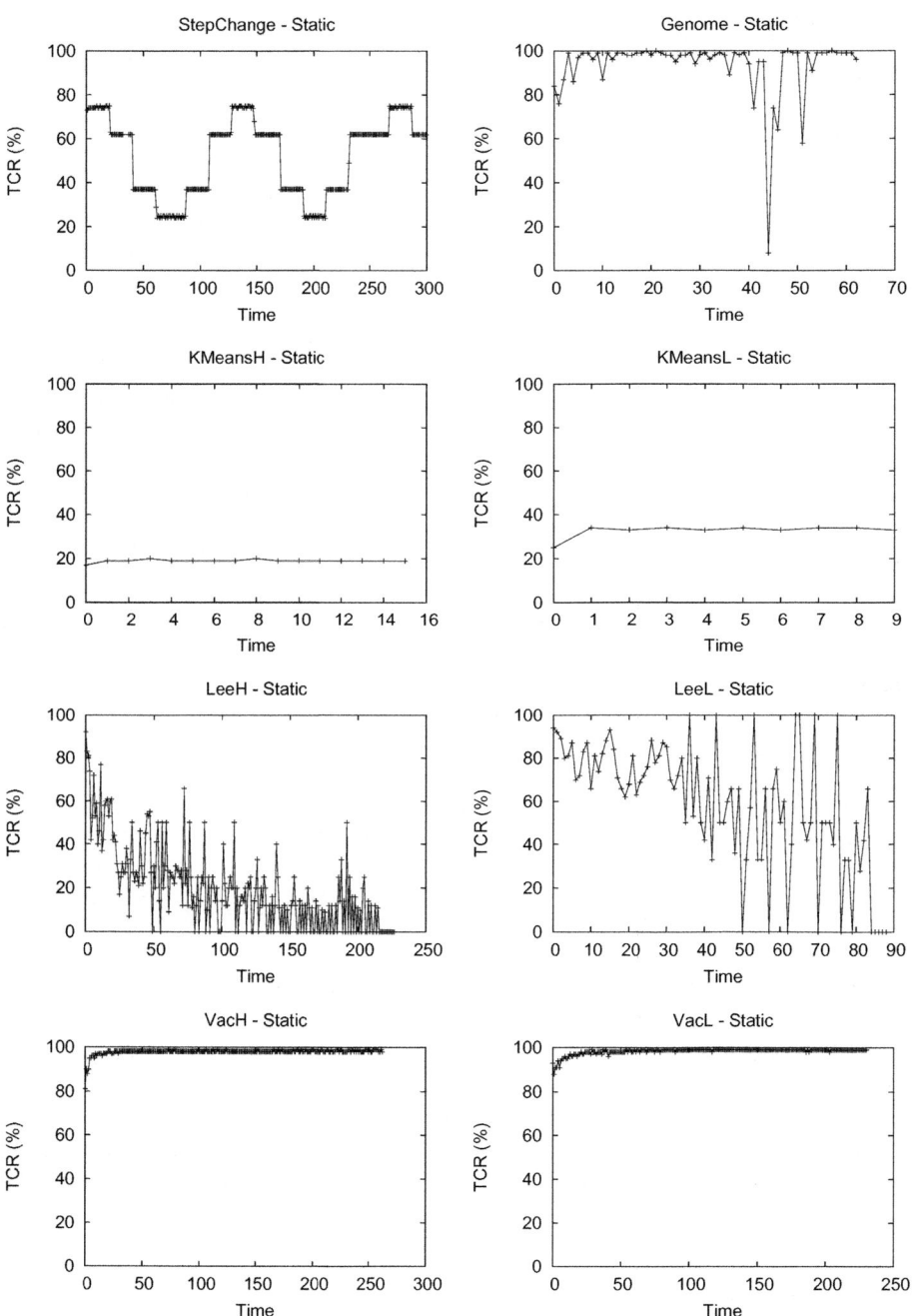

Fig. 4. TCR profiles of the benchmarks used, executing with 8 threads

remaining benchmarks are reported with all controller models, but only the Priority contention manager, as it is generally one of the better performing contentions managers. Using one of the better performing CMs will generally show the *minimum* benefit of using transactional concurrency tuning.

For each benchmark, dynamic execution should: (a) reduce execution time, over static execution with an initial number of threads that under-exploits the available parallelism, (b) reduce execution time, over static execution with an initial number of threads that over-exploits the available parallelism, and (c) reduce variance in execution time over different numbers of initial threads, compared to static execution time variance.

Figure 5 shows normalised execution time results for LeeH with all CMs. For static execution Aggressive, Kindergarten, and Priority CMs provide the best execution times, with a maximum difference of 3.2% between their respective best cases, and are the only CMs to show improving execution times up to 8 threads. The remaining CMs' performance degrades from 4 to 8 threads, indicating that either the proportion of time spent executing aborted transactions, or the time spent in resolving access conflicts, or both, has increased.

Intuitively, the 8 thread execution time improvements with dynamic execution for some CMs suggest that, at this number of threads, there are phases of execution where the available parallelism is low. With fewer threads, although such phases of low available parallelism may have occurred, they were not significant enough to cause a noticeable difference in execution time performance between static and dynamic execution.

Dynamic execution satisfies goal (a) above: execution time is always reduced when compared to static execution with 1 thread. Goal (b) is satisfied: dynamic execution improves execution time with 8 threads for five CMs. Goal (c) is also met: dynamic execution reduces variance in execution time compared to static execution, although execution time variance is not negligible for any controller model.

Additionally, for each CM (excluding Backoff), dynamic execution time for all numbers of initial threads is within 10% of the *best* static execution time. For Backoff this rises to 21% with EC. This shows that dynamic execution performance varies insignificantly with the CM used, including the best performing CMs (Aggressive, Kindergarten, and Priority). The results also show there is no clear winner amongst the controller models for any CM, but the variance amongst them is far smaller than amongst the CMs.

Figure 6 shows normalised execution time results for the benchmarks with only the Priority CM. Amongst these benchmarks only KMeansH and VacL do not improve execution time all the way up to 8 threads. KMeans experiments run for less than 20 seconds on average, thus the graphs have noise due to small execution time differences resulting in large variation in normalised execution time.

Looking at the 1 thread results, dynamic execution improves execution time results when static execution under-exploits available parallelism. In Genome and LeeL, EI and EC improve execution time better than SA and EA. Although

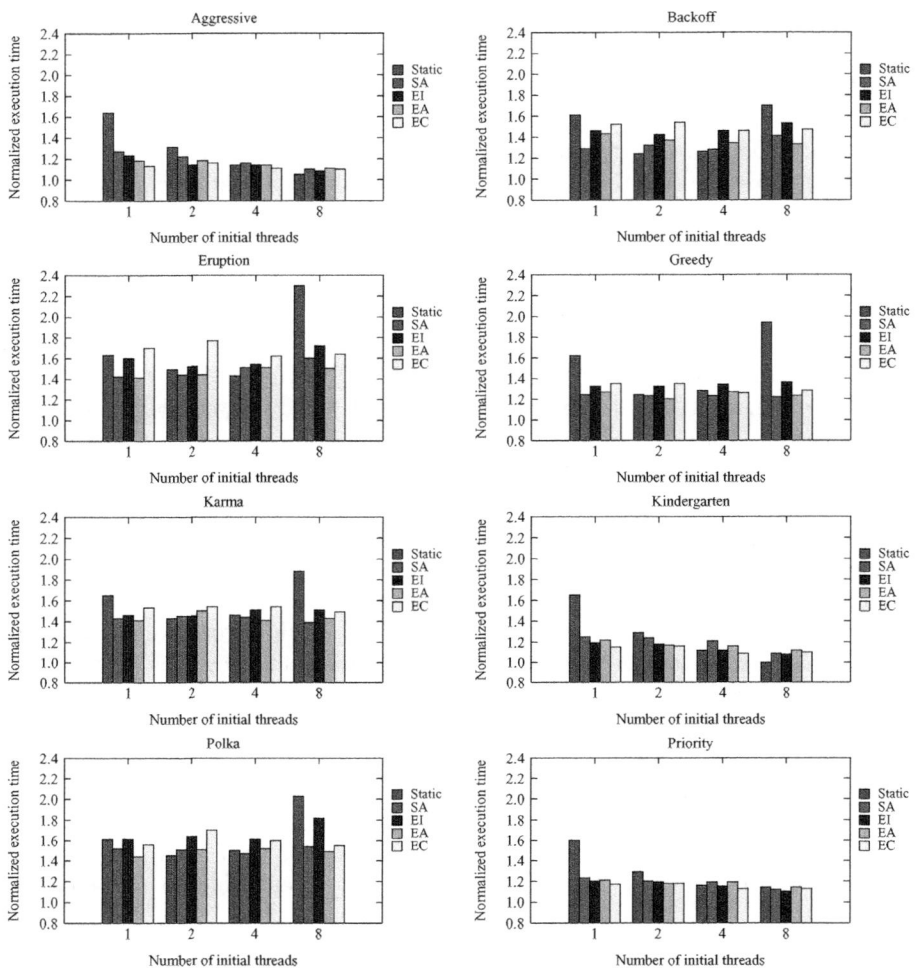

Fig. 5. Execution time for LeeH for each CM, normalised to overall best case static execution time (Aggressive with 8 threads). Less is better.

EC does not fare well in KMeansH, the difference is not significant once execution time is taken into account.

Looking at results across all threads and all benchmarks, dynamic execution reduces variance in execution time results, with EI and EC showing less variance than SA and EA. Looking at the 8 thread results, dynamic execution only improves execution time when static execution over-exploits available parallelism in KMeans, because the falling execution times up to 8 threads show most of the benchmarks don't suffer from over-exploitation. Furthermore, the significance of the KMeans results is devalued by its short execution time.

Although the performance of the controller models with respect to best case static execution time is more variable in these experiments, the best case

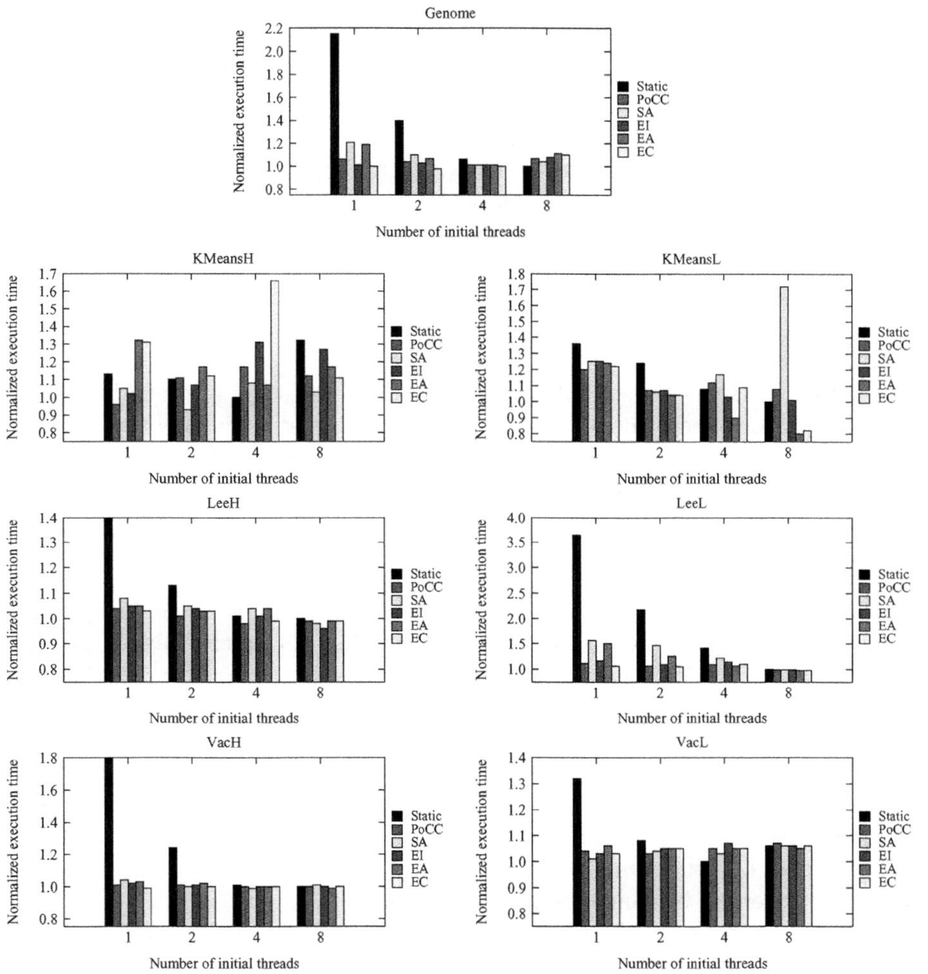

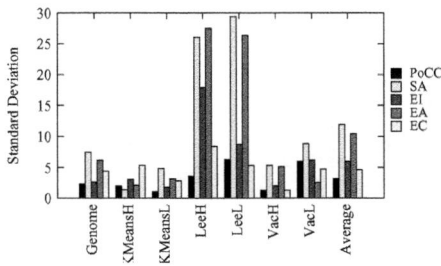

Fig. 6. Execution times for non-trivial benchmarks using the Priority CM, normalised to the best case static execution time for each benchmark configuration. StepChange benchmark omitted as it executes for a fixed duration. Less is better.

Fig. 7. Execution time std deviation over all initial threads. Less is better.

controller model for each benchmark degrades performance by 6% or less. Finally, again there is no clear winner amongst SA, EI, EA, and EC.

Generally, there is little difference in performance between PoCC and the first four controller models, but only PoCC consistently performs well across all benchmarks, whereas SA, EI, EA, and EC all show poor execution times in some benchmark configurations. Furthermore, averaging speedup of each controller model over static execution for each benchmark configuration, PoCC is second-best with an average speedup of 1.26, and EC is best with a marginally better speedup of 1.27. Averaging speedup of each controller model over best-case static execution for each benchmark, PoCC is joint-best with EC with an average slowdown of 5%, while EI, EA, and SA suffer an average slowdown of 6%, 7%, and 10%, respectively.

Figure 7 presents the execution time standard deviation for each benchmark to compare the effectiveness of the controller models at reducing execution time variance. The results show PoCC is the best on average, reducing standard deviation by 31% over the next best, EC.

3.5   Resource Utilisation

Resource usage is calculated by summing, for all TCR samples, the sample duration multiplied by the number of threads executing during the sample. For each benchmark, dynamic execution should improve resource usage over static execution with an initial number of threads that over-exploits the available parallelism. Resource usage is compared for 8 initial threads, the system maximum, as applications that scale past 8 threads should show little resource usage improvement, and applications that do not scale past 8 threads should get maximum resource usage saving at 8 threads with dynamic execution, and thus allow comparison between the controller models. Again, the analysis is in two parts: LeeH with all CMs first, then all benchmarks with the Priority CM.

Figure 8 shows resource savings for all CMs with LeeH. Dynamic execution shows significant resource usage savings with many results in the 40-50% range. In particular, even the best performing CMs (Aggressive, Kindergarten, and Priority) have substantial resource savings, and, as presented earlier, dynamic

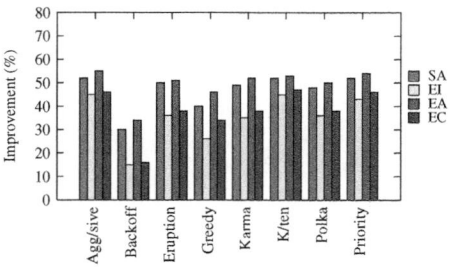
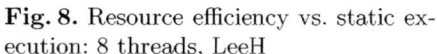
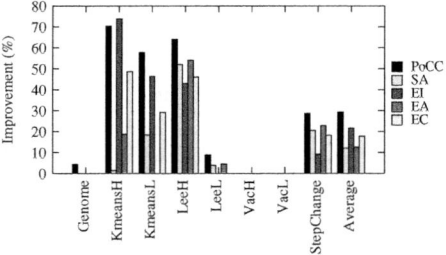

Fig. 8. Resource efficiency vs. static execution: 8 threads, LeeH

Fig. 9. Resource efficiency vs. static execution at 8 initial threads. More is better.

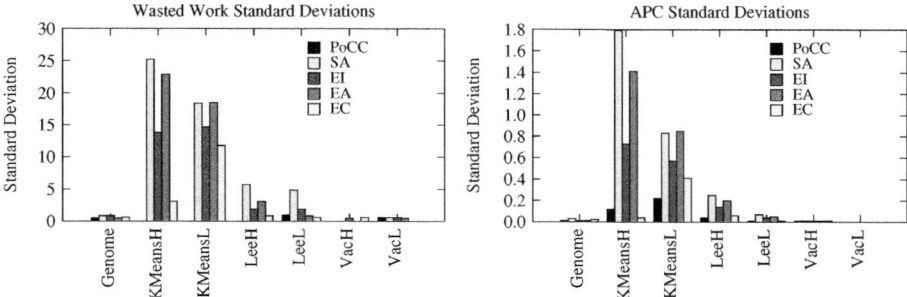

Fig. 10. Wasted work standard deviations for the benchmarks. Less is better.

Fig. 11. APC standard deviations for the benchmarks. Less is better.

execution still results in execution times that are similar to the best case static execution. The results also show that the relative savings between controller models is not affected by the CM used: EA always has the best savings, and EI the worst, for LeeH.

Figure 9 shows resource savings for all benchmarks, all controller models, with the Priority CM. Genome, Vac, and LeeL have little resource savings because they do not have low available parallelism at 8 threads. Relative savings are the same for LeeH and StepChange, but inverted for KMeans: EI offers larger resource savings amongst the first four controller models. However, PoCC is the best in every benchmark except KMeansH where EI is 3.7% better. On average, PoCC improves resource savings by 24% over the next best, EI.

3.6 Transaction Execution Metrics

Two transaction execution metrics are presented: *wasted work* and *aborts per commit* (APC), first presented in TM literature by Perfumo *et al.* [25]. Wasted work is the proportion of execution time spent in executing transactions that eventually aborted, and APC is the ratio of aborted transactions to committed transactions. Both metrics are a measure of wasted execution, and are thus of

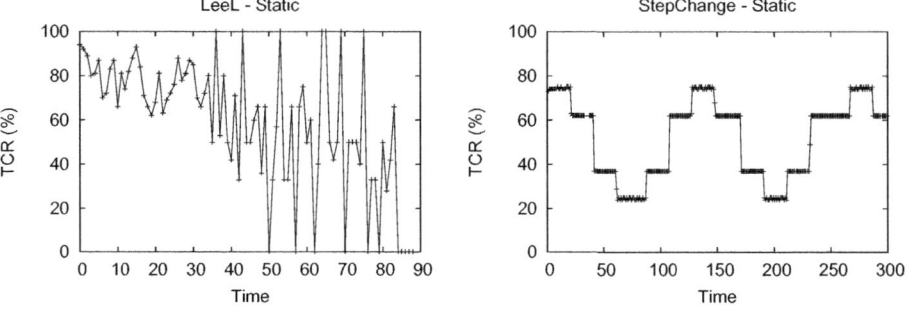

Fig. 12. TCR profiles of LeeL and StepChange, executing with 8 threads

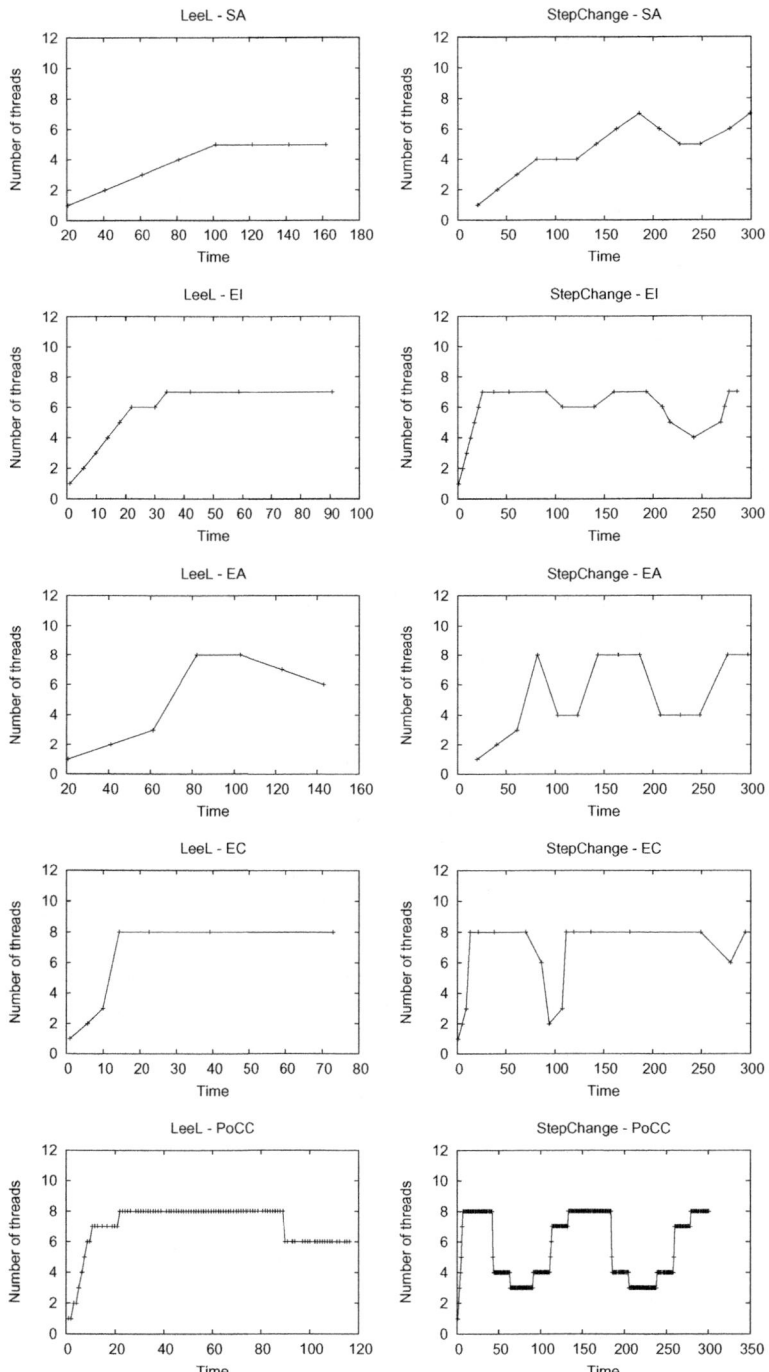

Fig. 13. Number of threads dynamically changing in response to changes in TCR using the Priority CM. All experiments start with 1 initial thread.

interest since transactional concurrency tuning attempts to reduce variance in TCR, which should result in reduced variance in these metrics.

Figure 10 presents wasted work standard deviations. PoCC significantly reduces variability in wasted work: on average its standard deviation is 88% lower than the next best controller model, which is EC. Figure 11 presents APC, and again PoCC reduces variability: on average its APC standard deviation is 26% lower than the next best controller model, which is EC. Furthermore, PoCC reduces average wasted work by 16% over the next best controller model, which is EC, and reduces average APC by 11% over the next best controller model, which is also EC.

3.7   Response Characteristics

This section examines how the controller models respond to changes in TCR. Specifically, this section investigates how fast, how much, and how robustly, controller models respond. The responsiveness analysis is restricted to StepChange and LeeL. Both exhibit TCR profiles that stress the controller models as shown sampled at 1 second intervals in Figure 12. StepChange changes TCR by large amounts at fixed intervals, and LeeL has a wildly oscillating TCR due to the fast sample rate used to capture the data, but earlier sections have shown it has high available parallelism up to 8 threads.

Figure 13 shows the how the controller models respond to the changes in TCR. The first four controller models are robust to the noise in LeeL as the sample rate of the controller models is 10 seconds, not 1 second, which acts as a noise filter. The 50–80% *setPointRange* reduces the chance of unstable behaviour further.

However, these advantages turn into disadvantages for StepChange, where the first four controller models respond poorly. The *samplePeriod* gives the controller models response gradients that are not as steep as StepChange's changes in TCR. The *setPointRange* prevents the controller models from responding to smaller changes in TCR, despite all steps altering TCR by 15% or more. Finally, the *samplePeriodRange* used by EI, and EA, have an upper bound that is too high (60 seconds), resulting in EC failing to respond to the second trough in StepChange's TCR.

PoCC shows good response to both benchmarks: it is robust to noise in LeeL due to the *minTransactions* filter, and it responds to StepChange quickly due to the 1 second *samplePeriod*. The first four controller models trade robustness to noise for responsiveness by using a larger *samplePeriod*. PoCC removes the trade-off with its *minTransactions* filter, giving high responsiveness without compromising robustness.

4   Limitations

Transactional concurrency tuning has been shown to improve performance and reduce resource usage for a number of non-trivial benchmarks; in particular, PoCC has shown good response characteristics. Transactional concurrency tuning has also been implemented to support existing TM applications with only trivial changes. This section discusses two issues in relation to its widespread use: the practicalities of using transactional concurrency tuning, and the implications of using a thread pool to execute transactions.

The key to effective transactional concurrency tuning, as the earlier evaluation has shown, is the ability to quickly and adequately respond to changes in TCR. The system can only respond as fast as the selected *samplingPeriod*, and care needs to be taken to set this short enough to respond to the application's fluctuating TCR. However, if the TCR fluctuates at a rate near to, or faster than, the time it takes to execute the transactional concurrency tuning loop, then it is unlikely the system will be able to offer meaningful improvements in resource usage and performance. Hardware support for the control loop, for example maintaining the statistics needed to calculate TCR in hardware registers, may improve the loop's execution time, and improve the system's ability to support rapid TCR fluctuations.

A short *samplingPeriod* also adds overhead; the thread that executes the transactional concurrency loop code uses processor resources. However, with the increasing number of cores in multi-core processors, we do not foresee this to be an issue. Indeed, it may even be recommended to have the thread running continuously on its own core.

The thread pool is a different programming model from that seen in TM research, although it is not unfamiliar to the world of database transactions, on which TM is based. The thread pool has been refined to improve its scalability by implementing multiple work queues, and work stealing, and it is likely that further research in thread pools will continue to reduce their overhead as existing thread pool based applications move to multi-cores.

One issue is the increase in the total number of threads: application threads plus worker threads. Increasing the number of threads adds context switching overhead. However, it is likely that this overhead will be significantly reduced in multi-core architectures for two reasons. First, the increasing numbers of cores makes it natural to increase the total number of threads. Second, many multi-cores have added support for hardware context switching, which can switch thread contexts per processor clock cycle.

Other overheads that have not been investigated in this work include creation of data structures representing transactional jobs, job submission, and synchronisation when using synchronous job submission. Such overheads may be significant when executing very small transactions.

5   Conclusion

This paper has presented the first application of transactional concurrency tuning to TM with the aim of improving resource utilisation and execution time performance by adapting the number transactions executing concurrently to the available parallelism. A new metric, transaction commit rate (TCR), was introduced as a measure of available parallelism. Four transactional concurrency tuning algorithms (controller models) that varied in response strength were initially evaluated against a number of benchmarks and contention managers. The results showed transactional concurrency tuning led to execution time within 10% of the *best* non-transactional concurrency tuned execution time, whilst significantly reducing processor resource usage (over 40% in many cases) for those applications that exhibited phases of low available parallelism. The saved resources could be used by other applications, or powered down to save energy.

However, analysis of the controller models' response characteristics showed that they traded off robustness to noise in sampled TCR data, with responsiveness. This meant that the controller models' potentially needed their transactional concurrency tuning parameters re-tuning for every application they used, limiting their general applicability. A fifth transactional concurrency tuning algorithm, called PoCC, was created to address this problem, and incorporated a relative gain formula and a minimum transaction count filter. Evaluation of PoCC showed it maintains average execution time similar to the best controller model, has the least performance deficit vs. best-case fixed-thread execution, and improves over the other four controller models by at least 24% average resource usage, 16% average wasted work, and 11% average APC. PoCC improves over the other four controller models standard deviation by at least 31% in execution time, 24% in resource usage, 88% in wasted work, and 26% in APC. Thus PoCC matches or improves in all benchmark performance metrics analysed. Finally, an analysis of all the controller models' response characteristics shows PoCC to be more responsive to, and more robust to noise in, changes in TCR. This is due to the new features in PoCC allowing fine-grain response to changes in TCR, and allowing the sample period to be application-independent.

References

1. Olukotun, K., Hammond, L.: The future of microprocessors. ACM Queue 3(7), 26–29 (2005)
2. Olukotun, K., Nayfeh, B.A., Hammond, L., Wilson, K., Chang, K.: The case for a single-chip multiprocessor. In: ASPLOS 1996: Proceedings of the 7th International Conference on Architectural Support for Programming Languages and Operating Systems, pp. 2–11. ACM Press, New York (1996)
3. Kongetira, P., Aingaran, K., Olukotun, K.: Niagara: A 32-way multithreaded sparc processor. IEEE Micro 25(2), 21–29 (2005)
4. McDougall, R.: Extreme software scaling. ACM Queue 3(7), 36–46 (2005)
5. Herlihy, M., Moss, J.E.B.: Transactional memory: Architectural support for lock-free data structures. In: ISCA 1993: Proceedings of the 20th Annual International Symposium on Computer Architecture, pp. 289–300 (May 1993)
6. Shavit, N., Touitou, D.: Software transactional memory. In: PODC 1995: Proceedings of the 14th Annual ACM Symposium on Principles of Distributed Computing, pp. 204–213. ACM Press, New York (1995)
7. Larus, J.R., Rajwar, R.: Transactional Memory. Morgan and Claypool (2006)
8. Watson, I., Kirkham, C., Luján, M.: A study of a transactional parallel routing algorithm. In: PACT 2007: Proceedings of the 16th International Conference on Parallel Architectures and Compilation Techniques, pp. 388–400. IEEE Computer Society Press, Los Alamitos (2007)

9. Ansari, M., Kotselidis, C., Jarvis, K., Luján, M., Kirkham, C., Watson, I.: Lee-TM: A non-trivial benchmark suite for transactional memory. In: Bourgeois, A.G., Zheng, S.Q. (eds.) ICA3PP 2008. LNCS, vol. 5022, pp. 196–207. Springer, Heidelberg (2008)

10. Minh, C.C., Trautmann, M., Chung, J., McDonald, A., Bronson, N., Casper, J., Kozyrakis, C., Olukotun, K.: An effective hybrid transactional memory system with strong isolation guarantees. In: ISCA 2007: Proceedings of the 34th Annual International Symposium on Computer Architecture, pp. 69–80. ACM Press, New York (2007)

11. Herlihy, M., Koskinen, E.: Checkpoints and continuations instead of nested transactions. In: TRANSACT 2008: Third ACM SIGPLAN Workshop on Transactional Computing (February 2008)

12. Riegel, T., de Brum, D.B.: Making object-based STM practical in unmanaged environments. In: TRANSACT 2008: Third ACM SIGPLAN Workshop on Transactional Computing (February 2008)

13. von Praun, C., Bordawekar, R., Cascaval, C.: Modeling optimistic concurrency using quantitative dependence analysis. In: PPoPP 2008: Proceedings of the 13th ACM SIGPLAN Symposium on Principles and Practice of Parallel Programming, pp. 185–196. ACM Press, New York (2008)

14. Herlihy, M., Koskinen, E.: Transactional boosting: a methodology for highly-concurrent transactional objects. In: PPoPP 2008: Proceedings of the 13th ACM SIGPLAN Symposium on Principles and Practice of Parallel Programming, pp. 207–216. ACM Press, New York (2008)

15. Felber, P., Fetzer, C., Riegel, T.: Dynamic performance tuning of word-based software transactional memory. In: PPoPP 2008: Proceedings of the 13th ACM SIGPLAN Symposium on Principles and Practice of Parallel Programming, pp. 237–246. ACM Press, New York (2008)

16. Kotselidis, C., Ansari, M., Jarvis, K., Luján, M., Kirkham, C., Watson, I.: Investigating software transactional memory on clusters. In: IWJPDC 2008: 10th International Workshop on Java and Components for Parallelism, Distribution and Concurrency, IEEE Computer Society Press, Los Alamitos (2008)

17. Herlihy, M., Luchangco, V., Moir, M.: A flexible framework for implementing software transactional memory. In: OOPSLA 2006: Proceedings of the 21st Annual Conference on Object-Oriented Programming Systems, Languages, and Applications, October 2006, pp. 253–262. ACM Press, New York (2006)

18. Blumofe, R.D., Joerg, C.F., Kuszmaul, B.C., Leiserson, C.E., Randall, K.H., Zhou, Y.: Cilk: An efficient multithreaded runtime system. Journal of Parallel and Distributed Computing 37(1), 55–69 (1996)

19. Ansari, M., Kotselidis, C., Jarvis, K., Luján, M., Kirkham, C., Watson, I.: Adaptive concurrency control for transactional memory. In: MULTIPROG 2008: First Workshop on Programmability Issues for Multi-Core Computers (January 2008)

20. Astrom, K., Hagglund, T.: PID Controllers: Theory, Design, and Tuning. Instrument Society of America (1995)

21. Scherer III, W., Scott, M.L.: Contention management in dynamic software transactional memory. In: CSJP 2004: Workshop on Concurrency and Synchronization in Java Programs (July 2004)

22. Scherer III, W., Scott, M.L.: Advanced contention management for dynamic software transactional memory. In: PODC 2005: Proceedings of the 24th Annual Symposium on Principles of Distributed Computing, pp. 240–248. ACM Press, New York (2005)

23. Guerraoui, R., Herlihy, M., Pochon, B.: Toward a theory of transactional contention managers. In: PODC 2005: Proceedings of the 24th Annual Symposium on Principles of Distributed Computing, pp. 258–264. ACM Press, New York (2005)
24. Herlihy, M., Luchangco, V., Moir, M., Scherer III, W.N.: Software transactional memory for dynamic-sized data structures. In: PODC 2003: Proceedings of the 22nd Annual Symposium on Principles of Distributed Computing, pp. 92–101. ACM Press, New York (2003)
25. Perfumo, C., Sonmez, N., Cristal, A., Unsal, O., Valero, M., Harris, T.: Dissecting transactional executions in Haskell. In: TRANSACT 2007: Second ACM SIGPLAN Workshop on Transactional Computing (August 2007)

Efficient Partial Roll-Backing Mechanism for Transactional Memory Systems[*]

M.M. Waliullah

Department of Computer Science and Engineering
Chalmers University of Technology
SE 412-96 Göteborg
Sweden
waliulla@chalmers.se

Abstract. Transactional memory systems promise to reduce the burden of exposing thread-level parallelism in programs by relieving programmers from analyzing complex inter-thread dependences in detail. By encapsulating large program code blocks and executing them as atomic blocks, dependence checking is deferred to run-time. One of many conflicting transactions will then be committed whereas the others will have to roll-back and re-execute. In current proposals, a checkpoint is taken at the beginning of the atomic block and all execution can be wasted even if the conflicting access happens at the end of the atomic block.

In this paper, we propose a novel scheme that (1) predicts when the first conflicting access occurs and (2) inserts a checkpoint before it is executed. When the prediction is correct, the only execution discarded is the one that has to be re-done. When the prediction is incorrect, the whole transaction has to be re-executed just as before. Overall, we find that our scheme manages to maintain high prediction accuracy and leads to a quite significant reduction in the number of lost cycles due to roll-backs; the geometric mean speedup across five applications is 16%.

1 Introduction

As we embark on the multi-core roadmap, there is a major quest for strategies to make parallel programming easier. One of many difficulties faced when designing a parallel program is to orchestrate the program in such a way that dependences are respected among threads. While lock-based constructs, such as critical sections, have been popular, they can introduce serialization bottlenecks if ?the critical sections are too long and also deadlocks. Transactional memory (TM) [1,4,5,6,8,12,13,14,15] can avoid the serialization imposed by coarse critical sections. This is done by allowing threads to execute critical sections in parallel while preserving atomicity and isolation. As long as there are no data conflicts, thread-level parallelism is uncovered; otherwise, transactional memory forces some transactions to re-execute in a serial fashion.

---

[*] This research is sponsored by the SARC project funded by the EU under FET. The authors are members of HiPEAC – a Network of Excellence funded by the EU under FP6.

Transactional memory system proposals abound in the literature and can be classified broadly in hardware (HTM) [1,4,5,8,12] and software (STM) [14] transactional memory systems. Whereas the former does data-conflict resolution in hardware, the latter emulates data-conflict resolution in software. Recently, some researchers are investigating hybrids between the two (HyTM) [6,13,15]. Based on the observation that STM imposes significant overhead, we target HTM systems in this paper although our contributed concepts can be applied to STM and HyTM systems as well.

In the transactional memory systems proposed so far, data conflicts are detected either lazily or eagerly [8]. HTM systems built on lazy data-conflict detection, such as TCC [4], typically take a checkpoint when a transaction is launched for execution and record the read and the write set for each speculatively executed memory access, i.e., the set of locations that are speculatively read or written. Data-conflict resolution occurs when a transaction finishes and is about to commit. If the read-set of an unfinished transaction intersects with the write-set of the committing transaction, the unfinished transaction has to be squashed and rolled back to the beginning. Clearly, if the conflicting access happened at a late point, useful execution can get wasted which may lead to a significant loss in performance and power.

In HTM systems built on eager data-conflict resolution, such as in LogTM [8], ongoing transactions are notified immediately when a location is modified. As a result, the decision of what transaction should be re-executed is not postponed until the commit point. On the contrary, the faulting read access is sometimes delayed so that the conflicting transaction is not squashed. However, when two transactions happen to have a conflicting read access with respect to each other, one of them is squashed and has to be rolled back to the beginning. Again, the faulting read access may have happened much later and lots of useful execution can get wasted. Of course, the longer the transactions are, the more useful execution can get wasted by conservatively forcing a transaction to re-execute from its beginning.

Recent proposals for supporting nested transactions [7,10] insert checkpoints at the start of each transaction nested inside another to reduce the amount of useful execution to be wasted. Unfortunately, they do not solve the general problem of squashing only the execution that depends on the conflicting access. This paper provides a solution to this general problem.

In this paper, we propose a new HTM protocol that records all potentially conflicting accesses when a transaction is executed. When a transaction is squashed, the set of conflicting addresses that are part of the write set of the committing transaction are book-kept. Next time a transaction is executed, a check-point is inserted when any of the book-kept conflicting addresses is accessed. If the transaction is squashed, it is rolled back to the check-point associated with the first conflicting access. We show that this scheme can be supported with fairly limited extensions to a TCC-like protocol and that it manages to save a significant part of the useful execution done by a squashed transaction.

We first establish the baseline system and frame the problem in Section 2. Section 3 presents our scheme for inserting intermediate check-points – our main contribution. We then evaluate our concept starting with describing the methodology in Section 4 and the experimental results in Section 5. We discuss how our contributions position themselves in relation to prior work in Section 6 and finally conclude in Section 7.

2   Baseline System and Problem Statement

We first describe the baseline system assumed in the study in Section 2.1. Section 2.2 then describes the problem investigated in this paper.

2.1 Baseline Architecture

Without loss of generality, but to assume a concrete design point, we consider TCC [4] as the baseline system. In TCC, all the processors are connected to the main memory through a central bus. To support transactions, the private data cache is modified to track speculative read and write operations of an ongoing transaction. The speculatively read and written locations for a whole transaction form the read and the write set, respectively. The read and the write set are kept track of with an R and a W bit associated with each block as shown in Fig 1.

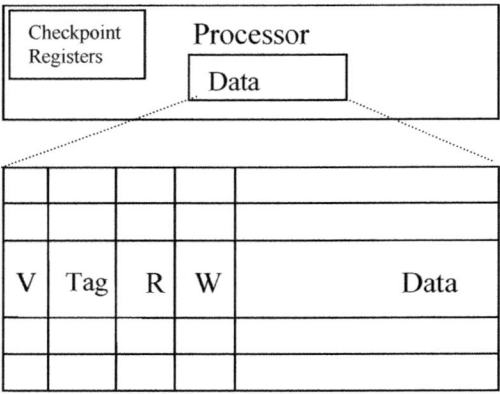

Fig. 1. The modified private data cache proposed in TCC. The cache is extended with two single-bit metadata: a speculative read (R) and a speculative modification (W).

When a read or a write operation occurs in a transaction, the respective R or W bit is set and reset on a commit or on a miss-peculation. Before a transaction is launched, the internal state of the processor is check-pointed. On a commit, all the modified values of the write set are propagated to the main memory and all the information regarding the read and the write set is reset by resetting the R and W bits. When the values associated with the write set are propagated to the main memory through the central bus, all other caches snoop the addresses associated with it on the bus. It is important that a commit is carried out atomically. As a result, no other memory transaction can be in progress during a commit process.

If any address in the write set of the committing transaction conflicts with an address in the read or the write set of another cache, the processor attached to that cache squashes its current transaction and restarts it from the beginning. Squashing involves invalidating all speculatively modified cache blocks and resetting all the R and W bits. While the metadata is allocated at the block level in the original implementation it can be maintained at the word granularity too, to avoid false miss-speculations.

Fig 2 shows the execution of two conflicting transactions. Processor P1 finishes and commits its first transaction. While P1 broadcasts its write set, which contains Wa, P2 detects a conflict with the read set of its ongoing transaction and squashes its transaction. The squashed transaction wastes a lot of execution time but nevertheless maintains the correctness of the program.

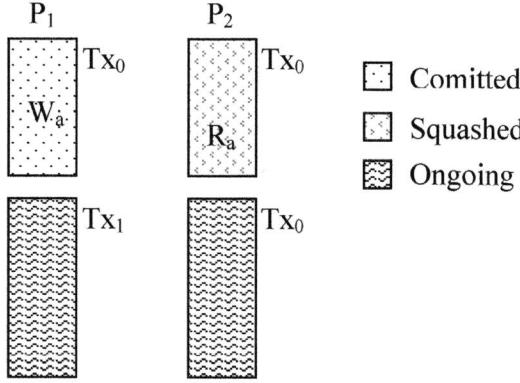

Fig. 2. An execution pattern of transactions running in two processors

In accordance with the TCC hardware model, and for clarity, we assume that the whole program will be decomposed into transactions. Hence, a transaction will start followed by a successful commit of the previous transaction.

2.2 Problem Statement

In Fig 2, we have seen that an access conflict between a modified location of a committing transaction and a read access to the same location by an ongoing transaction forces the ongoing transaction to squash and restart from the beginning. While the transaction restarts from the beginning, it ignores the position of the conflicting access which is 'Ra' in this case. To preserve the correctness of the program, it is necessary and sufficient to restart from a position before the first conflicting access. Therefore, by restarting from the beginning, useful execution is wasted which may impede performance and lead to power losses.

The effect of this waste in execution bandwidth can be huge if the conflicting access occurs late in a long-running transaction. To concretely show the losses, let's consider an execution scenario illustrated by the following micro-benchmark.

The micro-benchmark presented in Fig 3 implements an algorithm that can solve many other search problems. In the benchmark, checking each character in the string segment by a worker forms a transaction. If the character is a member of a set (e.g. vowel), the shared variable, count, is incremented and the next character is examined in a new transaction. Note that the only shared variable, count, is accessed as the last operation in a transaction if the character is a vowel. If the character is not a vowel, the transaction doesn't access any shared variable at all. Therefore, in a conflicting situation re-executing only the last operation is sufficient for correctness of the program. Nevertheless, by re-executing from the beginning, a significant amount of useful work is lost.

```
char *str, *vowels;
int count;

worker(low, high)
{
    for(i=low;i<high;++i){
        XTRAN
        for(j=0;j<n_vowels; ++j){
            if(str[i]==vowels[j]){
                ++count;
                break;
            }
        }
    }
}

main()
{
    for(i=0; i<n_proc; ++i){
        x = str_size / n_proc;
        low = i * x
    high = low + x;
    if(high > str_size)
        high = str_size;

create_thread(worker,low,high);
    }
}
```

Fig. 3. A micro-benchmark that counts the number of vowels in a string. The string is divided into segments and each processor works on one segment. When a vowel is found the processor increments the global shared variable count.

In the next section, we present a mechanism that allows a transaction to re-execute from an intermediate place on squash. Thus, by avoiding re-execution from the beginning we can save a significant amount of execution time and the experimental results in the following section confirms our claim.

3   The Intermediate Check-Point-Insertion Scheme

This section presents the scheme we propose to reduce the execution losses due to roll-back of transactions. We first provide an overview of the scheme in Section 3.1 and then present the structures and algorithms needed to implement it in Section 3.2.

3.1 Overview of the Scheme

Our solution is to insert intermediate check-points to enable a transaction to avoid re-execution from the beginning on a squash. The intention is to insert a checkpoint prior to each conflicting access. As this point is not known beforehand, our approach is to predict the set of conflicting accesses in a transaction based on the set of conflicting accesses recorded in previous transaction executions. The hypothesis is that this set is (1) highly predictable and (2) of a manageable size. The intuition behind the first hypothesis is that when transactions are launched from a particular piece of code e.g., a loop, the set of locations touched are the same in one invocation of the loop as in a subsequent invocation. This hypothesis will be tested in the experimental section. As we will see, the accuracy of this prediction methodology is surprisingly high.

With this hypothesis in mind, we track the history of conflicting memory addresses during the execution of a program. The set of conflicting addresses is called critical addresses (CA). Every time a transaction is squashed, the addresses of the memory accesses that cause the conflict are identified and added to the set CA for future reference. While a processor performs a read operation, the address is matched against the CA in parallel. If the read address is found, the read is considered as a potentially conflicting access. If the potentially conflicting access is the first one to that location within the transaction, a check-point is taken just before the read operation is performed. The goal is that on a squash it is possible to re-execute the transaction from this checkpoint if the prediction is correct.

The code segment starting from a checkpoint to another checkpoint or the end of the transaction is called a sub-transaction. Optionally, an intermediate checkpoint is avoided if the sub-transaction becomes too small to trade off with the check-pointing overhead.

When a processor ends up in a conflicting situation and decides to rollback, it determines the earliest accessed memory location that is involved in the conflict. The processor can rollback to any position before that access without violating the correctness of the program if it is possible to reconstruct the state in which the related part of the system was at that position. In our scheme, a processor restarts from the latest checkpoint that maintains the correctness of the program. As a special case, the checkpoint at the beginning of a transaction could also be the latest one if no intermediate checkpoint serves the purpose. In other words, the transaction restarts from the beginning of the sub-transaction to which the earliest conflicting access belongs.

3.2 Implementation

One key mechanism to support the intermediate checkpoint-insertion scheme is a buffer, called critical address buffer (CAB), attached to each processor that stores the critical addresses as defined in the previous section. Our hypothesis is that the set of critical addresses is small; hence the CAB is implemented as a cache with typically few entries. This hypothesis will be tested later in Section 5. The CAB is checked at every load and store operation in order to determine whether an intermediate checkpoint should be inserted. In order to not have an impact on the cache hit time, we assume that the size of the CAB does not exceed the associativity of the first-level cache. Hence, in the experiments, we will assume CAB size of 4. Further, we assume that the replacement policy of the CAB is LRU.

When an intermediate checkpoint is taken, a transaction is divided into sub-transactions and it is important to be able to roll-back to any of them. Support for rolling back to the beginning is already provided by the basic TCC scheme and involves installing the architectural state and resetting the R and W bits in the first-level cache. To be able to roll-back to an intermediate check-point, however, as many extra sets of check-pointing registers as the number of intermediate checkpoints are needed. This is illustrated in Fig 4.

What goes beyond the mechanisms assumed by TCC is a capability to restore the memory state at the intermediate check-points. There are two mechanisms that facilitate this: (1) a separate read and write set is maintained for each sub-transaction and (2) a single undo log – the ILog buffer as shown in Fig 4 – is used to store the old value of a private cache location that is modified by a sub-transaction so that the modifications by the sub-transaction can be undone. The old value is recorded in the ILog only if the old value is generated speculatively in some previous sub-transaction. Otherwise the old value could be restored from the non-speculative memory. A subsequent modification in the same location within the same sub-transaction doesn't need to be recorded in the ILog buffer. This helps keeping the buffer relatively small.

Each entry in the ILog buffer is associated with the sub-transaction number, STN, in which the transaction is executing while the entry is inserted. When a transaction is rolled back to an intermediate checkpoint, say N, all modifications recorded in the ILog buffer from subsequent sub-transactions (STN>N) are undone by starting from the last entry in the buffer. Undoing in reverse-order ensures that a correct value is restored in case of multiple entries for the same location. When a value in the ILog is restored, the R and W bits corresponding to the squashed sub-transactions are reset. To keep track of the sub-transaction that is executing, a log2 n-bit counter (STN) is also required where n is the maximum number of sub-transactions. Every time a checkpoint is taken the transaction enters into a new sub-transaction and STN is incremented.

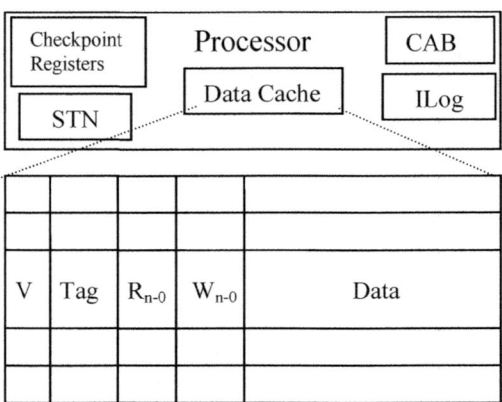

Fig. 4. Processor model of our system including the modified private cache structure

Finally, on a commit, the broadcast write set is matched against the read set of each of the ongoing transactions. When an address in the write set matches an address in a read set, a conflict is detected and the earliest sub-transaction that accessed the memory block is determined from the status of the individual R bit associated with the block. This procedure is repeated for all addresses in the write set to identify the earliest sub-transaction that accessed any of the conflicting location. When invalidating a cache location all R and W bits associated with the location are reset.

To summarize, in Fig 4, we show all the mechanisms needed to extend the baseline TCC with support for the intermediate check-pointing scheme. Apart from the extra set of check-point registers, the CAB, the STN, and the ILog, the first-level cache must also be extended with as many instances of read and write sets as the number of supported intermediate checkpoints. In our experiment, we assume 1-, 2-, and 4–bits in three different configurations. Similar to the baseline system, these fields keep track of the speculative read and write associated with a specific sub-transaction.

4 Experimental Methodology

In order to evaluate our proposed mechanism, we have implemented a simulation model for the baseline system and our proposed extension of it to support the intermediate check-pointing scheme. We also model an oracle system, called the ideal system, which takes a checkpoint at exactly the position of the first conflicting access. Hence, the performance gained in the ideal system reflects what execution can be ideally saved from squashes and is used to compare how good our scheme is and whether there is room for improvement.

The system is configured with 16 processors. Each processor runs a single thread of the application. A traditional three-level memory hierarchy (two levels of caches and the memory) is used in the implemented system. Unlike the private L1 cache, the L2 cache is shared by all the processors. The detailed memory configuration is given in Table 1. L1 and L2 caches are connected through a bus interconnect. As far as the bus capacity, we assume an ideal bus with a FIFO arbitration mechanism. While an ideal bus is not realistic we believe that the performance of our scheme is not sensitive to this assumption as our scheme will not generate more bus traffic than the baseline system. In our scheme, the decision to insert an intermediate check-point is taken locally in a processor to reduce the amount of wasted work. Since it is a local decision it does not generate any bus traffic. The traffic generated in a commit, the write set, is the same as it would have been in the baseline system. We use a victim buffer of 1K entries for storing the evicted cache blocks whose speculative R or W bit is set. Since the scheme does not deal with cache overflow we choose a victim cache that is large enough not to overflow the private buffer. In case of further overflow, the overflowing transaction grabs the bus and executes non-speculatively by holding it until the transaction commits.

Table 1. Memory configuration in the implemented system

Level-1 data cache	64KB, 32-byte/blocks, 4-way ass.
Miss penalty to Level-2	15 cycles
Shared Level-2 cache	8MB, 32-byte/blocks, 64-way ass.
Miss penalty to main memory	200 cycles

A commit overhead of 10-cycles is assumed for each block of data written back. 15-cycles overhead is considered for checkpointing the architected registers [18]. Therefore, we don't take a checkpoint if the resulting sub-transaction size becomes less than 15 instructions. We consider a single-cycle overhead for each reinstalled block from the iLog in case of rollback to an intermediate checkpoint. As for the ideal system, we assume a perfect (zero-cycle) memory system.

In our experiment, we use three applications from the SPLASH-2 benchmark suite [17] and two applications from the Olden applications [2]. We also evaluate the performance of the system with the micro-benchmark presented in Fig 3. In each application, the main work is divided into 16 processors by invoking 16 threads and one thread is allocated per processor. Each thread is decomposed into transactions.

Since the representative or common-case transactional behavior is not yet well understood, the following method is used to 'transactify' the applications. We analyze the source code and insert XTRAN manually that has the semantics to end the ongoing transaction and start a new one. Furthermore, we start a new transaction at every barrier synchronization point while ending the old one. In Health and Raytrace, we also start a new transaction after 2k instructions at runtime having the constraint that a transaction cannot begin or end inside a critical section. It is important to know that our transaction size is not the same as the size of critical sections since we adopt to the transaction-all-the-time approach in [4]. The input parameters and related information of the applications are given in Table 2.

Table 2. Input parameters and benchmark-suite of the applications

Application	Benchmark Suit	Inputs
Raytrace	SPLASH2	Teapot.env
Ocean	SPLASH2	34x34 grid
FMM	SPLASH2	512 particles
MST	Olden	level: 1024
Health	Olden	level: 5, time: 30
Micro-bench		String size: 10000 Set Size: 10

The experimental system is driven by the application traces gathered by running the application in the full-system simulator, Simics [9]. We run the applications on Simics by using the original synchronization primitives in the applications. Each such synchronization primitive (Lock/Unlock, XTRAN, and Barrier) is associated with a magic instruction that will instruct the memory system simulator to either start a transaction or commit a transaction. We systematically remove all synchronizing instructions, e.g. busy waiting at barrier, from the traces before letting the traces drive our implemented system. Nevertheless, all the synchronization and XTRAN primitives are still annotated in the trace to assist the emulator. Only the parallel sections of the applications are considered in generating traces.

We model an in-order, single-issue processor model. While this to a large extent simplifies how to insert checkpoints, the issues involved in inserting check-points in an out-of-order core are well-understood and have been studied in e.g. the context of kilo-instruction processors [16].

The metrics used in the following sections are (1) useful cycles, the number of cycles needed to execute the actual workload; (2) useless cycles, the number of cycles lost in squashed transactions; (3) idle cycles, the number of cycles the processor is waiting for synchronization in ordered transactions; and finally (4) overhead cycles, the number of cycles spent on checkpointing, committing, and restoring the old values of a private cache while roll-backing to the intermediate checkpoint.

5   Experimental Results

Section 5.1 first investigates the potential benefits from intermediate checkpointing. Then we show the performance gains for the micro-benchmark in Section 5.2 followed by the performance gains of SPLASH2 and Olden applications in Section 5.3. The accuracy of the prediction scheme is established in Section 5.4. Finally, in Section 5.5, we study how our results depend on the size of the transactions.

5.1   Potential Gains by Inserting Intermediate Checkpoints

By inserting a checkpoint at the first conflicting access in a squashed transaction, the hope is that some of the execution can be saved. If the first conflicting access happens early, the amount of saved execution is low whereas if it happens close to the point where the transaction is squashed, the amount of saved execution is high. To get intuition into the potential gains, we recorded the fraction of work that can get saved for all squashed transactions. This fraction is calculated as the number of instructions executed before the first conflicting access divided by the total number of instructions executed for the transaction when it was squashed. These numbers are generated by running the applications in the ideal system since the exact information regarding the first conflicting access is not known in the baseline implementation. The cumulative distribution of this ratio is shown in Fig 5.

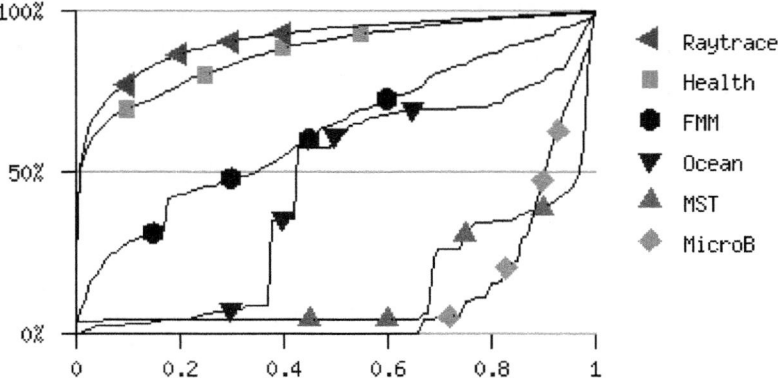

Fig. 5. The cumulative distribution of the fraction of work that can be saved by ideally checkpointing the earliest conflicting access

Fig 5 shows that in MicroB (the micro-benchmark), MST, Ocean, and FMM, the conflicting accesses happens late in the squashed transactions. For example, in MST in about 70% of the squashed transactions, the conflicting access happens after 80% of the transaction has been executed. As a result, the intermediate checkpointing scheme could save a significant amount of work. By contrast, in a large number of squashed transactions in Health and Raytrace, the conflicting accesses occur at the beginning of the transaction and intermediate checkpointing might not be of much help. Overall, while intermediate checkpointing seems to have a great potential, we next study the impact of the gains on the overall performance starting with the micro-benchmark.

5.2 Micro-benchmark Performance

Fig 6 shows the execution time of each of the 16 threads in the micro-benchmark. We consider three systems (from the left to the right bar for each thread): the baseline system, our proposed scheme using a single checkpoint, and an ideal intermediate checkpointing scheme. The execution time for each thread is normalized to the slowest thread of any system because the slowest thread determines the execution time of the parallel application. Further, the execution time is broken down into five parts: useful, useless and idle cycles, transactional overhead and memory latency. For the ideal system, we do not show the memory latency. Therefore, when comparing the execution time of a certain scheme with the ideal, one should not consider the memory latency part of that scheme.

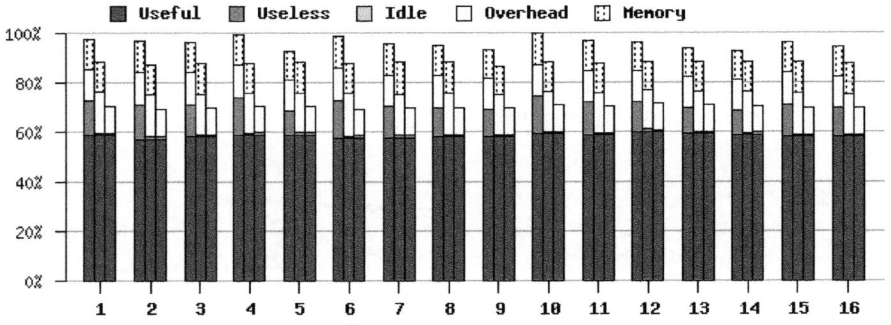

Fig. 6. Normalized execution of all 16 threads in the micro benchmark running on the three systems (from left to right): baseline, single checkpoint, and the ideal system

Fig 6 shows that a single checkpoint suffices to reap most of the gains of intermediate checkpointing. This is expected as the micro benchmark has only one shared variable that can cause any conflict. However, the execution time of the single-checkpoint scheme is higher than that of the ideal scheme because of the single pass of training needed to learn about the conflicting address, checkpointing overheads, and the dominant memory latency which is absent in the ideal scheme. However, in a fair comparison between the schemes (disregarding the memory latency), the single-checkpoint scheme performs almost as well as the ideal scheme.

5.3   Performance Gains for all Applications

In order for the CAB (critical address buffer) to not impose any cycle-time penalty on the micro-architecture, we have assumed that its size is constrained by the associativity of the level-1 cache which is four entries. In this section, we study the impact of inserting up to four checkpoints. Fig 7 shows the execution time of all the applications, dictated by the time when the slowest thread terminates. For each application, the five bars (from left to right) correspond to the baseline, one-checkpoint, two-checkpoint, four-checkpoint and the ideal schemes. The execution times of the four systems are normalized to that of the baseline.

A first interesting observation in Fig 7 is that a single checkpoint is almost as effective as a higher number of checkpoints. To quantify the overall performance using different checkpointing schemes we use the geometric mean over the speedups of all applications. More specifically, we use the following formula considering one checkpointing scheme at a time to calculate the speedups:

$$ speedup \ = \ \sqrt[n]{\prod_i^n \frac{Execution \ - \ time \ _{baseline}}{Execution \ - \ time \ _{checkpo \ \text{int} \ ing \ - scheme}}} $$

where i is the ith-application and n=5. We measured 16%, 17% and 17% speedup using our proposed scheme with one, two and four checkpoints respectively, over the baseline scheme. These numbers suggest again that a single checkpoint is good enough to reap significant benefits.

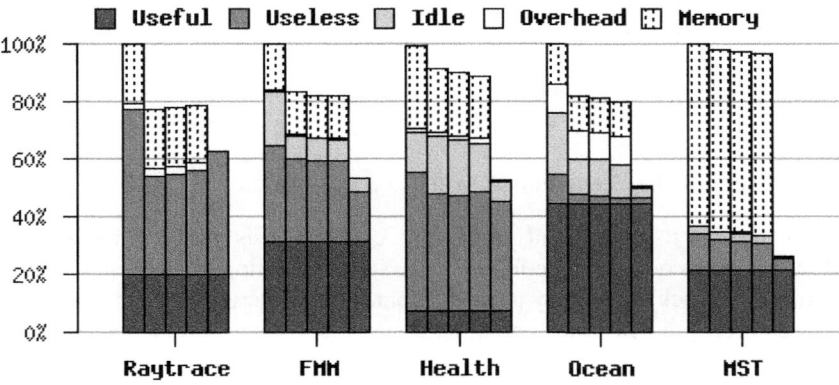

Fig. 7. Normalized execution time of the busiest thread of the applications running on five different system configurations

In case of Raytrace, the higher number of checkpoints seems to increase the useless cycles. This is because the self-scheduling effects cause different interleaving of transactional commits in the different schemes which provokes different violation behaviors. In addition to the execution time, our scheme manages to reduce the number of busy cycles (useful + useless) which is very important from an energy point of view since the processor can go into sleep mode in an idle state.

One concern is that the additional overhead of checkpointing sub-transactions could limit the gains. However, the overheads of execution are very low except for Ocean. To understand the scenario better we presented some relative runtime statistics in Table 3 where application names are specified in the first column. The second column indicates the average transaction size in number of executed instructions. The third column shows the average write set size which is broadcasted as part of transaction commit. The values are counted in terms of number of L1-cache blocks which is 32 bytes. Finally, the fourth, fifth and sixth columns show the average number of ILog entries for one, two and four checkpointing schemes, respectively. As we described in Section 3.2, ILog is used to restore the memory when roll-backing to an intermediate checkpoint.

Table 3. Application execution statistics

Application	Avg Transaction Size (instructions)	Avg Write Set Size (blocks)	Avg iLog Size (blocks)		
			C1	C2	C4
Raytrace	2.6K	25	2	2	3
FMM	16K	38	4	7	8
Health	1.6K	55	1	2	3
Ocean	1.8K	41	1	1	1
MST	4.7K	13	0	0	0

There are three different sources of overhead: (a) checkpointing the architectural registers, (b) broadcasting the write set, and (c) walking through the log table in case of an intermediate rollback. From Table 3, it is clear that the numbers of blocks in ILog are very small. Compared to the size of the transactions, the write set size is significant only for Health and Ocean. And the 15 cycles overhead for each checkpoint is also insignificant in relation to the size of the transactions. In general, our scheme manages to keep the overhead low as depicted in Fig 7.

5.4 Accuracy of the Prediction Scheme

It is interesting to understand whether a checkpoint is inserted before the first conflicting access or not. In the former case, some execution is saved and in the latter, we have to rollback all the way to the beginning. Considering the first case, we could have accurately predicted the conflicting access (called exact prediction) or simply be lucky that another non-predicted conflicting access happened after the checkpoint (called additional coverage). Fig 8 shows the prediction statistics.

Fig 8 shows that the prediction scheme works quite efficiently except in FMM. In FMM, although the effective prediction accuracy is high, the number of exact predictions is low. From the trace of the execution, we have observed that the number of shared variables accessed in a transaction is quite high so the CAB is not able to keep the correct conflicting addresses.

When we relate the data in Fig 8 and the data presented in Fig 5 and Fig 7, we find a discrepancy that the useless cycles in the proposed scheme for MST is not close to that of the ideal scheme while the prediction scheme (Fig 8) shows high accuracy and

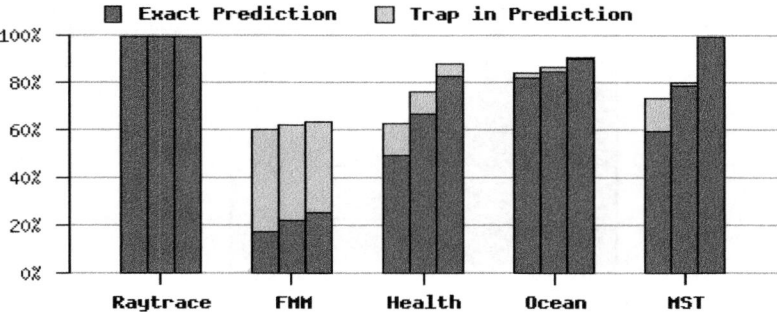

Fig. 8. Percentage of squashed transaction where the first conflicting access is identified or covered by the prediction scheme. Each of the three bars in a cluster represents (from left to right) the number for the scheme with 1, 2, and 4 checkpoints.

Fig 5 shows promising. To analyze this we should keep in mind that in MST, transactions are created only at barrier synchronization point. Therefore, the corresponding transactions in different threads start at the same time. In Fig 5, we observe that most of the violations in MST happen very late and few happen very early in the transactions. However, this data is generated from a run on the ideal scheme where parallel threads tend to execute at the same regions at a specific time. When memory system effects are taken into account, some threads that encounter cache misses lag behind others even though all threads start at the same time. In this way, a huge number of late conflicts disappear from the scene and the percentage of early conflicts dominates. However, to tradeoff with the overhead we didn't take any checkpoint at an early stage in a transaction even though our prediction scheme predicted the conflicting access accurately. In addition to that, the small number of transactions that conflicted very early weight heavy in terms of the number of instructions executed by them.

Table 4. Statistics of variation's transaction-size

Application	Smaller		Initial		Larger	
	Tran-size System Parameter	Average Tran-size Dynamic	Tran-size System Parameter	Average Tran-size Dynamic	Tran-size System parameter	Average Tran-size Dynamic
Raytrace	1K	1.5K	2K	2.8K	4K	4.6K
FMM	5K	4.2K	50K	13.2K	20K	16.8K
Health	1K	0.85K	2K	1.6K	4K	2.95K
Ocean	1K	0.89K	50K	1.9K	4K	1.4K
MST	2K	1.5K	50K	4.8K	8K	4.8K

5.5 Variation Analysis

The results presented in the previous sections were collected using a methodology that decomposes the application into transactions essentially when a synchronization primitive is encountered (a barrier, a lock or unlock primitive) as described in

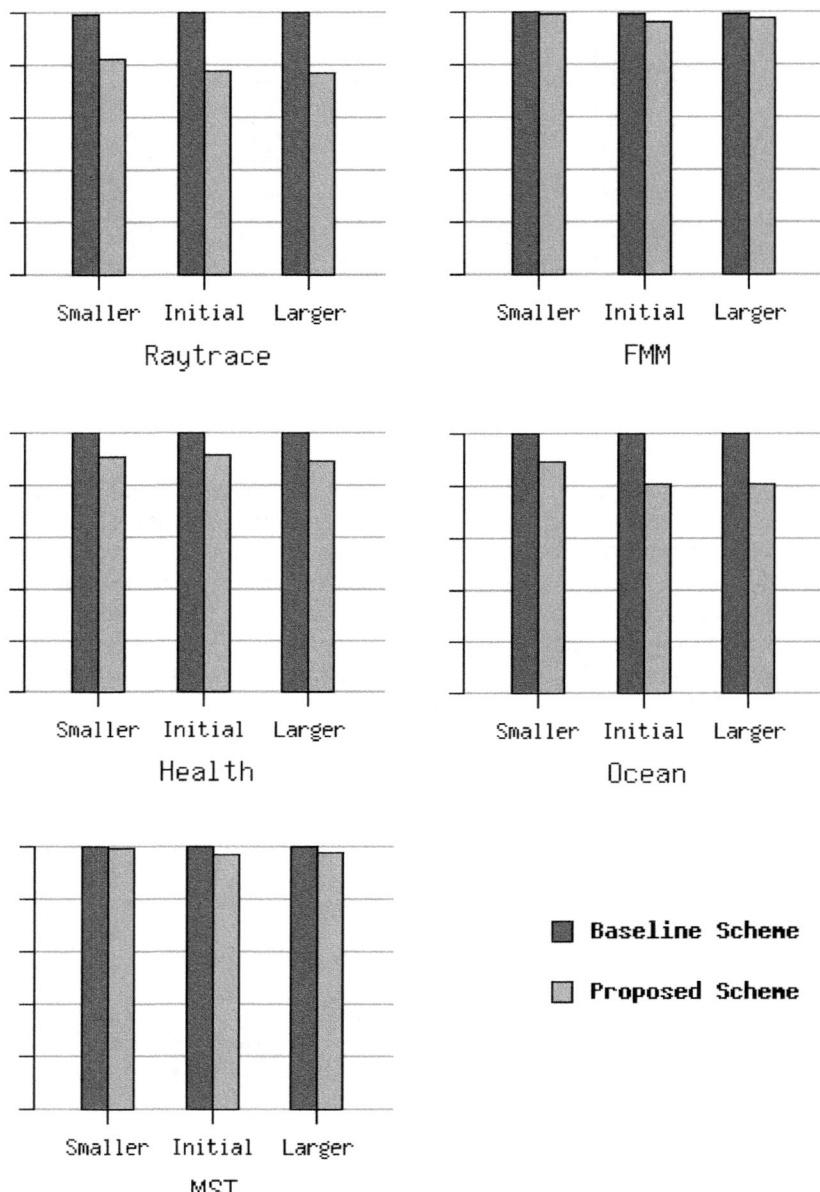

Fig. 9. Execution time for each application normalized to the baseline system. The left and right bars in a cluster represent the execution time under the baseline and the proposed scheme, respectively. Each of the three clusters represents execution time with different transaction sizes.

Section 4. Table 3 represents the average size of transactions that is manifested in the runtime system. In this section, we will see how the proposed system performs when running the same applications but using different transaction sizes. To capture that, we run the applications in three different system configurations in terms of transaction sizes (Smaller, Initial, and Larger) where each system terminates and starts a new transaction after a certain number of instructions are executed. For the system configuration that is termed 'Initial', the number of instructions for a transaction size is fixed as the average transaction size represented in Table 3. For the Smaller and the Larger system configurations, the size is set as half and double, respectively, of the transaction size set in the Initial configuration. The detailed information regarding the transaction sizes in these different setups is presented in table 4.

In Table 4, we associate two columns with each application under a specific system configuration. The first column, Tran-size System Parameter, represents the given system parameter as if the system will terminate the ongoing transaction and start a new transaction after executing that number of instructions. The second column, Average Tran-size Dynamic, represents the dynamically manifested transaction size for each application under the specific system configuration. For each configured transaction size, we also run the baseline and our proposed system with 2 checkpoints.

In Fig 9, we present the execution time of each application in a separate graph. For each application, there are three clusters that represent the execution time of the application run under Smaller, Initial and Larger configurations from left to right. Within the cluster, the left bar represents the execution time under baseline and the right bar represents the execution time under our proposed system.

From Fig 9, we can see that the performance improvements in our system over the baseline sustain over various size of transactions. However, the ratio of improvements is higher in larger transactions than the smaller transactions. The results are also consistent with our hypothesis in Section 2.2 that long-running transactions suffer more.

One may assume that the execution time that is represented by the third bar of each cluster in Fig 7 and the execution time represented by the right bar of the Initial configuration in Fig 9 should be same. However, they are different because the configured transaction size in the Initial setup is the average manifested transaction size of the original setup whereas the transaction size of the original setup was as described in Section 4.

6 Related Work

In this paper, we have presented a scheme that enables us to have intermediate checkpoints while a transaction is running so that we can re-start the transaction from an intermediate point rather than from the beginning of the transaction on a squash.

The work that is most related to our study is [3] by Colohan et al. In that paper, the authors proposed sub-threading in the context of TLS where the sub-transactions (called sub-threads in their work) are created after executing a fixed number of instructions. However, our work extends it by proposing and evaluating a novel scheme for when sub-transactions should be created based on the prediction of conflicting access. Additionally, our paper also describes the memory state recovery mechanism needed to restart from an intermediate checkpoint which is lacking in [3].

Prior to [3], Vallejo et al. proposed the use of implicit transactions [16], as a means to allow memory accesses to overlap each other in kilo-instruction multiprocessors. They sketch another intermediate checkpointing scheme that shortens the length of sub-transactions when conflicts are common. By contrast, we keep track of the source of the miss-peculation.

Moss and Hosking [11] describe closed and open nesting semantics for transactional memory systems. McDonald et al. also outline the implication of using different types of nesting transactions in [10]: (1) closed nesting that enables independent abort and (2) open nesting that enables independent abort and commit both. Moravan et al. proposed an infrastructure for supporting nested transaction [7] in LogTM.

In aforementioned work, nested transactions are considered to facilitate software composition using different program modules where one module is called inside another module. The independent abort of nested transactions enables the system to have partial rollback. However, it is a software embedded sub-transactification. In our approach, long running flat transactions are sub-transactified to reduce rollback overhead. This is a dynamic effort that resembles closed nested semantics. More importantly, it can coexist with the nested transactional concept. Furthermore, Most of the nested transaction semantics advocate merging the read/write set with the parent at commit and after that partial rollback is not possible. In our approach, partial abort is possible during the entire execution.

In transactional memory systems that detect conflicts eagerly, e.g., LogTM, on a conflict, a transaction can wait and retry after a back off time and hope that the other will commit by the time and avoid unnecessary squashes. But this is not possible in all conflicting situations as transactions may be involved in a cross dependency where one of the transactions must rollback to the beginning. Our scheme does not suffer from that weakness.

7   Concluding Remarks

In this paper, we propose to take intermediate checkpoints to reduce wasted work from squashed transaction. In this scheme, on a commit, a conflicting transaction does not rollback to the beginning but rather to an intermediate checkpoint. One novel aspect of the approach is how it predicts conflicting accesses before taking checkpoints by just keeping a limited number of conflicting accesses in a cache-like structure from previous transaction conflicts. We have shown that this scheme performs almost as well as a system in which the conflicting access is known a priori and a checkpoint is inserted there.

We have evaluated this concept in a framework assuming lazy conflict resolution such as TCC. We have compared the performance of our scheme with the baseline TCC and an ideal system that can yield maximum gain. Experimental results show that the performance can be improved significantly and is often close to that of the ideal system. The reduction of busy cycles is also very important from the perspective of energy consumption. The prediction accuracy of conflicting accesses by our history based prediction scheme is also surprisingly high. The system also sustains its performance in different sizes of transactions.

References

1. Ananian, C.S., Asanović, K., Kuszmaul, B.C., Leiserson, C.E., Lie, S.: Unbounded Transactional Memory. In: Proceedings of the 11th International Symposium on High-Performance Computer Architecture (HPCA 2005), San Francisco, CA, pp. 316–327 (February 2005)
2. Carlisle, M.C., Rogers, A.: Software caching and computation migration in Olden. In: Proceedings of the Symposium on Principles and Practice of Parallel Programming, Santa Barbara, CA, pp. 29–38 (July 1995)
3. Colohan, C.B., Aliamaki, A., Steffan, J.G., Mowry, T.C.: Tolerating Dependences Between Large Speculative Threads Via Sub-Threads. In: Proceedings of the 33rd International Symposium on Computer Architecture, pp. 216–226. Boston, MA (June 2006)
4. Hammond, L., Wong, V., Chen, M., Hertzberg, B., Carlstrom, B., Davis, J., Prabhu, M., Wijaya, H., Kozyrakis, C., Olukotun, K.: Transactional Memory Coherence and Consistency. In: Proceedings of the 31st Annual International Symposium on Computer Architecture, München, Germany, June 19-23, pp. 102–113 (2004)
5. Herlihy, M., Moss, J.E.B.: Transactional Memory: architectural support for lock-free data structures. In: Proceedings of the 20th International Symposium on Computer Architecture, pp. 289–300 (1993)
6. Minh, C.C., Trautmann, M., Chung, J.W., McDonald, A., Bronson, N., Casper, J., Kozyrakis, C., Olukotun, K.: An Effective Hybrid Transactional Memory System with Strong Isolation Guarantees. In: Proceedings of the 34th Annual International Symposium on Computer Architecture (June 2007)
7. Moravan, M.J., Bobba, J., Moore, K.E., Yen, L., Hill, M.D., Liblit, B., Seift, M.M., Wood, D.A.: Supporting nested transactional memory in LogTM. In: Proceedings of the 12th International Conference on Architectural Support for Programming Languages and Operating Systems (ASPLOS-XII), pp. 359–370 (2006)
8. Moore, K.E., Bobba, J., Moravan, M.J., Hill, M.D., Wood, D.A.: LogTM: Log-based Transactional Memory. In: Proceedings of the 12th Annual International Symposium on High Performance Computer Architecture (HPCA-12), Austin, TX, February 11-15 (2006)
9. Magnusson, P.S., Christianson, M., Eskilson, J., et al.: Simics: A full system simulation platform. IEEE Computer 35(2), 50–58 (2002)
10. McDonald, A., Chung, J., Carlstrom, B.D., Minh, C.C., Chafi, H., Kozyrakis, C., Olukotun, K.: Architectural semantics for practical transactional memory. In: Proceedings of International Symposium on Computer Architecture (June 2006)
11. Moss, E., Hosking, T.: Nested Transactional Memory: Model and Preliminary Architecture Sketches. In: OOPSLA Workshop on Synchronization and Concurrency in Object-Oriented Languages (October 2005)
12. Rajwar, R., Herlihy, M., Lai, L.: Virtualizing transactional memory. In: Proceedings of the 32nd International Symposium on Computer Architecture, pp. 494–505 (June 2005)
13. Saha, B., Adl-Tabatabai, A., Jacobson, Q.: Architectural Support for Software Transactional Memory. In: Proceedings of the MICRO-39, Orlando, FL (December 2006)
14. Saha, B., Adl-Tabatabai, A., Hudson, R.L., Minh, C.C., Hertzberg, B.: McRT-STM: a High Performance Software Transactional Memory System for a Multi-core Runtime. In: Proceeding of 11th ACM SIGPLAN Symposium on Principles and Practice of Parallel Programming (PPoPP 2006), pp. 187–197 (March 2006)

15. Shriraman, A., Spear, M.F., Hossain, H., Marathe, V., Dwarkadas, S., Scott, M.L.: An Integrated Hardware-Software Approach to Flexible Transactional Memory. In: Proceedings of the 34th Annual International Symposium on Computer Architecture (June 2007)
16. Vallejo, E., Galluzzi, M., Cristal, A., Vallejo, F., Beivide, R., Stenstrom, P., Smith, J.E., Valero, M.: Implementing Kilo-Instruction Multiprocessors. In: Proceedings of the IEEE Conference on Pervasive Services, ICPS 2005, Santorini, Greece (July 2005)
17. Woo, S.C., Ohara, M., Torrie, E., Singh, J.P., Gupta, A.: The SPLASH-2 Programs: Characterization and Methodological Considerations. In: Proceedings of the 22nd International Symposium on Computer Architecture, Santa Margherita Ligure, Italy, pp. 24–36 (June 1995)
18. Martinez, J.F., Torrellas, J.: Speculative Synchronization: Applying Thread-Level Speculation to Explicitly Parallel Applications. In: Proceedings of the ASPLOS X, CA, USA (2002)

Software-Level Instruction-Cache Leakage Reduction Using Value-Dependence of SRAM Leakage in Nanometer Technologies

Maziar Goudarzi[1,3,*], Tohru Ishihara[3], and Hamid Noori[2,3]

[1] Computer Engineering Department, Sharif University of Technology,
Azadi Avenue, Tehran, Iran
goudarzi@sharif.ir
[2] School of Electrical and Computer Engineering, Faculty of Engineering,
University of Tehran, Tehran, Iran
noori@cad.ut.ac.ir
[3] Kyushu University, Fukuoka, Japan
{goudarzi,ishihara}@slrc.kyushu-u.ac.jp,
noori@c.csce.kyushu-u.ac.jp

Abstract. Within-die process variation is increasing in nanometer-scale process technologies. We observe that the same SRAM cell leaks differently under within-die process variations when storing 0 compared to 1; this difference can be up to 3 orders of magnitude at 60mV variation of threshold voltage (V_{th}). Thus, leakage can be reduced if most often the values that dissipate less leakage are stored in the cache SRAM cells. We take advantage of this fact to reduce instruction-cache leakage by presenting three binary-optimization and software-level techniques: we *(i)* reorder instructions within basic-blocks so that their bits better match the less-leaky state of their corresponding cache cells, *(ii)* statically change the register operands of the instructions with the same aim, and *(iii)* at boot time, initialize unused cache-lines to their corresponding least-leaky values. Experimental results show up to 54%, averaging 35%, leakage energy reduction at 60mV variation in V_{th}, and show that with technology scaling, this saving can reach up to 84% at 100mV V_{th} variation. Since our techniques are one-off and do not affect instruction cache hit ratio, this reduction is provided with only a negligible penalty, in rare cases, in data cache.

Keywords: Leakage power, software techniques, compiler optimization, process variation, power reduction, cache memory, instruction rescheduling.

1 Introduction

Cache memories, as the largest component of today's processor-based chips (e.g. 70% of StrongARM [1]) are among the main sources of power dissipation in such chips. In nanometer SRAM cells, the trend is that most of the power is dissipated as leakage [2] due to lower threshold-voltage (V_{th}) of transistors and higher V_{th} variation (caused by

---

* Corresponding author.

P. Stenström (Ed.): Transactions on HiPEAC III, LNCS 6590, pp. 275–299, 2011.

random dopant fluctuations [3] and other sources of variation) when approaching atomic sizes. This inherent variation impacts stability, power and speed of the SRAM cells. Several techniques exist that reduce cache leakage power at various levels [4]-[22], but none of them takes advantage of a new opportunity offered by this increasing variation itself: *the subthreshold leakage current (I_{off}) of a SRAM cell depends on the value stored in it and this difference in leakage increases with technology scaling.* When transistor channel length approaches atomic sizes, process variation due to random placement of dopant atoms increases the variation in V_{th} of same-sized transistors even within the same die [25]. This is an unavoidable physical effect which is even more pronounced in SRAM cells as area-constrained devices that are typically designed with minimum transistor sizes. Higher V_{th}-variation translates to much higher I_{off}-variation ($I_{off} \propto exp(-v_{th}/(s/\ln(10)))$ where s is the subthreshold swing [25]) even in the transistors of a single SRAM cell. Since some of these transistors leak when storing a 1 and others when storing a 0, cell leakage differs in the two states. Thus cache leakage can be reduced if the values stored in it can be better matched with the characteristics of their corresponding cache cells; i.e., if most of the time a 0 is stored in a cache cell that leaks less when storing a 0, and vice versa. To the best of our knowledge, no previous work has observed this saving opportunity. Monte Carlo simulations in Section 3 show that theoretically 70% leakage saving opportunity (comparing full match to full mismatch) would be available in a technology node with 60mV standard deviation of within-die V_{th} variation.

In this paper we use the above phenomenon to reduce instruction-cache leakage by three software-level techniques: we *(i)* reschedule instructions inside each basic-block (BB) of a given application to let them better match their corresponding cache cells, *(ii)* at the same time, we change register operands of the instructions (i.e. static register-renaming) to further improve the match between the instructions and their cache cells, and *(iii)* the least-leaky values are stored in the cache-lines that won't be used by the embedded application. In total, these techniques result in up to 54% leakage reduction (35% on average) on our set of benchmarks, with only a negligible penalty in the data-cache caused by the instruction-reordering since techniques *(i)* and *(ii)* are applied offline and *(iii)* is only applied once at the processor boot time. Furthermore, it is important to note that these techniques reduce leakage not only in the standby-mode, but also in the active-mode of system operation (even when the memory cells are being accessed in case of techniques *(i)* and *(ii)*) and moreover, it is orthogonal to current circuit/device-level techniques.

This paper is an extension of our previous work [26]. We have added the following further investigations in this paper:

- To avoid the need to store different binary executables per chip instance, we store the same executable in all of them, and then the RTOS modifies the binary in field upon first execution and stores the modified binary back to the programmable ROM to bypass this step in subsequent executions.
- Further detailed evaluation is presented for the overheads of the approach concerning performance and power of instruction and data caches.
- The proposed techniques and our assumptions on the input are explained in more details and are compared to several other related works.
- Detailed explanation is given for our experiments setup, simulation methodology, and power calculation method.

In the rest of this paper, Section 2 reviews related previous works. Section 3 motivates our work outlined in Section 4 and describes the new saving opportunity in presence of within-die V_{th} variation. Section 5 formulates the problem and presents the algorithm. Experimental results are presented and analyzed in Section 6, and finally, Section 7 concludes the paper.

2 Related Work

Leakage in CMOS circuits can be reduced by power gating [4], source-biasing [2], reverse- and forward-body-biasing [5][6] and multiple or dynamic V_{th} control [7]. For cache memories, selective turn-off [8]-[10] and dual-supply drowsy caches [11] disable or put into low-power drowsy mode those parts of the cache that are not likely to be accessed again. All these techniques, however, need circuit/device-level modification of the SRAM design while our proposal is a software technique and uses the cache as is. Moreover, none of the above techniques specifically addresses the leakage variation issue (neither variation from cell to cell, nor the difference between storing 0 and 1) caused by within-die process variation. We do that and we work at system-level such that our technique is orthogonal to them. Furthermore, all previous works focus on leakage power reduction when the SRAM cell is not in use or not likely to be accessed later, but our above *(i)* and *(ii)* techniques save power even when the cell is actively in use.

The leakage-variation among various cache-ways in a set-associative cache is used in [12] to reduce cache leakage by disabling the most-leaky cache ways. Our techniques, in contrast, do not disable any part of the cache and use it at its full capacity, and hence, do not incur any performance penalty due to reduced cache size. Moreover, our techniques are applicable to direct-map caches as well.

There are several compiler techniques to reduce power [13]-[19] but most of them focus on dynamic power and do not target leakage power dissipation. Compiler-inserted special instructions are used in [18] to deactivate (i.e. put into low-leakage mode) those cache lines of the data cache whose data are not used by the current computation. This approach, however, requires that each cache-line can be individually put in low-leakage mode, and furthermore, the processor core needs to be extended by special instructions to activate/deactivate cache-lines. Our technique needs no hardware modification in the processor or cache and can also reduce leakage even in the cache lines used by the current computation.

Special instructions for dynamic voltage scaling and adaptive body biasing are inserted by the compiler in [19] to reduce total power consumption, including leakage, of embedded processors. Our work does not need any extra actions or core-control instructions during program execution; our cache-initialization technique is only executed once at processor boot time, and our OS-based binary adaptation technique is a one-off task for each processor core—see Section 4.

In logic circuits, value-dependence of leakage power has been identified and used in [22] to set the input vector to its leakage-minimizing value when entering standby mode. We show this value-dependence exists, with increasing significance, in nano-scale SRAM cells and can benefit power saving even when not in standby time.

Asymmetric SRAM cells are proposed in [23] and [24] to reduce leakage in the 0 state based on the fact that most stored bits are 0 in data as well as instruction cache memories. The SRAM cells that we investigate are designed to be symmetric, but they *become randomly asymmetric* during manufacturing due to process variation. Thus, the reasons of asymmetry are fundamentally different, and it is uniform in [23] and [24] vs. random in our case; nevertheless, our techniques can also be used to reinforce advantages of asymmetric cells in [23] and [24].

Register-renaming is a well-known technique that is often used in high-performance computing to eliminate false dependence among instructions that otherwise could not have been executed in parallel. It is usually applied dynamically at runtime, but we apply it *statically* and obviously for a different aim. To the best of our knowledge, register-renaming has not been used in the past for *leakage* reduction.

Optimal allocation and binding of registers to minimize power has been investigated in literature [20] [21]. Assuming that the probability distribution function for the values of primary inputs is known, [20] defines a mathematical formulation for switching activity of a set of registers shared by different data values and assigns variables to registers such that total switching power is minimized. [20] chooses number and binding of registers as part of hardware behavioral synthesis process whereas our work concerns registers in an embedded processor, and hence, in our register-renaming technique the set of registers is fixed by the given processor core and only the register operands of instructions change. Gebotys uses a network flow technique [21] to optimally assign a given set of variables in a basic-block to a memory module and a set of registers such that total dynamic power consumption of memory and registers is minimized for executing that basic-block. Our work is a binary-optimization and post-compilation technique that does not change the partitioning of variables to memory and registers, and also our register-renaming is not restricted to a basic-block. Nevertheless, the algorithms and techniques in [20] and [21] can be properly modified to use for a new goal such as the one in our work.

Cache-initialization, normally done at processor reset, is traditionally limited to resetting all *valid*-bits to indicate emptiness of the entire cache. We extend this initialization to store the least-leaky values in all those cache-lines that won't be used by the embedded application.

3   Motivation and the New Saving Opportunity

Leakage is increasing in nanometer-scale technologies, especially in cache memories which comprise the largest part of processor-based embedded systems. Fig. 1 shows the breakdown of energy consumption of the 8KB instruction-cache of M32R embedded processor [27] when running 1 million instructions of MPEG2 application. We used CACTI versions 4 and 5 [28] to obtain cache dynamic and static power values in various technologies, and obtained the simulation time and number of accesses to the cache and to the off-chip memory by simulating M32R instruction cache (an 8KB 2-way set-associative cache with 16-byte line-size) for the MPEG2 instruction-trace obtained from M32R instruction-set simulator. Processor clock frequency is 200MHz (corresponding to our M32R implementation on 180nm technology), miss-penalty is 40 clock cycles, and a cache-line-fill from off-chip memory consumes 40nJ of energy (pessimistically constant in all technologies).

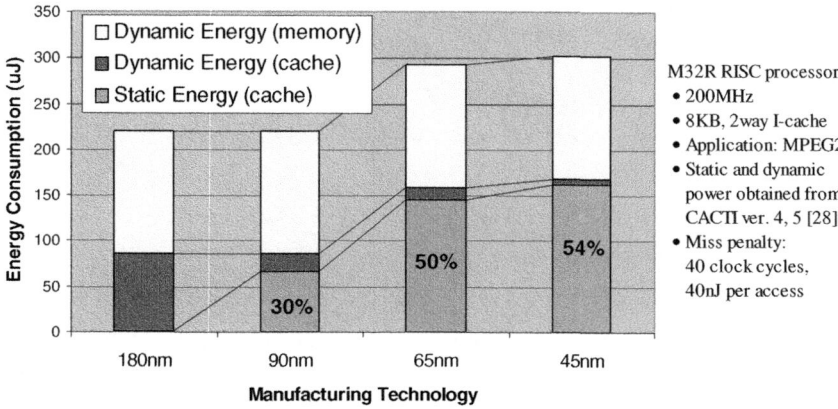

Fig. 1. Cache energy consumption in various technology nodes. Share of leakage increases with technology scaling.

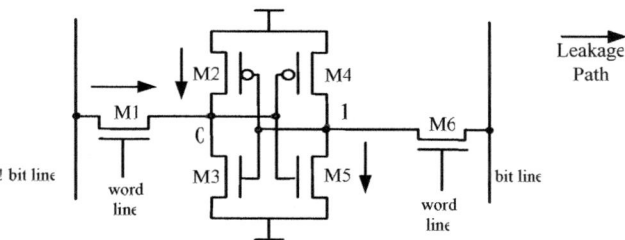

Fig. 2. A 6-transistor SRAM cell storing a logic 1. Arrows show leakage paths.

The figure clearly shows that although dynamic energy decreases with every technology node, the static (leakage) energy increases such that, unlike in micrometer technologies, total energy of the cache increases with the shrinking feature sizes. Thus it is increasingly more important to address leakage reduction in cache memories in nanometer technologies.

We focus on I_{off} as the primary contributor to leakage in nanometer caches [25]. Fig. 2 shows a 6-transistor SRAM cell storing a 1 logic value. Clearly, only M5, M2, and M1 transistors can leak in this state while the other three contribute to leakage only when the cell stores a 0 (note that bit-lines are precharged to supply voltage, V_{DD}). Process variation, especially in such minimum-geometry devices, causes each transistor to have a different V_{th} and consequently different I_{off} value, finally resulting in different subthreshold leakage currents when storing 1 compared to 0. Since the target V_{th} is in general reduced in finer technologies (in order to keep the circuit performance when scaling dimensions and V_{DD}) the I_{off} value is exponentially increased, and consequently, the above leakage difference is no longer negligible.

To quantify this effect, we used Monte Carlo simulation to model several similar caches and for each one computed maximum leakage difference once in each cell and once more in the entire cache. Notations and formulas are:

- **leak0 (leak1):** leakage power of the cell when storing 0 (1).
- **low** = min(leak0, leak1)
- **high** = max(leak0, leak1)

$$per-cell \quad saving = \frac{high-low}{high} \tag{1}$$

$$Upper \quad bound \quad of \quad per-cache \quad saving = \frac{\sum_{all \ cells} high - \sum_{all \ cells} low}{\sum_{all \ cells} high} \tag{2}$$

Eq. 1 gives leakage difference between less-leaky and more-leaky states of a single cell, while Eq. 2 gives, in the entire cache, the difference between the worst case (all cells storing more-leaky values) and the best case (all cells storing less-leaky values).

Variation in transistors' V_{th} results from die-to-die (inter-die) as well as within-die (intra-die) variation. We considered both in these experiments. Inter-die variation, which results in varying average V_{th} among different chips, is generally modeled by Gaussian distribution [29] while for intra-die variation, which results in different V_{th} values for different transistors even within the same chip and the same SRAM cell, independent Gaussian variables are used to define V_{th} of each transistor of the SRAM cell [30][31]. We used the same techniques to simulate inter- and intra-die process variation in 1000 16KB caches (direct-map, 512-set, 32-byte lines, 23 bits per tag) to obtain average values for Eq. 1 and 2 when $\sigma_{Vth\text{-}intra}$ (i.e. standard-deviation of intra-die V_{th} variations) varying from 10 to 100mV. We assumed each cache is within a separate die and used a single $\sigma_{Vth\text{-}inter}$=20mV for all dies. The mean value of V_{th} was set to 320mV corresponding to a commercial 90nm process.

Fig. 3 gives the simulation results showing the maximum theoretical per-cell and per-chip leakage savings. Our experiments with V_{th} mean values other than 320mV showed that the diagrams are independent of the V_{th} mean value; i.e., although the absolute value of the saving does certainly change with different V_{th} averages (and indeed increases with lower V_{th} in finer technologies), but the maximum *saving ratio* (Eq. 1 and 2) remains invariant for a given $\sigma_{Vth\text{-}intra}$, but the *absolute value* of the saved power increases with decreasing V_{th}. This makes sense since this saving opportunity is enabled by the V_{th} *variation*, not the V_{th} *average value*.

Since $\sigma_{Vth\text{-}intra} \propto 1/\sqrt{L \times W}$ [3], where L and W are effective channel length and width of the transistor respectively, the V_{th} variation is only to increase with technology scaling, and as Fig. 3 shows, this increases the significance of value-to-cell matching. In 0.13μm process, empirical study [32] reports $\sigma_{Vth\text{-}intra}$=22.1mV for W/L=4 which by extrapolation gives $\sigma_{vth\text{-}intra}$>60mV in 90nm for minimum-geometry transistors; ITRS roadmap also shows similar prospects [33]. (We found no public-domain empirical report on 90nm and 65nm processes, apparently due to sensitiveness and confidentiality of these data.) Thus we present results at various $\sigma_{vth\text{-}intra}$ values, but consider 60mV as a typical case. Note that even if the extrapolation is not accurate for 90nm process, $\sigma_{vth\text{-}intra}$=60 finally happens at a finer technology node due to relation $\sigma_{Vth\text{-}intra} \propto 1/\sqrt{L \times W}$. Fig. 3 shows that maximum theoretical saving using this phenomenon at 60mV variation can be as high as 70%.

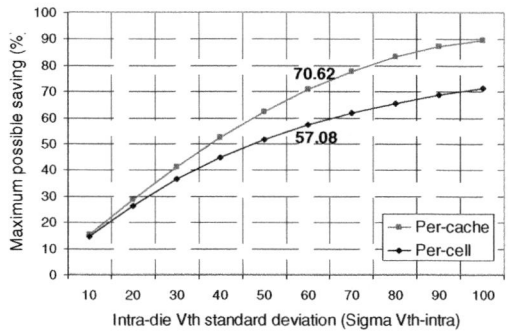

Fig. 3. Leakage saving opportunity increases with V_{th}-variation

4   Our Techniques for Instruction Cache Leakage Reduction

We propose three techniques applicable to instruction-caches: rescheduling instructions within basic-blocks, static register-renaming, and initializing unused cache-lines. We first illustrate the techniques by examples that are simplified for presentational purposes.

Illustrative Example 1: Intra-BB Instruction Rescheduling. This technique reorders the instructions within a basic-block, subject to instruction dependencies, so as to maximize the number of matches between instruction bits and the less-leaky state of their corresponding cache cells. Fig. 4 illustrates this technique applied to a small basic block (shown at left in Fig. 4) consisting of three 8-bit instructions against a 512-set direct-mapped cache with 8-bit line size. The arrow at the right of instruction-memory box represents dependence of instruction 2 to instruction 1. For simplicity, we assume *(i)* all the 3 instructions spend the same amount of time in the cache, and *(ii)* the leakage-saving (i.e., |*leak0-leak1*|) is the same for all bits of the 3 cache lines. A SRAM cell is called *1-friendly* (*0-friendly*) or equivalently *prefers 1* (*prefers 0*), if it leaks less power when storing a 1 (a 0). This *leakage-preference* of the cache lines are given in gray in the middle of Fig. 4; for example, the leftmost bit of cache line number 490 prefers 0 (is 0-friendly) while its rightmost bit prefers 1 (is 1-friendly). The *Matching table* in Fig. 4 shows the number of matched bits for each *(instruction, cache-line)* pair. Due to instruction dependencies, only three schedules are valid in this example: 1-2-3 (i.e., the original one), 1-3-2, and 3-1-2 with respectively 3+1+3, 3+3+7, and 1+7+7 number of matched bits (see the *Matching table* in Fig. 4). We propose to reschedule basic-blocks, subject to dependencies among the instructions, so as to match up the instructions with the leakage-preference of cache lines. Thus, the best schedule, shown at right in Fig. 4, is 3-1-2 which improves leakage of this basic-block by 47% (from 24-7 mismatches to 24-15 ones).

Obviously, the two simplifying assumptions in the above example do not hold in general. Potential leakage-saving differs from cell to cell, and also the amount of time spent in the cache differs from instruction to instruction even in the same BB. We consider and analyze these factors in our formulation and experiments. It is

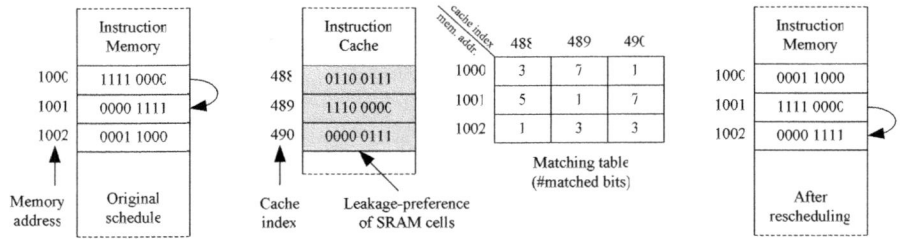

Fig. 4. An example illustrating instruction-rescheduling

important to note that location and length of basic-blocks do not change; thus, the instruction-cache access-pattern remains intact, and hence, no performance or power penalty is imposed concerning the instruction-cache.

Illustrative Example 2: Static Register-Renaming. This technique statically changes the register operands of instructions so that less-leaky values are stored in the corresponding SRAM cells as far as possible. Assume that the two right-most bits of each instruction in Fig. 5 represent a source register and the two left-most bits give the other source which is also the destination register. Fig. 5 depicts a simple example of static register-renaming on the same cache as previous example; for presentational purposes, we ignore instruction rescheduling here and merely apply register-renaming although our algorithm applies both at the same time. When applying merely register-renaming to these instructions, R0 can be renamed to R3 in the first two instructions (note that this implies similar renaming in all predecessor, and successor, instructions that in various control-flow scenarios produce, or consume, the value in R0; this is not shown in the figure). Similarly, original R3 in the same two instructions can be equally-well renamed to either R1 or R0; it is renamed to R1 in Fig. 5. For the third instruction, there is no better choice since source and destination registers are the same while their corresponding cache cells have opposite preferences (renaming to R1, which results in only the same leakage-preference-matching, is inappropriate since the instruction would then conflict with the now-renamed first instruction).

It is noteworthy that some register operands, e.g. stack pointer, cannot be renamed due to its special functionality. We took this point into account when implementing this technique.

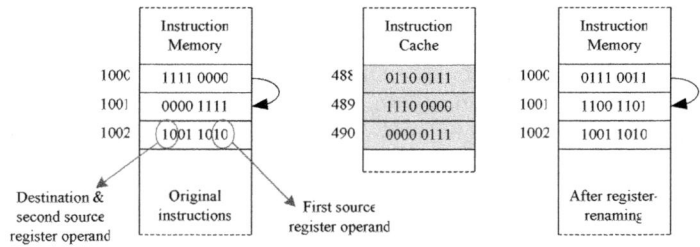

Fig. 5. An example illustrating static register-renaming

Illustrative Example 3: Initializing Unused Cache-Lines. Depending on the cache size and the application, some parts of the instruction cache may never be used during application execution. Fig. 6 shows the histogram of *cache-fill* operations in the 8KB instruction cache of M32R processor [27] (a 32-bit RISC processor) when executing FFT application. 69 out of the 512 16-byte cache-lines are never used in this case. We propose to initialize such unused cache-lines with values that best match the leakage-preference of their SRAM cells. Many processors today are equipped with cache-management instructions (e.g. ARM10 family [34] and NEC V830R processor [35]) that can load arbitrary values to every cache location. Using these instructions, the unused cache-lines can be initialized at boot time to effectively reduce their leakage-power during the entire application execution. For instance, if in Fig. 5 cache-line number 490 were not to be used at all by the application, it would be initialized to 0000_0111 to fully match its leakage-preference. A minimum power-ON duration is required to break even the dynamic energy for cache initialization and the leakage energy saved. We consider this in our problem formulation and experiments.

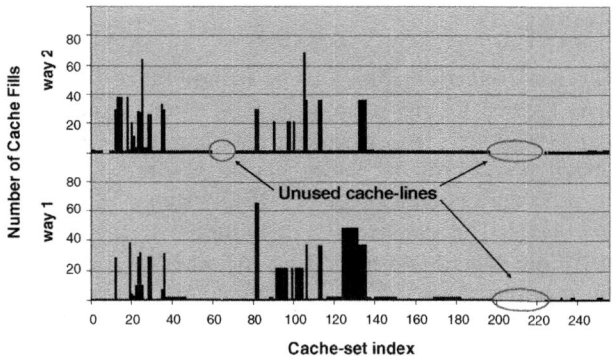

Fig. 6. Unused cache-lines when running FFT application on 8KB two-way set-associative cache with 16-byte cache-lines

Leakage Reduction Flow. Our proposed techniques imply optimizing each binary executable based on the core that it is actually running on. This may not be practical in large-scale production. To address this, we propose an alternative that takes advantage of Real-Time Operating Systems (RTOS) which are widely used in today embedded systems: in this approach, shown in Fig. 7, the same binary executable is stored in all chips and the RTOS applies our rescheduling and register-renaming algorithm; this is done only once per chip and the modified binary is stored back in the programmable ROM to avoid future repetitions of the above task. Even if an embedded system does not contain such RTOS, a small initialization routine can do the same task instead.

Fig. 7 shows the RTOS-based leakage reduction flow. At very first execution, an offline test procedure (the lower left box in Fig. 7—described below) detects the leakage-preference of all cache lines. This information is used by the rescheduling

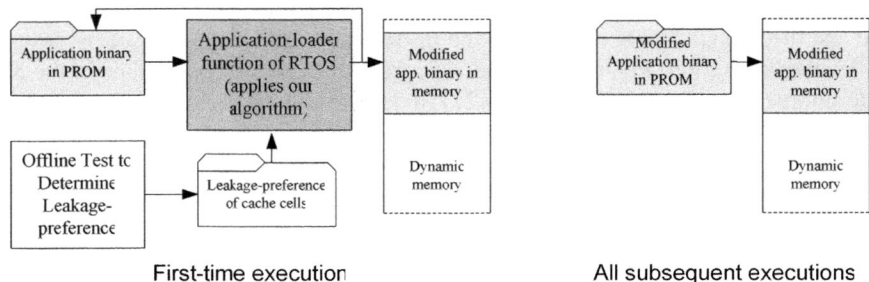

First-time execution   All subsequent executions

Fig. 7. RTOS-based alternative for leakage-reduction flow

algorithm, in the dark grey box, to reorder the instructions and rename registers of the application binary before putting them in the dynamic memory and executing. The modified binary is also written back to the PROM so that subsequent executions of the application directly load the program to memory without needing modification (right-hand side of Fig. 7).

Leakage-Preference Detection. This can be incorporated in the manufacturing test procedure that is applied to each chip after fabrication. Usually several march test sequences (such as walking-1 and walking-0) are applied to memory devices [36] to test them for stuck-at and bridging faults. Leakage current can be measured at each step of this test procedure (similar to delta-IDDQ testing [37]) to determine the leakage-preference of cells. This can even be done in-house since today commodity ammeters can easily measure down to 0.1fA [38] whereas the nominal leakage of a minimum geometry transistor is 345pA in a commercial 90nm process available to us. For some cells, this difference may be negligible, but one can detect more important cells that cause larger leakage differences.

Test time depends on the speed of current measurements. In the simplest approach, two measurements per bit are done: once writing a 0 to the bit-under-test to measure *leak0*, and once more writing a 1 there to measure *leak1* while all other bits have an arbitrary but invariant value in both measurements; this yields 128K measurements for an 8KB cache. Current-measurements can be done by off-chip Automatic Test Equipments (ATE) or on-chip circuitry called Built-In Current Sensor (BICS). Off-chip measurements need no change to the chip design, but impose test-time overhead and need additional memory to convey leakage-preference data to the optimizer program; such ATE equipment can provide a test rate of 100KHz at a resolution of 100nA [39-41] resulting in 1.28s of test time which would not be big compared to typical test time of processor chips (several seconds [42] depending on the complexity of the chip), but test results need an additional agreed-upon memory (say an on chip PROM) to be delivered to the optimizer program. The other alternative, BICS, instruments the cache with on-chip leakage detection circuitry (similar to the one presented in [43]) to let the optimizer software detect the leakage-preference in field; such BICS circuits are a long-known technique in CMOS testing [44] and can provide more accurate measurements (e.g. 500pA in a 0.7μm technology [45]) and higher speeds (e.g. 500MHz in a 2μm technology [46] or 100MHz in [47]) even in very old technologies; newer BICS designs in 0.18μm process [48] additionally provide tolerance to temperature and process variations at high speeds (230MHz) with a tiny footprints (0.0021mm^2) [48]. Choosing the BICS alternative not only eliminates the need to deliver data from testing phase to in-field operation, but also has the additional advantage of eliminating burden of any additional test overhead for manufacturer, and furthermore, allows running the optimization again from time to time so as to adapt to changes in cells leakages due to aging. Noting that recent research on memory testing in nanometer era has revealed the necessity of on-chip facilities for test-and-repair [49] and self-calibration for stability [50], adding a BICS for leakage sensing in a cache memory would not be unordinary when justified by its power-saving advantages.

5   Problem Formulation

We formulate the problem using the following notation:

- N_s, N_w: The number of sets and ways of the cache.
- N_{BB}: The number of basic-blocks in the given application.
- $N_i(bb)$: The number of instructions in basic-block no. bb.
- $L(i, bb, w)$: Leakage power dissipated by the corresponding word of the cache line at way w of the cache when instruction number i of basic-block number bb is stored there. Note that the cache set corresponding to the instruction is fixed, but the cache way may differ over time.
- $T(i, bb, w)$ or *cache-residence time*: The amount of time that instruction number i of basic-block number bb remains in way w of the corresponding cache set.
- E: Total leakage energy of the instruction cache:

$$E = \sum_{bb=1}^{N_{BB}} \sum_{i=1}^{N_i(bb)} \sum_{w=1}^{N_w} L(i,bb,w) \times T(i,bb,w) \tag{3}$$

Each term in this summation gives the leakage energy dissipated by instruction i of basic-block bb at way w of cache.

- T_{viable}: The minimum amount of time that the embedded system should remain ON so that the cache-initialization technique would be *viable* (i.e., would actually save energy).

The problem is formally defined as "*For a given application and cache organization (i.e. for given N_s, N_w, N_{BB}, and $N_i(bb)$ vector), (i) minimize E, and (ii) find T_{viable}.*"

Algorithm. We use a list-scheduling algorithm for problem *(i)* above to achieve high efficiency; register-renaming is performed at each iteration of the algorithm:

```
Algorithm 1: ListScheduling(G)
```
```
Inputs:  (G: control-data-flow Graph of application)
Output:  (S: obtained Schedule for instructions of the application)
```
```
1   S = empty-list;
2   foreach basic-block do
3     BA = Base-Address of the basic-block;
4     L  = Length of the basic-block;
5     for addr=BA to BA + L do
6       lowestLeakage = +INFINITY;    bestChoice = 0
7       for each instr in ready-list(G, BA) do
8         (new_instr, new_src, new_dst) = applyRegRenaming(instr, addr);
9         leak = get_instruction_leakage(new_instr, addr);
10        if leak < lowestLeakage then
11          lowestLeakage = leak;       best_choice = new_instr;
12          best_regs = (new_src, new_dst);
13        endif
14      endfor
15      propagateRegRenamings( G, instr, best_regs );
16      S = S + {best_choice};
17      Mark {best_choice} as scheduled in G to update ready-list(G, BA);
18    endfor
19  endfor
20  return S
```

The algorithm sequentially processes each basic-block in the application binary and stores the new schedule with the new register-names in S as output. It needs the control-data-flow graph of the application for register-renaming so as to figure out live registers and the instructions that produce and consume them. For each basic-block, all *ready* instructions (i.e. those with all their predecessors already scheduled), represented by ready-list(G, BA) in line 7, are tried and the one with the least leakage is chosen (lines 9-13) and appended to the schedule (lines 16, 17); line 9 computes the leakage corresponding to the instruction by giving the innermost summation of Eq. 3. Register-renaming is also applied to each *ready*-instruction (line 8) and if chosen as the best, its corresponding new register-names are propagated to all predecessor and successor instructions (line 15); these procedures are given below:

```
Procedure 1: applyRegRenaming(i, addr)
```
```
Inputs:  (i: the instruction binary to manipulate),
         (addr: the address of i in memory)
Outputs: (new_i: instruction after register-renaming),
         (new_src, new_dst: new source and destination register operands)
```
```
1   new_src = first-source-register of i;
2   new_dst = destination-register of i;
3   if new_src not affixed then
4     new_src = get_best_src1_choice(i, addr);
5   if new_dst not affixed then
6     new_dst = get_best_dest_choice(i, addr);
7   new_i = i with new_src, and new_dst;
8   return new_i, new_src, new_dst;
```

This procedure checks the two source and destination registers (in M32R, the destination register and the second source register are the same) and if each of them is not *affixed*, tries to rename it to the best available choice. A source or destination register is *affixed* if due to an already-applied register-renaming it is previously determined and should be kept unchanged; the below procedure pseudo-code shows this. In some cases, it may be beneficial to reconsider renaming since the leakage reduction by the new register-renaming may outweigh the loss in previously renamed instructions; we did not consider this for simplicity and efficiency.

Procedure 2: propagateRegRenamings(G, i, new_src, new_dst)

Inputs: (G: control data flow Graph of application),
        (i: instruction before register-renaming),
        (new_src, new_dst: new source and destination registers)

---

1 org_src = first-source-register of i;
2 org_dst = destination-register of i;
3 **if** (new_src != org_src) **then**
4   rename org_src to new_src, and mark it affixed, in all predecessors
     and successors of i in G
5 **if** (new_dst != org_dst) **then**
6   rename org_dst to new_dst, and mark it affixed, in all predecessors
     and successors of i in G

The algorithm has a time complexity of $O(m.n^2)$ and memory usage of $O(m.n)$ where m and n respectively represents the number of basic-blocks in the application and the number of instructions in the basic-block. Note that the algorithm correctly handles set-associative caches since the innermost summation in Eq. 3 considers individual leakages of each cache-way. The algorithm does not necessarily give the absolute best schedule neither the best register-names, but comparing its experimental results to that of exhaustive search in the feasible cases, which is still prohibitively time-consuming, shows the results are no more than 12% less optimal than the absolute best schedule.

6   Experimental Results

Experiments Setup and Methodology. Fig. 8 shows the setup of the experiments. We used benchmarks (Table 1) from MiBench [51], MediaBench [52], and also Linux compress in our experiments. We implemented our techniques on an in-order

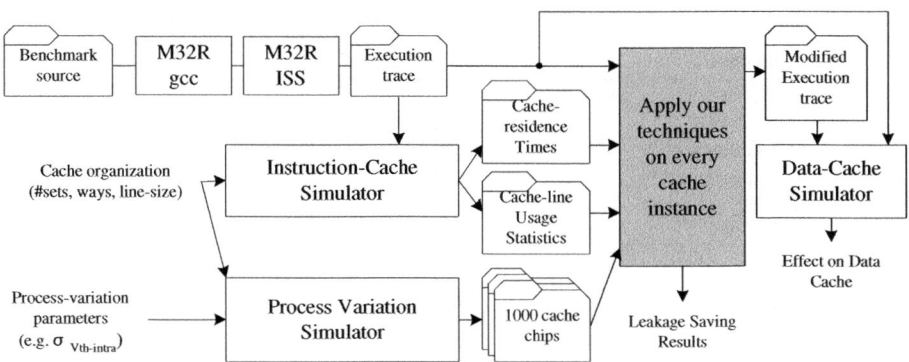

Fig. 8. Simulation setup of the experiments

single-issue 32-bit RISC processor, M32R [27]. Benchmarks were compiled once with no compiler optimization option and once more with –O3 full optimization option (the lower half of Table 1) and were simulated using M32R instruction-set simulator (ISS) to obtain execution traces for 1 million instructions (FIR ran up to completion). These traces are given to M32R instruction-cache simulator (the middle box in Fig. 8) to obtain cache-residence times and cache-line usage statistics.

To simulate process variation effects, Monte Carlo simulation was used to model within-die process variation (lower part of Fig. 8); independent Gaussian random values for V_{th} of each transistor of the cache were generated with 320mV as the mean (which corresponds to a commercial 90nm process) and 60mV as the standard deviation for the minimum-geometry transistor. Since $\sigma_{V_{th-intra}} \propto 1/\sqrt{L \times W}$ [3], V_{th} variation is different for different-sized transistors. Thus, we considered the length (L) and width (W) of SRAM transistors (Fig. 9) when generating the above V_{th} values. To consider the randomness of process variations, we simulated 1000 chips. Die-to-die variations do not change the saving percentage (see Section 3) and were not modeled in these experiments.

For each benchmark, the execution-trace and cache usage statistics are used by our techniques (the gray box in Fig. 8) which are applied to each individual 1000 cache instances. This gives 1000 leakage-saving results each corresponding to one of the simulated caches. The average and maximum of these savings are reported later in this section. Another output of the gray box is the execution trace modified according to our rescheduling and register-renaming techniques. The original and modified execution traces are simulated by M32R data-cache simulator to obtain impact of the techniques on the data cache.

Reported power consumptions correspond to a commercial 90nm process. To compute the power consumption, SPICE transistor models of the 90nm process are used to obtain transistor leakage as a function of its V_{th}. Then for each cache instance, the leakage power of each SRAM cell is computed by adding up leakages of the transistors that leak in each state: 0 and 1. Thus, $L(i,bb, w)$ (see Section 5) values can be computed which in turn is used in Eq. 3 to get total leakage power dissipated for storing the instructions.

Table 1. Benchmarks specifications

Benchmark	No of basic-blocks	Basic-block size (#instr.) Average	Largest
MPEG2 encoder ver. 1.2	16000	5.36	596
FFT	12858	4.83	75
JPEG encoder ver. 6b	11720	5.68	248
Compress ver. 4.1	9586	5.11	718
FIR	450	7.59	57
DCT	508	4.96	64
MPEG2 –O3	26483	3.99	547
FFT –O3	22507	3.80	76
JPEG –O3	22062	3.78	126
Compress –O3	18455	3.94	1404
FIR –O3	706	5.99	37
DCT –O3	715	4.28	30

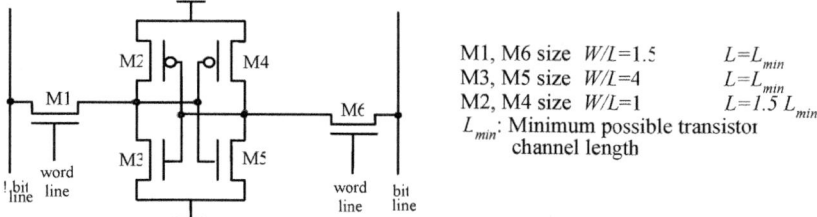

Fig. 9. Transistor sizes of our SRAM design used in the experiments

6.1   Evaluation Results

Fig. 10 shows the average leakage powers before and after applying our leakage-saving techniques, obtained over 1000 8KB direct-mapped caches with 16-byte cache-line size. Each bar is composed of two parts: the leakage power dissipated by the cache-lines that were used during application execution, and those that were never used. Our rescheduling algorithm reduces the former, while the cache-initialization technique decreases the latter.

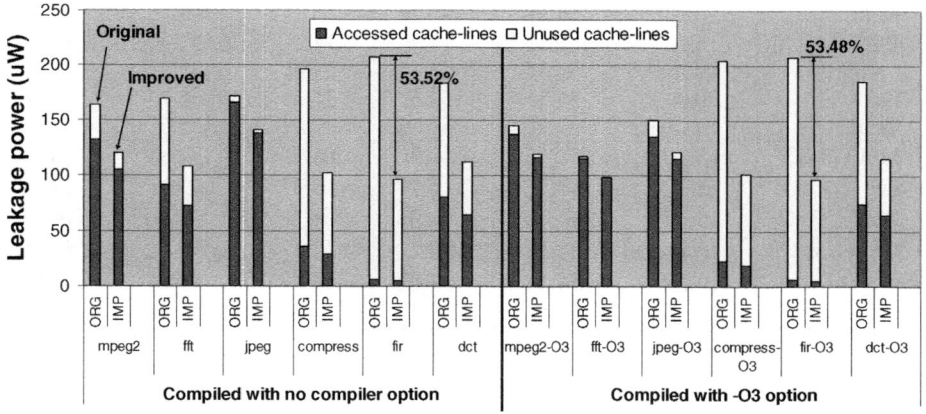

Fig. 10. Average leakage power on 1000 8KB direct-map caches

Table 2 gives the individual average and maximum savings obtained by each technique over the above 1000 chips; note that the values in *rescheduling* and *initializing* columns respectively correspond to the leakage savings *only in used* and *only in unused* cache-lines. The lower half of the table gives results for benchmarks when compiled with "-O3" compiler optimization option. The rescheduling and register-renaming technique saves up to 31.31% of power for FIR while savings by the cache-initialization technique reaches 63.68% for FFT-O3 benchmark. Average saving obtained by cache-initialization is always around 55% for all benchmarks since we assumed that before initialization, SRAM cells in the unused cache-lines randomly contain uniformly distributed 0 or 1 value.

The "-O3" compiler optimization has reduced effectiveness of the rescheduling and register-renaming techniques from 19% to 15% on average over the 6 benchmarks; this is due to the tighter pressure on register usage and less freedom in reordering instructions. It has also resulted in a reduction of total leakage saving from an average of 37% to 32% over these benchmarks. Marginal increases are observed in the case of JPEG-O3 and Compress-O3; this is because the unused cache lines (where more leakage can be saved) have happened to slightly increase in case of these benchmarks. In case of MPEG2 and FFT, the "-O3" optimization has happened to substantially reduce number of unused cache lines, and hence, total leakage saving is decreased to nearly that achievable by only rescheduling and register-renaming.

Note that since optimization options enabled by "-O3" option do not specifically target better usage of available cache capacity, the above changes in number of unused cache lines are not deterministic and cannot be purposefully used.

Table 2. Average and maximum leakage savings by our techniques

Benchmark	Average Saving (%)			Maximum Saving (%)		
	rescheduling (used lines)	initializing (unused lines)	Together	rescheduling (used lines)	initializing (unused lines)	Together
MPEG2	20.10	54.51	26.78	21.67	56.16	28.25
FFT	20.50	54.51	36.28	22.43	55.7	37.36
JPEG	16.70	54.51	17.96	17.91	58.36	19.26
Compress	19.74	54.51	48.15	23.95	55.32	48.92
FIR	20.04	54.51	53.52	31.31	55.19	54.18
DCT	19.31	54.51	39.09	21.49	55.61	40.13
MPEG2-O3	15.19	54.55	17.30	16.59	57.89	18.35
FFT-O3	15.17	54.46	15.79	16.92	63.68	17.49
JPEG-O3	15.12	54.49	18.98	16.7	57.16	19.95
Compress-O3	16.14	54.51	50.20	20.31	55.22	51.50
FIR-O3	16.59	54.51	53.48	26.77	55.21	54.01
DCT-O3	13.86	54.51	38.15	16.44	55.48	40.10

Different cache-sizes result in different number of unused cache-lines, and hence, affect saving results. Fig. 11 depicts the savings for 16KB, 8KB, and 4KB direct-map caches with 16-byte line-size. As the figure shows, in general, the leakage saving reduces in smaller caches proportional to the reduction in the number of unused cache-lines. This, however, does not affect the results of the rescheduling and register-renaming techniques, and hence, increases their share in total leakage-reduction (see Fig. 11). Consequently, when finally all cache-lines are used by the application in a small cache (as in MPEG2 and JPEG cases in Fig. 11), the leakage reduction reaches its minimum which is equal to the saving achieved by the rescheduling and register-renaming techniques alone (compare MPEG2 and JPEG in Fig. 11 to their corresponding rows in Table 2 under *rescheduling* column).

Table 2 and Fig. 10 and Fig. 11 clarified the effect of compiler optimization options on the effectiveness of our proposed techniques. In the rest of the paper, experimental results correspond to benchmarks compiled with no compiler optimization unless otherwise specified.

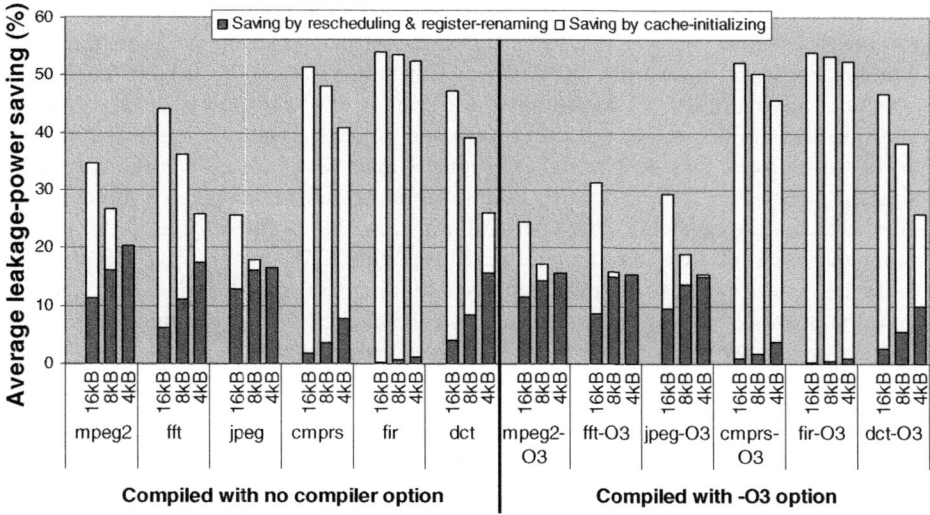

Fig. 11. Effect of cache-size on average leakage-saving results

Set-associative caches take better advantage of the available cache-lines and reduce the number of unused ones. Fig. 12 shows the leakage savings in an 8KB cache when the number of ways changes from 1 (direct-map) to 8. The leakage-saving by cache-initialization reduces in caches with higher associativity, and finally total saving reduces to that obtained by the rescheduling and register-renaming technique as is again the case for MPEG2 and JPEG in Fig. 12.

Furthermore, in set-associative caches, the location of each instruction in the cache cannot be precisely determined since there are multiple cache-lines in the cache-set that corresponds to the address of the instruction. This uncertainty is expected to

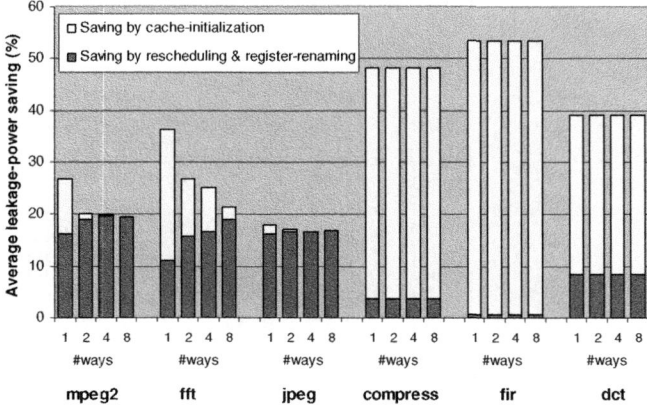

Fig. 12. Effect of set-associative caches on total leakage saving

decrease the saving results of the rescheduling algorithm, however, our cache simulator gives separate per-way residence-times for each instruction so as to direct the
matching process toward the cache-ways with higher probability of hosting the instruction. Saving results of Algorithm 1 are given in Fig. 13; as in Fig. 12, cache size
and line-size are respectively fixed at 8KB and 16-bytes while the number of cache-
ways varies from 1 to 8. The figure confirms that the number of cache-ways only
slightly affects the results due to the above-mentioned technique for directing the
algorithm towards matching the instruction against the more likely used cache-way.
Some marginal increases are seen in Fig. 13 for MPEG2, Compress, and FIR at higher
cache associativity; these are random effects that happen since the algorithm does not
give the absolute optimal schedule and also the cache-lines that correspond to each
instruction change when changing the number of cache-ways.

Execution-times of the rescheduling algorithm for the above caches are given in
Table 3; values are measured on a Xeon 3.8GHz processor with 3.5GB memory. The
execution time increases with the number of cache-ways, since more calculations are
necessary, but it remains reasonably low to be practical. In case of in-field optimization illustrated in Fig. 7, the optimizer runs on the embedded processor which could
be two orders of magnitude slower. Thus, it may take a number of seconds to finish
but needs to be done only once per product (say at *install time*), and hence, the execution-time is acceptable given its power-saving advantages.

Table 3. Algorithm execution-time (in seconds)

Benchmark	Cache configuration (sets×ways×line_size)			
	512×1×16	256×2×16	128×4×16	64×8×16
MPEG2	0.15	0.33	0.55	1.04
FFT	0.08	0.19	0.31	0.60
JPEG	0.18	0.40	0.70	1.35
Compress	0.05	0.10	0.15	0.26
FIR	0.01	0.01	0.02	0.04
DCT	0.03	0.06	0.12	0.23
Average	0.08	0.18	0.31	0.59

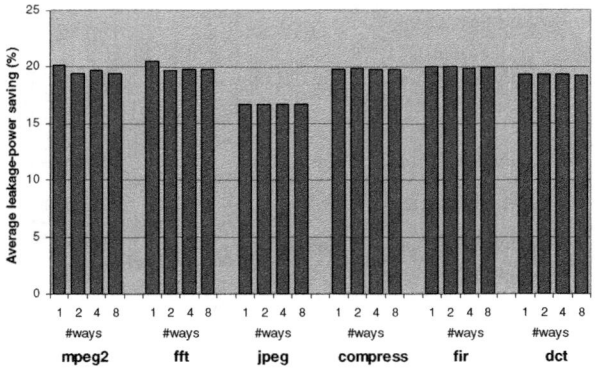

Fig. 13. Effect of set-associative caches on rescheduling algorithm

Fig. 3 suggests that the achievable energy saving rises with the increase in V_{th} variation caused by technology scaling. We repeated the experiments for 8KB, 512-set direct-map cache with $\sigma_{Vth\text{-}intra}$ of the minimum-sized transistor varying from 20 to 100mV (with mean-V_{th}=320mV in all cases). Fig. 14 shows the trend in saving results which confirm the increasing significance of the approach in future technologies where random within-die V_{th} variation is expected to increase [33] due to random dopant fluctuation which is rising when further approaching atomic sizes in nanometer processes.

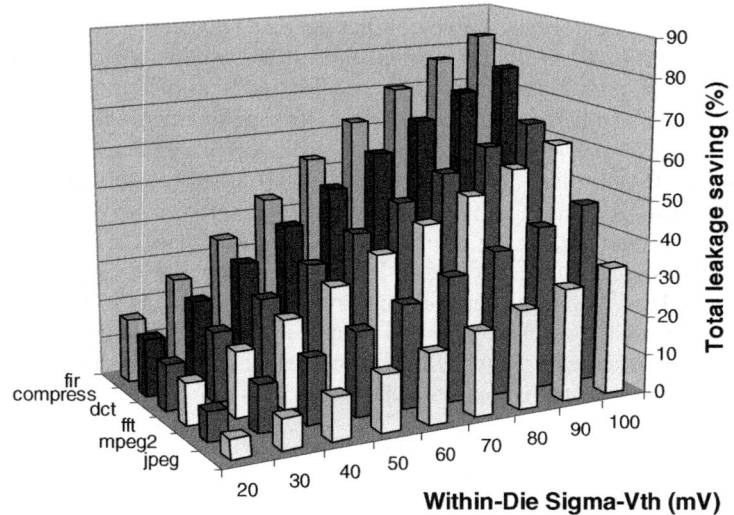

Fig. 14. Saving improvement with technology scaling

6.2 Analysis and Evaluation of Costs

Performance Impact of Intra-BB Rescheduling and Register-Renaming. Register-renaming imposes absolutely no penalty since there is no difference in performance among various registers. Intra-BB instruction-rescheduling has no impact on instruction-cache but may in rare cases marginally affect data-cache; these are explained below:

Instruction-cache performance is unaffected by our techniques because number, size, and memory address of basic-blocks remain the same. The execution time of each basic-block after rescheduling changes only due to data-cache misses in case of M32R processor (a 5-stage pipelined in-order single-issue RISC processor) since only two factors may affect this execution time: *(i)* data cache misses, and *(ii)* other pipeline stalls; but the latter does not change by instruction rescheduling in case of M32R since:

- M32R implements internal register-forwarding [27], and hence, no stall occurs if a producer-consumer pair of instructions execute back to back in the pipeline.
- According to M32R datasheets, the only other sources of pipeline stall in M32R are the *taken branch* instructions and *multi-cycle* instructions (multiply, divide,

and remainder) [27] neither of which is affected by our technique because *(i)* we do not change the position of branch instructions and they remain at the end of their corresponding basic-block, and hence, their imposed number of stall cycles remains the same after rescheduling, *(ii)* multi-cycle instructions also impose the same number of pipeline stalls irrespective of their position in the basic-block.

In data cache, however, reordering of instructions may change the sequence of accesses to data elements, and hence, may slightly change cache behavior. If a miss-causing instruction is moved, the hit-ratio is the same, but residence-times (and hence leakage power) of the evicted and fetched data items change negligibly. In addition, if two instructions that access cache-conflicting data elements change their relative order of execution, the cache hit-ratio changes if the originally-first one was to be a hit. This case may also change the data that finally remains in the cache after basic-block execution, and hence, potentially affects leakage power of the data cache. These cases are, however, very unlikely to happen when noting that due to locality of reference, two conflicting data accesses are unlikely to follow closely in time (and in a single BB). This is confirmed by our experimental results shown in Fig. 15; the total dynamic power and data cache hit-ratio varied no more than 1% in our experiments on 8KB 2-way data cache of M32R. It is noteworthy that the dynamic power in Fig. 15 includes dynamic power consumption of data cache as well as off-chip data memory. Since total dynamic power is dominated by off-chip memory accesses which correspond to data-cache misses, the bar corresponding to power consumption in Fig. 15 also represents the increase in data-cache miss ratio.

Memory Requirements. For set-associative caches, when using the in-field binary-modification proposal illustrated in Fig. 7, the rescheduling and register-renaming

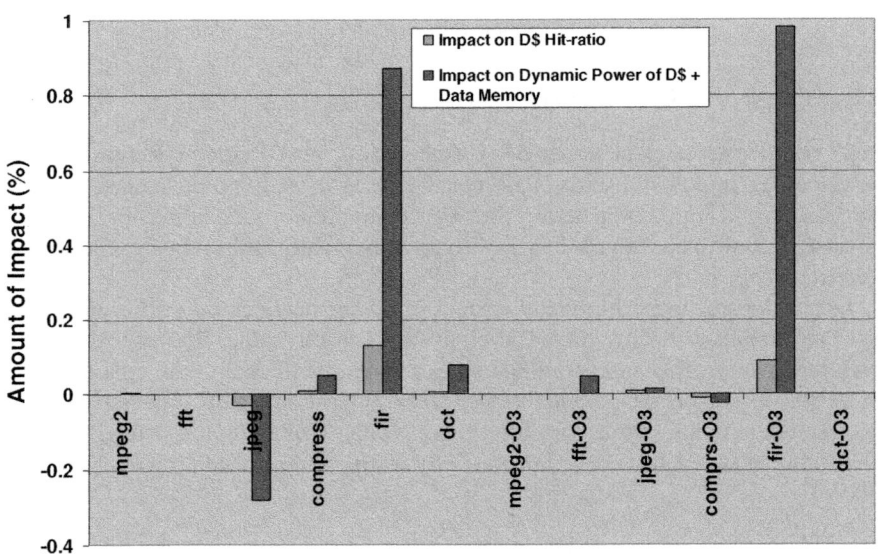

Fig. 15. The amount of decrease in data-cache hit-ratio and increase in dynamic power consumption of data cache and off-chip data memory after instruction rescheduling

algorithm needs to know which cache-way most probably hosts each instruction-block so as to know the cache location to which each instruction should be matched (obviously, no such information needs to be stored in case of a direct-map cache). Consequently, for a W-way set-associative cache, $log_2(W)$ bits per instruction-block should be stored along with each application binary; for example, in a 4-way set-associative cache with 16-byte line size on a processor with 32-bit instructions, 4 instructions reside in each cache line and hence 2 (i.e. $log2(4)$) bits should be stored per every 4 instructions.

One concern is that if the analyzed execution trace is not a good representative of actual execution traces, the above stored information may mislead the optimization algorithm and impact leakage savings. This is a general concern for all trace-based optimization techniques but an intensive benchmarking and analysis phase in order to obtain a representative trace can effectively reduce the chance of such drawbacks.

The optimizer itself should also be stored in the embedded system in case of in-field optimization illustrated in Fig. 7. We recompiled our developed optimizer without any change using M32R port of GCC to obtain M32R executable; the code size is 102KB which is nine times smaller than a JPEG application compiled for M32R. It is worthy of note that an implementation to actually run on an embedded system may differ in size since several source-level improvements can be applied and also the optimizer must work with binary executables as opposed to text files in these experiments.

Cost of Cache Initialization. As explained in Section 4, the cache-initialization technique consumes some dynamic power to execute the cache-management instructions before it can save leakage power. This introduces a break even point in time beyond which the obtained leakage-saving outweighs the consumed dynamic power. Our implementation of M32R processor with two separate 8KB instruction and data caches on a 180nm process technology consumes 200mW at 50MHz clock frequency. This gives, on average, 4nJ per clock cycle or pessimistically 20nJ per instruction in the 5-stage pipelined M32R processor. Assuming all 512 cache-lines of the instruction cache are to be initialized, 10.24μJ is consumed for cache-initialization. T_{viable} can now be calculated using the power-saving values obtained by cache-initialization (Fig. 10). Results are given in Table 4 which confirms that most often a small fraction of a second is enough to make the initialization technique viable. Even for the worst benchmark, FFT-O3, a number of seconds is enough. Assumptions in the estimations were intentionally pessimistic in order not to overestimate benefits: *(i)* processor implementation in a finer technology (e.g. 90nm) would consume less dynamic power, *(ii)* more than one instruction is often in the processor pipeline, and hence, average

Table 4. Upper bound of T_{viable} for different applications

Benchmark	MPEG2	FFT	JPEG	Compress	FIR	DCT
T_{viable} (s)	0.590	0.238	3.281	0.117	0.093	0.182

MPEG2-O3	FFT-O3	JPEG-O3	Compress-O3	FIR-O3	DCT-O3
2.419	10.020	1.279	0.104	0.093	0.169

power per instruction would be less than 20nJ, *(iii)* not all cache-lines need to be initialized (e.g. for FFT-O3 only 3 and for JPEG, only 14 cache-lines remain unused and should be initialized). Thus, values in Table 4 should be considered as upper bounds for T_{viable}.

7 Conclusion

Our contributions in this paper are *(i)* observing value-dependence of SRAM leakage and analyzing the corresponding new opportunity for reducing cache leakage in nanometer technologies enabled by the reducing V_{th} and the increasing within-die V_{th}-variation in such processes, and *(ii)* presenting first techniques that take advantage of this opportunity and reduce leakage up to 54% (35% on average) with negligible impact on system performance. It is important to note that our techniques *(i)* become more effective with technology scaling, *(ii)* reduce leakage also in the normal mode of system operation (in addition to standby mode) even when the cache-lines are actively in use, *(iii)* are orthogonal to other techniques for leakage reduction such as body- and source-biasing, and *(iv)* are software low-cost techniques that need no hardware modification in the cache or processor design (except for adding an on-chip leakage sensor in case of using BICS approach to eliminate test overhead). As future work, we are investigating techniques similar to garbage-collection so as to invalidate the cache-lines that won't soon have a hit and to store the least-leaky values in them. In addition, more aggressive optimizations such as moving basic-blocks around in the address space while considering its effect on instruction-cache access pattern are other directions of expanding this work.

Acknowledgments. This work is supported by VLSI Design and Education Center (VDEC), The University of Tokyo with the collaboration of STARC, Panasonic, NEC Electronics, Renesas Technology, and Toshiba. This work is also supported by Core Research for Evolutional Science and Technology (CREST) project of Japan Science and Technology Corporation (JST). We are grateful for their support.

References

1. Moshnyaga, V.G., Inoue, K.: Low-Power Cache Design. In: Piguet, C. (ed.) Low-Power Electronics Design. CRC Press, Boca Raton (2005)
2. Roy, K., et al: Leakage Current Mechanisms and Leakage Reduction Techniques in Deep-Submicron CMOS Circuits. Proc. IEEE (2003)
3. Taur, Y., Ning, T.H.: Fundamentals of Modern VLSI Devices. Cambridge University Press, Cambridge (1998)
4. Kao, J.T., Chandrakasan, A.P.: Dual-Threshold Voltage Techniques for Low-Power Digital Circuits. IEEE Journal of Solid State Circuits 35, 1009–1018 (2000)
5. Fallah, F., Pedram, M.: Circuit and System Level Power Management. In: Pedram, M., Rabaey, J. (eds.) Power Aware Design Methodologies, pp. 373–412. Kluwer Academic Pub., Dordrecht (2002)
6. De, V., Borkar, S.: Low Power and High Performance Design Challenge in Future Technologies. In: Proc. Great Lake Symposium on VLSI (2000)

7. Kuroda, T., Fujita, T., Hatori, F., Sakurai, T.: Variable Threshold-Voltage CMOS Technology. IEICE Trans. on Fundamentals of Elec., Comm. and Comp. Sciences E83-C (2000)
8. Albonesi, D.: Selective Cache Ways: On-Demand Cache Resource Allocation. In: Proc. Int'l Symposium on Microarchitecture (1999)
9. Powell, M.D., et al.: Gated-Vdd: A Circuit Technique to Reduce Leakage in Cache Memories. In: Int'l Symposium on Low Power Electronics and Design (2000)
10. Kaxiras, S., Hu, Z., Martonosi, M.: Cache Decay: Exploiting Generational Behavior to Reduce Cache Leakage Power. In: Proc. Int'l Symposium on Computer Architecture, pp. 240–251 (2001)
11. Flautner, K., et al.: Drowsy Caches: Simple Techniques for Reducing Leakage Power. In: Proc. Int'l Symposium on Computer Architecture (2002)
12. Meng, K., Joseph, R.: Process Variation Aware Cache Leakage Management. In: Proc. Int'l Symposium on Low Power Electronics and Design (2006)
13. Steinke, S., Wehmeyer, L., Lee, B.S., Marwedel, P.: Assigning Program and Data Objects to Scratchpad for Energy Reduction. In: Proc. of Design Automation and Test in Europe (2002)
14. Verma, M., Wehmeyer, L., Marwedel, P.: Cache-Aware Scratchpad-Allocation Algorithms for Energy-Constrained Embedded Systems. IEEE Trans. Computer-Aided Design of Integrated Circuits and Systems 25(10), 2035–2051 (2006)
15. Tomiyama, H., Yasuura, H.: Code Placement Techniques for Cache Miss Rate Reduction. ACM Trans. on Design Automation of Electronic Systems (ToDAES) 2(4) (1997)
16. Tomiyama, H., Ishihara, T., Inoue, A., Yasuura, H.: Instruction Scheduling for Power Reduction in Processor-Based System Design. In: Proc. of Design Automation and Test in Europe (1998)
17. Panda, P.R., Catthoor, F., Dutt, N.D., Danckaert, K., Brockmeyer, E., Kulkarni, C., Vandercappelle, A., Kjeldsberg, P.G.: Data and Memory Optimization Techniques for Embedded Systems. ACM Trans. on Design Automation of Electronic Systems (ToDAES) 6(2) (2001)
18. Zhang, W., Kandemir, M., Karakoy, M., Chen, G.: Reducing Data Cache Leakage Energy Using a Compiler-Based Approach. ACM Trans. Embedded Computing Systems 4(3), 652–678 (2005)
19. Huang, P.K., Ghiasi, S.: Leakage-Aware Intraprogram Voltage Scaling for Embedded Processors. In: Proc. Design Automation Conference, pp. 364–369 (2006)
20. Chang, J.M., Pedram, M.: Register Allocation and Binding for Low Power. In: Proc. Design Automation Conference (1995)
21. Gebotys, C.H.: Low Energy Memory and Register Allocation Using Network Flow. In: Proc. Design Automation Conference (1997)
22. Abdollahi, A., Fallah, F., Pedram, M.: Leakage Current Reduction in CMOS VLSI Circuits by Input Vector Control. IEEE Trans. VLSI 12(2), 140–154 (2004)
23. Azizi, N., Najm, F.N., Moshovos, A.: Low-Leakage Asymmetric-Cell SRAM. IEEE Trans. VLSI 11(4), 701–715 (2003)
24. Moshovos, A., Falsafi, B., Najm, F.N., Azizi, N.: A Case for Asymmetric-Cell Cache Memories. IEEE Trans. VLSI 13(7), 877–881 (2005)
25. Clark, L., De, V.: Techniques for Power and Process Variation Minimization. In: Piguet, C. (ed.) Low-Power Electronics Design. CRC Press, Boca Raton (2005)
26. Goudarzi, M., Ishihara, T., Noori, H.: Variation-Aware Software Techniques for Cache Leakage Reduction using Value-Dependence of SRAM Leakage due to Within-Die Process Variation. In: Stenström, P., Dubois, M., Katevenis, M., Gupta, R., Ungerer, T. (eds.) HiPEAC 2007. LNCS, vol. 4917, pp. 224–239. Springer, Heidelberg (2008)

27. M32R family of 32-bit RISC microcomputers, http://www.renesas.com
28. CACTI integrated cache access time, cycle time, area, leakage, and dynamic power model, HP Labs, http://www.hpl.hp.com/personal/Norman_Jouppi/cacti4.html and http://quid.hpl.hp.com:9082/cacti/
29. Agarwal, A., Paul, B.C., Mahmoodi, H., Datta, A., Roy, K.: A Process-Tolerant Cache Architecture for Improved Yield in Nanoscale Technologies. IEEE Trans. VLSI 13(1) (2005)
30. Luo, J., Sinha, S., Su, Q., Kawa, J., Chiang, C.: An IC Manufacturing Yield Model Considering Intra-Die Variations. In: Proc. of Design Automation Conference, pp. 749–754 (2006)
31. Agarwal, K., Nassif, S.: Statistical Analysis of SRAM Cell Stability. In: Proc. Design Automation Conference (2006)
32. Toyoda, E.: DFM: Device & Circuit Design Challenges. In: Proc. Int'l Forum on Semiconductor Technology (2004)
33. International Technology Roadmap for Semiconductors—Design (2006) (update), http://www.itrs.net/Links/2006Update/2006UpdateFinal.htm
34. Hill, S.: The ARM 10 Family of Embedded Advanced Microprocessor Cores. In: Proc. HOT-Chips (2001)
35. Suzuki, K., Arai, T., Kouhei, N., Kuroda, I.: V830R/AV: Embedded Multimedia Superscalar RISC Processor. IEEE Micro 18(2), 36–47 (1998)
36. Hamdioui, S.: Testing Static Random Access Memories: Defects, Fault Models and Test Patterns. Kluwer Academic Publishers, Dordrecht (2004)
37. Thibeault, C.: On the Comparison of Delta IDDQ and IDDQ Testing. In: Proc. VLSI Test Symposium, pp. 143–150 (1999)
38. DSM-8104 ammeter, http://www.nihonkaikeisoku.co.jp/densi/toadkk_zetuenteikou_dsm8104.htm
39. Ferre, A., Isern, E., Rius, J., Rodriguez-Montanes, R., Figueras, J.: I_{DDQ} Testing: State of the Art and Future Trends. Integration, the VLSI Journal 26(167-196) (1998)
40. Wallquist, K.M., Righter, A.W., Hawkins, C.F.: A General Purpose IDDQ Measurement Circuit. In: Proc. Int'l Test Conference, pp. 642–651 (1993)
41. Wallquist, K.M.: On the Effect of ISSQ Testing in Reducing Early Failure Rate. In: Proc. Int'l Test Conference, pp. 910–914 (1995)
42. Bushnell, M.L., Agrawal, V.D.: Essentials of Electronic Testing, for Digital, Memory and Mixed-Signal VLSI Circuits. Kluwer Academic Publishers, Dordrecht (2000)
43. Kanda, K., Duc Minh, N., Kawaguchi, H., Sakurai, T.: Abnormal Leakage Suppression (ALS) Scheme for Low Standby Current SRAMs. In: Proc. IEEE Int'l Solid-State Circuits Conference, pp. 174–176 (2001)
44. Feltham, D.B.I., Nigh, P.J., Carley, L.R., Maly, W.: Current Sensing for Built-In Testing of CMOS Circuits. In: Proc. Int'l Conference on Computer Design, pp. 454–457 (1988)
45. Stopjakova, V., Manhaeve, H.: CCII+ Current Conveyor Based BIC Monitor for I_{DDQ} Testing of Complex CMOS Circuits. In: Proc. European Design and Test Conference (1997)
46. Shen, T.L., Daly, J.C., Lo, J.C.: 2-ns Detecting Time, 2-μm CMOS Built-In Current Sensing Circuit. IEEE Journal of Solid-State Circuits 28(1), 72–77 (1993)
47. Antonioli, Y., et al.: 100 MHz IDDQ Sensor with 1μA Resolution for BIST Applications. In: Proc. IEEE Intl. Workshop on IDDQ Testing, pp. 64–68 (1998)
48. Liobe, J., Margala, M.: Novel Process and Temperature-Stable IDD Sensor for the BIST Design of Embedded Digital, Analog, and Mixed-Signal Circuits. IEEE Trans. Circuits and Systems 54(9), 1900–1915 (2007)

49. Marinissen, E.J., Prince, B., Keitel-Schulz, D., Zorian, Y.: Challenges in Embedded Memory Design and Test. In: Proc. Design Automation and Test in Europe (2005)
50. Ghosh, S., Mukhopadhyay, S., Kim, K., Roy, K.: Self-Calibration Technique for Reduction of Hold Failures in Low-Power Nano-Scaled SRAM. In: Proc. Design Automation Conference (2006)
51. MiBench (ver. 1.0), http://www.eecs.umich.edu/mibench/
52. MediaBench, http://cares.icsl.ucla.edu/MediaBench

Author Index

GPSR Compliance

The European Union's (EU) General Product Safety Regulation (GPSR) is a set of rules that requires consumer products to be safe and our obligations to ensure this.

If you have any concerns about our products, you can contact us on ProductSafety@springernature.com

In case Publisher is established outside the EU, the EU authorized representative is:

Springer Nature Customer Service Center GmbH
Europaplatz 3
69115 Heidelberg, Germany

Batch number: 09490872

Printed by Printforce, the Netherlands